# Adolphe Appia
## Essays, Scenarios, and Designs

# Theatre and Dramatic Studies, No. 57

## Oscar C. Brockett, Series Editor

Professor of Drama and Holder of the
Z. T. Scott Family Chair in Drama
The University of Texas at Austin

## Other Titles in This Series

No. 48   Le Sacre du printemps: *Seven Productions
from Nijinsky to Martha Graham*                          Shelley C. Berg

No. 49   *Revolutionaries in the Theater:
Meyerhold, Brecht, and Witkiewicz*              Christine Kiebuzinska

No. 52   *The Feminist Spectator as Critic*                        Jill Dolan

No. 53   *Wisecracks: The Farces of
George S. Kaufman*                                        Jeffrey Mason

No. 55   *Harold Prince: From* Pajama Game *to*
Phantom of the Opera                                        Carol Ilson

No. 56   *The Eugene O'Neill Songbook*          Travis Bogard, coll. and ann.

No. 59   *Edwin Booth's Performances:
A Critical Edition of the
Mary Isabella Stone Commentaries*          Daniel J. Watermeier, ed.

No. 60   *Pier Paolo Pasolini and the
Theatre of the Word*                              William Van Watson

# Adolphe Appia
## Essays, Scenarios, and Designs

Translated by
Walther R. Volbach

Edited and with notes
and commentary by Richard C. Beacham

 Research
Press

Ann Arbor / London

Produced and distributed by
UMI Research Press
an imprint of
University Microfilms Inc.
Ann Arbor, Michigan 48106


Library of Congress Cataloging in Publication Data

**Appia, Adolphe, 1862-1928.**
[Selections. English. 1989]
Adolphe Appia: essays, scenarios, and designs / translated by
Walther R. Volbach ; edited by Richard C. Beacham.
p. cm.—(Theatre and dramatic studies ; no. 57)
Translations from the French.
Bibliography: p.
Includes index.
ISBN 0-8357-1945-6 (alk. paper)
1. Theater. I. Volbach, Walther R. (Walther Richard), 1897-
II. Beacham, Richard C. III. Title. IV. Series.
PN2096.A6A25   1989
792—dc20                                                                89-31846
                                                                        CIP

British Library CIP data is available.

The paper used in this publication meets the minimum requirements of
American National Standard for Information Sciences—Permanence of Paper for Printed
Library Materials, ANSI Z39.48-1984. ∞ ™

René Martin, Portrait of Adolphe Appia in Front of His Setting of *Parsifal,* 1922

# Contents

List of Figures     *xi*

Preface     *xv*
  Walther R. Volbach

Acknowledgments     *xix*

Introduction: Adolphe Appia, 1862–1928     *1*

**Part One: Appia on Appia**

Introduction to Part One     *37*

  Introduction to My Personal Notes     *41*

  Theatrical Experiences and Personal Investigations     *47*

  An American Lecture     *73*

  Curriculum Vita     *77*

**Part Two: Appia on Wagner**

Introduction to Part Two     *81*

  Comments on the Staging of *The Ring of the Nibelungs*     *89*

  Ideas on a Reform of Our *Mise en Scène*     *101*

  Richard Wagner and Theatrical Production     *109*

  The Reform and the Theatre at Basel     *113*

**Part Three: Appia and Eurhythmics**

Introduction to Part Three    *119*

Return to Music    *127*

Style and Solidarity    *131*

Eurhythmics and the Theatre    *135*

The Origin and Beginnings of Eurhythmics    *141*

Eurhythmics and Light    *149*

About the Costume for Eurhythmics    *153*

**Part Four: Essays on the Art of the Theatre**

Introduction to Part Four    *161*

Preface to the Edition of My Essays in One Volume    *169*

Comments on the Theatre    *173*

Actor, Space, Light, Painting    *183*

Art Is an Attitude    *187*

Living Art or Dead Nature?    *191*

Theatrical Production and Its Prospects in the Future    *199*

Monumentality    *221*

The Art of the Living Theatre    *235*

**Part Five: The Aesthetic and Prophetic Essays**

Introduction to Part Five    *245*

Reflections on Space and Time    *255*

A Dangerous Problem    *257*

New Forms: A Fable    *269*

The Gesture of Art    *277*

After Reading *Port-Royal* by Sainte-Beuve    *305*

The Intermediary    *319*

The Theme    *333*

The Child and Dramatic Art    *343*

Costuming    *347*

Picturesqueness    *349*

Mechanization    *359*

The Former Attitude    *375*

Man Is the Measure of All Things    *379*

**Part Six: Selected Scenarios**

Introduction to Part Six    *389*

*The Walkyrie:* Commentary and Scenario for Act 3    *397*

*Carmen:* Act 3    *417*

The Staging of Aeschylus' *Prometheus*    *421*

*Iphigénie en Tauride*: A Scenario    *425*

Goethe's *Faust*, Part 1    *435*

Notes    *457*

Select Bibliography    *473*

Index    *477*

# Figures

René Martin, Portrait of Adolphe Appia in Front of His Setting of *Parsifal,*
1922    *Frontispiece*

1.  Appia's Design (1890s) for *Siegfried*, Act 1    *8*

2.  Rhythmic Design    *12*

3.  Appia's Hellerau Setting of 1912 and 1913 for Gluck's *Orfeo*, Act 2; The
    Descent into the Underworld    *16*

4.  Design of 1926 for *Orfeo*, Act 1, Similar to That Used Earlier at
    Hellerau    *17*

5.  Design for the Elysian Fields, *Orfeo*, Act 2, Scene 2, As Staged at
    Hellerau    *19*

6.  Design for *Tristan*, Act 3    *26*

7.  Design of 1924 for the Walhalla Landscape of *Rhinegold*, Scenes 2 and
    4, As Presented at Basel    *28*

8.  Design of 1924 for *The Walkyrie*, Act 3, at Basel    *32*

9.  Adolphe Appia, circa 1890    *36*

10. Bayreuth Setting of 1882 by Paul von Joukowsky, for the Flower
    Meadows of *Parsifal*, Act 3    *60*

11. Appia's Design of 1896 for *Parsifal*, Act 3    *61*

12.  Rhythmic Design, "The Staircase"    *64*

13.  Bayreuth Setting of 1896 for the Walhalla Landscape of *Rhinegold*    *83*

14.  Revised Bayreuth Setting for *The Walkyrie*, Act 3, Used in the First Decades of This Century    *87*

15.  Appia's Design of 1892 for *Rhinegold*    *96*

16.  Appia's Design of 1896 for *Parsifal*, Act 1    *111*

17.  External View of the Hall at Hellerau    *122*

18.  Eurhythmic Performance at the Geneva Fête de Juin, 1914    *125*

19.  Design of 1925 for *Götterdämmerung*, Act 1, Outside Gunther's Hall    *205*

20.  Design of 1922 for *Hamlet*, Act 1, Scene 1    *214*

21.  Rhythmic Design, "Scherzo"    *218*

22.  Adolphe Appia, circa 1923    *254*

23.  Rhythmic Design    *260*

24.  Rhythmic Design, "The Cataracts of the Dawn"    *281*

25.  Rhythmic Design, "The Last Columns of the Forest"    *293*

26.  Design of 1926 for *Lohengrin*, Act 2    *381*

27.  Design of 1926 for Gluck's *Iphigénie en Aulide*, the Closing Scene of Act 3    *393*

28.  Design of 1922 for the Conclusion of *Hamlet*, Act 5, Scene 2    *395*

29.  Design of 1892 for *The Walkyrie*, Act 3    *399*

30.  Design of 1892 for *The Walkyrie*, Act 3    *408*

31.  Design of 1892 for *The Walkyrie*, Act 3    *414*

32.  Design of 1910 for *Prometheus*     *422*

33.  Design of 1926 for Gluck's *Iphigénie en Tauride*, Act 1     *427*

34.  Design of 1926 for Gluck's *Iphigénie en Tauride*, Acts 2 and 4     *430*

35.  Design of 1926 for Gluck's *Iphigénie en Tauride*, Act 3     *432*

36.  Design of 1927 for *Faust*; Faust's Study     *442*

37.  Design of 1927 for *Faust*; Outside the City Gate     *445*

38.  Design of 1927 for *Faust*; Street     *452*

39.  Design of 1927 for *Faust*; Prison Cell     *454*

# Preface

This, the publication of many of Adolphe Appia's essays for the first time, which were originally written in French, but have now been translated into English, signifies much more for me than merely the presentation of a new book to the public. With this volume, a dream becomes a reality.

Since my student days, I had admired the eminent Swiss artist, and my admiration for him increased during the succeeding decades when I worked as a director in European theatres, and still later as a university teacher in the United States. It soon became clear to me that here, just as "over there," Appia's designs were unfamiliar and his various books and articles were almost entirely unknown. In the early 1950s I was convinced that a translation of his works into English would be greatly welcomed not only by colleagues and students, but also by others interested in the development of theatrical art. Appia's ideas and their theatrical realization would support the trend toward nonrealistic productions, a trend which was already evident on the professional stage, and avidly discussed and explored in university theatre. I was able to persuade colleagues in the American Educational Theatre Association that we ought to set up a committee whose task would be to support the translation and publication of little-known foreign books and articles on theatre. Soon, as chairman of this committee, I had a list of appropriate works, a list which included Appia's writings.

It was my good fortune at this time to learn that a friend of mine, the noted designer Donald Oenslager, had a collection of Appia essays—copies of the originals—which he had received from Edmond Appia, a distant cousin of the great designer, and himself an internationally known musician. He was head of the Foundation Adolphe Appia in Geneva. Fully in favor of our plan, Oenslager wrote to Edmond Appia, who soon responded, promising his support. Words are inadequate to describe the deep understanding and wonderful assistance I received from Mr. Appia. Through my contact with him and other members of the Appia Foundation, I was authorized to translate and publish in the United States all of Appia's writings. About the same time, the University of Miami agreed to take on the demanding task and responsibility for publishing a series of "rare books." Appia's two major works, *Music and the Art of the Theatre* and *The Work of Living Art,* were duly published in 1962 and 1960, respectively, the former translated by Robert Corrigan and Mary Dirks; the latter, by H. D. Albright.

I was eager to concentrate my efforts on examining as many of the French language essays as I could find. The Geneva foundation sent me all that they had, and with the addition of others obtained from theatre collections elsewhere in Europe, I acquired quite a large number of essays—more, indeed, than are published here. It was necessary to be selective, and it was not an easy task to decide which were the most important. Another problem arose in the case of the numerous scenarios that Appia had devised but which, with few exceptions, had never been realized on any stage. Only a small sample has been included here.

Whoever undertakes to translate a long essay or book has to deal with some difficult problems. If, for example, the translation into English is of a work written in a cognate language, the task is easier than if (as in the case of Appia's French), the language has few affinities with English. A further problem for me is that my native language is German; I had to ignore that language and rethink the original French directly into English. As always, it was frequently necessary to choose from among several possible English terms, and this was even more difficult when complex phrases in the original language had to be expressed in appropriate English.

In factual contexts the task was relatively straightforward, but became far more difficult in those of an abstract or philosophical nature. So long as the original author is in full control of his own means of expression, a translator's job is greatly assisted. However, this was not always the case with Appia, who had an extremely personal style, and whose complex presentation of theoretical ideas is not always easy to grasp, even in those fascinating essays he wrote towards the end of his life.

One of Appia's mottos was "style is the man," and consequently it was important to know the man himself before interpreting his writings. I set out to discover as much as I could about Appia's development and to trace its evolution throughout his life. I found that to some extent he never ceased to change and to experiment with new ideas. It was essential to learn as much as possible about the books he read, people he met, performances he had seen: everything that helped to influence his thinking. In order to do this, I consulted a great many friends and relatives of Appia, submitting questions to them about particular subjects in the essays. Jean Mercier and Oskar Wälterlin, both marvelous stage directors, had been very close to Appia and greatly assisted me. I am also deeply indebted to two of his cousins, Mme Blanche Bingham and Dr. Raymond Penel. An extensive memorandum written by Dr. Oskar Forel, who had been Appia's friend and physician for many years, was extremely useful in helping me to interpret certain passages. Above all, I received invaluable assistance from Edmond Appia who answered numerous inquiries in a most thorough manner.

It is not just a duty, but a particular pleasure to mention the colleagues who supported my work. First among these is Walton H. Rothrock, who took on the very onerous task of going over my initial draft, page by page, always ready to suggest a better version, and always mindful of the original text. Much later, Barnard Hewitt and H. Darkes Albright took on in turn the burden of checking the final manuscript, as I had assisted them in their own publications of Appia's works. I am also grateful for the financial assistance given me by the Research Committee of Texas Christian University and for the support of the Graduate School of the University of Massachusetts which assisted me in the final preparation of my manuscript.

Unfortunately, just at the moment when the publication of this and other "rare books" seemed assured, severe and very regrettable problems of organization, cooperation, and personal antagonisms arose, unexpectedly, and these resulted in the collapse not only of the "rare books" project but of the A.E.T.A. as well. The anticipated publication has had to be delayed by many years. Sad as that is, I am very pleased to state that "All's Well That Ends Well." The basis for this happy ending was provided by Richard C. Beacham, a most esteemed colleague whose depth of knowledge and sincerity of interest in Appia I became aware of after meeting him as a result of the research he was doing for his own recently published critical biography of Appia. When I told him that I was again looking for a publisher, he offered to help. Soon he informed me that UMI Research Press was interested, and shortly thereafter, there were contracts for me as translator and my friend Beacham as editor. This delightful and unexpected turn of events has made possible the realization at last of the hope and the dream I first conceived so many years ago. Both Beacham and UMI Research Press deserve the highest praise, and my most deeply felt "thank you."

WALTHER R. VOLBACH

\* \* \*

*This book is dedicated to Claire, my very dear wife, who has assisted me since 1924 whenever I have written a note for the program of a production, a review for a newspaper, an article, or a full-fledged book. To call her my special copy editor is too prosaic a title. I rather name her my guardian angel.*

# Acknowledgments

I would like to extend thanks for support and assistance in the editing of this book to a number of individuals and institutions. Foremost among these is Professor Volbach, the translator of Appia's essays, who entrusted his work to me, and gave me invaluable advice in preparing it for publication.

I would like to thank the staff of the Beinecke Rare Book and Manuscript Library at Yale for their cooperation, and to the Yale School of Drama both for making its collection available to me, and for permission to reproduce many of the illustrations appearing in this book. Other illustrations are used with the kind consent of the Swiss Theatre Collection in Bern. I am grateful too to its Director, Dr. Martin Dreier, and his assistant, Ms. Silvia Mauer, for their vital support.

The section of Appia's scenario for act 3 of *The Walkyrie*, reproduced here, was translated by Mr. Neil Monro-Davies, who also assisted me in preparing my manuscript. Portions of the commentary have appeared in my critical biography, *Adolphe Appia, Theatre Artist* and are used by permission of Cambridge University Press.

The complete French language edition of Appia's works is being published in five volumes by the Schweizerische Gesellschaft für Theaterkultur, under the editorship of Mme Marie L. Bablet-Hahn. At this time, the first two volumes have appeared, covering the period 1880–1905. Unless otherwise indicated, Appia's essays and scenarios written after 1905 appearing in this book have never before been published in any language.

# Introduction

# Adolphe Appia, 1862–1928

Adolphe Appia has long been revered as the most important innovator in the concept and use of stage lighting, but his imagination and work extended far beyond that to embrace fundamental reform of scenic design, directing, the use of theatrical space, and a greatly expanded conception of the nature and limits of theatrical art. Many of his ideas, which were extremely advanced for his time, have now been widely accepted and put into practice, but frequently Appia has not received the credit and attention which he deserves, and much of his most important work remains unpublished and largely unexplored.

A measure of such neglect is the fact that the great majority of the essays that make up this book have never before been published, and of those that have, hardly any have appeared in English translation.

And yet from the moment that Appia's ideas first became known, even to a limited readership, a few far-sighted and imaginative critics recognized their fundamental importance and the implication they had for total reform of theatrical practice. The basis for the renovation of theatrical art—above all the recognition that the theatre could be an art—was already at hand when Appia set to work. Such demands for reform as Georg Fuchs passionately called for in 1905 were already in the air, and had been for some time: "Away with the footlights! Away with the wings, the backcloths, the flys, the flats, and the padded tights! Away with the peep-show stage! Away with the auditorium! This entire sham-world of paste, wire, canvas and tinsel is ripe for destruction!"[1] Appia's early and abiding importance was that he moved beyond such criticism to outline a positive and concrete alternative to the degraded theatre of his day. By providing almost all—and almost all at once—of both the theoretical and the practical guidance necessary to pursue fundamental theatrical reform, Appia cleared the path and lit it for a host of others to follow, throughout the first half of the twentieth century and beyond.

By the 1930s, Lee Simonson would assert that "most of what we call innovation or experiment is a variation of Appia's ideas, deduced from his original premises"[2] and suggest that the history of the theatre prior to Appia could simply be referred to as "B. A.," so fundamental and lasting were his reforms. And yet, paradoxically, Appia's own work and writings were never widely known in his lifetime, and have been extraordinarily neglected ever since.

This fact is perhaps not difficult to explain: Appia's own shyness, his aversion to publicity, and his inability to establish a wide range of connections with other influential theatre artists who might have spread his fame and perpetuated his memory help to account for it. As Simonson explained the paradox, "I do not imply that the designers of this generation read an out-of-date German volume and then rushed into the theatre to apply its precepts. They were already in the air. . . . [M]odern designers accepted a torch without knowing who lighted it; our experiments amplified Appia's theories almost before we knew his name, had seen his drawings, or had heard a quotation from his published work."[3]

Appia's creative life may be usefully divided into three periods, during each of which he significantly advanced the state of theatrical art. In the first of these, lasting roughly from 1885 to 1900, he concentrated on an analysis of Wagnerian opera and its implications for scenic reform. The second period, from about 1905 to the end of the First World War (or, perhaps, its beginning; Appia was able to do little work during the conflict) was devoted to exploring the potential which an understanding of the human body moving in space had for new forms of theatre. In the final period, from around 1919 to the end of his life in 1928, Appia moved beyond orthodox notions of theatre altogether to evoke and describe the shape of things to come, through a series of extraordinarily prophetic and deeply perceptive writings, based on his concept of "Living Art."

**The First, "Wagnerian" Period**

As a young man Appia was enthralled by Wagner's works, and goaded by the challenge they offered conventional stagecraft. In the period from 1885 to 1900 he used them to formulate a completely new definition of scenic art, which in large part provided the theoretical and practical basis for the modern theatre.

The first part of this period was of crucial importance to the development and refinement of Appia's ideas; these were to culminate in the unprecedented theories drawn together and published in the 1890s. Although ostensibly studying music, first at the Leipzig Conservatory between 1882 and 1884, and subsequently, until 1889, in Dresden, he was far more engaged in developing a comprehensive critique of contemporary stage practice. With few exceptions, what he saw about him in the theatre was profoundly disappointing and disheartening. Yet, however negative his impressions of the productions he witnessed, the thoughts that gradually he formulated in reaction to them began to coalesce into positive ideas for reform. His as yet uncertain, but deeply sensitive, mind responded to the affront of crass and inartistic staging by beginning to work out, slowly and hesitantly, first the practical and then the theoretical basis for a more beautiful and expressive *mise en scène.*

Preoccupied to the point of obsession with the problem of staging the works of Richard Wagner, Appia directed all his creative resources and mental energy to this task. In 1890 he returned to Switzerland and eventually settled at Bière, in the country a few miles north of Lake Geneva, where he was to make his home until 1904, and at once set to work preparing a scenic analysis of Wagner's titanic masterpiece, the *Ring.* His own accounts of his method are extremely revealing for they demonstrate how his approach was based directly and solely on the works themselves—on their integrity and expressiveness—and not on any pre-existent notions whatsoever about how they *ought* to be presented in the theatre. This was in itself a revolutionary concept, for, uniquely, Appia undertook not to provide the external historical or fictive locales—mere illustrations and background for the stories—but rather, to determine the setting dictated by the *music itself,* generated from within the work, through the drama. Only later, after comparing and analyzing the results achieved through the process of directly visualizing the work, did he step back and attempt to formulate a coherent theory and set of principles.

The achievement was prodigious and, in time, its effect upon contemporary staging—indeed upon the very concept of theatre—was revolutionary. Within a period of fewer than ten years, Appia articulated theories and bodied them forth in designs that swept away the foundations that had supported European theatre since the Renaissance. In their place he laid down what became the conceptual and practical basis for theatrical art for many years to come. As Simonson wrote, Appia's theories "elucidated the basic aesthetic principles of modern stage design, analysed its fundamental technical problems, outlined their solution, and formed a charter of freedom under which scene designers still practice. . . . [T]he light in Appia's first drawings, if one compares them to the designs that had preceded his, seem the night and morning of a First Day."[4]

Appia's passionate critique of traditional stagecraft was soon taken up by others, some of whom conceived similar although less comprehensive ideas independently of him. Before long, everywhere, the "new art of the theatre" was being promulgated, frequently by people with little direct knowledge of Appia or of his decisive contribution to the movement which they so ardently promoted.

But it was Appia alone, who in the 1890s, with extraordinary clarity of vision, first provided a complete assessment of the disastrous state of theatrical art, and who, with quite astonishing foresight, first suggested the solutions which in time, and frequently at the hands of others, laid down a new basis for the modern theatre.

Appia began his work by first trying to understand and explain Wagner's fundamental failure himself to develop an appropriate means of staging his own works, a failure that had resulted in a style of production which, with all its inadequacies, became enshrined as orthodox after his death. The expressiveness of Wagner's operas resides in the music and the dramatic actions generated by the music and libretto on stage. To attempt at the same time to give that music a completely realistic materialization was not only impossible, but, inevitably, it buried and obscured from the audience the essential qualities of the work.

Wagner failed to understand this, believing that direct scenic instructions from the author were necessary. But, according to Appia, "the musical score is the sole interpreter for the director: whatever Wagner has added to it is irrelevant. . . . [H]is manuscript contains by definition the theatrical form, i.e. its projection in space; therefore any additional remarks on his part are superfluous, even contradictory to the aesthetic truth of an artistic work. Wagner's scenic descriptions in his libretto have no organic relationship with his poetic-musical text."[5]

Appia began, then, by attempting to visualize, purely and simply, the settings that the music and necessary stage actions suggested to him. In the process he kept firmly in mind the central role of the performer as the intermediary between the composition and its realization on stage. He determined what the text and score required of the performer in terms of his location and physical movement within the scenic environment. The relative theatrical significance given to each scene and its setting should thus be a direct and proportionate expression of the demands made by each upon the performer. Anything else would be superfluous, mere window dressing, extraneous to the work and therefore not expressive of it. Wagner's composition as a work of art was conditioned by an overall unity of conception, and in performance this conception—the meaning of the work—was bodied forth on stage. Any genuinely artistic staging must therefore also exhibit a unity of expression which would be the sum of its parts: each scene, each event on stage, each setting must be carefully balanced and coordinated with the others to contribute its appropriate measure to the overall quality of the production.

While assessing this, based on the requirements which each scene makes of the performer, and the degree to which its actions advance the plot, Appia was careful to bear another factor in mind. A Wagnerian opera has, in addition to its story, an emotional and intellective plot: another level of meaning. This interior drama, which in Wagner contributes so massively to the impact of his work, must also somehow be expressed through staging. Otherwise the production, while representing the external circumstances of the action and its setting, would fail utterly to convey the real substance of the work. This was precisely the limitation of Wagner himself as producer.

Appia's reforms were based upon two major premises. The first of these was that theatre since the Renaissance had developed and perpetuated a set of conventions that were inherently contradictory, and that consequently the contemporary theatre was divided against itself.

Through the adoption and manipulation of the newly rediscovered and refined principles of perspective painting, which in the Renaissance soon came to dominate the visual form of dramatic art, the theatre could project carefully chosen and composed images to an audience which, in order to perceive those pictures correctly, had itself to be organized along systematic (and inevitably hierarchical) lines. Thus a potentially communal and democratic activity became instead an innately authoritarian enterprise concerned with arranging the outward appearance of things for display to a passive audience of spectators. The theatre was in the service not of genuine artistic expression and the communication and active experience of profound ideas and emotions, but rather had been confined to conveying external indications, to imitating surface reality, and, in a phrase, to putting on a show.

Theatrical staging had long been conditioned and controlled by the conventions and requirements of scenic illusion—of perspective *painting*—while, incongruously, the drama itself consisted of *actions* taking place in time and space according to another set of quite different, and indeed incompatible, conventions.

The second major premise out of which Appia's work developed in this period was that theatre was not a true art form at all and never could become one unless the process through which dramatic works were brought to the stage was fundamentally altered. What was demanded of theatre was an artistic integrity that it might acquire only if, like the other arts, it could be made to convey faithfully the expressions of the individual creative artist, the dramatist. This it quite patently failed to do. Theatre could never be an integral art form unless the conception, fashioning and ultimate realization of the art object—the production itself—could somehow be guided and controlled by the intentions of the original autonomous artist.

Appia asserted, then, that the contemporary theatre suffered two overwhelming defects. The first of these was the fundamental incompatibility between the conventions appropriate to the enactment of drama and those required for displaying painted perspective scenery. The second was the gulf separating the creative artist, the playwright, from the eventual presentation of his work in the theatre. Appia proposed to correct both fundamental faults by organizing theatrical production in strict obedience to a specific and inviolable hierarchy.

At the apex of this hierarchy Appia placed the artist, the composer-dramatist, who creates the music and its dramatic libretto. Music as notated in the score determines the time sequences and rhythms in production, while, simultaneously, the libretto dictates the actions required of the performer. The actions that occur in obedience to the music must take place within a particular space (as well as a particular time), and that space, the setting for the performance, provides the actor with the areas and objects necessary for his movement and gestures. Thus, according to Appia, music, which already controls the time of the production, comes to control its space as well: through the intermediary of the performer, it becomes in effect transported into space to achieve physical form. Therefore, Appia pointed out, through the medium of music the original composer-dramatist might express his artistry over all the separate elements of production to achieve a mutually subordinated synthesis of them—a work of theatrical art—which as finally realized in performance would maintain its artistic integrity.

It was essential that the entire process of production be coordinated by a supremely sensitive scenic artist—a designer-director—who would devote all his powers to the single complex task of applying the hierarchical principle to the particular work being presented. Although gradually evolving, the role of designer-director that Appia called for was still a relatively new concept in theatre, and Appia went further than any before him in providing a thorough and concrete description of the principles governing this largely untested idea.

The first of these was the recognition that the *mise en scène* was already immanent in the score. It was the original music-drama itself that contained not only the tempo and duration of the words, not only the necessary rhythms, gestures and movements, but by extension the setting as well, which the director must think of as music projected and visualized in space.

The second principle was that the performer was the intermediary between the music and its physical setting. Appia placed the actor at the very center of his revolutionary scenic theory; the scenic elements were not to be thought of as setting or background for the drama, but rather as an extension of the actor himself, as he in turn was given significance and motivated by the musical score. In order to fulfill this high office, the actor would have to mold himself into a supremely sensitive and responsive instrument capable of embodying the music. Appia called for a new type of musical gymnastics to train the body to be activated by music and to represent musical expression and nuance in its movements and gestures. Although in the 1890s he took the idea no further than briefly describing it, while borrowing for it the term "choreography," it was a subject that dominated and determined the second period of his creative achievement, which began about 1905.

In the meantime, in attempting to use the scenery to serve the actor as he in turn served the music, Appia realized that the conventions that had governed stage décor for centuries would have to be overthrown and replaced by a wholly new set of principles. Ever since the mid-seventeenth century, the stage had been in the thrall of a scenic arrangement essentially inimical to the presence of the living actor. The defects of this scenic system had long been noted and lamented, but little had been done to correct them. Appia demanded utter simplicity: the stage should be set "only so far as is necessary for the comprehension of the poetic text; a mere indication is enough to enlighten us to the nature of the visible environment."[6] He also demanded the abolition of painted scenery. He criticized the absurd conjunction of the three-dimensional actor with the two-dimensional *trompe l'oeil* flats. The scenic illusion was shattered the moment the performer intruded on to the stage, with results as ridiculous and inartistic as if a real nose were inserted from behind the canvas into an exquisitely composed portrait.

The normally flat surface of the stage floor should be replaced with a variety of levels, steps and slopes: there should be changes of height and depth, all calculated to establish the solidity and volume of the actor and the space supporting him. In place of two-dimensional flats, "practicables" must be used: solid objects whose mass and volume were articulated by their displacement of space. This space and setting, as used by the actor, became within Appia's hierarchy of production an *expressive* element: the visible embodiment of the music-drama that the composer had conceived. At the same time, and in contrast to those calling for more realistic detail in stage settings, he insisted that what was desired was not an accumulation of ever more lifelike rendering of the *external* appearance of dramatic settings, but rather, the suggestion by the simplest means possible of the artistically appropriate locale, as generated from *within* the drama itself and conveyed through the actor.

Appia's concept of the setting as an element of production and his call for three-dimensional scenery expressive of the drama were revolutionary; his achievement in identifying and describing light as the soul of the *mise en scène*, and, moreover, in accurately predicting in detail its subsequent technical development and use, can only be described as miraculous.

He began by observing that lighting as used in the contemporary theatre failed to fulfill either of its potential services to production: it neither supported the inner emotional expressiveness of the music nor, surprisingly, properly emphasized the plastic form of the actor and setting. Newly introduced electrical lighting, as practiced, was of a dull, over-bright uniformity, which effectively destroyed any quality of three-dimensionality, while providing no sense of the ebb and flow of action and meaning.

Appia charted out in detail the course that lighting must follow to reach the goal of becoming an aesthetic medium. Like the actor, it must first of all break away from its enslavement to painted scenery, which effectively denied and mocked its very existence. In order to enhance both a plastic setting and the music itself, it was necessary first to identify and then to utilize two types of light.

The first of these was general illumination and brightness, a *diffused* light, which provided a sort of luminous undercoat for later, more suggestive effects. The other was *formative* light, consisting of more intense, diverse and mobile radiance, which could be used as an extraordinarily subtle tool by the scenic

Figure 1.    Appia's Design (1890s) for *Siegfried*, Act 1

artist. With it he could highlight objects or cause them to disappear; he could, like a sculptor, build up or take away; distort, give mass to or dematerialize the physical objects on stage, including the performer.

The formative light that selected, differentiated and molded what it lit provided the means for enhancing both the external setting of the drama and its inner life as well. Appia was the first to develop the concept of employing light through the equivalent of a musical score—the lighting plot—to convey emphasis and counterpoint as a visible correlative to the flow of the music-drama itself. This represented an enormous advance in scenic art, since, for the first time, lighting could be employed to create, sustain and modulate mood and atmosphere. He went further. He outlined the technical reforms that would allow light to achieve its full potential, calling for mobile light sources, and for the use of different filters, colors and lenses to allow greater subtlety and adaptability. He demanded the abolition of the footlights, which so grotesquely distorted the actors' appearance, and described for the first time the vast potential which the use of projections had for expanding the range and expressiveness of scenic art.

Appia anticipated a number of technical developments which, at the time, had yet to occur, but his description of what was required and how it should be used was direct and precise. His call for mobile spotlights to replace the fixed overhead strip lighting which provided the major source of illumination on the contemporary stage was particularly important, since the fluid and dynamic formative light at the center of his reforms depended upon them. By controlling and modulating the intensity, color, movement and size of the beams projected by these lamps, the scenic artist could obtain a vast range of wonderfully expressive effects.

Appia's brilliant presentation of his ideas for the use of light completed and crowned his theoretical writings of the 1890s. While formulating them he had also created a set of extremely detailed scenarios for several of Wagner's operas, along with a large number of astonishing designs illustrating his descriptions of stage settings. Nineteen of these were included in his major work of the period, *Music and the Art of the Theatre,* which was published in 1899 in German translation—*Die Musik and die Inscenierung*—together with a complete scenario for *Tristan and Isolde* and a brief outline of the staging of the *Ring.* His study of Wagner's operas formed the critical core of his work for many years to come. His subsequent investigations, his practical experiments and his theoretical essays all radiated outward from the mass of these explosive ideas. As they became known, developed and put into effect by theatre practitioners everywhere, they were finally to sweep away both the theoretical and the technical foundations of post-Renaissance theatre.

**The Second Period: Eurhythmics**

However exemplary Appia's designs and ideas now seem to us—and in retrospect, how superior to the prevailing practice at Bayreuth—they were firmly rejected and ridiculed by Wagner's widow, Cosima, to whom suggestions of reform were most unwelcome. Appia's fervent hopes that her production of the *Ring* in 1896 might incorporate some of his suggestions were dashed. Although she later mellowed slightly to allow that his ideas might have some relevance to producing Shakespeare, who had left no instructions regarding the staging of his plays, she insisted that to apply them to Wagner was patently absurd, because "even as the creator of these works of art constructed his own stage, so also did he determine absolutely their staging."[7] The subject was closed as far as Bayreuth was concerned.

Appia was bitterly disappointed. Disheartened, but convinced that he had discovered through his Wagnerian investigations the key to the renewal of contemporary stagecraft, he continued to promulgate his as yet untested theories.

Like Wagner before him, Appia encountered the innate conservatism and inertia of the established theatre, an establishment to which, with cruel irony, Bayreuth itself now belonged. Change of any sort is difficult to carry out in the theatre, subject as it is to social restraints, the problems of coordinating a system of complex collaboration, financial and technical limitations and established custom. Unlike Wagner, Appia lacked both powerful friends and a strongly assertive personality, as well as the ability to organize and direct the talent and energy of other artists. His situation was made still more desperate by the sheer magnitude and thoroughness of the reforms he envisaged and prophesied. To destroy one theatre and erect another in its place from the ground up, was what Appia accomplished with such magnificent results *imaginatively,* as a wonderfully detailed theory; to carry out such reform in practical terms was more than one man alone could do.

Appia was indeed alone, an inspired but reclusive genius with little talent and less taste for intense collaboration with others. That in the end, his reform was realized through the efforts of others—a host of pragmatic men of the theatre—attests to both the essential efficacy of his concepts, and to his own unfortunate limitations as a man of action and practical affairs.

In May 1906 Appia encountered Emile Jaques-Dalcroze and the system of rhythmic exercises which he devised and taught, eurhythmics. Dalcroze, who taught harmony at the Geneva Conservatory of Music, had begun by composing "gesture songs" which used physical movement to accompany short pieces of music. Later he developed an entire set of "musical-gymnastic" exercises designed to enhance his pupils' perception of musical nuance, as well as their awareness of the responsive movement of the body in space. In effect he taught them to translate musical composition directly into space through the reactive medium of their own bodies, and his exercises trained students until this occurred almost automatically.

Appia attended one of Dalcroze's sessions in Geneva, and was astonished and greatly moved. He sensed, albeit as yet imprecisely, that eurhythmics could provide the solution to the problem he had faced earlier in his analysis of Wagner and the challenge of scenic reform: how to physicalize systematically the temporal by transferring musical time and consequent bodily movement into three-dimensional space. He wrote at once to Dalcroze, and shortly thereafter enrolled in a course in eurhythmics. He soon persuaded Dalcroze to vary the flat area in which the exercises were performed through the addition of some stairs and platforms. By adding a vertical element to their work, Appia increased students' awareness both of space and of their own mass and encouraged them to create dynamic three-dimensional exercises in place of mere moving tableaux.

Gradually over the next several years, during which Dalcroze and he worked closely together, experimenting and enlarging their vision of eurhythmics, Appia began to realize the full potential of the system for fundamental theatrical reform. For a time, however, he was perplexed over exactly how to translate this into actual production. His first attempts to compose designs appropriate as settings for eurhythmic exercises were disappointing. He tried simplifying the lines of his earlier Wagnerian scenes, but, in the absence of any score, found it difficult to conceive abstractly of suitable settings. Then he realized that what was essential was the very quality of three-dimensionality itself, an element which, although demanded in his earlier settings, was not always unequivocally manifested in the drawings themselves.

In the spring of 1909, Appia created about twenty designs which he termed "Rhythmic Spaces" and submitted them to Dalcroze, who viewed them with great excitement. Appia perceived that the way to bring these settings to life was by contrasting them with the human body. Their rigidity, sharp lines and angles, and immobility, when confronted by the softness, subtlety and movement of the body, would, by opposition, take on a kind of borrowed life. These designs, moreover, suggested far more than merely a series of settings for eurhythmic exercises: they could help clarify the relationship between music, time, space and movement and, ultimately, revolutionize stage performance and design. Appia and Dalcroze worked together with growing conviction to develop spaces and exercises that successfully embodied this relationship.

In 1909 they had a decisive opportunity to make practical progress towards their goal of basic reform. In October of the previous year Dalcroze had given a demonstration in Dresden with some of the students trained by him in eurhythmics. It was attended by a thirty-two-year-old, well-to-do gentleman named Wolf Dohrn. Together with his colleague, Karl Schmidt, Dohrn had established

Figure 2.   Rhythmic Design

in the outskirts of Dresden a small factory dedicated to the ideal of enabling workers to overcome the threat of dehumanization in modern industry and to regain a sense of satisfaction and pride in their work and its products. With the help of the German *Werkbund,* an enlightened organization devoted to the development of the applied arts in light industry, they founded a small settlement near the factory modeled on the English concept of the "garden city"; the first such town in Germany. The project was pursued as a noble social experiment. Dohrn, Schmidt, and their supporters hoped that within a harmonious natural surrounding, a new utopian community could be established and nurtured; one based on principles of social equality, liberal and universal education and the revival of unalienated art and labor. The settlement was called Hellerau.

For Dohrn, his encounter with eurhythmics was a revelation. He seized upon it at once, convinced that through it Hellerau could become "the future centre for a spiritual and physical regeneration, out of which a broad social renewal would follow."[8] Barely a month after first meeting Dalcroze, Dohrn invited him to found an institute at Hellerau to become the primary site for the practice, further investigation and propagation of eurhythmics. He offered to set up such an institute and construct it exactly according to Dalcroze's specifications. Dalcroze in turn suggested that Appia should be directly involved in every aspect, from the beginning. Consultations between Appia, Dalcroze and Dohrn began at once. The thirty-four-year-old architect Heinrich Tessenow was engaged to execute the design and building, and a Russian painter, Alexander von Salzmann, was brought in to oversee arrangements for lighting, which, given Appia's detailed but largely untested theories, promised to be complex and unprecedented.

The collaboration between Appia and Dalcroze proved highly successful. Dalcroze had a remarkable talent both for effective pedagogical work and for expressing and publicizing his methods enthusiastically and articulately to others. Nevertheless, he lacked autonomous inspiration and imagination; he needed theoretical and aesthetic support and structure for his work, as well as the identification and definition of ultimate goals. Appia (who was far too shy and introverted to present publicly his own ideas) provided Dalcroze with the creative analysis, the ability to formulate new objectives and, above all, the inspired vision of the possibilities for a new scenic art which were essential if eurhythmics were ever to become more than a species of refined gymnastics.

Dalcroze constantly sought advice from Appia (who remained for most of the time in Switzerland), particularly in regard to using the "practicables"— rostra, platforms, stairs, podia and the like—which made up his designs for rhythmic spaces. In addition, Appia advised about the crucial role of lighting and the influence it should have upon the expressive quality of the musically coordinated exercises. For some time he had envisaged a building which would help to abolish what, increasingly, he considered to be the unacceptable distinction between spectator and performer. For this to take place, he needed an entirely new theatrical architecture, and at Hellerau it was achieved for the first time.

As the central and largest room in the institute, he designed a great open hall, fifty meters in length, sixteen meters wide, and twelve meters high, which would enclose both performers and audience without any barrier or obstacle between them. The orchestra and its light were also hidden from view. Thus he abolished the proscenium arch and raised stage, using a completely open performance area for the first time since the Renaissance. For Appia this was not merely a practical development, but a deeply philosophical and social gesture as well, since it implied a wholly different attitude towards the function of art and the way in which men respond to it; a subject which was to dominate the final period of his creative life. Art was not to be contemplated passively, but engaged in actively. Theatre was not an illusion that one observed, but a real event that one experienced. The hall at Hellerau, which had seating for 560 spectators and space for about 250 performers, was constructed exactly according to Appia's plans.

Following the successful completion of the first year's classes in temporary facilities during the year 1910–11, the directors of Hellerau had decided that the institute should hold annual festivals presenting examples of its achievements to the general public, and as Dalcroze and Appia embarked on further experimental work with their pupils, plans for the first festival were already well advanced. These festivals were held only twice, in the summers of 1912 and 1913, but, in the event, became much more than simple demonstrations of school exercises and work-in-progress programs: they produced instead extraordinary and unique displays of a new kind of performance art, which proved enormously suggestive and influential, and assured both Appia and Dalcroze of an important (if inadequately recognized) role in the development of the modern theatre.

It was a curious collaboration. Because he shrank from practical work and sustained contact at first hand, Appia poured out his ideas and suggestions in abundant detail in his letters to Dalcroze, confidently answering every question put to him and virtually stage-managing the whole affair from a safe distance. Slowly he overcame Dalcroze's antipathy towards a fundamental attack on traditional staging, and as the plans for the first festival evolved, what emerged was essentially the consequence of his own prophetic vision of a radically new type of theatrical art. Throughout the school's session (1911–12) the work progressed.

Meanwhile, the newly completed hall was fitted with its—totally unprecedented—lighting system. In his earlier writings Appia had laid down the theoretical basis for modern stage lighting. yet he had not been able to realize his ideas in practical work, or to extend them through experimentation. Together with Salzmann, who thoroughly understood Appia's concepts and proved to be an ingenious interpreter of them in practical terms, he devised a system for creating diffused light, as well as for special spotlight effects. The entire hall at Hellerau—the area for performance as well as for viewing—was lit by means of thousands of lights, some of them colored, installed behind translucent linen that had been dipped in cedar oil and covered all the walls and ceilings of the building. This method created the diffused light that Appia had demanded years earlier. The space literally glowed.[9]

To obtain the formative, or plastic, light called for earlier, Appia suggested a system of movable spotlights placed in the ceiling of the hall behind sliding panels. Light could now express the emotional nuance of the music with great subtlety and variation while being operated centrally from a newly devised "light organ," a calibrated and extremely sensitive lighting console, operated by a single person. Light could, in effect, represent the music visually in space, and thus complement the physical embodiment of the music expressed through the eurhythmic gestures and movements of the performing students.

The first festival opened on 26 June 1912. In addition to part of act 2 of Gluck's opera, *Orfeo,* presented on each night, a varied program was offered, including a number of school exercises and improvisations, some pantomime dances and a rhythmic representation of selections of classical music. The presentation of the scene from *Orfeo*—his descent into the Underworld—caused a sensation. Orfeo entered at the highest point of the scenic structure, in a glare of light, and slowly descended the monumental staircase into ever greater darkness, confronted and opposed by the Furies. Dressed in black tights, they were in constant motion; carefully coordinated with the ebb and flow of the music. Arranged along the steps and platforms, their naked arms and legs seemed like snakes, and formed a veritable moving mountain of monstrous forms, before being overcome and subdued by the sound of Orfeo's playing and the poignancy of his pleas. The whole scene was bathed in an otherworldly blue light, the glow of Hades, and, as one spectator observed, "It was beyond imagination. The space lived—it was a conspiring force, a co-creator of life."[10]

The reaction to the music, staging, and, above all, the setting and lighting was overwhelmingly favorable. A number of perceptive critics recognized that the work at Hellerau presented a real and direct alternative to contemporary staging techniques and believed that, almost inadvertently, eurhythmics was in the process of opening up quite extraordinary new vistas for the theatre.

Greatly encouraged by the success and recognition achieved by the first festival, Appia and Dalcroze proceeded at once with plans for the following summer. They decided to concentrate their efforts this time on a full production of the entire Gluck opera. Again Dalcroze turned to Appia, not only for complete designs for the production, but for extensive notes and staging suggestions as well. Appia produced drawings for act 1, for the Elysian Fields and for the

Figure 3. Appia's Hellerau Setting of 1912 and 1913 for Gluck's *Orfeo*, Act 2; The Descent into the Underworld

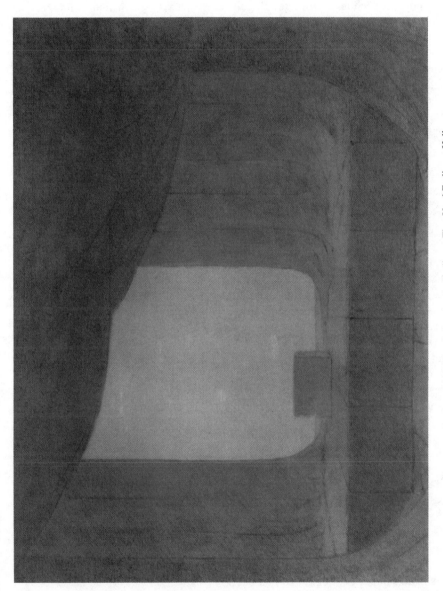

Figure 4. Design of 1926 for *Orfeo*, Act 1, Similar to That Used Earlier at Hellerau

closing scene. The descent into Hades was to be kept as it was, unchanged from the first festival.

The second festival was held at the end of June and beginning of July 1913, with the production of *Orfeo* forming the centerpiece of the institute's presentations. It was attended by five thousand in all, including a great many illustrious theatre artists and critics drawn from throughout Europe and America. Most were highly impressed by what they saw. As one remarked, they came in curiosity but returned as pilgrims. "[O]n no stage in Germany or anywhere else could one see a production which in purity and beauty of style could be compared to this."[11]

Another wrote:

[T]hrough all three acts one never had the feeling that one was at a presentation: we had before us real life, translated into music, magnificent music, which became living. It could not be otherwise, since all the performers were possessed by music; it possessed them both physically and emotionally; the music was for them a principle of life like the act of breathing. . . . [T]he radiating inner beauty was indescribable. Most impressive of all was the naturalness—one forgot that it was an opera—the most conventional and unbelievable of all arts.[12]

Upton Sinclair, the American writer, recalled: "It was music made visible; and when the curtain had fallen upon the bliss of Orfeo and his bride, a storm of applause shook the auditorium. Men and women stood shouting their delight at the revelation of a new form of art."[13]

The success of the collaboration at Hellerau between Appia and Dalcroze was prodigious, and its influence soon widely evident. Appia had been able to realize a portion of his audacious dream of re-creating the theatre. He had put into practice earlier theories, had tested new ideas and had seen them both work and attract the admiration of fellow artists and the larger public. Dalcroze had seen the promise of eurhythmics fulfilled beyond his furthest hopes and had triumphantly brought his work to the attention of a wide, appreciative and influential audience.

There were plans for a third festival in the summer of 1914, but the threat of war and its eventual outbreak destroyed them. Although Appia and Dalcroze were afterwards involved in several joint ventures, Hellerau, to which neither of them ever returned, marked the climax, triumph and effective end of their work together.[14] Few who came to Hellerau failed to admire the work they saw there; many recognized its startling potential for radically transforming orthodox theatre practice; some even came to share the ultimate vision of a world renewed through "living art." One such convert wrote, "Nietzsche expressed the hope . . . that one could found the State upon music. Who knows if this paradoxical prediction might not come true one day? The audience at the Hellerau festival has in any case seen the dawn of a new art and a new aesthetic life."[15] It was

Figure 5.  Design for the Elysian Fields, *Orfeo*, Act 2, Scene 2, As Staged at Hellerau
Gordon Craig wrote of this design: "How inviting it is, how
gracious—how silent—how perfectly temperate—how GOOD."

with such a vision dominating his imagination that Appia embarked on the third and final phase of his creative life.

### The Third Period: "Living Art"

Appia's earliest writings and his subsequent work with Dalcroze had far-reaching implications for theatrical development during the first decades of this century. The product of his last years—his book *L'Oeuvre d'art vivant (The Work of Living Art),* and a remarkable series of prophetic and philosophical essays—contained ideas which, although they had little immediate influence, did nevertheless display Appia's extraordinary and continuing ability to infer and predict future developments from contemporary conditions. As in the 1890s so again in the 1920s, Appia looked well beyond his time to evoke and describe new directions in the performing arts.

Eurhythmics, of course, and the exploration of the "unknown" which it invited, had helped to clear the way. Immediately after the Hellerau festival of 1913, Appia and Dalcroze began work on a pageant to be held in Geneva the following summer. The Fête de Juin was, on the surface, the continuation of a venerable Swiss tradition: patriotic festivals combining folk music, dance and drama to celebrate national occasions and commemorate historical events. But the event of 1914, marking the Geneva Republic's entry into the Swiss Confederation a century before, was in many ways strikingly different from its predecessors, and reflected the evolution of Appia's thought. While celebrating the historical and cultural experience of a particular community, he believed such an occasion could also provide the basis for new forms of popular art.

A series of *tableaux vivants* was presented in the context of carefully choreographed and synchronized performances of music and dance. These provided an emotional and emblematic accompaniment to parallel and underscore the explicit representation of historical scenes. A huge hall was erected on the shore of Lake Geneva. The spectators, some six thousand of them, sat facing a vast raised stage fifty meters wide, to the rear of which was a wall that could be opened up to reveal the lake and a distant vista of the countryside and mountains. There was no proscenium arch and no curtain.

Appia frequently referred to the statement by Schopenhauer that "music by and through itself alone never expresses the phenomenon, but rather the inner essence of the phenomenon."[16] He had made this one of the guiding principles of his reform of Wagnerian staging, and he now put the same idea to use in creating a work of "living art" for the Geneva production. Recognizing that behind every historical action were underlying and motivating human values and emotions, he sought not just to represent directly, but to express as well the inner content of the historical events being commemorated, through an evocative musical and eurhythmic accompaniment. A historical pageant could thus be raised to an altogether more universal plane: "The spectator had simultaneously before his eyes, first, animated historic themes whose progression in itself formed a majestic dramatic action, and second, the purely human Expression, stripped of all historic pomp, presenting a sacred commentary on—and a transfigured realization of—the events."[17]

With the conclusion of his work at Hellerau and the Geneva Festival, it is probably fair to infer that Appia believed a particular chapter of his creative life had closed. He was not in fact to work on any major projects with Dalcroze again. Instead, his time was increasingly devoted to exploring and developing new, more radical ideas about the nature and limits of theatrical art. In any case, the war severely curtailed the scope for direct practical work and encouraged Appia's innate tendency to solitary and theoretical investigations. In a letter to Gordon Craig[18] of November 1918, at the end of the war, he outlined the evolution of his thought:

> I've decided to do a series of essays linked one to the other by the same theme. The complete work will probably be called *The Living Art;* that's to say, the *moving art* (human body, light, etc.) as opposed to immobile art (all the rest!). . . . If this is successful I will then publish several of my numerous articles and prefaces similarly gathered into a volume. For this I will do some new drawings, always with a vision of *The Hall,* a kind of cathedral of the future, which reunites in a vast, free and *changeable* space, all the expressions of our social life, and in particular, dramatic art, *with or without spectators.* . . . From there we shall arrive, I have a strong and profound conviction, at majestic festivals where an entire people will give their cooperation, and where no one will be allowed to remain passive, and we will express all our joy, our passions, and our pains.[19]

The book that Appia was working upon was *The Work of Living Art,* which he completed in May 1919, and published late in 1921. The "numerous articles" are in fact numbered among those that are published here, in this volume, many of them for the first time.

Appia had long nurtured very radical notions about the changing nature of theatrical art and the need to transform audience expectations and reactions as well as to purify the role of the actor—and had put some of his insights into practice through his work with Dalcroze. He now consolidated these ideas in his book, which he regarded as an aesthetic "last testament," although he continued to explore and develop some of its more innovative concepts through the essays written during the final few years of his life.

The early chapters of the book are devoted for the most part to a restatement and refinement of his earlier wide-ranging (and already widely influential) principles. He discusses the essential elements of theatrical art, and analyzes their use, employing the headings "Living Time," "Living Space," "Living Color" and "Organic Unity" to sketch out his model of a reformed theatre. But running through these chapters, somewhat ambivalently, before rising finally to dominate the final portion of the book, are even more advanced ideas, which, in the end, overwhelm any remotely orthodox conception of theatre—even a theatre reformed along the lines Appia had laid down earlier and summarized in this very book!

Thus in the very process of consolidating his previous work, Appia's restless and prophetic thought surges beyond it. The final chapters, "The Great Unknown and the Experience of Beauty" and "Bearers of the Flame," border, as their titles suggest, on mysticism and the ineffable, while yet conveying through their sometimes extravagant imagination a sublime and inspiring vision.

Appia realized that his work, which had begun as an analysis and critique of the state of theatrical art, must end in a fundamental attack on contemporary culture itself, and, crucially, on the role that art was forced to play within it.

People observed art passively: if it moved them at all, it did so *artificially,* having lost most of its pristine power to disturb, excite or invigorate an audience who now might contemplate and collect it, but could no longer actively enter into it. It was necessary to return to the wellspring of all art, "the living experience of our own body"[20] and from there to express and understand both the reality of oneself and, simultaneously, one's communal relationship with the rest of society. Instead of being an isolated "eternal spectator,"[21] one could become whole again, reintegrated "into living contact with our fellow men."[22]

In confronting this crisis of art in society, and suggesting a solution, Appia once again places the actor at the very center of his concept of theatre. But the actor in Appia's more advanced theory is not, as earlier, in the service of the work: he becomes the work itself.

The earlier theory had emphasized the actor's function as the vital link through which the musical score and the dramatic text were realized in space, and through whose movement the scenic elements were in effect "generated." Now, even more radically, Appia conceives art forms in which the moving body simultaneously creates the work and, doing so, *is* the work. This redefinition was predicated upon his analysis of the basis of theatrical art, which he had come to believe lay not in the enactment of fictive stories, but in the immediate physical activity of living, moving bodies, motivated by light and music.

Previously he had been concerned to free and externalize the expressive elements of theatre as they were contained in a musical drama and conveyed through the medium of a dramatic plot. In enacting such stories, however, the actor is constrained to take on imitative and representational qualities, which are not themselves purely "expressive" elements, but constitute instead what Appia termed "indications" or "signs." If the dramatist and, in turn, the actor were to renounce these fictive encumbrances altogether—to use the expressive elements of their craft in their purest and most direct form—would it not be possible for them to create a theatrical art analogous to abstract painting, sculpture, or indeed to music?

It was necessary to experiment in creating less "literary" art forms in the recognition that theatrical art need not have a plot or story to sustain it any more than a symphony requires a title or notional program to make it expressive and sensible. An art form based upon the body moving to music in space was ultimately capable, Appia believed, of extraordinary expressiveness—communicating directly to all present—since all alike have bodies.

Thus, at the end of his life, as his later writings eloquently confirm, Appia had moved far beyond the revolutionary reforms proposed in his earlier theory into even more prophetic and advanced beliefs about the nature of new, emerging art forms, as well as the performance places and occasions at which they would occur. In his essays—those included in this volume—he writes enthusiastically and at length about the social implications of this new collaborative art, the benefits it may bring, and the need to begin exploration of the various forms it might take. These speculative treatments tend, inevitably, to be somewhat vague and exhortatory, as well as at times ecstatic, but they should not therefore be too readily dismissed as merely the final inconsequential bursts of flame from a burnt-out visionary.

At the close of his life Appia still retained that astonishing ability so evident in his youth, to peer into the future of "theatrical" art to trace (and sometimes to determine), however limited in practical detail, a proximate outline of things to come.

The extent to which Appia's ideas ranged far in advance of his time is devastatingly clear in the light of the practical work he undertook in the last five years of his life. It was not until 1923 that, at the age of sixty-one, Appia was at last given an opportunity to stage one of Wagner's operas according to the detailed plans which he had first drawn up in the 1890s. In June of that year, he wrote to Gordon Craig joyfully announcing that he had been invited by Arturo Toscanini to stage *Tristan and Isolde* at La Scala in Milan: "They offered me everything to realize my idea, and at last,—at last—the great, the beautiful dream begins."[23]

Back in 1899 Appia had included a masterful scenario for *Tristan* as an appendix to *Music and the Art of the Theatre*. That scenario and the designs accompanying it now served, with only slight modifications, as the conceptual and scenic basis for the Milan production. Both the lighting plot and the settings were virtually identical with the earlier plans, a fact which demonstrates how prescient Appia's "dream" had been, since at the time the lighting equipment necessary for its execution did not exist.

The radical nature of Appia's vision was further indicated by the fact that now, a quarter of a century later, his ideas still seemed too advanced for La Scala readily to assimilate them. The place was a bastion of conservative tradition within an Italian theatrical establishment almost wholly innocent of the reformist ideas now clearly evident (if not yet predominant) in much of the rest of Europe. Appia found "the agonies of Milan"[24] enormously taxing. His habitual reticence and sensitivity were exacerbated by the Italian style of production, which outraged his sense of order, control, and careful coordination of all the elements of production. A perfectionist by nature—a tendency which his relative lack of practical experience as well as his ever more refined theories reinforced—he found the pragmatic and sometimes haphazard compromise of actual production difficult to endure.

The personnel at La Scala, in addition to being rather disorganized, were also set in their ways, and reluctant to accept or adhere to the very different principles and technique which Appia's novel ideas entailed. Craig himself (to whom Appia confided) wrote later of his experience: "He was badly helped. His helpers exclaimed 'wonderful' and added the aside 'unpractical' without attempting to aid him with whatever poor practicality they might possess. . . . A large theatre like La Scala . . . is somewhat like an old fashioned court—intrigue is despicable in such places, and paramount."[25] Craig's conclusion was not wide of the mark: "Appia must have been staggered when it dawned on him that La Scala was about to tie him up and slip a sack over his head."[26]

Appia recorded after his ordeal that "up to the last *hour* nothing was sure, nothing arranged" and confessed, "Not for a million francs would I begin it all over again with these delightful gentlemen who have no firmness or consistency, and with whom day after day, one experiences the most awful anxiety."[27] *Tristan* opened on 20 December 1923 and was performed a further five times during the season. Despite all the problems, and his personal distress, in the end, Appia was satisfied that the scenic presentation conformed to his designs and intentions. The production was lavishly praised for the magnificence of its musical interpretation and for Toscanini's superb conducting. But there was little understanding and less sympathy for Appia's settings among the opera-going public, although they received a more mixed response from the critics, ranging from one who termed them "ridiculous, shameful, pretentious, and oppressing to the eye,"[28] to another who praised them for their "poetic use of light, psychological intimacy and sense of mystery."[29]

In general the negative criticism proceeded out of a literal-mindedness which objected primarily to what was perceived as nonrealistic and therefore illogical scenery. Paradoxically perhaps, it was precisely Appia's insistence that, scenically, the external world in *Tristan* must be deemphasized to encourage the audience's perception of the inner and spiritual essence of the opera that caused the greatest distress. Spectators were perplexed by the relative drabness of color, the absence of elaborately painted scenery, and the austere simplicity of the decor, without understanding that it was the opera's essential transcendent quality, impossible to convey through purely realistic and quotidian scenery, which Appia sought to express through more subtle means.

Although the lighting found greater understanding and approval, the Italian critics by and large failed to grasp the first and most basic principle and pre-requisite of Appia's reform: that stage settings must be designed not as static pictures arranged according to the requirements of perspective painting, but as plastic and dynamic spaces, constructed to meet the needs of the actor as he expresses and realizes a work of dramatic art. Toscanini, who greatly esteemed Appia's work, was discouraged and saddened by its reception at La Scala, and never presented the production again. Not until January 1931 was *Tristan* seen once more in Milan in settings that reverted to the old style, "that were not only static and stereotyped, but resembled lurid colored postcards sufficiently to make everyone happy."[30] Only a few at La Scala appreciated the genius and beauty of Appia's work, or the enviable experience of having seen it staged for the first time.

Despite the situation at La Scala, by the early 1920s Appia's demands for such elements as three-dimensional scenery, the expressive use of light, and the evocation of psychology and atmosphere in scenic presentation had been widely introduced, though frequently his influence was unacknowledged. As he himself remarked, late in his life, " 'Appia' and 'anonymity' belong together."[31] The experience of the First World War brought about fundamental and permanent shifts in artistic sensibility and practice, and such change was particularly evident and pervasive in the theatre. The old aesthetic of scenic illusion, already widely repudiated, was further discredited as part of a larger and general reaction—even a revulsion—against traditional cultural norms. Obviously, Appia's post-war manifestos concerning "living art" were directly relevant to this new spirit, but so too was his earlier work; in particular his designs for rhythmic spaces, which were found now to provide a ready practical and, in part, theoretical basis for experiment. Everywhere designers began to employ abstract scenery, frequently using the same elements—steps, podia, solid geometric forms and platforms which Appia had used with such superb effect in the rhythmic settings he first created during his collaboration with Dalcroze, which continued to characterize his work in the 1920s.

An international exhibition of theatrical design held at Amsterdam in 1922 included a large cross-section of current work, as well as examples of Appia's "old" designs dating from before the turn of the century. The greatly gifted and influential French director Jacques Copeau attended, and observed, "When we go into the other exposition rooms, we see that everything done after [Appia] stemmed from him but has been more or less deformed in the process."[32] In a similar vein, the American critic Sheldon Cheney, whose book *The New Movement in the Theatre* (1914) had been one of the earliest to deal comprehensively with reforms in theatrical art, was moved to remark: "Of course there are those who would say the Craig and Appia have become historical now, but after studying the other exhibits, I came back to the Craig and Appia room with the

Figure 6. Design for *Tristan*, Act 3
Tristan as he died was at the base of the tree, illuminated by the fading rays of the sun shining through the window.

feeling that it will be time enough to put these two on the history shelf when the rest of the world has caught up with them."[33]

At about this time Appia became acquainted with Oskar Wälterlin, a young theatre director who was to become one of his most dedicated and accomplished followers. Wälterlin, who was a stage director at the Municipal Theatre of Basel, was distressed that, although "in the realm of the theatre, Appia was a prophet,"[34] he was one virtually without honor in his own country, being far "better known to the connoisseurs and enthusiasts of theatrical reform, than in the theatre himself, or to the theatre-going public."[35]

After consulting with Appia, Wälterlin grew increasingly anxious to collaborate with him in the interest of seeing his work produced in Switzerland. In the summer of 1922 he visited a number of German theatres, and reported to Appia after his tour that everywhere he went, Appia's ideas were being put into practice, but sometimes inadequately. The superficial appearance of his designs was reproduced on stage with little regard for the synthesis of light and movement without which, as Appia insisted, the designs were meaningless. Directors were embracing the form, while neglecting or ignorant of the substance, and Wälterlin therefore urged Appia to become directly involved in the testing and promulgation of his theories.

These appeals and the logic behind them undoubtedly encouraged Appia to accept the invitation which came at just this moment to stage *Tristan* at La Scala. In the meantime, Wälterlin persuaded the management of the Basel Theatre to present an entirely new production of the *Ring,* to be executed according to Appia's conception and to commence in the 1924–25 season. Appia agreed to the project in August 1923. Now in failing health and with only a few years to live, it offered the chance to realize at last a goal which had eluded him throughout his career: to produce Wagner's great cycle according to the principles first painstakingly formulated at the turn of the century, and meticulously refined and developed in the course of his life's work.

Appia at once prepared for Wälterlin a new set of designs and scenarios for *Rhinegold* and *The Walkyrie.* Although the underlying goal of providing a staging directly expressive of Wagner's work remained the same, and Appia's basic principles were still valid, nevertheless, the means for achieving them needed revising. Under the influence of his experiments with Dalcroze, Appia had long since freed his later settings from the vestiges of romanticism still evident in those created in the 1890s. Prompted by Wälterlin, he now produced new "rhythmic designs" for the *Ring,* which incorporated the spatial concepts derived from eurhythmics.

The change of style can readily be discerned by comparing the Basel settings with the earlier compositions. Stage structures are similar, but the new designs are more sharply defined through the use of carefully articulated architectonic elements, whose crisp lines and geometric solidity are reiterated

Figure 7. Design of 1924 for the Walhalla Landscape of *Rhinegold*, Scenes 2 and 4, As Presented at Basel
Compare with Appia's 1892 design in fig. 15, as well as with the 1896 Bayreuth setting in fig. 13.

throughout all the new settings, and, moreover, underscored by the stage lighting. In place of the relatively subdued, occasionally diaphanous illumination employed earlier, which emphasized the soft contours of the sets, Appia now called for a heightened contrast between light and dark areas, corresponding to the bold lines of the practicables. Tightly focused beams of light were to be used further to define and underscore the plastic reality of the stage structure.

What Appia hoped to achieve through this new approach was to establish unequivocally the actual dimensions of the performance space and the solid elements within it. Traditionally scene design tended to abolish real space, together with its solid components, by substituting for it through perspective technique an extended *imaginary* space which was incompatible with that occupied by the audience on the other side of the proscenium arch. As a result of his experience and aesthetic analysis of eurhythmics, and his desire for "living art," Appia was determined to achieve the greatest possible proximity and affinity between performers and spectators and between the realms of stage and auditorium. This concept was emphasized in all aspects of the Basel production, and the necessary contact began by establishing unambiguously a common spatial ground for actors and audience.

Appia came to Basel on the first day of September, 1924—his 62nd birthday—to assist in rehearsals and consult further with the director, cast, and theatre personnel. Wälterlin appears to have fired the entire company with his own enthusiasm and sense of the importance of the experiment, and Appia could hardly have found elsewhere more enlightened or responsive support. Another factor favoring the project was the nature of the Basel public itself. The city took pride in its reputation for an open and responsive attitude to new ideas in art and culture, and for being, in general, a more tolerant and sophisticated community than other Swiss cities.

Such advantages, however, were balanced by a number of profoundly inauspicious circumstances. The Basel Theatre was a repertory company, which meant that the time allowed for rehearsing Appia's radically new type of production was severely limited, and to make matters worse, the unusual scenic and technical requirements of his designs quite exceeded the theatre's resources. Even with the best will in the world, moreover, the performers had hardly any appropriate training or experience out of which to fashion the relatively restrained but highly expressive and meticulously coordinated movement and gestures demanded by Appia's scenario. None of them had any prior training in eurhythmics.

The public, although generally well-intentioned and open-minded, was inevitably larded with reactionary elements. These were particularly liable to become aroused by what they must certainly view as an impudent challenge to the carefully tended and fervently revered Bayreuth "house-style," which, particularly in provincial theatres, was regarded as orthodox, if not indeed sacrosanct. Wälterlin, convinced of the importance of their project, was determined that the best possible arrangement backstage should be matched by equally energetic attempts to prepare things on the other side of the curtain. He was keenly aware of the radical and disorienting innovations both in setting and in underlying concept with which the Basel audience was to be faced: a confrontation which, as he clearly anticipated, some in the audience must view as a challenge and an affront. He did everything possible to prepare his public, mounting lectures, an exhibition, and providing newspaper articles in advance of the premiere.

The scenarios that Appia prepared were conditioned by his concept of "living art" and stress constantly that the characters and plot of the *Ring* must be viewed not as belonging to and contained by a mythical past, but rather as the agents of a theatrical event, here and now, which the audience must experience directly in all its visual, physical, emotional and intellective power. Because much of the staging of these operas was widely considered established and orthodox, they provided particularly interesting (if volatile) material through which to test such a concept and to observe its effect upon an audience.

*Rhinegold* opened at Basel on 21 November 1924. The performance went extremely well, and was favorably received both by the opening-night audience and by the critics. Most of the attention was, of course, focused upon Appia's settings and the stage direction. His attempt to rid Wagner's work both of its nineteenth-century ballast and of any suggestion that the opera should be revered as a romantic expression of German mythology was certain to encounter opposition, but, although at the premiere a few catcalls and boos were heard among an overwhelmingly approving audience, little, at first, of such hostility was evident in the press.

Most reviews appeared not only to concede the need for fundamental reform, but also to welcome Appia's specific innovations. Although there were slight objections raised here and there over details of staging, or technical limitations, all but one of the half-dozen or more papers reviewing the production found much to praise both in Appia's ideas and in their execution.[36]

While *Rhinegold* continued to play before generally enthusiastic audiences, rehearsals got under way for the next production of the cycle, *The Walkyrie,* and progressed through January 1925. Behind the scenes, however, intrigue developed, as members of a grossly intolerant and reactionary faction marshaled their forces to combat what they chose to see not merely as a controversial staging, but somehow as perverse and decadent, an affront to the Basel public, and a conspiracy against its morality and reputation.

The leader of this fringe, Adolf Zinsstag, was president of the Basel Wagner Society, and also the official representative in Switzerland of the Bayreuth Festival. He was in sympathy with the still-entrenched "old guard" there, headed by the indomitable Cosima Wagner, who, as ever, remained hostile to any fundamental reform. Shortly before the opening of *The Walkyrie*, Zinsstag wrote a scathing article condemning the *Rhinegold* setting and personally denouncing Appia and Wälterlin. Claiming to speak for a large and outraged public, he extravagantly castigated the production as "vandalism" and "profanity." He insisted that the task of director should consist solely in precisely representing the setting and action dictated by the stage directions and libretto. He ridiculed Appia's abstract scenery, the stylized movement of the actors and the unrealistic lighting. In place of the exact replication of nature called for by Wagner, and admirably executed at Bayreuth, Appia had substituted a perverted and farcical product of his own fantasy, which Zinsstag characterized as "artistic Bolshevism."

He was ready with a small band of supporters at the opening of *The Walkyrie* on 1 February. At the final curtain, as Appia and Wälterlin appeared before the predominantly appreciative audience, the dissidents erupted in a chorus of shouts, hisses and boos, which the rest of the audience, becoming aware of the tumult, tried to drown in applause. Then, for half an hour, there was pandemonium, while each side hurled abuse at the other. In the days following, the press comment, although qualified, was once more largely favorable and tolerant.

Not content with the opening-night furor, Zinsstag's perverse Wagnerites continued a relentless campaign of vilification throughout February. He wrote virulent articles referring to the "Prostitution of a Work of Art," in which he condemned the production as "so unnatural as to border on obscenity." Determined that the citizens of Basel should be aroused against this threat, he organized a petition, prepared handouts and, together with his followers, raised such a scandal that the Basel *Ring* became known far and wide, attracting in the process a good deal of sympathetic attention to its creator's ideas.

Appia was, nevertheless, devastated by the vicious attack. In the face of threats to its public subsidy, the theatre management was forced, under protest (its director resigned), to abandon plans for producing the remainder of the *Ring*. Appia returned dejected to Geneva. His disappointment was intense at seeing this last great effort to reform Wagnerian staging end so disastrously. The following spring (1926) the Basel Theatre belatedly presented another work from the *Ring:* a "new" production of *Götterdämmerung* which returned to the "authentic" and traditional Bayreuth style.[37] No one demonstrated.

The last years of Appia's life were a final period of astonishing creative work. Within a few years he produced a great many richly suggestive essays, as well as numerous designs, and scenarios for such works as, *King Lear, Macbeth, Lohengrin, Faust,* and Gluck's *Alceste, Iphigénie en Tauride* and *Iphigénie en Aulide.* As these writings and designs eloquently confirm, Appia had moved far beyond the revolutionary reforms proposed in his earlier theory into even more prophetic and advanced beliefs about the nature of new, emerg-

Figure 8.  Design of 1924 for *The Walkyrie*, Act 3, at Basel
Compare with the Bayreuth setting in fig. 14, as well as with Appia's
own earlier setting in fig. 29.

ing art forms. These radical concepts pulled him decisively away from any kind of traditional theatre.

He pointed this out in a letter to Gordon Craig: "My vision and all my thought are indeed much-advanced. I don't see the theatre anymore, it doesn't inspire me—and if one wishes to comprehend how I have developed, it can't be conveyed by my drawings. One must wait, therefore, until I've brought new elements." He went on to hint at the nature of the ideas he was now developing, "the great joy which I am charged with placing before my fellow men," noting that being "retained in the atmosphere of the theatre—the theatre such as it is—contradicts even my most profound convictions."[38]

In the same letter Appia mentioned that he intended to complement *The Work of Living Art* with a further volume developing its ideas in a more practical context. "Until then, I ought to work, work well, and . . . keep quiet, at least in public." Appia termed the essay written in August 1923, "Man Is the Measure of All Things," as "A Preface to a New Work," and a little later, wrote the piece entitled, "Preface to the Edition of My Essays in One Volume."

From these, and other references, it seems likely that Appia saw his late essays (to be assimilated into a single volume) as the culmination of his creative work: the furthest point attained by his restless imagination. They are found (in most cases published for the first time) in the latter sections of this book. Reading and evaluating them may therefore provide the best and most appropriate evidence of Appia's importance and foresight. They remain fascinating and at the same time poignant evidence of a genius who, however limited the scope for practical realization of his deeply felt and keenly intelligent ideas, never ceased to innovate, explore, prophesy, and inspire.

> In our search for the flame of aesthetic truth we had to extinguish, one after the other, the false torches of a false artistic culture. Now our own fire—yours and mine—can relight those torches.[39]

# Part One

# Appia on Appia

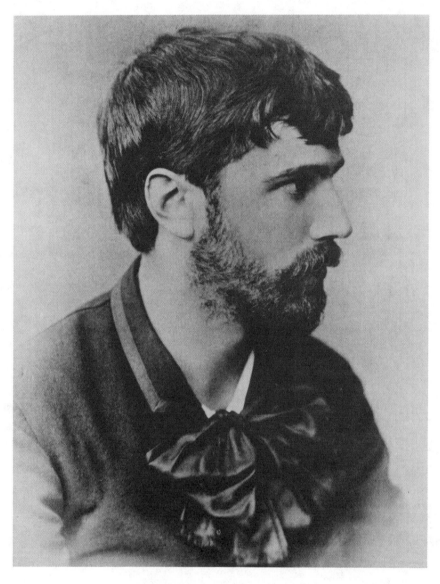

Figure 9.    Adolphe Appia, circa 1890

# Introduction to Part One

Appia was an inspired, but extremely shy and reclusive genius. He shunned publicity of any kind and despised those whom he felt put their personality before their art. Rarely in his writings does he make personal observations apart from expressing his views on—broadly conceived—aesthetic subjects. Even at the end of this life, when his ideas were being widely accepted and put into practice—frequently without any acknowledgment of their source—he was content for others to point out his influence, if they wished: "I am happy to have been able to show the way to a few people; to turn to the profit of others something which had been given to me."[1]

That, in the end, his reforms were realized largely through the efforts of others—a host of pragmatic men of the theatre—attests to both the essential efficacy of his concepts, and his own unfortunate limitations as a man of action and practical affairs. Both his family background—strict Calvinist—and his schooling had encouraged an inward-looking, and rather unworldly attitude, an inability to interact with others, or to understand how to secure their goodwill and cooperation. Moreover, he suffered acute difficulty in communicating because of rather severe stuttering: an obstacle which perhaps above all else prevented him from direct collaboration in practical work.

And yet, the relevance of Appia's contribution to so many widely diverse manifestations of modern theatre is due, strange to say, in large part to his failure to engage in substantial practical work himself. Forced to express his ideas predominantly through his designs and writings, he developed these along rigorously logical lines, with each new stage of his thinking and theory evolving directly and inevitably from that preceding it. Appia's vision of the development of theatrical art proceeded linearly and without distraction along a track upon which practicing men and women of the theatre came again and again as, through trial and error, they advanced along somewhat more meandering paths.

The "Introduction to My Personal Notes," written in 1905, indicates the nature and direction of things to come. It also provides an introduction to and brief summary of Appia's achievement by that time: his inspired analysis of the disastrous state of theatrical art, and comprehensive suggestions for reform. These had been published first in 1895, in *La Mise en scène du drame wagnérien (Staging Wagnerian Drama)*, and then, in 1899, much more fully in his great work, *Die Musik und die Inscenierung (Music and the Art of the Theatre)*. As yet, however, they had attracted little attention. His detailed suggestions for staging Wagner's operas had been scornfully dismissed by Wagner's formidable widow, Cosima, who was determined to preserve and venerate what she considered to have been the "last word" (Wagner's) on the matter of stagecraft at Bayreuth. Indeed, his ideas were not to be officially welcomed there for half a century.

Appia's bitter disappointment at this rebuff is evident in his "Notes." It was the moment when above all else he needed encouragement in testing his theories through practical application. Bayreuth was not only the obvious venue for realizing the ideas and scenarios over which he had labored so long with such passion, it was also the point from which his revolutionary call for a reform generally of theatrical practice might most readily have been heard and taken up by others throughout Europe.

"Theatrical Experiences and Personal Investigations," written almost twenty years later—but never before published—in addition to providing an overall summary of Appia's career, also supplies the most revealing record of his early years, and the personal background which determined his artistic development. It is also particularly useful in providing a retrospective analysis and account of his crucial early work on Wagnerian staging. Indeed, in some ways its description of the process by which Appia thought through and developed his scenic concepts is more fluent and immediately accessible than the initial outcome of that process, that is, his earliest scenarios and the critical writings referred to above.

The writings through which Appia first expressed his observations and ideas reflect the intensity of his passion, but sometimes, the struggle as well which he had in trying to capture logically and coherently perceptions and concepts that first came to him only visually and emotionally. One must bear in mind his own description of the process: how he first contemplated and reacted to Wagner's works by striving imaginatively to give them their appropriate and (somehow inevitable) theatrical realization, and only later attempted to extrapolate from the results of this process a conceptually unified aesthetic theory. It is not, therefore, surprising that his earliest writing is sometimes convoluted or vague, and occasionally repetitious and overwrought. He was, after all, attempting to use language to map out an altogether unfamiliar mental landscape.

In "Theatrical Investigations," Appia describes the misunderstanding that sometimes resulted, above all, when his theoretical writings (or worse still, merely the designs themselves) were considered without consulting the detailed scenarios which he had based upon them. Too often, the settings were copied, or elements lifted from them, without heeding Appia's essential requirement that they be closely coordinated with the emotional qualities as well as the stage action of the piece to be performed within them. The organic relationship between stage space and dramatic action was crucial, but frequently overlooked by those who merely looked to Appia for visually satisfying designs.

The topic next taken up in this autobiographical essay—eurhythmics—was, Appia believed, the key to understanding and, indeed, realizing the promise of his earliest work. Not only did it provide a method for coordinating stage movement (and by extension, stage space) with music, it also offered through the person of its inventor, Emile Jaques-Dalcroze, the vital opportunity to engage in fruitful collaborative activity. Thus, eurhythmics both as a theory, and an activity, fulfilled in turn Appia's critical and practical work. The culmination of his liaison with Dalcroze, their acclaimed presentation of Gluck's *Orfeo* at Hellerau in 1912 and 1913 is briefly noted by Appia, who, ever modest, does in this essay, for once allow himself a moment of triumph in asserting that "for the first time since the Greek era, a perfect fusion of all media of expression, closely and mutually subordinated, was realized."

The final portion of the essay, in delineating the effect of eurhythmics upon Appia's subsequent work, provides as well a summary of the ideas both aesthetic and social, which were presented most extensively in his book, *L'Oeuvre d'art vivant (The Work of Living Art)*, published in 1921.

Particularly provocative is his call (taken up too in several of the late essays) for the construction of "study sites" that would allow the greatest possible range of activity and collaboration to take place, while encouraging the collective involvement of all present. He envisaged buildings that could be arranged to contain a great variety of spaces—everything from an intimate studio theatre to a large open hall—in which the barriers between audience and performers would be progressively eliminated. Lighting would be the major scenic element, music would dominate the performance, attention and response would be focused on the moving bodies of those taking part, and the entire space would be kept as flexible and unrestrictive as possible. Improvisation and experimental work would be encouraged so that through such investigations new creative possibilities would be opened up and new forms of performance emerge. It was a liberating vision, to which Appia returned again and again, believing that it held out the possibility of not just aesthetic, but social and spiritual renewal as well.

A similar concept permeates the brief "American Lecture" which Appia wrote (about 1926) in the third person for presentation by a speaker to an American audience. Again he emphasizes the integrative function of art: its power to mitigate the alienation of contemporary life; to restore communal values and relations and combat a pervading sense of existential isolation.

The final piece in this section, "Curriculum Vita," written in 1927 near the end of Appia's life, provides in his own words the briefest summary and evaluation of his theoretical and practical work.

Appia was an intensely private person, and, apart from the purely factual biographical information they contain, these essays are intriguing for the glimpses that they afford of how Appia viewed and evaluated his own work and accomplishments. Of a life apart from that work, very little at all is said, and that too is significant for its indication that, for Appia, no separation between a genuinely expressive art and life was possible; ideally each permeated the other as "Living Art."

In "Theatrical Experiences," he records that at the very beginning of his creative work: "I began to sense my own inner resources and the responsibilities they imposed upon me. Shortly thereafter I retired to the countryside and set to work on what I regarded as my imperative task." The statement is revealing: Appia saw his undertaking as, simultaneously, a personal and an artistic mission. Personally, he recognized that after many years of real and figurative wandering, a period during which he had functioned as analyst, critic and iconoclast, it was now personally imperative as he approached thirty to enter into what he knew must be his true role: that of a genuinely creative artist. A variety of personal and psychological factors must have further urged this course upon him. Artistically he saw clearly that the challenge which Wagnerian opera presented to stagecraft had to be taken up and its implications followed relentlessly into completely uncharted areas. The same would later be true of eurhythmics.

This concept of a mission, one which fulfilled both existential and aesthetic imperatives, colored and characterized Appia's personality and work throughout his life. No one who knew or worked with him for any length of time ever failed to be profoundly affected by it. Perhaps because the quality and direction of his own life were so deeply influenced by the subjects of his aesthetic investigations, he always insisted on the uniqueness and centrality of art to man's existence generally.

# Introduction to My Personal Notes

## (1905)

"It is almost always symptomatic of frustration when an artist interrupts his creative work to appear before the world as a writer of theory. Depending on whether this frustration is due to an obstacle from the outside or to a conflict of two opposing forces within the artist himself, it will be perceptible to others with greater or less clarity."[2]

With these words Chamberlain begins his chapter on the writings of the master.

On the whole I should say the same, and this would suffice to introduce my personal notes to those of my friends who care to read them. But I cannot show any artistic work that would explain or demonstrate the frustration.

At best, a scenario—like a score that can be read by any musician—can be made of a *mise en scène,* based on the dramatic life of the actor; not on the purely decorative effect. Such a scenario would be annotated with a series of diagrams, sketches, etc., indicating the performer's actions. But unlike a musical score whose existence is independent of the actual performance, the scenario exists, even for the expert, only in the production. Those who have witnessed the performance and can reconstruct it in their mind will understand the setting, the diagrams, and the sketches and can detect the stage director's motivations for certain arrangements; they alone will be capable of doing this. To others who did not attend the theatre, all this material will remain unintelligible.

Thus my work and my ideas are virtually unknown, and my difficulties cannot attract attention. For this reason a few explanations preceding my personal notes seem appropriate.

As Chamberlain stated, the obstacles to be faced by an artist stem from two

---

Editor's note: A date in parentheses below the title of an essay indicates the year in which the piece was written. If an essay has appeared elsewhere, the publication history is given also.

sources: they come either from the outside or from within his own personality. As a rule, those deriving from the outside are the more serious, since the artistic passion is apparently always strong enough to overcome difficulties inherent in character or temperament. For the majority of artists, therefore, the problem remains simple. A painter needs leisure for painting and favorable conditions for the exhibition of his paintings. This is also true of the composer, although the "exhibition" of his work may be more of a problem. The dramatist encounters far more serious difficulties; nevertheless, he too, writes his play at his leisure in the quiet of his home. Its production can take place without him, because, after all, the play exists in its manuscript; like the score of a music drama, it can be disseminated in printed form.

The scenic artist, as I see him, is obviously a kind of painter; only the execution of his work and its "exhibition" are confused, perhaps not as far as he himself is concerned, but surely as it concerns everyone else. One can watch a picture being painted in a studio, or see it in its final form, before it is exhibited in the window of a dealer or in an art gallery. This cannot be done with the *mise en scène*. The labor of slowly developing scenic ideas; the notes and diagrams resulting from it; the sketch itself; nothing of all this resembles the projected work of art.

The work of the scenic artist is displayed to the audience at the very moment when it is being executed.

This seems to be the precise definition of the difficulties that may hinder the functioning of the scenic artist, for the consequence of the imperative necessity for a performance is that the work produced in the solitude of his home does not represent his entire task. Before his work can achieve final form, the theatre artist must learn to master a great number of unfamiliar details and a good many technical methods not directly related to his design.

Of course many individuals are capable of executing a painting in the quiet concentration of a studio and then of taking the few steps indispensable to a display of their finished work. But few artists have so many varied talents that they are able to create a décor, and, at the same time, direct, and even invent methods more technical than artistic—all the while coordinating, like a tyrant, the work of many minds towards a single goal.

Furthermore, it must be assumed that a particular stage is at the disposal of the artist for this purpose, since theatres are, at present, objects of financial speculation.

Thus, far more than other artists, the scenic artist encounters considerable obstacles—so considerable in fact that his freedom of action may become problematic. (The scenic artist I am talking about must, I insist, be equal in rank to first-rate artists in other fields.)

So much for the external problem. I have already spoken of the manifold gifts rarely combined, with which the scenic artist must be blessed. The problem regarding his inner attitude is hardly less difficult or less complex. If, moreover, an impediment or a particular character trait paralyzes him, his lot is truly pitiable. His artistic passion, his creative urge, are as indomitable as those of other artists. And yet, outside of the production, he has nothing to show!

Before I began to occupy myself with music I had already felt a passionate curiosity for everything connected with the theatre, with the presentation of any kind of drama. The study of music defined and purified that taste, and my experience with Wagnerian productions directed me irresistibly towards the idea of reform. Unable to accept the ridiculous contemporary mode of staging, I conjured up one that seemed to me truly suitable for Wagner's music dramas. A creative period thus preceded that of theoretical deliberation; for this reason the artistic integrity of my scenic visions seems to me guaranteed. First I "saw," undoubtedly within myself yet with perfect distinctness; and only then—the essential point—did I reflect theoretically on the value and suitability of what I had seen. Through this abstract labor I gained the conviction that the *mise en scène* was the natural outlet for my talents, and that no other specialization would allow a full expression of my artistic vision.

Accordingly, at my age (43), I should head a large shop for constructing and painting settings, possess a private studio for composing and executing diagrams and sketches. I should constantly be on the stage, carry out a long series of rehearsals, and supervise performances.

To this end I should have steadfast relations with as many artists as possible; painters, sculptors, musicians, writers, architects, et al., with as many actors and singers, as many people as feasible, in every social stratum. There would be few who could not be of value to me. I, myself, should write, travel, see, listen, read, without respite, everything within reach. I should train myself in exercising authority and giving commands, and acquire from this training clear judgment that would strengthen my influence.

All my activities should be focused upon this single purpose, the *mise en scène*, the importance of which I know so well. Probably I am one of the very few who do, since I also know what a multitude of elements must combine to create the *mise en scène*.

For the sake of my moral health I should, above all, frequently enjoy the incomparable happiness of seeing my work fulfilled—a goal that, as I have said before, is achieved only in a production.

But nothing of all this happened.

Instead, I became ever more isolated, ever more alienated from the theatre and from artists in all fields.

A private theatre and subsidies sufficient for large projects have been placed at my disposal. I do nothing about them, decline both, and, instead, I take up the pen, for which my hand is not suited at all, but which, nevertheless, must serve as substitute for everything!

In this situation a brief explanation is probably not superfluous. I shall try to enumerate as briefly as possible the obstacles standing in the way of my normal activity and to state the reason for my inability to overcome them.

To begin with, I discover an hereditary disposition that is perilous to define. I inherited it from my father, and it consists of a kind of interruption in the normal functioning of my social faculties. Friendly contacts and purely social relations come relatively easily to me despite my stuttering, of which I shall talk later. But as soon as it means becoming involved in the activity of others or arousing their interest in my aims, I suddenly find myself utterly incapable of action, not because of shyness but rather because of complete ignorance.

Ignorance of what?

At this point the definition becomes troublesome.

My education encouraged and strengthened the development of this inherited disposition, which a different education would certainly have subdued.

My mother raised her children for heaven, not for this world. She knew how to keep busy without a real concept of work. Religious compassion dominated her life.

Brought up without a sense of work and without the least knowledge of worldly matters, I had been living outside of life for a long time.

At the age of twenty when I had to find out after all what Reality was, I of course took the wrong route. Within a few months everything that gives a passionate zest for living was revealed to me. I surrendered to it completely, enchanted to the point of not recognizing for years that my ignorance of Reality had increasingly deepened. There were the pleasures of art—as far as I could appreciate them at the time—mixed with the entirely new happiness of comradeship, friendship, of events enjoyed together, of freedom from convention. Enthusiasm over anything we undertook: an exuberance too sudden, too violent to be controlled.

Among my friends one soon dominated all the others. The influence of an extraordinary intelligence, the advantage of contact with him, pride in being the most intimate friend of a great man, all this contributed to my definite attachment. My friend had a marvelously organized mind, but poor taste. He formed a flattering image of my artistic tendencies which I readily adopted. This relationship replaced Life for me, and it became my first step towards an illusion. Artificially I assumed the kind of personality that my friend and, to a certain degree, the others saw in me. A catastrophe became inevitable.

I recovered from that debacle (1902–3) but not before I suffered profound damage. I had known Reality only in pleasures, and I had known myself only in a flattering though fictitious image. To my total ignorance in matters of everyday living was added the almost intentional ignorance of myself.

This is the biographical side of that inherited disposition of mine. Let us examine the other aspect of it!

My father once said: "Men have written quite interesting things, they have created sublime pieces of art . . . but getting out of bed and into my slippers interests me more."

In this particular manner he expressed his consciousness of himself, and I might say the same of my own case. For my father, solitude was the only intimate company, the only company at all that did not bore or tire him; the one that always held his interest. "The highest bliss of all mortals is to be a personality."[3]

Goethe's words embrace a great number of phenomena. It always takes a strong personality to enjoy one's own company, painful as such a *tête-à-tête* may sometimes be. Furthermore, a powerful pathological element enters the picture if this personality finds harmony only in solitude; if this attitude that deprives him of the faculties necessary to communicate with his fellow men, even renders him incapable of acquiring these faculties. This was my father's situation, and it is mine too. Contact with others disturbs my peace of mind as it did his, and I long for my friend's fictional image of myself—which would enable me to create an appearance of harmony before others.

Yet it is understandable that this expedient is effective only with friendships and purely social relationships. When the interest and the services of indifferent people have to be obtained, that fictional image, aggravated as it is by ignorance, poses an obstacle that no effort can overcome.

Besides, I stutter. Those not suffering from an impediment can guess its effect upon the handicapped, but only theoretically. In daily life, they expect the afflicted one to react to his defect like a normal person. "Don't think of it!" I would be told, whereupon I would answer, "But the stuttering thinks of me!" as if I thought anyone could understand me. Even now I do not think it useful to elaborate on this matter.

My stuttering and my kind of education aggravated my inherited disposition. I may be permitted to assume that, without this handicap and with a different education, the obstacle within me would eventually have yielded to my effort, instead of growing ever more insurmountable.

To summarize: a natural calling, *mise en scène,* involves continuous relations with a multitude of people from all walks of life. To gain the good will of these people, to secure their collaboration in the realization of my artistic dream, I must know how to proceed diplomatically. This again implies above all precise, incisive, and commanding speech. I have just demonstrated that I utterly lack all these qualities. Therefore, in my study and in solitude I shall do the work that must compensate for everything else.

# Theatrical Experiences and Personal Investigations

(ca. 1921)

For some time I have been asked to write about my work in general, how I create and execute a stage setting and—in particular—how I arrived at my present style. Such requests are undoubtedly quite natural in view of a reform that has taken root and of certain principles which have been adopted without clear perception of the origin of this reform and frequently without recognition of its significance.

The study I have in mind will be divided into three parts: first, a brief statement of my theatrical experiences; then the report of my personal investigations; and finally the conclusions I have drawn from them.

The idea of theatre, even the word, was banned in our family circle, and its absence was doubtless a stimulant to my imagination. Children are attracted to all types of fiction; and, since theatre, its most fascinating form, had been excluded from my childhood, it inevitably drew my attention. When I was eighteen years old, my parents decided to let me study music, so I had to go to the theatre to become acquainted with opera. Until that time our conversation rarely turned to opera; when it did, it was rather perfunctory and by no means told me what I wanted to know. Only once did I pose a question which revealed a propensity as yet unconscious, but which seems to mark the beginning of my career.

One of my friends at the boarding school had seen *Tannhäuser* in Germany and gave me vague reports of it. I tried to pin him down and inquired whether the characters were really "in a place" and what this "place" looked like. He did not understand me. I remember having been rather insistent and having finally asked almost in despair: "Where were their feet?" To be sure, such preoccupation is characteristic of a fourteen-year-old boy; I am now sixty and still greatly concerned about where the actor's feet are.

Thus, in my ignorance of the theatre it was the location assigned to the actor that drew my primary interest. During this period we amused ourselves with the construction of a little cardboard stage. It did not work out well and so it led to arguments. I always wanted to place real objects on the stage, i.e., three-dimensional pieces; whereas my friend insisted on crowding it with painted cutouts which, to me, were meaningless. For the sake of peace, the whole thing was solemnly burned. I wish this fate would befall the majority of our contemporary settings.

The first real opera I saw was *Faust* by Gounod,[4] and I shall mention only my impressions directly related to the *mise en scène,* from the viewpoint with which we are concerned.

From the moment the curtain opened, to my amazement, I was conscious of the flimsiness of the settings and the flatness of the stage floor. I had assumed that a diversity of levels would improve the positions and the movements of the performers. I clearly sensed this, but could not precisely explain it. During the performance my sympathy, focused almost exclusively on the characters, grew steadily. I found it strange that their movements were so poorly arranged. Again this was more felt than formulated. The performers appeared to wander about haphazardly as in a public square and consequently the passionate love scene in the garden seemed out of place. And seeing only the flat floor, I wondered why Valentine had to die at the same spot. Afterwards I toured the theatre alone, murmuring to myself: "Is it for this that these thick walls were built, this massive construction!"

Of course, I experienced a kind of pleasure; yet for a long time I vaguely felt a moral and artistic betrayal of my innermost being. The moral disappointment was a natural consequence of my education; the artistic one, however, was more significant. The result was that, for a long time, my interest in the theatre centered on music, and that, with very few exceptions which I shall discuss later, the following years in the theatre were a period of a rather negative experience, as brilliant or mediocre spectacles unfolded before my eyes. I accepted these productions as children accept what they assume is inevitable, although they left my desires latent and did not inspire me to work.

In Paris, where I spent two years, the theatre taught me nothing except the advantage of numerous rehearsals and solid preparation. It was the precision of Parisian productions which, for all their conventionality, seemed remarkable to me, primarily because they emphasized the actors, my own main interest. I saw many productions, and the memory I have preserved of them is one of regrettable monotony.

During the same period I went three times to Bayreuth, where I saw *Parsifal* (the premiere was in 1882 under Wagner, who was then still living) and *Tristan*. Later on, I returned there three other times to see *Tannhäuser, Lohengrin, The Mastersingers,* and the *Ring*. Even now I have trouble sorting out all I learned there. I was not mature enough for such an experience, and since I did not understand the implications of the plot, I was totally unaware of the social and aesthetic ideas involved in these extraordinary creations. The *mise en scène* in Bayreuth, conceived in the pictorial tradition of the day, impressed me only by its unusual luxury; the acting of the singers, on the other hand, attracted my attention, and not without good reason. Yet even the careful treatment of the characters left an emptiness, because there was no harmony between scenery and acting except in the Temple of the Holy Grail. The arrangement of the auditorium did not impress me until later, and the marvel of the proscenium and curtain, as fascinating as it was, had not the impact upon my imagination that it should have had. Again, the music held all my attention.

At that time, the stage director of the theatre in Brunswick, reputedly a painter, was a fine cultured artist.[5] He tried to utilize the rather sketchy and conventional material at hand and without intending to reform anything, obtained, through ingenious arrangements and appropriate illumination, impressive settings, which were surprisingly effective in their simplicity. There I witnessed for the first time the proper use of platforms, which in those days might have seemed daring, but was nevertheless perfectly appropriate; and I became firmly convinced that a variety of stage levels had a favorable effect on the acting in addition to the support and stimulation it gave to lighting. Act 2 of *Carmen* and several scenes of Shakespeare's *Midsummer Night's Dream* impressed me most. Without trying to maintain what then was called illusion, this director attained a vision of superior reality, a dream for the eye to behold. The impression was very great, but not yet based upon sufficient technical knowledge nor upon aesthetic convictions.

In the spring of 1883 Leipzig announced a series of unusual presentations of both parts of Goethe's *Faust,* staged by Devrient,[6] the renowned actor, who was also to play the part of Mephistopheles. I never regretted having seen them. When a very great actor determines the *mise en scène* he naturally has his own body and movements in mind, even though he may imagine his conceptions to be derived from an entirely different and independent viewpoint. So it was with Devrient. In the case of *Faust,* at least, he insisted on settings designed according to a principle that was rather artificial and needed comment and explanation in a voluminous program. Nevertheless, his creations were extraordinary, especially for what might be called bodily imagination. In order to be more explicit I shall describe one of the settings devised by this remarkable man.

The reader will please imagine himself strolling in a small medieval German town. On a high platform, surrounded by tall linden trees, the cathedral dominates the ramparts. From the supporting wall our gaze plunges onto gardens which fill the moats and shelter little houses overgrown with greenery. A flight of steps from the wall leads down to a little street that crosses the outskirts of the town. A fountain is wedged into the foundation of a small house. In a corner nearby a Madonna decorated with a few flowers stands in the shadow of a niche. Opposite a little door opens into a garden, where flower beds extend to the front of a cottage. All this is well composed. Each motif calls for another; each seems to depend on and to influence another.

Let us now take a seat in the theatre in front of this segment of a town. My descriptions refer to left and right from the spectator's view. In the foreground slightly to the right, the street rises from the footlights and joins the stairs in the third wing. Martha's garden opens to the left of the stairs at the level of the stage floor. In the rear of this garden, against the wall that faces us, is the arbor. The wings to the left are hidden by Martha's house. On the right side of the little street is Gretchen's house, which is separated from the ramparts by a narrow passage of which only the entrance is to be seen. Opposite Martha's door is the niche with the Madonna, bedecked with flowers, fitting into the corner of this house. Downstage the narrow street turns to the right, vanishing in the wings. At the base of the house, in front of the spectator, is the fountain. The flight of steps, descending from the cathedral, stands out against the supporting wall and reaches halfway down, meeting a small platform at the level of the blind alley that leads to the rear door of Margaret's house. The door itself is not visible. The entrance to the alley is all one can see. From the platform, steps descend towards the audience and join with the little street, which, as we have seen, extends to the foreground, where it turns to the right along the fountain and the wall of the house. Gretchen's house has no windows at street level; she occupies the upper floor. A bay window at the corner, directly above the Holy Virgin, permits us a glimpse of the action inside the room.

This is truly an extraordinary scenic arrangement. It brings all these settings within one and the same picture: the cathedral (we shall see how), the square and street for several scenes, the Madonna *(Mater dolorosa),* the public fountain, Gretchen's room, Martha's garden, the arbor, and finally Martha's house. Everything belongs together, and provides both for effortless continuity of scenes and for clear and suitable movements by the actors. They walk freely about places familiar to them as well as to us, giving us the illusion that we accompany them wherever they go; so much so indeed that it is sometimes, for the audience, difficult to remain seated. Unfortunately, this fascinating effect is achieved by too great a compromise. The advantages of the setting are striking, but its shortcomings are equally significant. Here they are:

We are in front of the cathedral under the tall linden trees of the terrace. Bells ring while people are going to Mass. Gretchen comes out of her house; trembling, she supports herself by clinging to the wall and climbs the stairs that separate the house from the terrace; arriving at the portal of the church, she hesitates to mingle with the faithful. The organ begins to play; some latecomers brush against Gretchen, who does not dare to cross the threshold but humbly kneels among the timid beggars. This is as the church scene should be played. There is nothing impossible in it. And yet, is her humility not exaggerated, and is this exaggeration not too high a price to pay for a lively picture of the surroundings?

Devrient interprets the evil spirit, who in Goethe's *Faust* is not Mephistopheles, as Gretchen's own conscience. This is surely correct. But how can this be made clear to the audience? Devrient has Gretchen speak with two different voices. It is not difficult to vary them and the actress apparently took a special interest in this perfectly justified dramatic device. The *Dies irae* resounded through the open portal and the faint twilight gave the whole a very impressive atmosphere. In this setting Gretchen's anguish acquires a new and surprising value. But the scene was certainly not so conceived by the author; the violence done to it is obvious. A terrace with linden trees and a church seen from the outside cannot compare with the solemn emptiness and the chiaroscuro of a big nave. The contrast of the place to Gretchen's torturing agonies is not expressed. The choir does not sufficiently dominate the terrors of her thought; there are no pillars, no vault to stifle her. Her house and Martha's garden really are too close. The scene is not exactly sacrificed, still it does not hold the importance the poet has given it. This is a betrayal. Let us continue.

Frau Schwertlein, instead of occupying herself inside the house, tends her flowerbeds. Gretchen, descending from her house, crosses the narrow street, opens the door and finds her neighbor in the garden. This is very animated, to be sure, but it is not natural for Gretchen to put on jewelry out in the open. To the far left on the level of Martha's house, but downstage, a kind of door with a tiny window supposedly opens into an alley. Mephistopheles, still invisible, knocks at the door and Martha, opening the little window, finds herself nose to nose with the rather amazing head of her visitor. She opens the door and Mephistopheles enters the garden from a concealed passage. An excellent effect, perfectly fitting for this scene. But the next one is out of place in a garden with a low fence along a busy lane. Moreover, it is unfavorable for the scenes between Faust and Margaret, in which the spectator gains the impression of an anticipated deflowering.

Later on, Faust and Gretchen, Martha, and Mephistopheles stroll in the garden. The place itself is all right, but any passer-by, either on the terrace of the church or in the street, could look into the garden. One is particularly aware of this in the intimate scene between Faust and Gretchen. Devrient goes even so far in the liberties he takes that he has Gretchen speak her lyric monologue *Meine Ruh* (My peace) on Martha's bench while she waits for Faust. Their dialogue seems then to begin with Gretchen's *Versprich mir* (Promise me);

whereas the author intends her to be speaking before she is seen by the audience. Above all, he does not have this scene immediately follow the preceding one. Further betrayals!

Faust and Mephistopheles slip into the blind alley that leads to Gretchen's door. The effect is good. Soon thereafter they enter the room on the upper floor, and here we must emphatically state that in this scene our wish to see and hear what happens in that room outweighs any interesting and picturesque spectacle. But obviously even the spectators in the best seats can witness, through the open windows, just a bit of this scene or of Faust's monologue. The majority of the audience can catch no glimpse at all. Gretchen crosses the terrace in front of the cathedral, descends the steps, disappears behind her house and, shortly thereafter, enters her room. In order to be within sight of the audience, Gretchen is obliged to stay near the window virtually all the time. Twilight invades the narrow street; Gretchen's candle illumines the windows and casts moving shadows inside her room. It is charming and suggestive. If this scene were set to music, and if a considerable increase in expression by other means compensated for these sacrifices of sight and words, everything would be fine. But this is not the case, and so we recognize the error of staging a scene to the detriment of the scene itself!

The *Mater dolorosa* in the passageway, on the other hand, is too much in the open and hence makes the spectator fearful of an unpleasant interruption. Devrient weakens this effect by having the evening bells ring softly, as a few faithful walk to the threshold of the cathedral, making Gretchen more isolated. The fountain scene moves rapidly and naturally, and Grethen re-entering her house, has a suitable place for her monologue.

The serenade of Mephistopheles and the death of Valentine draw the greatest benefit from the scenery. A description will explain why: twilight creeps out of the shadows around the cathedral. Faust and Mephistopheles enter from the right, high up on the terrace. Through a stained glass window Faust can distinguish the eternal light. On the steps opposite Margaret's house, Mephistopheles, standing in profile against the supporting wall, takes a place precisely meant for him. The utter perfection of this impressive picture makes us forget the preceding compromises. Night falls; there is only the faint light of the sky. Valentine comes from his sister's house and steps onto the terrace which cuts into the stairs, finding himself, quite naturally, face to face with Mephistopheles. The rest of the scene is staged partly in the narrow street and partly on the lower section of the steps. In the moonlight the *Mater dolorosa* and the fountain can be distinguished. Martha's garden breathes its fragrance, the terrace at the top is lit with torches brought in by people. Valentine dies on the steps almost in the center of the stage, facing the audience. From here he can denounce Martha, who has not left her garden. A better arrangement for the last scenes could not be conceived. The spectators feel complete satisfaction, and one senses that the actors share it.

I have dwelt on this setting because it is significant from all possible viewpoints. It holds together the scenes, which unfold as an unforgettable whole, leaving a very favorable imprint on the memory. Its purpose seems to be to place each episode clearly and to give the performers the best area for their acting. It strikingly curtails the function of the curtain through extensive use of lighting and thus reduces the work of the stage crew. Finally, as we have seen, this setting lends perfection to the last two scenes. But it sacrifices for a general impression the significance of the majority of scenes, and in this way it betrays the ideas of a great author like Goethe.

In connection with the scenes in Gretchen's room, I mentioned the possibility of incidental music. This is a significant point of great importance. The staging of a scene and all the procedures leading to it are closely related to the means of expression used by the author. The hierarchic principle must not be violated. The author will not do justice to his text by imagining a setting ingenuously picturesque, historically or geographically true. What matters above all is the technical quality of the text; this alone is the determining factor. If this sounds strange it is nevertheless indispensable. The content of the play takes second place. For instance, when Gretchen mentions her window, the greenery surrounding it, the twilight throwing a gloom over it and so forth, these things actually do not have to be shown in the *mise en scène* unless they are warranted by the author's technical form. The mere mention of these facts should not necessarily influence the stage director's decision.

The manner in which the author expresses his dramatic intentions must be grasped through the technical quality of his text. What the performers have to speak or sing is less essential than how they present it to the audience. If the author uses the spoken word alone, the technical scope is restricted. The text then oscillates between a lyric medium preserving just an appearance of rational meaning and a definitely realistic dialogue. If, on the other hand, he considers a musical intervention as indispensable for his communication, freedom in delivering the words becomes almost unlimited. Between the two poles—the recitative in which music is subordinated to speech for the sake of purely verbal expression, and passages where music alone is the revealing element—all nuances are possible and the *mise en scène* must adapt itself to them.

The imagination of the author or the stage director, even though stimulated by the words of the text, should not be the source of scenic invention; that source should always and exclusively be the quality of the poetic or music-poetic text. The normal hierarchy of the stage is confirmed throughout. Music brings about modifications in timing and, through it, in space. Since my other works deal with this subject, I shall discuss here only the balance between the visual representation and the expressive possibilities of the text. Let us recall, for this purpose, the scenes in Gretchen's room. Here the words stand alone and must be perfectly understood; furthermore, the actors, as the sole interpreters, must be clearly visible. Since the quality of the text takes a happy medium between purely lyric expression and rational discourse, all the director has to do is to conform by giving the setting the precise amount of suggestion needed to support the text. Should the author be more inclined towards realism, the director would have to use fewer nonfunctional, suggestive elements in order not to distract the spectator's attention. If, however, the author leans toward lyric expression, the performer is no longer the only interpreter, because the quality of the text transcends the mere presence of the actor on stage. The text approaching realism bestows upon the actor the responsibility and authority of an interpreter. Conversely, if pure lyricism is predominant, the actor loses some independence and tends to become an instrument in the author's hand.

These factors should guide the director in planning his scene. Somehow the actor in Devrient sensed this, and that is what I am coming to. He had a musical theme composed to accompany Gretchen's entrance into her room. Gretchen begins to talk before the music ends. During this brief moment there is no need to hear or see better. But as soon as the music stops the power of suggestive expression declines considerably; then the actor must be clearly seen and understood, for, charming as this picture is, it is no substitute for the lyric quality of music. Devrient tried to reconcile two conceptions of staging, but the spectators were well aware of his error. At a second performance Gretchen's windows opened up wider like a folding screen, permitting the audience to see easily into the room, but nullifying the scenic effect without adequate compensation. The entrance music no longer suited the scene, which now seemed to have lost its balance. This was quite instructive to me.

Since the *mise en scène* is and can only be empirical, it is from such examples that a basic principle is to be discovered.

Some time later, I saw *The Ring of the Nibelungs* in Dresden. Overwhelmed by the work and bewildered by the scenery with which it was burdened, I began to sense my own inner resources and the responsibilities they imposed upon me. Shortly thereafter I retired to the countryside and set to work on what I regarded as my imperative task.

Apart from the endeavors of the Brunswick stage director and the Devrient setting, the theatrical experiences that I took with me into my retreat were more extensive than profound, more negative than inspiring. This was probably fortunate, although that baggage remained with me a long time and constantly burdened my imagination through sheer force of habit. Wherever the absolute necessity for freedom did not make itself felt, I still clung to the earlier impression, adjusting it as much as possible to my rigorous demands concerning the actor's role. For I directed all my efforts to make the actor free. I was very conscious of this principle; only its application and consequences were not yet clear to me, although they were beginning to evolve. Technique yields to infallible logic and rejects bondage.

So I approached the *mise en scène* of the *Ring* with the sole desire of being true to my own vision. My honesty did not fail me; on the contrary, it prevented me from violating a work of art whose character and complexity could have presented a great difficulty. Such was my disposition at the beginning of my work. After long years of experiences, or rather after years of recording them in a necessarily unmethodical way, I began to practice a completely unknown art, for which neither my environment nor my memory could offer me any ideas, and for which all the elements had yet to be discovered and organized. Still, I was convinced that, following my own vision, I would find the truth.

**Investigations**

A theorist gains a thorough knowledge of the work he is studying; then he seeks a general principle to which it may be reduced. From this basis he develops a theory and applies it to lesser details of the work. Through that artificial procedure he, of course, obtains a unity, but this unity does not emanate from the work itself; hence it remains an illusion, and the real meaning of the work escapes; the theorist has not even touched it. A work of art comes to life only when in contact with an artist to whom alone it confides its secret. If the author of these lines has become a theorist, it was because of the impossibility of realizing his dream. The work of art revealed itself to him earlier, and the two consummated a mysterious pact that freed him from all prejudices and enabled him to come to its assistance. Obstacles were of no concern to either of them.

I turned to the first scene of *Rhinegold* without the slightest notion of how to achieve a technical unity that would apply to the four parts of the *Ring* with all their differences, as Wagner himself would have desired if he had had my natural talent for synthesis.

In this connection I can assert the value of my scenic vision: spontaneous from the very beginning, and derived directly and somehow chronologically from the score, it naturally implied the theories which I discovered only later on.

I was well aware that my irrepressible desire was based on indisputable realities. No matter how long my investigations might have lasted, I should never have hesitated a moment after I had made this discovery. Furthermore, when I maintain that I found a solution for my *mise en scène* exclusively in the score, I merely state a fact, but clearly a fact stemming from my own personality and not equally valid for another person. Thus I have at my disposal a tool that eludes analysis, and this obliges me to say that my presence on the earth has been good for something. First I obeyed the dictate of my vision, and only later did I discern the reasons that make it possible to establish a theory.

Deep in my heart and before my drawing paper I knew that for me the *mise en scène* means the performer. So I took the score of *Rhinegold* (the quarto vocal score by Klindworth)[7] and studied the first scene exclusively from this viewpoint. I shall attempt to give the reader an idea of my method. First of all I try to single out the episodes of the action and to determine their distinct features, keeping in mind what holds them together, much as a mason does with his mortar. Wagner's romanticism must be preserved; this is an obligation for the stage director. However, he must know how much romanticism is necessary. I therefore search among the assorted episodes for the one that requires the most romanticism, in order to establish a scale of values on this point. Taking this episode as the maximum, I can determine the amount of romanticism due each of the other episodes.

A further indispensable evaluation concerns the theatrical significance of the episodes, independent of their romanticism. A still more important point, however, remains for final consideration. It is the part an episode plays in the inner drama, i.e., its importance in the eternal meaning beyond visible action and its casual appearance. This final consideration, indeed, surpasses the others, but, as it does not directly concern the scenic substance, it can be settled only on the basis of already given situations. In the scene under discussion, the moment when one of the Daughters of the Rhine informs Alberich of the frightening qualities attributed to the ring must be regarded as a climax towering over all the other episodes.

Having the essential facts under control, we can now begin to design the setting, bearing in mind that the second consideration, theatrical significance, depends on what we have established for the performer. Here I use a method that, if used with caution, is sanctioned by experience, and that alone enabled me to overcome the difficulties inherent in this undertaking. Everyone will agree that the arrangement of an interesting bouquet requires more flowers than are actually used. So it is with the *mise en scène,* and accordingly I *prepare* a number of drawings of interchangeable and suggestive locations, somewhat like a word puzzle in which not all the given letters are needed to compose a specific word. I would be ridiculous to attempt this without preliminary classification of the episodes. But with the knowledge thus acquired we may risk this game, evocative in its flexibility and not at all binding. It certainly involves guesswork, and this in turn calls for a general sense of form. Of course, it demands a faith in the unconscious which, strangely enough, has never deceived me. One can even venture further, and place all these provisional scenes within a framework, suggested by the place of action without strict observance of the hierarchy. It is then a unit setting that is approximate and can be modified at will until finally it fits each episode. Here the mortar—the connecting link—enters the game, and it may happen that a scene that we thought was worth an episode is now a transition, while one that had appeared to us only transitional is found to be worthy of an episode.

Imagine all the elements involved in this work: text, music, external dramatic design (plot), the hidden reality of the inner drama, peculiarities and social status of the characters, their actions and reactions, their mode of delivery, the area assigned to them, organic relationships, lighting with its changes, shades, and shadows, color. All these to be maintained within the scope of technical possibilities and all made to converge on a single moment, the time of the performance! No single method could bring this about; the field is too vast and too complex to fit into a uniform frame. Whatever is suitable for one fragment is unsuitable for another; each element needs to be treated differently, and what I have called the "dosage" is infinitely varied.

The question may now arise whether unity is desirable at all for the *mise en scène;* whether the director may not employ different devices in the same work, in spite of the fact that the score ought to suggest but one mode of attaining the style that captures the poetic image of the music? Perhaps we should pose the question in another form, namely, "What is the nature of the unity of production?" This is, indeed, how the problem should be stated to reveal the principle that entails all the rest.

For the poet-musician, unity lies in the dramatic intention that inspires a specific work and that work alone, so much so that we are tempted to find in each of Wagner's last four dramas a motive that generates all the others in a particular opera. The idea is a little childish, for who would doubt this even before it is verified? But it is the height of childishness to dare assume the master was aware of it and acted accordingly! The origin of a Wagner score is forever inaccessible to us. Our knowledge begins with the technical employment of such means of expression as are relayed in the score. Since these means are subservient, the unity they manifest cannot be ascribed to them. By the same token the unity of the *mise en scène* does not depend on its means, because they too are subordinate. To what? This is the question!

At present the *mise en scène* is the order of the day, and any pretext for launching a new experiment is good. But too often the drama is no more than a pretext. If the dramatist is dead and cannot defend himself, so much the better; if he is alive, he will work with the director, because, all appearances notwithstanding, the scenic artist is so independent that he may experiment with the setting for a play without first considering its needs. Formerly, it is true, when settings were simply used again and again, scenic art enjoyed less consideration. The procedure, however, remains the same; the settings are one matter, the drama is another, and the two are put together like ready-made shoes and a customer's feet. We have freed ourselves only to tumble into new servitude; in our desire to establish an independent scenic principle, we have become its slaves. The truth is that the dramatist should be free, not the director. Like the commander of an army after a victory, the director should present his weapons and subordinate himself to his sovereign. Freedom is for the dramatist first of all, for the stage second. From this viewpoint, the war of independence which the artists have undertaken has missed its goal, and the authors know it.

The subordinate position that the scenic artist must accept reveals what we mean by the unity of this work. In the theatre, as elsewhere, we have unfortunately brought about a division of labor. Normally the dramatist might be his own leading actor, designer, and stage director; if he is a composer, he should be a singer and a conductor. In the good old days of the theatre he was just that. Of course, this is asking too much of him! But, lacking such versatility, he should at least perform as many of these functions as is feasible. A modern production increasingly tends to grant him this possibility—which is already of considerable benefit—so long as he remains the master. For the unity of a production depends not on the technician but on the dramatist and, returning to Wagner, the master will give us this unity. A Wagnerian score is a medium between the inviolable origin, which is moreover inaccessible, and the projection of that original concept in space. Wagner himself did not understand this, and that is the reason for his failure. The scenic descriptions at the beginning of each act, in particular, acts 2 and 3 of *Tristan,* prove this. As I have for the time being presumed, we do not have to seek a unity on the stage analogous to that in the score: this unity is implied in the score, ready to be discovered. Therefore, Wagner wrongly believed we need direct instructions from the dramatist. The musical score is the sole interpreter for the director: whatever Wagner has added to it is irrelevant. On this point the hierarchy is merciless.

We begin to grasp the importance of the score for the scenic artist; he can not do without it. The score serves him as imagination, regulator, guide and balance; it alone has the word of authority to which we must listen and respond obediently like the slaves in *A Thousand and One Nights.* If the director listens well and responds obediently, unity is guaranteed. It is thus imperative for the scenic artist of a Wagnerian music-drama to be a musician; indeed it is deplorable that we have to state this fact.

Resuming our investigation where we left off, we now understand the power that permits us to make so many varied elements converge on a single point, i.e., the production. This power is not within ourselves. A Wagnerian score demands of the scenic artist an act of faith, and his *mise en scène* testifies to this complete trust, which alone makes the production impressive. The author of these lines has frequently had this experience with his designs. That also explains why Wagner's is the only work today that confers such powers upon the scenic artist. Unfortunately this power has its limitations. Wagner did not know the hierarchic principle which ought to have shaped his *mise en scène,* without the images that his imagination placed in the final version of his music-poetic libretto. Therein lies the root of all the misunderstanding. Imagine a dramatist with an unbelievable gift for music-poetic expression using it with abandon, and, at the same time, meticulously setting down every minute detail in his score! His manuscript contains, by definition, the theatrical form, i.e., its projection in space; therefore, any additional remarks on his part are superfluous, even contrary to the aesthetic truth of an artistic work. Wagner's scenic descriptions in his libretto have no organic relationship with his music-poetic text. If the production in Bayreuth had not given us so perfect a proof of this misunderstanding, we would question our own judgment.

We must conclude that because he does not know the scenic hierarchy the poet-musician does not enjoy the freedom in his score that is granted by trust in this principle. Wagner believed himself completely independent, but it is inconceivable that he was not influenced by his vision of the modern stage. Certainly he cracked its framework, but he by no means broke it. The stage director must take cognizance of this fact.

Understanding the director's position, we can now review it in relation to the Wagnerian drama. On the one hand, the director is faced with Wagner's traditional conception of staging; on the other, with a music-poetic text apparently free of that tradition and not at all influenced by the modern stage. This is the external phase of the problem. The contradiction, however, reveals a deep conflict in the dramatist's thinking, and the director can solve it only by seriously compromising with the normal hierarchy. The consequence of such a compromise is that the *mise en scène* of a Wagnerian drama will never be derived exclusively from the score. Considerations of another order will always interfere. There is, furthermore, the question of romanticism, the outgrowth of a traditional vision; Wagner's purpose was entirely directed at transforming a legend or a myth into a truly human action. In his music he achieved this, but his scenic vision remained paralyzed, and his music-poetic text encumbered by tradition.

Such technical considerations seem quite trifling in the face of so tragic a conflict, and so great a figure as Richard Wagner. They are, however, inspired by the deepest respect and the most enthusiastic admiration for a master who indubitably failed in his scenic conception. All the more reason, then to salvage what remains of his incomparable work. I consider it my task to help in this attempt.

Through my complete scenario for the *Ring,* I acquired the fundamental principles of a Wagnerian production and summarized them in my small volume entitled *Staging Wagnerian Drama* (Paris: Chailley, 1895). Realizing that we are masters only of what we have taught, a year later I began to prepare a complete volume on this subject. It was *Music and the Art of the Theatre* (Munich: Bruckmann, 1899). I still relied on the work of Wagner for, at the time, it was the only work that could serve me as a point of departure. But while

Figure 10.   Bayreuth setting of 1882 by Paul von Joukowsky, for the Flower
Meadows of *Parsifal*, Act 3

Figure 11. Appia's Design of 1896 for *Parsifal*, Act 3

writing, I became aware how far my thinking had detached itself from Wagner's work in order to treat the subject in all its fullness and general scope.

That book can, therefore, no longer by properly called Wagnerian. As its title indicates, it offers a theoretical and technical account of relations that exist, and must be recognized, between music and the stage, i.e., between sounds that meet our ears and moving images that are presented to our eyes. This account is based on a clear definition of music from a dramatic viewpoint since, in drama, music is time—not a length of time but the idea of time itself. When I wrote this, such an affirmation appeared to be enigmatic. We have come a long way since then and the idea of musical time is now generally accepted.

A discussion of the book here is unnecessary, for it has gradually become widely known and influential on scenic art. It may be regarded as having been the initial impetus for all current reform, and it contained the elements necessary to continue the movement and consolidate it. Some designs are included in the volume. For the scenario of the *Ring,* I had already tried sketches with positions indicated to facilitate the reading of the libretto and its transfer to the stage. But these attempts were very timid. While writing *Music and the Art of the Theatre* I felt it necessary to indicate to the reader my precise vision; and to this effect I executed large designs whose compositions, though suggestive, would clearly show the construction of the scenery. These designs served as illustrations for the production of *Tristan* and the *Ring* which I summarized in an appendix. They broke with traditions, going beyond anything that could, at that time, be expected of reform, and hence they compelled attention at least. If at first they were adopted only in certain of their details, eventually they were accepted as a whole.

Yet, nobody had the key to the designs! Nobody even comprehended that the key, the scenario, was indispensable for the setting, which remained an unsolved problem without this key. Misunderstandings were the result. The letter was taken from the spirit, and my claim that I found my entire *mise en scène* exclusively in the score met with disbelief. Yet these settings contained something that defied analysis and gave the impression of a finality which was attributed to me because my inspiration for it was not understood. I could explain no better than I had in my book. I had to let this false impression stand. Bayreuth refused to take cognizance of my scenario for the *Ring,* although it arrived there in plenty of time for the preparation of the production in 1896. I had forwarded it in 1892! Bayreuth also refused to consider *Music and the Art of the Theatre* and accused my designs of being reminiscent of Nansen's expedition.[8]

In 1906, seven years after the book's publication, I attended a demonstration of eurhythmics by Jaques-Dalcroze, then just beginning. Already in *Music and the Art of the Theatre,* I called for "musical gymnastics" as essential for the singing actor, but of course, I had no idea how to go about organizing these.

Dalcroze revealed them to me and, from that day on, I saw clearly the route my development was to take. The discovery of basic principles for the *mise en scène* could only be a point of departure; eurhythmics decided my further progress. I became free of the restrictions attached to a circumscribed work of art, and I could perceive the elements of production independent of the theatre, that is, as existent by themselves without the need for an audience. But I am anticipating!

One summer in Geneva I myself experimented with eurhythmics, and that clinched my determination. Yet, despite all the enthusiasm with which I went to work, I needed a period of incubation. Hitherto, only the musical movement of the body had been revealed to me, not its echo in space as yet, and I suffered from this fact without analyzing it too much. I prevailed upon Dalcroze to provide stairs and some platforms. Intuition was indeed there but I still lacked the vision to realize it.

In the spring of 1909, Dalcroze invited me to attend a production he had carefully prepared with his own unpublished music, costumes, colored light, etc. I left the performance depressed and made a resolution: seizing paper and pencils I composed feverishly, every day, two or three *space designs* intended for rhythmic movements. When I had about twenty I sent them to Dalcroze with a letter telling him his pupils were constantly moving on a flat surface, thus giving the impression of alpinists trying to climb Mount Cervin[9] on a bas-relief that lay flat on the ground! My designs aroused great enthusiasm, and I was convinced that I had accomplished as much for him as I had for myself. This is how the style of space for the rhythmic movements of the body was founded. All we needed was to gain experience and flexibility to adapt it to everyday requirements. After some fumbling, the stairs, that fine accomplice of the body, became a safe guide.

In 1912, for the first time since the Greek era, a perfect fusion of all media of expression, closely and mutually subordinated, was realized in the descent to Hades in Gluck's *Orfeo*.[10] It was the final solution and, try as we may, we shall always come back to it. The body would admit of no other surfaces, no other lines!

Let us return to the designs I made in order to suggest and establish the style, which I shall call *corporeal space* and which becomes *living* space when the body animates it. Still under the influence of Wagnerian romanticism, my first attempts showed only a greater simplification of lines but, alas, this time, without the support of a score! This lack troubled me greatly; I was not accustomed to work without a specific object or to rely on my imagination alone. Whereas, in the case of Wagner, I proceeded exclusively from the performer, here for lack of a score, I believed I could start from space itself, but I failed miserably. At last I understood! If I had no score, I had at least the living body and could rely on its help. My designs for Wagner had trained me to indicate

Figure 12.    Rhythmic Design, "The Staircase"

clearly the construction of the setting. I observed that many of the lines I had used for the Wagnerian compromise could not be executed in three dimensions, and that, though inevitable for Wagner's romanticism, they should be omitted in a space intended for the body itself and its movements, one that had no dramatic goal. This conclusion set me free. Atavism, doubtless, made me still retain a backdrop, essential perhaps for the design, but not always for its execution. Wherever the pencil touched paper it evoked the naked body, the naked limbs. The active role of light resulted naturally from a construction that called for it, and thus everything assumed an *appearance of expectancy:* the quality of the space rendered the presence of the body indispensable. I was then so fortunate as to win Dalcroze over to this normal, organic vision which was, in fact, based on his work and without which in turn his work would have remained static.

I can now review my path to this point.

My artistic disposition drew me irresistibly to the theatre. Before I ever attended any performance, my imagination was exclusively focused on the actor. My first experience was deeply disappointing; but although at first sight it was the inconsistency of the canvas settings that disturbed me, my attention was soon caught by the vague position of the actor and a stage floor that remained invariably the same. The following years in the theatre provided only two examples that were interesting and really instructive for the *mise en scène,* namely, the artistic director in Brunswick and Devrient's setting for *Faust.* My understanding of Wagner's music dramas became increasingly deeper and made me ardently yearn to give them a production appropriate to them; yet music was then still my prime interest, and it was not until the *Ring* aroused an irrepressible desire that I became determined.

I retired to the countryside, where I concentrated on the settings for a production of the *Ring.* Later I turned to writing a book with the idea of publishing it, something that had never occurred to me before. My designs took shape. In the course of composing *Music and the Art of the Theatre,* I felt the necessity for the actor to be trained in rhythmic gymnastics, and in 1895, I wrote about this in the manuscript, which was not published until 1899. The method of rhythmic gymnastics was revealed to me by Dalcroze in 1906. Without changing my orientation, rhythmic gymnastics freed me from too inflexible a tradition and, in particular, from the decorative romanticism of Wagner. In order to impress upon Dalcroze the importance of varying rhythmic movements from their original arrangement on the floor alone, I drew a variety of space designs. They fulfilled their purpose. Through these designs I gradually attained a purity of style which consisted mainly of lines and forms. Their resistance to the movements of the body enhances its expression and creates plasticity. The performance of *Orfeo,* in 1912 and 1913, in Dresden-Hellerau firmly established this style.

Thus, from my childhood, the living human body dominated my vision and determined my career. It was the driving force in my reform of the Wagnerian *mise en scène;* it led me towards the art of the human body, which was revealed to me by the Dalcroze method. It remains to mention the influence of this emancipation upon my view of the world and its relationship to the individual and society. But first, a digression is necessary!

My study of Wagner's dramas was concerned primarily with the score alone. I therefore gained an extensive knowledge of the scores, but it was lacking in depth and would have remained so had not my friend H. S. Chamberlain given me great assistance. Very likely this deficiency would have gravely handicapped my development and deprived me of principles essential for a reform of the theatre.

Chamberlain, with whom I enjoyed close relations for several years, began his literary activity with critical and analytical essays on Wagner's compositions. He knew these very well and also the master's writings, the ten volumes so neglected, yet so vital for the understanding of his personality. My friend was a scholar and a philologist; he applied to everything that interested him a scholarly discipline and comparative judgment derived from the study of languages. A good musician endowed with an artistic feeling that was more intellectual than intuitive, he was well equipped to defend a work that was still much disputed or misunderstood. His authority was established in 1892 with a booklet called *The Wagnerian Drama* and, later on, was thoroughly confirmed by a complete study of the master and his works under the title, *Richard Wagner,* published in 1896. This brilliant book seemed definitely to have clarified the personality and words of the master and thus rescued it from all misunderstandings. It was a boon for Wagner's writings, including the scores, but not for the production of his music dramas.

From Chamberlain I received a fully rounded and documented picture of Wagner's personality seen through the enthusiasm and adoration of a thoroughly informed artistic disciple. He gave me precisely what I could not obtain otherwise and what he alone, due to his affectionate awareness of my own individuality, was able to make me absorb. The purely artistic phase of the work was easily accessible to me; my friend gave me then all I needed to enter the sanctuary and to support my artistic ideas with firm and sound convictions. This conferred upon my work a knowledge, I might even say, an evidence that it would never have attained without him.

The art of the body, as my dreams would call it long before I knew of Dalcroze's eurhythmics, applied only to the actor. I have always been and I still am a theatre man. Auditorium and stage, one opposite the other, appeared to me as something normal and self-evident; so did the curtain; and that the director's preparation of the cuisine should go unnoticed by an audience that is to be offered only hot and well-prepared dishes. My most advanced ideas always concerned the *performance* alone. And if I ever thought of the audience I did so only to hope that it would understand my efforts. The darkened house and the invisible orchestra in Bayreuth filled me with delight.

In a fanciful little story of that period, I went still further, imagining a rich man who invites his friends to spend an evening with him. In a large parlor these gentlemen are seated on cushions on the floor; coffee and cigarettes are placed on low, small tables. Imperceptibly the lights fade, one of the walls opens, and very softly and gradually there can be seen the beginning of a miraculous spectacle of which the host's friends had not the slightest notion, as they were also completely ignorant of the tremendous installation arranged by the owner on a vast site adjoining this residence. The passivity of the spectators could not be carried further, neither could the definite separation of the place of action! It seemed to me, then, a dream: impossible, to be sure, but desirable!

The first time I attended a session of eurhythmics my impressions were complex and surprising. At first, I found myself moved to tears, remembering how long I had waited. But soon I sensed the awakening of a new force utterly unknown to me! I was no longer in the audience, I was on the stage with the performers! The following day I wrote Dalcroze, whom I did not know. My letter expressed the key to the problem, the explanation of my deep trouble, the name of the force which had taken possession of me the evening before; it was communion in art, not art brought within reach of all, but art lived together.

Today in the light of further experience, I realize that this revelation, however suddenly it occurred, was already contained in my previous vision. My passionate concern for the full development of the actor betrayed a way of feeling that went beyond the egoistic satisfaction of the spectator. Whenever I explained my scenic vision to others I mimed it, quickly arranging the furniture at hand not for somebody else but for myself as I needed it for my acting; and often I was said to have been quite convincing. My suffering during Wagnerian performances became increasingly unbearable for me, because, identifying myself with the actor, I suffered with him, for him, and in him; I myself was the actor, who wanted better treatment.

The Dalcroze exercises that I witnessed were all right as a demonstration, but for a performance they should have been arranged differently, not confined to a formula that obviously was of interest to no one but the performers themselves. This flaw could not escape my perception. Suddenly the curtain appeared to me ridiculous and barbarous; one after another, my traditional notions collapsed, and I fancied myself alone with the students in an unlimited space. I did not realize, though, that my revelation remained incomplete. A big step had still to be taken—the step from a vividly envisioned intuition to the living experience of one's own body. Accompanying a friend to the dentist and going oneself are two different things, however much sympathy one may feel; and when Hamlet feels the sword pierce his chest, he becomes very much aware, if somewhat late, of the fact that reality has a character all its own!

My personal experience with eurhythmics completed my evolution, defined it precisely once and for all, and decided my future. I was not alone, taking a private lesson; no, we were a whole group set on a common course under the same flag, and when one of us temporarily retired, he continued the exercises—in his thoughts—with the inner satisfaction of being thus able to rejoin the ensemble whenever it suited him. His place was not numbered, and the footlights did not separate him from his colleagues; he belonged so inseparably to the performance that there was no longer a performance and, most importantly, no one to look at him, since he was not presented to anyone.

The consequences of such a revelation and their multiple results could not become evident in one day. This is the reason why I spoke of a time for incubation. I shared the lot of eurhythmics almost from its birth, assisting in its development and its struggle for existence. In an essay entitled "The Origin and Beginnings of Eurhythmics," I delineated its history. Now I can talk of a past that was succeeded by the flowering of a cultural principle recognized by all and assured of life.

First of all, eurhythmics shares the fate of all living organisms; it never stands still, but incessantly develops in constantly-renewed, never-crystallized forms; its study is solidly based on a method, but this method is subject to continuous changes; it lives with the work. So Dalcroze, the ingenious originator, lives with his students, inextricably united with them. He can do nothing without them; eurhythmics is their common work; it is a microcosm, a little world within the big one. This little world is founded on an educational principle and dominated by an art, music; movement is its element, and its medium of operation is obedience. Obedience to whom? Communion of ideas implies subordination, and this brings us back to the theme of this study.

Hierarchy is not an invention; fortunately, it is a discovery. I have discovered the reciprocal subordination through which the elements of expression at our command obtain life, or, rather, the right to exist. Here, more than anywhere else, the law of solidarity applies. Theatre is a creation, no doubt, but through its hierarchic requirements this creation becomes a significant symbol. The composition of a piece and its production seem at first sight to be at the mercy of the author's and the stage director's whim. But actually it is not so, and if one or the other infringes upon the laws dominating him, his work is no longer really viable. Indeed it falls into anarchy or turns into mechanical movement, which is the opposite of art, and that is just what our current repertory theatre is.

Art is an instrument, produced by our hands, which records thoughts and feelings collectively experienced; theatre is the symbol of these thoughts and feelings in a fictitious form; it is their indication but not their reality. In the theatre, fiction is, after all, in the auditorium, not on stage. It is the passive reaction of the audience that renders the stage fictitious; without an audience, scenic action enters immediately the domain of real existence, and the actors are human beings who, at one and the same time, create a work of art and participate in it; relations have become normal. One can very well observe that fact during a good rehearsal.

It is normal to look at a statue or a painting, because we cannot at the same time see and create them; it is abnormal, however, to be yourself the piece of art and to exhibit yourself to others who, although just as alive as you are, do not wish to participate in your creation. I have dealt in detail with this whole problem in my book, *The Work of Living Art:* a painting locked up in a box does not exist as such. A moment of living art with no other witness than the performers themselves exists fully and with greater dignity than when reflected in the eyes of passive spectators. The living body, as a means of expression in itself, not as the mere bearer of a dramatic action (the actor), is independent; but it is not isolated, for henceforth it participates in the rhythm of other bodies. Even if alone, it feels and will always feel the solidarity that directs it. It has become social in the powerful grip of art. This remarkable fact is recognized by all those who have submitted their bodies to eurhythmics.

Theatre would thus be an intermediary form between the static fine arts and living art. It should not be considered a finished and definite form. On the one hand, it tends towards literature or pure music; on the other, it seeks instinctively to liberate itself from the tutelage of the audience and to develop in a free atmosphere. The audience still restrains it and will probably continue to restrain it, for mankind is indolent even in its recreations, but eurhythmics and its rich promises for the future have released us from the constraints imposed upon our imagination by an exclusively representative form. We can now conceive a nobler form which, no longer isolating us in a passive reaction, will bring us in living contact with our fellow men. This is the revelation of eurhythmics. One can easily judge the influence it would exert on a man of the theatre!

The designs I first made for Dalcroze were still more or less oriented towards a spectacle presented to the eyes of others; hence they only partially included the auditorium. Today I have arrived at extreme conclusions of the hierarchic principle for the *mise en scène*. Reaching beyond theatre, it will serve all living art. I conceive an oblong, empty, and unadorned wall with complete lighting installations. On the sides large outbuildings would contain sections of three-dimensional units. These would be constructed in such lines and proportions as the human body will admit and divided into matching parts to be fitted into all possible kinds of levels, horizontal, sloping or vertical. They would be combined with drapes, folding screens, etc., and the whole would be covered with canvas of uniform material.

This would be called the "study site." Its various parts should be so light that they could be shifted by one or two students. The walls of the hall are to be kept in a subdued neutral tone, similar to or matching those of the platforms; the whole should have the effect of an arrangement that makes the performers feel at home, without encountering any obstacles except those they impose on themselves. Whenever a set of exercises or a piece is to be presented to a group of people, movable rows of seats can be easily arranged, first on one side, then on the other. Yet, as a rule, the entire hall belongs to the students, with no indication of an audience in it. Music participates in the general flexibility; there is a piano, or two, or some other instruments up to an entire orchestra sitting together or dispersed in groups. Soloists and choristers can likewise be arranged at will, all the more so as the singing might be entrusted, wholly or partly, to the dancers themselves. Since the studies are based on movement, whose expression radiates from the body, a quasi-nudity is essential. Short tights, preferably black, may be chosen for the beginning (arms, neck, legs and feet uncovered); but whatever costumes are assigned, they should not impede the movement during practice nor conceal it from spectators who happen to be present. The latter distinction will occupy us for a moment.

Today, it is actually the audience who determines the place that the performer must take in the theatre as well as in the concert. We are accustomed to being *offered* a concert or a performance. This is an integral part of our general view of the situation; music is played on one side and listened to on the other. Likewise a performance is presented on one side and watched from another. We cannot even think of any other arrangement, and yet this one is arbitrary. One objects to having the chorus with orchestra presented in this or that manner lest its acoustic effect be disturbed. Very well; but who will be disturbed by this effect? Certainly not the performers, I imagine! Or, for instance, a play will not be understood if actors whose every facial expression must be seen and every word clearly heard, turn their back. The actors see and understand each other very well. The principle of facing each other is implanted in us: the book *and* the reader; the picture, the statue *and* the public! But what about architecture? Can one imagine a building existing for the eye alone? Even the pyramids have an entrance! And music? The shepherd singing in his mountains, does he not make music? Does the tourist listening to him contribute anything to the singing? Does the roundelay danced by little girls in a meadow gain much by being heard and noticed? Far from it! We confuse living with feeling; he who has participated as a singer in the first chorus of Bach's *The St. Matthew Passion* and the listener who has received the thundering message are two entirely different beings: the singer has lived the work; the listener has felt its effect; and if he assures us that he too has lived it deep down in his soul, he uses the word living in a figurative sense.

Experience always surpasses everything else. So all of us should experience art, the living art, each one according to his gifts and the share of culture granted him. Is the experience of living art necessarily superior to the impressions of the spectator-listener, sometimes so extraordinarily alive and profound? This is not the question. We always base our scale of values on individualism. Art is, as its name indicates, an artifice which we learn to utilize for the purpose of doing greater justice to life than we could under the rule of accident. Individualism is a second artifice within the first; it demands always more of art, forcing it to strain its capacity and hence to diminish its power. All our arts can attest to that. We preach simplicity, but individualism will not listen; though satiated, it desires ever more; it is the corrupter of art and knows no limits, or, at least, confuses them with its desires. Individualism thus violates the divinity of art but never blames itself for art's disappointments and failures.

To live art means to offer oneself to its artifice, as it is, without adding anything to it; the gesture of art is giving, not receiving. The presence of an audience is, therefore, not necessary for living art, and the gift of his work and effort made by the performer to an audience does not directly concern the life of art; it derives from our specific condition of culture and civilization. To speak of egotism is to be sentimental; all of nature teaches us egotism. To conquer it one must have something to offer, consequently one must first have acquired something. If we want to offer art to those who are incapable of living art, let us live it first. The apostle Paul had to undergo the frightful experience of the flame himself before he could communicate it in a beneficial form. Today, we want only to receive another's flame or to impart it without having received it; and so our churches are hothouses as are our theatres, concerts, and exhibitions. . . . To live art is to live in a grand manner. Art must not be measured and limited by our sensitivity, any more than a sick man's desire for a necessary drug should determine the dosage. Appealing only to this sensitivity, that is, the wishes of the audience, makes poison out of art. Alas! this is what has happened; our resilience is worn out; it takes violence to make us react. Let us just think of Richard Wagner's excessive force . . . and we were barely aware of it! What we need therefore is health.

Art is the source of health if we give ourselves to it instead of dragging it down to our inadequacies. We receive art in proportion to our surrender. Since we are sick, we need a remedy; and we cannot yet foresee what we may be capable of in a state of health. This remedy amounts to a decision from which a rescuing action will result. Instead of being everywhere on the lookout like a bibliophile, we must give up collecting impressions, enriching our private museums and burying within our four walls this booty of unsound coinage gained from an evil war. The sacrifice is considerable. We readily speak of a sacrifice for a cause; the future of art deserves such a cause; we, of course, are old, but our grandchildren will thank us and praise our courage.

The current civilization, opposed to culture, divides both our attention and our work; we cannot follow it as a whole; each part advances by its own effort and its own particular direction; the most dissimilar objects go together. Never were circumstances more suitable for any kind of experiment; but there was never a greater lack of the faith that moves mountains, because modern obstacles are unopposed by any conviction, and only the presence of the obstacle suggests the faith that will be required to remove it.

The obstacle to living art is the audience. We are in it, and it is in us! Therefore the very idea of the audience, the expression of passivity, must be neutralized by an attempt to overcome this passivity. But to give up everything that suggests and supports passive reaction would, in our day, mean to eliminate three-fourths of our public life! So we must temporize for the time being and let our attitude work from within. Then we shall understand how and why art is a great educator.

Culture recoils from our civilization, which resembles a large cardboard filing case with many differently labeled drawers. By contrast, the distinctive sign of all true culture is mutual penetration. In the progressive mechanization of life, art alone has preserved its flexible independence; art objects and protests, but it also waits; and it can wait, for it is confident of its power and expansive strength. We must not try to make it fit the departmentalized elements of our civilization. Nothing originating in art is fragmentary; everything is integrated; the discipline of living art, far from being an isolated manifestation, exerts a general influence. It has done this for many, teaching them gradually how to use wisely the glittering applications of science and the monopolies of industry. To submit to this discipline means to possess a touchstone for the *mise en scène;* but, of course, it does not matter which aspect of art is to be the guide as long as the artist has a sense of responsibility that integrates his work with all other activities. Mandarinism is passé, and artificial flowers are no longer fashionable. This is perhaps a pity, but the page is turned. To return to it, we should have to begin the book all over again.

The fact that the actor has been taken as point of departure is indeed significant. Man is the measure of all things, said Protagoras. If we are convinced of this (and how can we not be?), our scale of values will not deceive us. Yet it can be true only under one unique condition, i.e., that man, who furnishes this measure of values, is not a mechanical but a *living* organism.

# An American Lecture

## (ca. 1926)

I believe I cannot begin better than with a brief account of Appia's fundamental ideas. From these ideas Appia draws his aesthetic principles, and we must always return to them to test the reality of these principles and to understand their many ramifications. After having stated them without commentary we shall examine them by means of illustrative examples that will clarify them. Here they are: Appia is convinced that our relations to Art have been slowly and progressively distorted; that without realizing it, we have lost the thread which unites us *organically* with what we call the work of Art, and that thus the work of Art has developed an artificial life of its own.

To this conviction Appia adds a second which is its corollary: If Art lives an artificial life among us, our own lives are greatly injured, greatly weakened by this.

Indeed, not only can we not do without Art, and our efforts to uphold it at any price bear witness to this, but the influence on our life exercised by Art is essential. If, therefore, this influence is artificial and stems from a distorted and inorganic relationship, it will be pernicious.

The relation between Art and Life is reciprocal: a misguided Art corrupts our existence; a corrupted existence mortally injures artistic creation. Yet by definition Art is the expression of Life. It is thus the supreme touchstone, the only touchstone, we possess to regulate our life and to prove *its quality*. Hence, it is perfectly legitimate to consider the artistic question fundamental and to look at all the problems of modern life from this aspect. This does not delimit the question, quite the contrary; it seizes it at its most perceptible and important aspect. Accordingly, Appia believes that, in attacking modern art, he attacks our entire culture. To understand Appia's train of thought it is imperative that we ourselves believe in this fact and understand its importance; this is the first idea we should receive from Appia's demonstration. He reminds us that *every-*

*thing is included* in Art, and that, in dealing with a specific form of art, one implicitly touches Art in general. If, therefore, Appia begins with dramatic Art, the conclusion must not be drawn that he means to talk only of Theatre. We shall see later on how he can reconnect this special question with all the others and why he prefers to tackle first the problem of the theatre.

Appia's second essential idea will perhaps be more difficult to comprehend, but it will become evident to you in the course of this presentation. It is this: in a normally established social life, Art is not an exception, a luxury, *an ornament* of life. On the contrary, it forms part of life and is involved in all its manifestations. This mutual penetration is for Appia the condition *sine qua non* of the life of Art. The fact that Art can no longer find a place in our social life is precisely the very proof that our social life is profoundly corrupted. We place Art outside ourselves; we have become spectators of or listeners to Art. This isolates Art and consequently puts it in an abnormal position where it develops fictitiously; its roots no longer sink into *our* social soil; its flowers and fruits are no longer nourished by *our* sap. Art has little by little become an artifice, nothing else; and as we, its spectators, feel the need for change in Art, to please us, we must vary it continually. Its development depends solely on our own will. We ought to be responsible for it as we are for our life, but we have thrown that responsibility far away from us. The artist has become a lonely man, but the fault is not his; we are all to blame.

This is Appia's second idea: we place ourselves *opposite* Art instead of living it and making it an intimate part of our lives. We call all artistic manifestations "works of art"; and we are very much embarrassed when someone asks what Art itself is, for we know merely its works.

For him who accepts or attempts to understand fully these premises of Appia's general vision a single question will arise: how can we return to normal relations with Art? In other words: how can we again live Art instead of merely contemplating it in its works? This question and this alone Appia tried to answer. All his thinking is contained in this question and . . . in his answer. Here it is: Let us remember once again that although Appia speaks of a specific art form, he also means Art in general. (Insert here some biographical data about my theatrical experiences.) Thus we see the road Appia has followed almost in spite of himself.

Starting from the pain he suffered at the discord between Wagner's poetic theatrical expression and its realization in space on the stage, a discord he believed to be purely artistic, Appia eventually came to understand that this discord is to be found in ourselves—in us, the spectators and listeners—not in a distorted relationship between the means of expression as employed by the dramatist. This is a crucial point because it shows us that Appia's entire thinking is not a more or less arbitrary construction stemming from his personal artistic sensitivity, but that it has its deep roots in his very conception of our personal and social existence. On this point, therefore, we must dwell longer, because it is still the goal towards which all the previous observations lead.

What characterizes Appia's thought and gives it all its power is the importance he confers upon *technique*. Appia is convinced that all efforts towards a reform or progress in any field must rest on a solid technical basis, and that, without such basis, those efforts will remain arbitrary, sterile and hopeless. There is technique in life, and above all, in social life. It is a principle of order, to which we must subordinate ourselves. Appia never tires of repeating this. Yet, he readily adds that our freedom lies in this subordination. Who would not agree with this assertion! Do we not all know that an arbitrary action, no matter in what sphere, is never a free action, nor can it ever lead us to freedom! Here is Appia's great secret, the secret he entrusts to those who are willing to give it their full attention. This is also the reason why he has not hesitated to use the work of Art as the means of his demonstration. He is an artist and avails himself of the materials his own art provides. It matters little to Appia whether somebody else begins with a different subject, provided the principle of technique and the principle of subordination, which is its corollary, are the basis of all discussions, direct all inquiries, and dominate all conclusions.

Appia goes still further; for him, these two principles require an attitude that has a religious meaning. Some will give them a more or less dogmatic, some a more or less mystic, some merely an aesthetic meaning. This is of no importance to Appia. The attitude of submission to laws that one accepts and tries to obey has taken on a religious character for him. If we obey the technical laws imposed upon us by Art instead of continually trying to regulate them arbitrarily and whimsically, we shall have the "religious" attitude that Appia considers inseparable from an orderly life. For him the laws of aesthetics are deeply rooted in pure Humanity, in Humanity that is not yet polluted by a false civilization and culture. The return to these laws alone can make us worthy of talking about Art and, consequently of *living* it. Until then we can only remain spectators of an artificial production which, although it seems to be addressed to us, does not concern us. Under such conditions the artists are separated arbitrarily into an isolated group, and their personal lives are cruelly affected by this inhuman isolation. We have seen all too briefly the technical forms that Appia proposes for a return to the laws of an aesthetic life. Art is the affirmation of Life. If this affirmation is subordinated to aesthetic law it becomes capable of revitalizing our whole existence.[11]

# Curriculum Vita

## (1927)

Adolphe Appia, born in Geneva in 1862, son of Dr. Louis Appia, founder of the Red Cross. Studied music at Geneva, Leipzig, Paris, and Dresden. In 1888 Appia resolved to reform the *mise en scène*. Explored theatres at Dresden and Vienna. Retreated to a country place in 1891, where he actually set to work on this project in earnest.

Principles: the performer has three dimensions, and he moves. Scenery painted on flat canvas has two dimensions and represents imagined objects, light and shadow effects. The performer is a living reality not affected by these painted lights and shadows and unable to make any real contact with them. Although the light that must make the painting visible is not intended for the performer, it does strike him, while the light intended for the performer strikes the painting, distorting its pictorial effect. From these contradictions Appia concluded that it was necessary to establish a rational hierarchy among the means of scenic expression. And of course he ranks the Performer first. Then comes the Spatial Arrangement, whose secondary position implies that it should serve exclusively the Performer and his three dimensions. Next is the all-powerful Light. Lastly, Painting, which is definitely subordinated to the three preceding elements. Color is not only involved in the Painting but in the Performer as well as the Spatial Arrangement and the Light, the latter by definition.

This hierarchy imposes upon the stage director a series of important technical consequences that are independent of his imagination and his free choice. The Spatial Arrangement, especially, must, through its lines and its rigidity, oppose the living forms of the Performer; for in resisting these forms and their mobility Space acquires Life and contributes to the harmony of the production.

Such a hierarchy must not become crystallized; it is not dogmatic; on the contrary, it readily adapts itself to the playwright's changing intentions. One law, however, will always dominate it, namely, the definite supremacy of the

Performer in the scenic Space. Everything must be offered him; everything must be sacrificed to him.

In 1895 Appia published *La Mise en scène du drame wagnérien (Staging Wagnerian Drama)* at Chailley in Paris. Later he devised scenarios for the *Ring, The Mastersingers, Tristan and Isolde, Parsifal,* and several other works. In 1895 he began to write *Music and the Art of the Theatre,* which was published by Hugo Bruckmann, Munich, in 1899. He published a large number of essays and designs in periodicals. In 1906 he became acquainted with Dalcroze's Eurhythmics, which confirmed ideas expressed in *Music and the Art of the Theatre.* In 1921 he published his last book, *The Work of Living Art* (Atar, Geneva), which he regards as the most significant and complete expression of his ideas.—Thereafter followed designs for several new productions of operas and plays (Gluck, Bizet, Shakespeare, Goethe, Ibsen, Aeschylus, etc.).

Productions: Geneva, Hellerau, Paris. His two main and last complete achievements: *Tristan and Isolde* under Toscanini at La Scala in Milan, 1923–24, and *Rhinegold* and *The Walkyrie* under Wälterlin in Basel, 1924–25. (In *Rhinegold* the Daughters of the Rhine did not use a swimming device, hence were not suspended.) Several productions of scenes for various theatres; collaborations; and private experiments.

Exhibitions: Darmstadt, 1909.[12] Zurich (international exposition), February 1914. Cologne, June 1914. Geneva, Institut Dalcroze, 1918. Amsterdam (international exposition), February 1922. London (international exposition), June 1922. Milan, La Scala, 1923. Stockholm, 1924. Basel, October 1924. Zurich, April 1925. Leipzig, Music Congress, June 1925 (with lecture and slides). Magdeburg, 1927.

# Part Two

# Appia on Wagner

# Introduction to Part Two

Richard Wagner succeeded in his later operas in creating a new art form—a union of drama and music—which overturned the conventional concept of opera, and, in time, that of theatre in general. Having joined within himself the roles of composer and dramatist, he achieved an extraordinary creative breakthrough, fashioning a new type of musical drama in which a work's inner values as expressed through the music were conjoined with its outward meaning as articulated through dialogue and plot. The new medium thus achieved could become, as Wagner both practiced and prophesied, a uniquely expressive art form.

He recognized, moreover, that if the autonomous artist, the composer-dramatist, were to present his work successfully before an audience, it would be essential for him to master and, ideally, control all the disparate elements of production. Since his operas were simultaneously music and drama, the latter not fixed for performance by a score, their integrity could be maintained only through rigorous attention to all the details of theatrical production.

Yet despite drastic and far-reaching reforms, in the end, Wagner himself failed to carry through any genuine revolution in staging. To be sure, his purpose-built theatre, the Festspielhaus at Bayreuth, completed in 1876, was highly unusual. Its semicircular amphitheatre, modeled upon ancient example, in theory allowed every spectator an equally good and unimpeded view of the performance. From it he banished the customary distinctions of social hierarchy, as well as all elaborate décor or ornament—anything that could draw attention from the stage itself. For the first time, the auditorium was darkened during performance, and even the orchestra was hidden from view to allow the spectators to observe the world of the opera without distraction.

On stage, however, the situation was different. Wagner spared no expense or effort in equipping his theatre with the most advanced technology of the period, but it was all essentially in the service of the traditional aesthetic of scenic illusion. It is difficult to assess the extent to which Wagner himself was aware of or troubled by the incompatibility between his works and their realization on stage. Whether consciously or not, by placing his performers within a relentlessly illusionistic scenic environment where little or nothing was left to the imagination, he ensured that, visually, the settings could never express the inner spiritual world suggested by the music. Although his librettos abound with precise stage directions and scenic descriptions, Wagner was generally less than satisfied with the results, and he seems to have desired more than he could visualize—something at any rate other than the romantic naturalism which his craftsmen invariably produced. At the end of his life, he lamented that "in this field of musical dramaturgy, alas, all is still so new and hidden in the dust of bad routine."[1]

Appia first saw Wagner's own final production, that of *Parsifal* in 1882; and later attended Cosima Wagner's faithful re-stagings of *Tristan and Isolde* and *The Mastersingers* in 1888. In Dresden he witnessed a production of the *Ring*. He was overwhelmed by the impact of these works as music, while goaded by the unshakable conviction that their potential as pieces for the theatre, and as the basis for an entirely new form of theatrical art, had not only been left unexplored and unexploited, but also had been all but totally obscured under the gross burden of contemporary stage practice. Here, at last, in Wagner, Appia recognized an artist whose titanic genius might redeem theatre and raise it to the level of true art. Here were sublime works whose full power and beauty could only emerge, be revealed and realized, could only *exist* in the theatre itself—but only if a theatre could first be fashioned to contain them.

With the help of his friend, Houston Stewart Chamberlain,[2] Appia was able to spend time at Bayreuth, observing and analyzing both the productions themselves and the technical intricacies of the Festspielhaus. He acquired a direct and concrete understanding that challenged him at the time to develop his own theory further, and later ensured that the theory when it emerged was firmly grounded in sound technical expertise and practical knowledge.

By the end of 1890, Appia was ready—indeed, he felt himself impelled—to fashion into writing and designs his scenic ideas, which over the years had come to possess his mind, virtually to the exclusion of everything else. For the next ten years he devoted himself with an extraordinary singleness of purpose to expressing and consolidating through his writing, scenarios, and designs the wealth of ideas inspired by his observation and analysis of Wagnerian production.

His first extended essay, written in 1891–92, but never published in his lifetime, was entitled "Notes de mise en scène pour *L'Anneau de Nibelungen*" ("Comments on the Staging of the *Ring of the Nibelungs*") and is included here. In a concise and straightforward format, Appia discusses, essentially through concrete description, the problems that Wagner's work presents and his own solutions to them, solutions that required fundamental reform of contemporary stagecraft, although not as yet of its technical resources. His second essay,

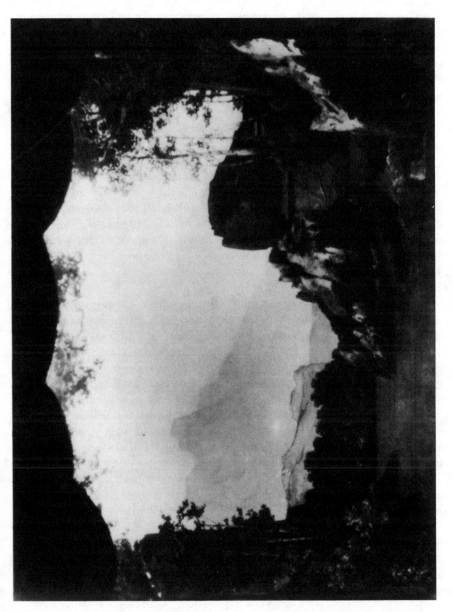

Figure 13.   Bayreuth Setting of 1896 for the Walhalla Landscape of *Rhinegold*

published as a small book in 1895, was *La Mise en scène du drame wagnérien (Staging Wagnerian Drama)*. This was a further developed and considerably more theoretical rendering of the earlier work, presented now in the context of a totally new analysis of the principles governing the relationship between music, stage actions and setting. Finally in 1895 Appia began to write his major work, *La Musique et la mise en scène (Music and the Art of the Theatre)*, which both summarized and revised his two earlier essays, while moving beyond Wagner altogether to describe the implications of his theories generally for a radical and fundamental reformation (amounting virtually to a rebirth) of theatrical art. It was published in German in 1899, as *Die Musik und die Inscenierung*.

Throughout this period, and in close coordination with his writing, Appia worked upon a series of extensive scenarios for the *Ring,* elaborately illustrated by his own quite unprecedented designs, and executed according to the theories presented in the essays. A portion of one of the scenarios, act 3 of *The Walkyrie* along with Appia's designs indicating the setting and lighting for the act, is included in the selection of scenarios in part 6 of this volume. Analysis of the scenarios reveals his astonishing ability (quite unprecedented at the time) to integrate all the elements of production *dramaturgically* into a unified work of theatrical art. In an approach far in advance of conventional practice, Appia displays consummate skill not merely as an innovative theorist, but as a talented director as well.

Around 1902 Appia wrote the short essay "Comment reformer notre mise en scène" ("Ideas on a Reform of Our *Mise en Scène*"). It provides a succinct summary of the principles that Appia had formulated out of his close analysis of Wagnerian opera and also takes up certain questions not fully developed before. Appia notes that sensitive theatre practitioners are now everywhere becoming aware of the inadequacy of current stage conditions, without, however, yet undertaking the type of systematic reform that he proposed. He approves of the widespread interest in naturalism, and the gradual replacement of painted scenery with solid objects, but notes that although such reforms may produce admirable results with realistic plays, they are irrelevant to highly stylized works, including those by Wagner.

In a passage which became a famous epitomization of his concept of scenic art, Appia points out how the performer must come to dictate the manner in which the audience itself responds to scenery, and emphasizes the importance of atmosphere and psychology in determining stage setting: "We shall no longer try to give the illusion of a forest, but the illusion of a man in the atmosphere of a forest." Such an approach soon became prominent—most obviously in expressionist productions, but through more subtle manifestations in theatre everywhere.

It illustrates the relevance which Appia's principles, based initially upon the problem of staging Wagner, had for nonrealistic drama generally, at a point when partly through three-dimensional scenery and better lighting technique, realistic plays were at last being given plausible stagings. Realistic décor by itself was an aesthetic cul-de-sac offering nothing towards achieving more expressive rendering of the great body of non-naturalistic drama and opera. Appia proposes a direct attack on current practice and the testing of new techniques by staging a series of "experimental" productions.[3]

For the next twenty years, Appia's own theoretical and practical work was dominated by such experiment, particularly that growing out of his investigation of eurhythmics. But in the last years of his life, he turned his attention once more to Wagner. In 1923, at the age of sixty-one, he at last was able to stage one of Wagner's operas using a scenario he had prepared as a young man in the 1890s. Arturo Toscanini invited him to stage *Tristan and Isolde* at La Scala, Milan, where Toscanini was artistic director. The following year he was engaged to produce the *Ring* cycle at the Basel Municipal theatre. An account of both productions is given in the introduction to this volume. What is particularly remarkable is that, as both the critical and popular reaction indicate, years after Appia had first formulated his ideas (and following a period of far-reaching reform in theatre practice), they were still widely viewed as radical and innovative.

This view was due in large part to the extraordinary conservatism of the orthodox Wagnerian production style. Steadfast resistance to reform continued for many years under Cosima Wagner and her successors: a source of lifelong frustration and disappointment for Appia; for Bayreuth, artistic stagnation. The moribund approach unnaturally preserved there attempted the impossible: to create on stage an absolute replication of nature's appearance down to the smallest detail and nuance—pictorial realism. Such an approach, as Appia had pointed out, was fundamentally inappropriate to Wagner's work in the first place, and in time became theatrically out-dated as well: initial stylistic error, compounded by anachronism.

Thus, in 1925 when Appia wrote the short essay "Richard Wagner and Theatrical Production," soon after the debacle at Basel, his analysis was no less appropriate for briefly repeating in essence an argument he had first put forward some thirty-five years before. His brief but generous account of his experience at Basel, "The Reform and the Theatre at Basel," only hints at the disappointment and distress he felt in the face of the "intolerant fanaticism" which at the end of his life, his prophetic and enlightened ideas still sometimes encountered: not least at Bayreuth itself.[4]

The history of production at the Festspielhaus after Wagner's death provides an example—charged with irony—of the gradual displacement of traditional staging by reforms conceived and initiated by Appia. Bayreuth's patrons, as well as its directors, were loath to change. Increasingly frequented by a conservative, if not reactionary, elite, it departed from Wagner's concept of a place for communal and classless celebration and "threatened to become merely a rendezvous for snobs."[5] The failure to take up the opportunity for fundamental stylistic reform presented by technical innovations was epitomized by adherence to the old scheme of overhead lighting long after the Festspielhaus had acquired electricity. Until 1906 the stage illumination was provided solely by strip-lighting, arranged in parallel banks as it had been used during the gaslight era, which in turn was based on the centuries-old system of wings and borders. Under such lighting, as Appia had protested, solid scenery, as well as solid performers, appeared grotesque.

In 1906 Cosima officially surrendered artistic control to her son Siegfried, who, until his death in 1930, a few months after Cosima herself died, undertook some tentative—but still loudly protested—reforms. Gradually the scenic décor of Bayreuth productions was modified along Appian lines, although the reforms were nearly all external, ignoring Appia's insistence that the stage setting only had significance or integrity when conceived as emanating from the dramatic work itself. Siegfried slowly reduced or eliminated many naturalistic details, made far greater use of solid elements and gave clearer and smoother lines to the décor, but the productions still suffered from an obstrusive stylistic ambiguity: the set remained an amalgam of painted and plastic elements, and conveyed little sense of any organic relationship to the music-drama itself.[6]

Even Siegfried's modest changes encountered severe criticism from Wagnerian traditionalists. Some even accused him of having become a disciple of Appia, a charge he vigorously denied. After so many years of arrogantly and sometimes self-righteously defending an increasingly beleaguered position, Bayreuth could not meekly capitulate, and did not, for another quarter of a century. As gradually, basic change did come, little credit was given to Appia. He suffered the double indignity that initially he was a prophet so far ahead of his time, that he was ridiculed and ignored; and then, when ultimately his ideas gained widespread acceptance, few remembered or cared to know their source.

Not until 1951 did Wieland Wagner, when he became Bayreuth's director, offer belated recognition, admitting that "it is part of the genuine tragedy of Wagner's work that Appia's ingenious conceptions were not realized on stage. . . . Cosima Wagner's ban . . . rendered Bayreuth for decades the province of a long dead artistic style, and thus converted its once revolutionary role into the opposite."[7]

In his attempt to make a clear break with the past after the debasement of Bayreuth under the Nazis (with, it must be said, the connivance of its director during the period, Winifred Wagner), Wieland at last embraced Appia's theories in full and presented stagings which were in fundamental harmony with them. Appia's acceptance at Bayreuth was finally confirmed in 1955, sixty years after he had first placed his ideas before Cosima, and twenty-seven years after his death. The festival program for that year noted:

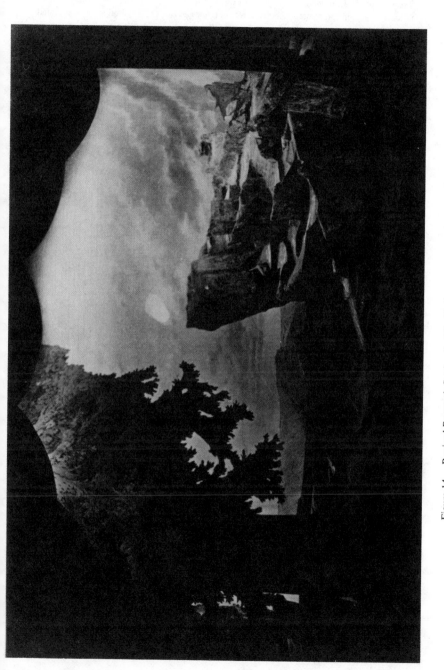

Figure 14. Revised Bayreuth Setting for *The Walkyrie*, Act 3, Used in the First Decades of This Century

That which Adolphe Appia demanded, and in the first quarter of our century created: a performance space fashioned out of the spirit of the music itself, and a sense of three-dimensionality; his recognition of the symbolic power of color and of light, rhythmically coordinated with space—these were the first expressions of the reform of operatic production which developed ultimately into the "New Bayreuth Style."[8]

# Comments on the Staging of
## *The Ring of the Nibelungs*

(1891–92)

Although written much earlier, these comments were first published in *Revue
d'histoire du théâtre* (1954), 1–2

In these comments on staging I have regarded the theatre as a festival house;
even apart from the work under discussion it is only in the festival house that
the art of staging can be firmly established.

This art is still in its infancy, not, to be sure, because of the means available
but because of the manner in which they are used. The appended project demonstrates better than an essay could explain the nature of the reforms indispensable
to obtain a production in harmony with the other means of expression that
Wagner has given us.[9] But it needs justification.

The realization of the drama on the stage, difficult to begin with because
of the numerous media required at present, is completely thwarted by the impossibility of bringing these diverse efforts together with even relative precision.
The creator alone could undertake this. Lacking his omnipotence, the work of
art, dissected for the purpose of study, can, at the moment it takes on life,
present only a conglomeration of its pieces, living, since they tend to approach
one another, but living a distressing life.

The impossibility of integrating those pieces derives from the disproportion
of the intentions, not of the media. On the one hand, the means of expression
are wantonly exhausted; on the other, we must be content with the worst in the
visual field, which has been developed separately and on its own, and which
has accustomed us to subtleties of its own.

The intentions concerning the *mise en scène* (choreography in the full sense
of the word) are inferior to those which motivate the creation of the lyric drama

itself. The reasons for their inferiority are too obviously related to the current theatre to need further discussion here. A single point is to be considered: unlike abstract (music) drama, theatrical production is composed of several parts or divisions; the orchestral performance of a musical drama is not, because the composer has the means to regulate the nuances *theoretically*. There is, by dint of circumstances, a disproportion here, since the creator of an ordinary drama cannot direct the staging of his work theoretically. He could do so if the interpreters of the roles were articulated machines; the only insurmountable difficulty therefore arises from the fact that life can be controlled only relatively.

The problem is thus to reduce as much as possible the uncontrollable portions of the performer's work, and to let him have the minimum of freedom he needs to develop his individual abilities. Therefore, just as the musical annotations minutely determine the singing and the recitative, just as conventional signs regulate the requirements of the music, so a method must be discovered to determine the choreography. The other representational elements, being inanimate, are completely manageable; and though they are at present still left in the hands of the ignorant or foolish, they will in the future obviously become an integral part of the score.

So defined, the scenic conception will work hand in hand with the very composition of the drama. The two will be united if not always in one person, at least in the most intimate unity of purpose.

The following observations can therefore in no way claim to materialize this progress, much less so since the drama which they mean to assist is not fundamentally different from those conceived according to the current mode of staging. Yet this drama needs, more than many others, a representational unity; and under the prevailing circumstances this unity will always be relative, that is, less dependent on the choice of means than on the unity in the intent of that choice. As a result, the value of precise directions given by the creator himself is dependent on the other contributing intentions. In a complex system such as that of the theatre, everything changes all the more quickly since its diverse means of expression do not develop at an equal pace. This is another source of unbalance, for the lyric drama remains immutable and develops only in relation to the audience. On this shifting ground, there is, as we shall see, just one single point that is certain: the unity of purpose—and if for the work under discussion it can only be relative, at least an effort must be made to reduce this relativity to a minimum.

This is the aim of this essay, which is definitive in nothing but the conviction which prompted it. I have written it in total ignorance of the staging conditions at Bayreuth in 1876. The author's wishes were known to me exclusively through his indications in the text and the score; if I have occasionally deviated from them I have no other justification for having done so than my strong feeling of deep reverence. The stage is taken as it is, and I shall use only accepted devices whose possibilities are evident; the purely technical part will be presented with all proper reserve, for I could not acquire the experience necessary to contrive the installations myself. (With some exceptions, the performances in Dresden and Vienna have been of a negative help, but this help nevertheless should not be disdained.) As to acting, I adhere to the generally accepted style, attempting merely to lift it to the high level of the drama under discussion; some passages, however, seem to require a style that aims higher than this. The entire description presents consistently my own vision and never an abstract purpose. Whenever this vision permitted no alternative, I presented it as it appeared to me. Whenever the freedom of choice was too obvious or my vision not precise enough, I was content with more general indications or simply guiding remarks. The choice of a particular interpretation (gesture, pose, setting, etc.) may sometimes seem arbitrary when taken out of context. Yet by making the character of each scene derive from the conception of the whole, that is to say, by giving this conception the fabric of enough secondary characteristics, I have striven to create a unity organic in all its parts, parallel to that of the musical expression. But evidently such an interpretation (the staging) is definitive only through a unification of everything that precedes and follows it; if this whole is diverted to another purpose, that interpretation collapses of itself. Certain gaps cannot be filled without the actual use of the stage, which calls forth and suggests what imagination alone cannot determine even after long experience. On the other hand, that very use of the stage can lead to a considerable change in a scenario planned independently of the stage.

While I have adhered as much as possible to the present conditions of staging, radical reforms seem to me absolutely indispensable: the part played by lighting and the part played by movements in depth and height; in other words, the necessity of creating an atmosphere through lighting and of utilizing the setting. The difficulties brought about by the second reform are compensated for, or may even disappear, through a rational use of lighting.

As far as the performers are concerned, I am aware of the obstacles with which the current state of affairs hinders this plan, since only its creator can hope to secure the disinterestedness necessary for the execution of so precise a scenario. To attempt these reforms seemed to me nevertheless useful, although experience alone can prove the artistic value of my suggestions.

## Lighting

In a drama such as the author of the *Ring* has given us, the expressive means are apparently exhausted: the music drives to the limit the suggestion and development of the most subtle nuances furnished by the libretto. Under favorable conditions, acting shows us this passionate world in a frame suited to increasing its significance. What then causes that extreme weariness, that disappointing void, in spite of all the indispensable and honest efforts of the imagination as regards the scenic part of the performance, the part which is the author's only indirectly? Why does the throughgoing spectator, who is enraptured in this marvelous world, which the music suggests to him and the libretto substantiates, feel the need to complete his esthetic satisfaction? Why this weariness of expectation rendered unbearable by the drama's persistence in its course? Because a living element, vibrant with excessive life, is offered him in a lifeless atmosphere. Because, as previously stated, on the one hand, the expressive means are wantonly exhausted and, on the other, the preeminent medium is missing, namely, *lighting,* without which plasticity and mimetic expression are inconceivable. The drama, all shadow and highlight, sharp contrasts and infinite nuances, is projected on a uniform surface all parts of which are monotonously clear. That this monstrous incongruity affects our receptive organs is not astonishing. Unfortunately, the drama itself is affected by it—primarily in its musical phase, whose effects are enriched or impoverished in direct relation to the lack of corresponding light effects (a light effect is not an isolated factor; the entire production is affected by it).

This persistent flaw is sanctioned by the audience-at-large, whose need for expression in the performance consists in the desire "to see" as much as possible, to have the best possible view, to miss no facial expression, none of the smallest gestures, no detail of a costume, of brush strokes, or parts of a setting. Accordingly, a night scene calls for blue light less bright than day light but, just the same, permitting the audience "to see" everything. In an interior setting, a room, one must be able to probe the tiniest recesses; the same room at night lighted by the glimmer of a weak lamp must still be sufficiently illuminated lest the least detail of living persons and lifeless objects be lost, etc. The result is—and let no one accuse me of exaggerating—that nothing is *seen* at all. An object lit from three or four directions throws no shadow and, from a theatrical viewpoint, does not exist. Today's staging, almost without exception, is merely a collection of such non-existing objects, the characters included. The drama, trying desperately to manifest itself, uses for this end only abstractions less alive than the pages in the score where it waits to be born.

Scenic painting (spatial arrangement included) developed independently of lighting, leaving the latter behind to make the modern inventions serve its own convenience; consequently the artist does not consider the lighting offered him equal to his scenic ideas and counts on it only in the most general way. He sees himself thus obliged to create, through deceptive painting, the effects denied him through actual light and shadow. Those charged with lighting very beautifully painted drops naturally have no other worry than to make the picture visible lest any detail be lost. Variations in the ground plan have induced these technicians to employ more or less ingenious devices, but solely to illuminate the painting; they have gone a long way towards perfection in the field of special effects (moon, water, clouds, etc.) always however applied separately to each of these phenomena, with little concern for the scenic painter and without regard for the consequences which the success of any one of those special effects is bound to provoke.

At present, conditions are such that, if the question of stage lighting is raised, one is answered with the supposedly unsolvable problem of the painted shadows. And indeed the two suppliers of decorative elements, the scenic painter and the electrician (I limit myself to these two in order to simplify the explanation—the technician serves both) are so far apart that it is difficult to imagine their collaboration in creating a harmonious agreement regarding the setting. Before his canvas pieces the painter believes he has complete freedom, and rightly so since he knows his picture will be illuminated so that not one of his ideas is lost; and this is his aim. The electrician asks few questions about the setting-in-preparation; he knows that the painter is acquainted with the electrical equipment and its recognized possibilites for light changes. So he leaves the field to the painter, ready, when the goods are delivered, to manipulate with inconceivable indolence the wonderful media at his disposal. The requirements of the characters are taken care of, almost all of them, at the last minute, and in the same old way, with which the painter has nothing to do and in which the living drama merely has to assist.

There are no doubt exceptions, accidental passages for which nobody is responsible and which remain hidden in the scenario of one or another work, until they are brought about unconsciously. And the amateur takes careful notice of them, delighted when the work, with its packaged staging, presents anew the incomparable effect, which stands out from the staging, slavishly repeated in every production. Due to its requirements, the realistic theatre has introduced some progress. Individual enterprises, on their part, have done for better or for worse what they could to escape the stagnation; but in the older and warped frame these revolutionary attempts can lead only to unrestrained luxury, to petty interests in trifles, or, what is more dangerous, to an excessive simplification that makes of the theatre a literary pastime.

The more restricted the setting (painting and spatial arrangement), the more independent and flexible is the lighting. One may even assert that, through light, anything is possible in the theatre, for it suggests unmistakably, and *suggestion* is the only basis on which the art of staging can expand without encountering any obstacles; material *realization* is of secondary importance.

The increase and perfection of the lighting equipment presents no real difficulties under the extraordinary conditions of a festival, but the manner of utilizing it cannot be determined by any rule. This remains flexible, dependent on a thousand esthetic problems. Based on experience, a list might perhaps be compiled on which the painter could rely; yet by the same token, experience turns into routine and if the aims are foolish the routine will be foolish too. It is therefore necessary not to confuse the artist who gives the order with the technician (electrician) who will always search for new and better ways to satisfy the artist's demands. Between the two no absolute understanding is possible; each of them needs to be entirely independent, they will meet always in agreement.

One reason for the current childish settings undoubtedly is that the scenic artist and the technician believe they are mutually dependent and thus paralyze their efforts. It is evident that the construction of the contemporary stage, which serves the sole purpose of facilitating the practice of established conventions, cannot admit as complete a reform as would be desirable, but light in its superb flexibility somehow adjusts itself to everything and thus lessens the difficulties that the setting, itself, could not overcome alone.

The worse way to illuminate the contemporary setting (without taking into account concessions that an attempt at reform would bring about) is first to light *naturally* as for the place indicated by scenery (exterior, interior, etc.), then to add *artificially* what is needed to modify the natural lighting to the quality of the picture and the requirements of the ground plan. It is obvious that the setting must be brought to life by the characters for whom it is built and that these characters must be considered an *important part* of it.

Yet, it is evident that if faces, gestures, groups and the entire pattern of movement are to have life, they must be given *shadow*. Therefore the current use of fixed footlights must be irrevocably done away with and replaced by portable strip lights completely subordinated to lighting from above with the single aim of creating artificially the *diffused light* of day. With more freedom, borderlights will serve the same purpose.

Light, in the precise sense of the word, will invariably be furnished by means of movable instruments. There are two distinct methods: one for exteriors, another for interiors. For exterior settings, the light will *always* come *from above* save for some few exceptions; the height of the characters is taken as the maximum angle and all comes from the same direction. For the interior setting the light will enter very obviously through the openings (never horizontally) reinforced extremely subtly by footlights or by special instruments to provide diffused light.

Since the action of the *Ring* occurs outdoors almost entirely, the former lighting method will prevail.

*Projection*, which has reached such marvelous perfection, although it is employed merely in isolated cases for special effects (fire, clouds, water, etc.) is indisputably one of the most powerful scenic devices; as a connecting link between lighting and setting it dematerializes everything it touches. Easy to handle, it lends itself to all kinds of effects.

This should not make us satisfied with just any, more or less improved, magic lanterns; rather, the numerous instruments must satisfy the same standard as portable lighting equipment; the functioning of projectors must be the best possible today, the choice of lens satisfactory and the specific effects required for each production executed by an artist of the first rank.

Projection thus prepared takes an *active* role on the stage—it must now and then even supersede the part played by the characters (see the sky in act 3 of *The Walkyrie*). It is rarely absent and when its purpose is not definitive, at least it supports lighting in the creation of a variable atmosphere for the entire setting. Moving gauze (simulating clouds, fog, et al.) will never be obtained without projection, whose use conceals the unnatural crudeness of this device. It must include the whole gamut from a vague, hardly noticeable motion to the most striking images.

When electric projections become a regular device for the stage they will deserve the epithet all-powerful as there will be few assignments they will be unable to fulfill.

For the time being the following plan requires merely a larger number of machines (and stagehands) and more versatile equipment for shifting. It gives projection a truly active part, sometimes even a *role* that the diverse machines will share but that will nevertheless be guided by a single purpose.

**Setting**

Since each part of the Trilogy has indeed its own characteristic style, the interrelationship of the parts in a production would benefit if each part could be staged in a similarly distinct style. Unfortunately, the repeated use of the Rock of the Walkyrie forbids this. *The Rhinegold* alone is privileged to permit a treatment independent of the three other parts. This condition must be profitably used to give *The Rhinegold* strong individuality.

The dominant character of the *Ring* settings is the rocky landscape covered with some vegetation. Exclusive of *The Rhinegold* it comprises six out of nine settings and among these six, four show a cave (a fifth cave is seen in act 1 of *Siegfried*). There is thus a danger of monotony and every precaution must be taken to avoid it.

In this plan two major divisions are noticeable as regards the general idea of staging: one includes everything related to the Gibichungs; the other, to the remaining settings (see introduction to *Götterdämmerung*). In the first division preceding the Gibichungs, in which *The Rhinegold* forms a separate part, the Style will consist in characterizing the design of each setting exclusively in accord with its dramatic intent as indicated, and by reducing it to the bare necessities.

For its staging, Wagner's *The Ring of the Nibelungs* can rely only partially and indirectly on its mythological background. The "symbolic" is so prominent in it that the drama is raised far beyond any local or mythological atmosphere.

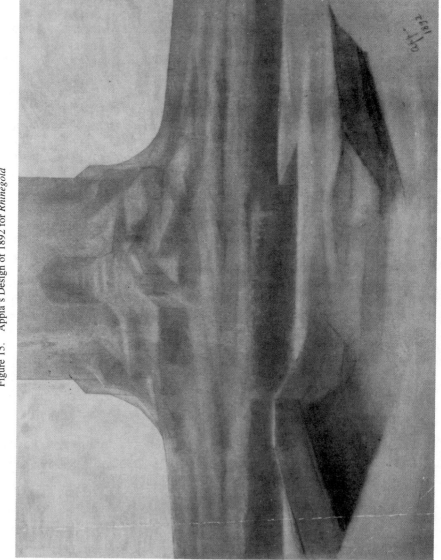

Figure 15.   Appia's Design of 1892 for *Rhinegold*

Yet this "symbolism" is of such nature that, in order to bring it closer to us, we wish to be able to dress the characters according to our taste, and to place them in a corresponding frame. There is only one way to satisfy this desire, namely, to keep costume and setting extremely simple. This is easy for the costume, although we must not forget that at all times dramatic necessities are involved. As to the setting, the problem is more complicated because of the diversity of the requirements. The second act of *The Walkyrie* offers a striking example: this setting must plunge the spectator into a mood of imposing heroism or at least not weaken the effect of grandeur created by the music. A few minutes later one must be able to follow a Walkyrie dashing across the same setting, which unfortunately necessitates some change in the setting. Soon thereafter the dramatic action tightens again and acquires an intensity that calls for an extreme simplification of setting. Then follows the emotive expansion (Siegmund and Sieglinde) which adapts itself quite well to a composite setting. The final scene requires all scenic resources. With its three-dimensional construction and a few cut-outs the setting alone cannot solve the problem, but light remains independent and through it the concessions are masked and the disproportions balanced. The setting presents a suggestive *atmosphere* to the eye by deceiving it about the real conditions. As will be seen, its task in this act can be reduced to a simple and single procedure.

The style of the second division, the Gibichungs, consists of being free of any worry by leaving its *mise en scène* to the imagination and to knowledge, intensifying it as much as possible, and doing everything to distinguish it from the preceding division. Lighting, although prominent in itself in this part, is capable of maintaining the indispensable unity of the whole. Of course the characters carried over from the first division are unchanged and so they stand out strongly alone over the stifling medley in which they represent the higher world already known to the audience.

Thus these two divisions solve the problem of avoiding monotony in the settings of act 2 and the beginning of act 3 of *Götterdämmerung*. The dramatic character of each of the remaining four settings is too clearly defined to be mistaken. The appended scenario carries the details which can provide the repetitions within the general character of each picture.

Nature in all its aspects supplies the decorative elements in the *Ring*. Therefore all effects will be based on *light*. The decorative abundance must be curtailed in its own interest, whereas the *practicability* has to be maintained as much as possible since it provides the contact with movement. To simplify the outline of the stage picture (by eliminating anything "picturesque") means to raise it to the level of the music (*Götterdämmerung* is subject to other laws). Practicability properly understood can contribute to the same goal, for it requires a relatively simply arrangement; moreover it is soothing to the eye, because it suits the three-dimensional bodies that are so jarring when placed in front of consistently vertical canvas flats; it also encourages the *use* of the setting (see *Characters*) in such a way that the latter could in turn evoke through *its construction,* the entire drama of the *Rock of the Walkyrie.*

In this plan the very dim footlights, by keeping the downstage area dark, force setting and characters to stay upstage of the front wing, if they want to be seen. The consequences for the scenic arrangement can easily be deduced, but the glimmer rising from the orchestra must be reduced to a minimum and the darkness of the house regulated in relation to this minimum.

The special staging of the introduction of *The Rhinegold* indicates an innovation in the manner of reducing the scenery, which is applied also to three settings of the other parts.

The designs here included are intended merely to facilitate the reading of the scenario.

The darker designs are intended to suggest general effect to the imagination. The stakes approximately mark the perspective; they have no direct connection with the scenario.

**Characters**

In the *Ring* the characters *form part of the setting* (in contrast to *Tristan*); the only exception is Wotan in act 2 of *The Walkyrie.* Their acting area will therefore be arranged in accord with their requirements or, to put it differently, they must become familiar with their environment. The harmony of the production depends on the working together of characters and setting.

Lighting and practicability (see *Lighting* and *Setting* in the *Ring*) tend to blend the performer with the scenic surroundings, the first by enveloping him with the same atmosphere as the inanimate picture, and the other by suggesting to him his movement, in which he thus makes the picture participate. Yet declamation must be included in this intended unity. The task is delicate when dealing with a work whose minor details of staging are not strictly contained in the musical conception; on the other hand, these very conditions necessitate the changes that are imitated on stage, and the movements selected are based on musical sounds. For, just as shade—i.e., not to see everything—is one of the best means of expression for the face, the body and the group, so not always to have a maximum of sound, musical sound, is an indispensable source of dramatic life. For a long time to come we are condemned to suffer the blemish with which opera has marred our taste; and we must always more or less compromise as long as the action is a decorative factor, that is to say, as long as the characters must be part of the setting and do not present an inner action whose life depends on the mood, as in *Tristan.* The following statements furnish many examples of the application of this principle, which brings declamation into the same unity of intention that the performer has already experienced in practicability and lighting.

"Musical" movements, particularly in crowd scenes or small groups, set out from the same principle to integrate sound (while always taking account of the dramatic intention). Sometimes the harmony is imperceptible, but the spectator who has once unconsciously partaken of this blessing will miss it if it is not there.

The recurrence of a gesture, a pose related or unrelated to the three-dimensional setting, a likeness suggesting a portion of the drama that is past, can become a powerful dramatic contrivance if carefully employed. But it is a method which does not necessarily match the recurrence of musical motifs. The arrangement of the setting must take this into consideration—it is part of the general harmony whose effects are rarely isolated one from the other.

The description of the simplest costumes is merely a preventive. It will take all the experience of a competent costumer to achieve the utmost in simplicity which is required in the first part of the *Ring;* as to the other part, the Gibichungs, the same costumer will be in his element.

The performer who is incorporated in the stage picture and supported by all the expressive media it gives or suggests to him must retain no inappropriate tradition of the past. To achieve this, a reform of the hair style (and the footwear) is imperative: to ease the task of the performers, everything in the setting as well as in their costumes that could create unforeseen hazards or complicate the execution of their roles is removed. Thus wigs are all of the same massive and solid type so that all the performers have to do is to see that they do not slip. Serious difficulties may occur if this convenient type is abandoned, but here as in other cases, no compromise is possible. Hair style is an essential means of expression. The new method being after all probably just a question of money, the task is to distinguish the characters for whom a flexible wig is a mimetic necessity from those who use it merely decoratively, and then to do everything possible to provide the *most flexible* material for the first group and, for the second group, to reduce the quality of the hair used without changing its shape, that is, to give them different *grades* of hair for the same role. As to the general impression, certain effects (*Götterdämmerung*) require here and there in the crowd a large display of hair. For Erda, the Daughters of the Rhine, Freia and less directly for Sieglinde, the flexibility of the hair is part of their costume (that is of their role in the unity of the scenario); in acts 1 and 2 of *Siegfried* the hero's hair is of prime importance. By contrast, such flexibility is immaterial for Fricka and Gutrune. Brunnhilde falls in both categories.

The use of *heels* for the "primitive" footwear gives the characters, whom we wish to see far removed from our life, the gait we are accustomed to, along with the ugliness of that gait. Therefore heels should be eliminated and the sandals (no matter whether more open or less so) should be unadorned, their leg straps limited or omitted.

# Ideas on a Reform of Our *Mise en Scène*

(ca. 1902)

*La Revue des revues* 1, no. 9 (1 May 1904)
Toby Cole and Helen Krich Chinoy, eds., *Directing the Play* (New York, 1953)

For several years dramatic art has been on a path of evolution. Naturalism on the one hand, and Wagnerism on the other, have violently shifted the earlier boundaries. Certain things which, twenty years ago, were not "theatre" (according to that ridiculously hallowed expression), have become almost commonplace. Hence some confusion: these days we hardly know the style appropriate to a particular play; and the liking we have for foreign productions will not guide us.

Such circumstances alone, however, would not be so harmful if the scenery we do use were adapted to each new experiment. Unfortunately, this is not the case. Theoretically the author with his manuscript (or the composer with his score) may fully agree with the actors on a basic conception; but on the stage under the glare of the lights, the new idea must be squeezed into the old frame—and our stage directors mercilessly cut out anything that does not fit.

Several people assert that it cannot be otherwise, that scenic convention is rigid, etc. I, for one, maintain the contrary. On the following pages I have tried to establish the basic elements of a *mise en scène* which, instead of paralyzing and immobilizing dramatic art, follows it faithfully but at the same time also provides an inexhaustible source of suggestions for the author and his interpreters.

Our present stage scenery is entirely the slave of painting—scene painting—which pretends to create for us the illusion of reality. But this illusion is in itself an illusion, for the presence of the actor contradicts it. In fact, the principle of illusion obtained by painting on flat canvas and that obtained by the plastic and living body of the actor are in contradiction. A homogeneous and artistic production, therefore, cannot be achieved by separately developing the manners of these two illusions—as is done on our stages.

Let us examine these two conceptions and their effect on modern scenic art.

It is impossible to transfer real trees, real houses, etc., to our stages; besides, it would hardly be desirable. We think that all we can do is to imitate reality as faithfully as possible. But imitation of three-dimensional objects is laborious, often impossible, and at any rate very expensive. One might think that this would compel us to reduce the number of items to be shown; our stage directors, however, are of a different opinion. They think the stage should present everything that seems appropriate to it; hence, whatever cannot be executed in three dimensions has to be painted. There is no doubt that painting permits us to show the spectator an infinite amount of detail. It also seems to give the *mise en scène* its desired freedom, and here the reasoning of our director ends.

The essential principle of painting, however, is to reduce everything to a flat surface; how, then, can it fill space, i.e., the stage and its three dimensions? Ignoring this problem, directors cut up the painting and set the pieces on the stage floor, leaving the lowest part of the scenic picture unpainted: if it represents a landscape, for example, the top will be a canopy of green, to the right and left there will be trees, upstage a horizon and sky—and on the floor . . . the bare boards. The picture that is supposed to represent everything has to renounce, from the very beginning, any portrayal of the ground: since the fictitious forms the picture represents must be exposed to us vertically and since there is no possible relationship between the vertical flats and the more or less horizontal floor or the canvas covering it, our designers add some padding to the lower end of the wings and backdrop.

The floor, therefore, is not really included in the picture; yet the floor is precisely where the actor moves. Our stage directors have forgotten the actor. *Hamlet* without Hamlet, once more!—Will they sacrifice a little of the dead painting in favor of the living and moving body? Oh no! They would rather renounce the theatre. But as this too lively body nonetheless has to be taken into consideration, the picture does consent to place itself, here and there, at the command of the actor, at times even so generously that it looks peculiar; at other times, however, it definitely concedes nothing; then the actor looks ridiculous. The antagonism is complete.

We started with painting; now let us see what direction the problem will take if we begin with the actor—the plastic and human body, considered solely from the viewpoint of its effect on the stage—just as we have done with the scenery.

An object appears plastic to our eyes only because of the light that strikes it. Its plasticity cannot be artistically emphasized except through an artistic use of light; this is self-evident. So much for the form! The movement of the human body needs levels to express itself. All artists know that the beauty of bodily movements depends on the variety of support provided by the floor and other objects. Therefore, the mobility of the actor can be artistically realized only in relation to an appropriate structure of objects and floor.

The two primary conditions for an artistic appearance of the human body on the stage would then be: light that enhances its plasticity, and a setting constructed in three dimensions that enhances the actor's postures and movements. Here we are far away from painting!

Dominated by painting, the *mise en scène* sacrifices the actor and, in addition, as we have seen, a great part of its own pictorial effect—since, contrary to the basis principle of this art, the picture has to be so cut up that the stage floor cannot participate in the illusion created by flats and drops.

What would happen if we subordinated it to the actor?

Above all, the light could be given full freedom. Ruled by painting, light is in fact completely absorbed by the setting. The details shown on the flats must be seen; hence, lights and shadows painted on canvas are illuminated . . . and from this kind of lighting, alas, the actor obtains whatever he can. Under such conditions there can be no question of true stage lighting or, consequently, of any plastic effect whatsoever.

Lighting is an element in itself whose effects are limitless; set free, it becomes for us what his palette is for the painter; all combinations of color can be created with it. By means of simple or complex, fixed or moving, projections—by justified obstructions, by diverse degrees of transparency, etc.—we can achieve infinite modulations. Thus by means of light we can in a way materialize colors and forms, which are immobilized on painted canvas, and can bring them alive in space. No longer does the actor walk in front of painted shadows and highlights; he is plunged into an atmosphere that is uniquely his own. Artists will easily understand the extent of such a reform.*

Here we are at the crucial point: namely, the plasticity of setting necessary for the beauty of the actor's posture and movement. Painting has in the past taken the upper hand on our stages by providing two-dimensionally whatever could not be realized plastically, and for the sole purpose of creating the illusion of reality. Are images thus accumulated on flat canvas indispensable? By no means! There is not a single play that demands one hundredth of them—for, mind you, these images are not alive; they are merely indicated on canvas in a sort of hieroglyphical language, merely signifying the items they purport to represent, all the more so since they cannot make real organic contact with the actor.

---

*A well-known artist in Paris, M. Mariano Fortuny, has invented a completely new lighting system based on *reflected light*. Its results are extremely fortunate—this excellent invention will bring about a radical transformation of the *mise en scène* in all theatres . . . to the benefit of light.[10]

Plasticity as required by the actor aims at an entirely different effect, for the human body does not try to create any illusion of reality; it is reality! What it demands of a setting is merely support for this reality. Naturally such a conception completely changes the purpose of the setting; in one case it is the realistic appearance of objects that is sought; in the other, the highest possible degree of actuality for the human body.

These two principles are technically opposed to each other; one or the other must, therefore, be chosen. Are we to choose a mass of dead images and an overly decorated abundance of flat canvas, or the performance of a mobile and plastic human being? If we hesitate—a most unlikely possibility—let us ask ourselves what it is that we are looking for in the theatre. Beautiful paintings may be seen elsewhere, and fortunately not cut up into pieces; photography permits us to travel all over the globe in an armchair; literature inspires us with the most charming pictures; and very few people are so poor in spirit that they are unable to see, from time to time, beautiful sights in nature itself.

No! We go to the theatre to witness a dramatic action, set in motion by the presence of characters on the stage; without them there is no action. The actor is, thus, the essential factor in the production; it is he whom we go to see, he from whom we expect the emotion we seek. It is then imperative to base a production on the presence of the actor, and in order to achieve this, to clear the stage of everything that is in conflict with him. We now have the technical problem clearly stated.

One may reply that this problem has been occasionally rather well solved on certain of our Parisian stages—the Théâtre Antoine, for instance, or others.[11] No doubt about that, but why always for only one type of play and one type of setting? How would directors mount *Troilus* or *The Tempest, The Ring of the Nibelungs* or *Parsifal?* At the Grand Guignol they know perfectly well how to present the room of a concierge, . . . but what would they do, for instance, with a garden?

There are two distinct sources for our *mise en scène:* opera and spoken drama. Hitherto, opera singers, with a few exceptions, have been treated like fashionable singing machines, and the painted setting constituted the most obvious visual aspect of the performance; hence its prodigious development. It is different in the spoken drama. Here the actor necessarily takes first place, because without him there would be no play. And if the director feels he must occasionally borrow from the luxury of opera, he does so discreetly, without losing sight of the actor. (Let us compare the decorative effect of spectacular plays with any opera.) Still the principle of illusion is the same in drama as in opera, and it is the scenic illusion, of course, that is most seriously impaired. Thus dramatic authors are well acquainted with the two or three combinations in modern staging which, in spite of the actor's presence, can create a bit of such illusion—and they strive never to go beyond them.

During recent years, it is true, conditions have somewhat changed. With the Wagnerian drama, opera approaches the spoken drama and the spoken drama seeks (except for extreme realism) to go beyond its former limitations in order to approach music drama. Strangely enough our contemporary *mise en scène* suits the requirements of neither of them! The ridiculous display of painting in opera has at this point nothing to do with a score of Wagner (Wagnerian directors in Bayreuth, like others, apparently do not yet suspect this). The scenic monotony of the spoken drama no longer satisfies the subtle imagination of most playwrights. Everyone feels the necessity for reform, but the force of inertia still drags us along in the same rut.

Under such conditions theories are useful, but they do not lead us far; scenic practice itself must be directly attacked and gradually transformed.

The simplest method, perhaps, would be to select one of our plays that has already been staged to show how scenery based on the principles delineated above could be employed. Of course, the selection must be made carefully: a play specifically written for present staging or an opera perfectly fitting the décor of our Académie de Musique[12] would be of little help. Instead, a dramatic work should be chosen whose requirements are in obvious conflict with our present methods: a play by Maeterlinck[13] or any other play of that same type, even a music drama by Wagner. The latter would be preferable, because music, precisely defining duration and intensity of expression, is a valuable guide. Furthermore, here the sacrifice of illusion would be less obvious than in a play. As we move along, we should note each aspect of the old scenery that opposes our aims. At the same time, concessions may have to be made which could be quite instructive. The question of light will occupy us first of all. This will give us the opportunity to experience the tyranny of painting on vertical flats and will make us understand, not merely theoretically, but very tangibly, the immense injustice still done to the actor and, through him, to the playwright.

Undoubtedly the attempt would have to be a modest one. It is difficult to achieve such a reform at one stroke, for it involves as much the reform of public taste as it does the transformation of our style of production. Besides, the result of a practical development in a familiar field is perhaps more certain than that of a more or less radical experiment.

The second set of *Siegfried* may serve as an example. How are we to present a forest on the stage? First let us have an understanding on this point: is it a forest with characters or characters in a forest? We are in the theatre to see a dramatic action. In the forest an action takes place which, of course, cannot be expressed through painting. This is our point of departure: so and so does such and such, says this and that, in a forest. In order to create our setting we need not try to visualize a forest, but we have to imagine in detail the entire sequence of events that occur in this forest. Thorough knowledge of the score is therefore indispensable. It completely changes the nature of the vision that can inspire a stage director; his eyes must remain fixed on the characters. He will then think of the forest as an atmosphere around and above the performers—an atmosphere that can be realized only in relation to living and loving beings, on whom he must focus. Thus he will never envision the setting as an arrangement of lifeless paintings: on the contrary, it will always remain alive. The *mise en scène* thus becomes the composition of a picture in time. Instead of beginning with a painting, ordered no matter by whom for whom, and afterwards reserving for the actor those pitiful devices with which we are familiar, we commence with the actor. It is his performance that we want to stress; we are ready to sacrifice everything for that. It will be Siegfried here and Siegfried there, but never the tree for Siegfried and the path for Siegfried.

I repeat, we shall no longer try to give the illusion of a forest, but the illusion of a man in the atmosphere of a forest. Man is the reality, and nothing else counts. Whatever this man touches must be intended for him—everything else must contribute to the creation of a suitable atmosphere around him. And if, leaving Siegfried for a moment, we lift our eyes, the scenic picture need not give a complete illusion. It is composed for Siegfried alone. When the forest, gently stirred by a breeze, attracts Siegfried's attention, we—the spectators—will see Siegfried bathed in ever-changing lights and shadows but no longer moving among cut-out fragments set in motion by stage tricks.

Scenic illusion is the presence of the living actor.

The scenery for this act as it is now offered to us on all the stages of the world leaves much to be desired! We shall have to simplify it a great deal; give up illuminating painted flats as is now required; almost completely rearrange the stage floor; and, above all, provide a control board for the light—one that is conceived on a large scale and that must be handled with meticulous care. Footlights, those astonishing monstrosities, will hardly ever be used. We may add that the larger part of this reform will have to be done with the performers, and it cannot be achieved without several orchestra rehearsals (a strict requirement which, at present, seems exorbitant but is indeed fundamental).

An attempt of this kind cannot fail to show us how to transform our rigid and conventional staging into an artistic medium, alive, flexible, and suitable for the realization of any dramatic vision. We may even be surprised that we have neglected for so long an important branch of art by leaving it to people who are not artists, because we thought it unworthy of our attention.

As far as the *mise en scène* is concerned, our aesthetic judgment is still anesthetized. A person who would not tolerate in his apartment an object that does not conform to his very exquisite taste is perfectly willing to pay a high price for a seat in an ugly hall constructed contrary to good sense, and to witness for hours a spectacle of such poor taste that, in comparison with it, colored lithographs sold by a peddler are delicate pieces of art.

The manner of stage designing, as in any other art, is based on forms, on light and on color. Since these three elements are actually at our command, we can employ them artistically in the theatre as elsewhere. Hitherto, the *mise en scène* has been expected to achieve the highest possible degree of illusion, and this principle—unaesthetic, at the very least—has doomed us to immobility. I have tried to demonstrate in the preceding pages that scenic art should be based on the one reality worthy of the theatre, the human body. And we have learned something about the primary and elementary consequences of this reform.

The subject is difficult and complex mainly because of the misapprehensions that surround it and of the rigid habits to which modern spectacles have conditioned us. My idea would have to be developed much further in order to convince very many people. It would be necessary to talk about an entirely new duty incumbent on the actor, the influence of expressive and artistic scenery on the dramatist, the power of music to create style in a production, the modifications needed in the building of stages and theatres, etc.

That is impossible for me within the scope of this essay, but perhaps the reader has glimpsed in my aesthetic longing something akin to his own, and thus will find it easy to continue this work for himself.

# Richard Wagner and Theatrical Production

## (1925)

The genius of all great artists has by far exceeded the particular dimensions of their personality. But these dimensions are inflexible. ("And neither time nor power can break up the form developed through life itself.")[14] Personality is a phenomenon; nothing in this world can alter it, just as the worst pen and the most unfavorable conditions cannot mislead the graphologist. Personality will always betray itself.

The artist genius suffers from human duality more than anyone else. Although all of us try to realize the superior being whose presence we feel in ourselves, the artistic genius alone has the disturbing power to express this ideal being in a language which is and remains alien to his everyday personality. So the duality is emotionally upsetting. The genius of the artist expresses what we all wish to realize without ever being able to and what gives our life its immortal quality; yet the artist is unable to bring this into accord with the everyday manifestations of his personality. His genius seems to direct his hand as if he were in a trance. Then, when the personality awakens and wants to read what it has created, it does not understand, and is in danger of making little rational use of a work that escapes it. The genius always lacks the perfect adjustment which is so typically present in the merely talented man, because the genius tries to adapt his mysterious and infallible work to the contingencies of his personality, which is subject to error.

Anyone who ponders this problem will discover that it is far more technical than psychological. The less hold the genius retains on his finished work, the more chance is there that it will be offered to us intact. On the other hand, if this work, once completed, must then be subjected to the arbitrary will of the artist's personality and, worse still, if this will is in turn influenced by outside pressures, then the work will run the risk of becoming seriously distorted.

This last is unquestionably the case with Richard Wagner. Michelangelo standing before his David or in his Sistine Chapel might well have said: "There it is! I understand nothing about it, but nevertheless there it is!" Wagner, armed with his scores, did not have this out-and-out good fortune. Before it reached us, his work had to undergo the most dangerous of tests, the theatre, and so it is quite clear that it has partly gone astray, and has not come to us intact.

Was Wagner aware of this? Perhaps; although everything suggests the inference that his notions about the nature of his genius were as imperfect as those about the conditions needed to reach whatever audience there was. Wagner, in short, did not know how to present his dramatic work to the audience of his time in a form that would fully reveal his genius. This caused, from the very beginning, a misunderstanding which by now has become such an established and untouchable tradition that it prevents any audience from approaching his work with the lack of bias that the work deserves.

In the music-poetic score of a Wagnerian drama we possess the work in its purest form, if we disregard all the directions added by the master. Who can doubt it? But Wagner is a dramatist and consequently a man of the theatre, for a dramatist of the library is a nonsensical Latin idea, and Wagner is a German. Does the vision he applied to the stage match all the power he unfolds in his score? Today nobody could hesitate to say that the master put his extraordinary work in a traditional stage frame of his period. And while everything in the auditorium of Bayreuth expresses his genius, everything behind the footlights contradicts it.

And such conditions are supposed to be perpetuated!—"Have you eyes!" Hamlet cries; Wagner's genius is like the dead noble King whose crown is still being placed upon the unworthy head of the usurper Claudius.

But—you will ask—how will this crown be restored to the majestic head which alone must bear it?

First of all, we must have unlimited love and respect for Richard Wagner. Then we must act. Now, to act in the theatre means to transfer a written work on stage and thus to reveal to our eyes the life latent and hidden in the manuscript. By regarding Wagner's scores as manuscripts, which means throwing behind us the traditional rubbish that has forced its way between these scores and ourselves, we adopt the preliminary attitude, indispensable to the liberation of the stage. The resulting freedom will be most favorable to the thorough and detailed study of the Wagnerian music-poetic score. To this score alone we shall turn. The scenic directions of the master are to be treated with caution, since they all originated from a dead tradition, or, at least, were influenced by it.

For instance, Wagner recommends for *Parsifal* the Gothic style of northern Spain. Does this manuscript express this geographic and historic idea? In no

Figure 16.  Appia's Design of 1896 for *Parsifal*, Act 1
The transition from forest to temple was to be accomplished for the most part by lighting.

way! Besides, would music be capable of expressing this in any way except through folktunes of the area, and is there anything of this kind in the score of *Parsifal*? Another time Wagner describes meticulously the neglected garden of the Breton castle on Tristan's estate. Is there any trace of it in the music-poetic score? We get there only a vision of a benign evening in a sorrowful light; in addition we learn that Tristan is bedded outdoors, that Kurvenal can look across the sea when he reaches a specific spot in the setting, which does not imply that we see the sea; and further, that a door in the rear is to be opened. That is all.

But, alas, Wagner did not understand it so; he obstinately insisted that his music be given not merely adequately but completely realistic materialization on the stage; and he believed this to be possible! He ignored the correlation of the senses, which presupposes a radical differentiation in their stimuli. Wherever his genius altered the harmony to give a situation or a phenomenon excessive musical expression, his temperament demanded the same of the production. What he had told our ears more than sufficiently he insisted on offering literally to our eyes by way of a production that is regrettably overloaded. Thus he buried his own work, and his example was followed by his adept disciples who, though surely sincere and enthusiastic, were nevertheless blind or blinded.

Yet this work, which is probably unique in the annals of humanity, is still alive under the heavy slabs that have been heaped on it! Let us lift these slabs and return those scores, those miracles of a genius and a persevering will, to the fresh air, the light, and the clear sky. Our reverence must go so far as deliberately to violate the wishes of the man whose formidable musical power unbalanced the aesthetic harmony. Art lives by collaboration; otherwise it is a beautiful body without life. Let us collaborate on the work of Richard Wagner and let us open our eyes for him—for him who has so royally enchanted our ears and deeply moved our souls.

Modern stage technique—not in Latin, but in German countries—has reached a point of correct and almost scientific visual expression which can correspond to any musical intensity and can do so, let us mark it well, without overloading the production. The majority of spectators is ready and willing to accept modern stage technique. Only the traditionalists must still be convinced. Under the new technique the actor alone is accountable, since he is the first and foremost to be considered. The proper direction of the characters determines the use of the inanimate parts of the setting and thus achieves the miracle, the inexpressible and wondrous miracle of making the actor create the space in which he lives his happiness and his suffering, a scenic atmosphere whose secret he alone possesses and which does not exist without him.

We go to the theatre to participate in this life, not merely to attend it. Every work of genuine art demands this contribution on the part of the audience. At last theatrical production understands this. Let us respond affirmatively!

# The Reform and the Theatre at Basel

*Gazette de Lausanne,* May 3, 1925

The problem of the theatre, or, properly stated, the very complex problems of dramatic art are the order of the day, although for many of us, their solution seems to be merely a financial matter. Can it be that our lake that is ever changing—yet, thanks to a perhaps too generous providence, fortunately ever remaining the same—has rendered us indifferent to certain aesthetic questions? It is possible, but it would be regrettable if, living in indolence like spoiled children, we should remain ignorant of events close to us in our own country.

We know, for instance, that we have to go to the German part of Switzerland in order to enjoy good operatic productions. Do we also know that we possess an incomparable theatre where every performance, musical or non-musical, is staged with precision and, moreover, in a pure style, shrewdly adapted to the requirements of each work and safely guided by a good taste and an artistic integrity that are perhaps unique in our day? This theatre cannot be called avant-garde. It is a modest repertory theatre in which tragedy, comedy, operetta, and opera are performed. How is it possible under the given conditions to obtain such a high degree of excellence? In this manner:

The manager of this theatre is an artist and, in addition, a designer of great ability. The conductor is an artist of the first rank, both in his technique and in his concept of music. The leading director is an artist, a doctor of philosophy, a man of great learning and solid culture. The technical director is an artist and a virtuoso, acknowledged in his field (he is considered one of the best experts at the Théâtre des Champs-Elysées in Paris), who has written a very interesting booklet on the tradition of stage technique.[15] Experience acquired in our theatre is for this courageous man only a springboard to leap further toward a higher goal. He is not a preserver, but a pioneer; as a matter of fact, I do not think that this theatre feels the need for a preserver. The collaborators on this stage pursue their ideal with little disagreement and they discuss it quickly and intelligently.

In such an exceptional atmosphere the actors cannot help being stimulated with great zeal, seized by a spirit of emulation that has nothing to do with rivalry. They cannot help but submit their pride to a discipline that will lead them toward a fulfillment so homogeneous and alive that each of them seems to be its creator. The spirit of initiative is so much the rule in this theatre that any opposition to it meets with contempt or, at least, open repugnance, whereas daring endeavors are quickly accepted as so many steps forward.

Do we know all this?

The writer of these lines recently had an unforgettable experience there. Upon the manager's invitation he submitted a most radical scenic reform for a tremendous drama which was in danger of being strangled by antiquated tradition, namely *The Ring of the Nibelungs* by Richard Wagner. Presenting Wagner's trilogy in this theatre was somewhat equivalent to staging *Aida* in the Théâtre du Vieux Colombier.[16] The comparison is poor, for the stage I am speaking of is of good size, yet it expresses the courage of the manager—who, although perfectly aware of my principles and my inability to compromise, honored me with his complete confidence, a confidence he never lost. All the singers went along too. The new effort demanded of them, and fearlessly accepted by them, apparently sustained them and carried them higher with each rehearsal. The orchestra was superb, giving an interpretation so rich that it almost seemed to share the three-dimensionality of the settings. The technical director considered it an honor to put his great virtuosity at the service of a style that made his work appreciated only by professionals.

Lastly, to crown this beautiful edifice, the stage director, promoter as well as inspirer of the venture, did not hesitate to subordinate his personal taste to the unity of ideas whose motives he respected and whose importance and value he recognized. Unostentatiously and with a rare psychological tact he offered his service to the Idea. He supervised the complicated interworkings of the theatre so that nothing could go wrong. Tireless and overlooking nothing, he devoted all his strength to the task. If the production achieved success, the city of Basel should give thanks to Oskar Wälterlin, its leading director.

It is, in fact, the theatre at Basel with which we are concerned here, a theatre of which a larger city could justly be proud! Traditionalists clinging to the letter and opposed to life, from which art must always draw new nourishment, formed a clique and succeeded in suspending these performances after two months of success. This sad fact emphasizes even more the value of this noble gesture and the unselfishness of the whole venture. The press, leading German newspapers included, understood this and harshly denounced the tactics used by a minority to impose their opinions—opinions respectable enough in themselves, but here rendered intolerant by narrow fanaticism.

The indulgent reader will understand, I hope, the deep gratitude a French Swiss feels toward all the members of this theatre in German Switzerland. He has a profound wish to express this feeling to his French-speaking compatriots. We all have our sorrows and our disappointments, so let us share our delights and admirations.

# Part Three

# Appia and Eurhythmics

# Introduction to Part Three

Appia's encounter with the system of musical gymnastics, eurhythmics, taught by Emile Jaques-Dalcroze, was of overwhelming importance to his work, enabling him first, to extend the application of his theories for reform beyond Wagner's operas into other works of music-drama, and later, to propose entirely new forms of theatrical art. Wagner himself had called for the regeneration of music by emphasizing what he termed the basis "of all pure human art, the plastic bodily movement expressed through musical rhythm";[1] Appia in turn, in his earlier writings, had proposed that stage movement should be dictated by the music, although he had not yet determined any formal means, method, or mechanism whereby this musically motivated movement was to be controlled and measured in space.

Appia recognized at once the relevance of eurhythmics to his work, and wrote to Dalcroze introducing himself and announcing that "the externalization of music (which is to say, its rehabilitation) is an idea that I have desired for many years. . . . Nothing can save music from sumptuous decadence except externalization. It must expand in space, with all the salutary limitations which that must have for it. On the other hand, the life of the body tends towards anarchy and therefore towards grossness. It is music that can liberate it by imposing its discipline upon it."[2]

Dalcroze recalled many years later this first contact with Appia, "a long letter in which . . . in the very clearest fashion he identified the future course of my efforts."[3] In response to this letter, Dalcroze invited Appia to his home, after which he in turn wrote to Appia proposing the friendship and collaboration which in fact came to pass: "I am happy to know you and hope with all my heart that we may see each other often. . . . I am again fresh and well, and work with zest, supported by your sympathy and complete understanding for my work. . . . [T]he future belongs to us, while we live, and we have the duty to explore it."[4]

Appia's first written expression of faith in what was to become a veritable aesthetic religion for him was published in August, 1906, barely three months after his initiation. "Return to Music" outlined very briefly the nature of eurhythmics—its attempt to internalize musical training by "making music an integral part of the organism"—and invited readers to participate in a two-week summer course. Appia himself took part and described the experience briefly in his essay of 1911, "The Origin and Beginnings of Eurhythmics."

Appia quickly perceived that the implications of the system were not limited to musical sensitivity or consequent bodily movement, but that they extended to scenic design as well. He saw the need for sets which established and emphasized their mass and volume unambiguously for the viewer, because only within the context of such an arrangement could the actor's body itself be seen to occupy and require space rhythmically—that is, to be engaged in active and living movement—which could be perceived and measured in terms of the static objects around it. Henceforth he insisted that scenic artists must "design with your legs, not with your eyes."[5]

The result was the series of about twenty "Rhythmic Spaces" which he prepared and submitted to Dalcroze in the spring of 1909: "Whenever the pencil touched paper it evoked the naked body, the naked limbs . . . the quality of the space rendered the presence of the body indispensable."[6] At about the same time, he wrote the article "Style and Solidarity," which was published in September. In this he began to develop ideas which he had touched upon earlier, and which would come to dominate his later theory: the need to overcome the passivity of the spectators by directly involving them in the work of art. Through rhythm, the body could be actively engaged in music and enter what Appia (in one of his earliest uses of the term) designated as "Living Art."

In the same article, he referred in passing to the potential of public festivals for reaffirming "solidarity" through a sense of reciprocity between a community and its collective expression in art. Dalcroze and Appia had hoped to present a selection of their work that summer as part of a fête to be held in Geneva, using the foremost dancers of the day, including Isadora Duncan, Maud Allan, Ruth St. Denis and Olga Desmond. Unfortunately, nothing came of these plans, although in formulating them, they continued to expand their awareness of the implications of their work for a decisive reform of theatrical art and its role in society. In the autumn, when the invitation was extended to Dalcroze and Appia to establish an institute at the Garden City of Hellerau, the way lay open to realize such ideas in their fullest form. The establishment of eurhythmics as the defining and motivating spirit of the Hellerau experiment became the primary goal of its founder, Wolf Dohrn, "and from that moment on he devoted to this idea all his strength, extraordinary personality, confident will and great perseverance."[7]

By March 1910, Dalcroze was able to write an exuberant and optimistic letter to Appia, confirming that generous financing for the project was available, and rejoicing that their mutual dream of establishing a genuinely popular aesthetic enterprise seemed about to be fulfilled. This new, nonelitist activity would be created and sustained by its broad appeal; it would directly reflect and respond to society's needs and aspirations. He concluded: "Take heart, my dear collaborator . . . for our efforts and plans are almost realized."[8]

It was Appia's gift of a far-reaching and visionary imagination that made this collaboration so productive. Originally Dalcroze conceived of eurhythmics almost exclusively as a basis for musical training and consequent musical reform. Only gradually, under Appia's influence, did he come to recognize and accept that what had begun as training in musical sensitivity had vast implications for theatrical reform, an area which, initially, had held little interest for Dalcroze. He continued to insist, "Eurhythmics is not an art form—I want to shout that from the rooftops—but a path towards art,"[9] while gratefully accepting the help provided by Appia along that path.

Dalcroze resisted thinking of eurhythmics either as a technical method on the one hand or as a spectacle on the other. It was meant to enable the student to react to and express whatever music he applied it to, without lapsing into the purely abstract or improvised creation of pleasing visual effects. At the same time, he hoped and expected that its practitioners would move beyond a totally mechanical relationship to the music, to use the music so that its expression through the body became a deeply personal and liberating experience.

However, as he made clear in "Eurhythmics and the Theater," an article written in April 1911, Appia nurtured even more expansive hopes. In that month the cornerstone of the institute at Hellerau was laid, and this building—which later observers have claimed marked the beginning of the modern theatre[10]— was to embody many of Appia's most advanced ideas, and would in turn, provide the vital testing ground for still others. As he noted in his article, "Eurhythmics has taken a positive step toward a complete reform of our scenic and dramatic conception." Gradually Appia helped Dalcroze to glimpse the ultimate implications of eurhythmics: that, if the necessary connections could be made, it provided not simply a means towards greater sensitivity to music, or even to a Greek-inspired reintegration of body and mind through dance, however worthy such an achievement might be; it was, Appia became firmly convinced, potentially an independent creation, born out of elements of music, dance and drama, but capable of maturing finally into a wholly new and wondrously expressive art form. Slowly the conception and generation of the new art became the guiding principle and chief goal of the Hellerau institute. In his article, Appia announced plans for a series of summer festivals which would "certainly constitute the most significant, the most decisive step on the road to the victory of *living art.*"

Although Appia was extremely modest about his own role, and always generous in the praise and credit he gave to Dalcroze and others, clearly in the

Figure 17.  External View of the Hall at Hellerau
Note the yin-yang symbol on the pediment.

course of the institute's work, Appia became the motivating, somewhat mysterious, but always benevolent genius of the place. Reticent, sometimes remote, and rarely seen, he determined and guided its development.

A little later, in July of that same summer, after returning from Hellerau, Appia wrote a second article, "The Origin and Beginnings of Eurhythmics." In it he described the evolution of the system, and of the process of "synthesis" through which Dalcroze himself had developed and progressed. It expressed the highest admiration for what Appia characterized as Dalcroze's "educational genius," and hardly hinted at the role he himself had played in its enlightenment.

Dalcroze, although a gifted teacher, was also by nature rather cautious, and tended to cling to his original pedagogical principles and goals. Of rather conservative taste aesthetically, he displayed a certain Calvinistic scepticism towards the theatre in particular. Initially he was disinclined to present theatrical activity at all, still less to undertake any radical reform of existing stage practice. "I certainly have no intention of establishing a theatre at Hellerau," he wrote; "I am no friend of the theatre, this playing which—usually with no conviction—is served up to blasé spectators."[11] At the same time, Appia's own rejection of the current state of theatrical art would have met with sympathy and, potentially, understanding and support from Dalcroze. Building on this, Appia's ideas and enthusiasm, the force of his convictions and the prophetic, inspired quality of the written expression he gave them proved irresistible.

During that summer of 1911, as the institute was being constructed, Appia was, typically, analyzing, reviewing and developing his theories, while Dalcroze, just as characteristically, was actively engaged with his students on an exhibition tour. While on it, he attended a production of Gluck's *Orfeo ed Euridice,* which disgusted him with its heavy and traditional staging. It occurred to him to offer the second act of that opera as part of the institute's presentations at the first festival. Initially he only wished to demonstrate eurhythmics' usefulness in achieving a purer and simpler staging, while essentially adhering to the traditional tenets and conventions of the illusionistic theatre. But the designs which Appia laid before him were startling, and so unprecedented that they quite precluded the possibility of any remotely orthodox production. They dictated an altogether different approach.

Dalcroze worked on the choreography for *Orfeo* from the first day of classes in the autumn of 1911. He was extremely disconcerted, however, to discover how different practicing in the recently completed hall was from work in more traditional venues; his initial plans and exercises were invariably altered when the students tried to perform them in the new building. This, in turn, made him even more dependent upon Appia's confident advice and encouragement. Throughout the year they continued to refine their ideas and plans.

The evolution of Appia's's ideas during this period is evident in the article "Eurhythmics and Light," written in 1912, prior to the first festival that summer, but never published in his lifetime. The extraordinary system of flexible lighting, which he had devised at the institute, was to be used to achieve two of his major objectives: first, to emphasize the living and expressive quality of the human body in rhythmic movement in space; and second, to break down the barriers which, traditionally, had governed and restricted the spectators' perception of the work of art in performance. At the same time, because of its great flexibility and control, the "light organ" devised by Appia, allowed what he termed "luminous sound" to be employed. Light, music, and movement could be carefully coordinated and integrated to create subtle and expressive effects which previously had been virtually unimagined, much less achieved.

Appia recognized that light provided an invaluable medium for linking music, movement, and stage setting in "a perfect fusion"[12] and creating thereby uniquely expressive works of art. His attention to the detail of such expression extended to every aspect of production, one of which he delineated at this time (1912) in the essay "About the Costume for Eurhythmics." He recognized that costume not only had direct practical implications for the effect of the lighting, and for signifying the nature of the aesthetic event (pedagogical exercise, fictive representation, shared communal event, etc.), but acted forcefully upon the psychology of the participants as well. Indeed, it could help to unite both performers and spectators in a single act of artistic expression.

In an age in which ordinary clothing was quite modest and restrictive, and had the effect of deemphasizing the physical (not to mention the sexual) nature of the body, both the wearing in public, and the viewing, of scant, form-fitting leotards (with bare legs and feet!) were profoundly disorienting. The reaction to this might frequently be one of shock or disapproval, but it could also lead to a strong sense of both physical and psychological liberation. Indeed, part of the extraordinary appeal of eurhythmics to its adherents (many of whom embraced it as a veritable secular religion; a "cult without gods")[13] undoubtedly is due to such factors. Appia's analysis shows him to be entirely aware of this phenomenon, and of its aesthetic potential.

In the same essay Appia looks forward confidently to future festivals at Hellerau and the promise there of further marvelous achievements. But, despite the astonishing reception of the 1913 festival, plans had to be dropped for 1914, and with the outbreak of the War, the association of both Appia and Dalcroze with Hellerau ceased.[14] Instead, in July 1914, the two men were involved in a patriotic festival in Geneva, the Fête de Juin. For it they employed some two hundred pupils of eurhythmics along with the same number of supernumeraries for the presentation of *tableaux,* performing a very elaborate, intricately organized presentation: a synthesis of the arts of music, dance, drama and singing. The students functioned rather as a Greek chorus, a great crowd whose words and gestures commented upon and interpreted the dramatic action, and whose movements were themselves a powerful element of artistic expression.

Figure 18.  Eurhythmic Performance at the Geneva Fête de Juin, 1914

Unfortunately, despite the very profound success of the Geneva production, Appia and Dalcroze did not work together frequently afterwards. In 1915 Dalcroze opened a new institute for eurhythmics in Geneva and continued to present the type of exercises and performances seen at Hellerau. Appia from time to time participated in the work there. In June of 1920 they presented a new staging of the pantomime *Echo and Narcissus,* first performed at Hellerau and now, its settings adapted to the institute, with considerable acclaim in Geneva. A production of *A Midsummer Night's Dream,* for which Appia provided some very novel designs during the same period as he prepared settings and a scenario for *Hamlet,* was planned for the winter of 1921–22, but failed to take place.[15]

Gradually, however, Dalcroze reverted to his former attitude, to emphasize the pedagogical aspects of his work as musical training, and largely abandoned any further work of significance aimed at extending and expanding its relevance to theatrical presentation or to dance. For his part, Appia, building upon the ideas suggested by and explored through eurhythmics, moved ever more deeply into theoretical investigations, which further estranged him from Dalcroze. He resigned from the Geneva institute in June 1923. Nevertheless, eurhythmics remained for him an indispensable element, both for effective production of orthodox theatre (he used it in his 1924–25 Basel productions of the *Ring* and of *Prometheus*) and for new forms of "living art." He considered it to be his "aesthetic homeland."[16]

# Return to Music

*Journal de Genève,* 20 August 1906

Do we not often feel ill at ease when we recognize our passive attitude towards a work of art?

Our collaboration, what does it amount to! Good will ... sometimes; at best, a contribution of tidbits of education and culture. In short, we approach a work of art,whatever it may be, like samplers; it is there, we are here, always separate; and we aggravate the situation still further through our tendency to make the least possible effort. Thus, culture, having endowed us with the means to grasp art at our convenience, seems to keep it apart from us, outside us; and, indeed, our education introduces this situation by teaching us the elements of knowledge as something completely external to us.

In this respect, however, a reaction may be setting in. Contemporary pedagogy—searching for a basis of knowledge within the child itself—is beginning to help him assimilate also whatever can really be transmitted to him only from the outside.

In certain schools whose aim is a healthy balance of mental and physical hygiene, instruction has made appreciable progress in this direction. Modern development of the plastic arts has, in some measure, brought the artist and the lover of art closer together. But music remains what we have made of it: a speculation, less and ever less inspired, a combination quite apart from us, outside of us, susceptible of being conveyed only as knowledge. Hence, we consider music a virtuosity, a group of elements unrelated to our personal, physical, and mental life, in brief, a phenomenon that, for all its specifically sensual appeal, has become completely intellectual.

Thus the teaching of music remains external.

We have discovered without question that music finds a uniquely precise and fascinating expression in the movement of the body. Wagner wished—though he did not accomplish it—to give his dramatic presentation a visual appeal appropriate to the musical expression; at our folk festivals, music is sometimes very eloquently expressed through the attitudes of the body; people spellbound by music occasionally do express it for the eye; [Isadora] Duncan[17] has charmed us with her interesting, if fragmentary art, etc. And yet music remains, nevertheless, at present and for us Occidentals an intellectual combination drilled into human beings—who then think they understand it. For example, instead of being taught the origin of rhythm, we learn only the conventional signs of certain rhythms; and so it is with modulation, whose established forms are transmitted to us only to be discarded later as antiquated, a procedure which leaves the game of tonalities to the discretion of the temperament and, thus, rapidly degrades art or drives it to anarchy.

At the same time music goes its own way, formidably developing its own means and technique—means and technique that (in spite of their entirely intellectual origin) do not keenly interest our mind, but instead needlessly play upon our nerves and frequently evoke a life of somehow disordered sensations. The art that we believe we exalt most, that we seem to sustain with the greatest care, and with which we brazenly fill our existence, is the very art we have lost track of and must find again and rehabilitate.

A musician and teacher, a scrupulous seeker of new forms, has become convinced of this decline. His conviction does not stem from any personal speculative impression; rather it has forced itself upon him gradually, yet firmly, in the course of his teaching, until he has felt compelled to conclude that "music is within man." He adds that "the task of the mind is merely to control and classify, to harmonize and balance, the natural functions from which we have broken away." His desire is to "restore eurhythmics to the body," to "make music vibrate in it." He dreams of "making music an integral part of the organism," of "playing this wonderful keyboard, the muscular and nervous system, in order to express plastically his measured thought in space as well as in time."

Instruction in music must, therefore, begin, above all, with a search for music in the student himself, by "awakening his consciousness of the relationship between body and mind." Knowledge of the conventional signs needed for musical notation takes second place, and even the correct execution of these signs on any instrument remains optional. Only the voice as the expression of our will, as offspring of our body, has a central place from the very beginning.

Yet how can such instruction be organized? What methods can help us regain "these natural functions from which we have broken away"?

This is what Jaques-Dalcroze plans to show us in a very complete course specifically devised for teachers. (Duration: two weeks beginning 23 August.)

The course obviously represents the result of strenuous labor. For—although a particularly gifted and sincere person may easily reach the above mentioned conviction—the achievement of the idea, the patient study necessary to its realization, requires unusual perseverance. Only a profound sense of obligation towards his fellow men could sustain such selfless effort when other roads lead easily to apparent success. To be understood, this reform, like every other, demands our passionate desire to prepare for the future at any price what the present cannot give us.

To strive to re-establish the relationship between music and our bodily organism and thus to recover the ancient eurhythmics—so long forgotten that it seems almost a fantastic novelty today—is indeed a daring project! It takes magnificent temerity to conceive it! It is now our turn to shake off our indolence and dilettantism, to discard our preconceived ideas and our collected prejudices, and courageously follow the road towards a renaissance so infinitely desirable. The immediate results are surprising enough. There is every reason to hope that the future will gradually return music to us!

# Style and Solidarity

*Le Rhythm* 1, no. 6 (September 1909)
*Der Rhythmus* 1, no. 6 (September 1909)

*Uns vom Halben zu entwöhnen,*
*Und im Ganzen, Guten, Schönen,*
*Resolut zu leben.*

Wolfgang Goethe[18]

The word *style* is said to come from the stiletto which was used in ancient times to write on tablets of wax. The great significance we attach to style derives, therefore, from the phenomenon of writing.

As soon as we take our pen and let it glide in a regular fashion across a piece of paper to set down our thoughts, we feel *responsible* for the lines it makes. The slightest irregularity at once appears to us to be false, for this mute language is the outcome of our most secret intentions; it is the very image of ourselves. If graphology sometimes loses its powers in the face of fortuitous circumstances which it is unable to overcome, it nevertheless remains a judge, and a judge especially formidable because it serves on a permanent basis.

In addition to the handwriting itself, style means also the manner of organizing our ideas and of expressing them in writing. So we rightly say: style is the man himself. As in the characteristics of our handwriting, we reveal ourselves in the ideas we set down for others. Anyone with a sense of the art of writing knows, for example, just where the writer is truly himself, regardless of the content of a letter—and, consequently, the psychological importance of a given sample of correspondence.

Style is the man himself! But in order to widen further the meaning of the term, let us apply it to all the arts, but distinguish between two facets of it. We speak of being in style and of *having* a style. The former denotes a classification only. Obviously those who created a form of architecture or a fashion of painting did not give these a name, any more than a warrior could say he departed for the Hundred Years War. To work in this or that style means to copy it. The other concept, to *have* style, denotes a personal and living quality, and derives directly from our feelings about handwriting or about writing itself: it is a quality for which the artist in us is responsible.

At this point, however, a new element appears: the audience. In exposing his work to everybody's view the artist must ask himself whether his dream, the subject of his work, merits the particular expression in which he clothes it. He feels responsible for what he is and, consequently, for what he gives of himself.

Is this feeling solely the concern of the artist? Are we only his audience, taking no part whatever in the object of his dream?

What respectful person can feel happy and calm today among the columns of the Parthenon, in St. Mark's Cathedral, in any Egyptian sanctuary? Do we not hesitate to enter the Louvre, the Pinakothek? And does it not seem strange to leave our seats placidly after listening for two hours to the Ninth Symphony? Finally, do we not in all these places carefully avoid looking at ourselves in the mirror—a mirror that is held up so well by our modern conscience?

Yes, indeed! We have a sense of *responsibility* toward the work of art, and it is this feeling that makes us lie. We know perfectly well that art must be lived, not only contemplated, and we despise the idea of dilettantism . . . because on this point we despise ourselves.

There is, then, *solidarity* between us and the artist; yet warily we arrange pictures and statues in our museums, pieces of music in our programs; what else could we do with them? Warily also we keep our auditoriums dark and try always and everywhere to separate, as sharply as possible, the work from its audience, art from ourselves.

But in doing this we forget that the artist draws, or should draw, his inspiration from us! We deprive the artist of his true objective and force upon him an artificial creation. It is we who commit the aesthetic crime—and then we accuse the artist of alienating himself from us, of no longer *offering* intelligible works! For heaven's sake, what do we *offer* him, that we have the right to make such demands?

We consider art in terms of manufactured luxury objects; they are shown to us, and we select, as in a pastry shop, those that flatter our taste. We have compelled a good many artists to become pastry cooks. We leave the works of those who do not cater to our taste in the showcase and know them only by sight. Without having lived, for a moment, the life of a work that thus remains foreign to us, we classify, accept, or reject it. But how can we ever feel a work of art without having identified ourselves with it, from the very first? Do not our happy tears of aesthetic joy flow only when we recognize ourselves in the work? Who else then would shed them?

All of us are responsible for style in our arts. If music lives like a harlot it is our fault. And if painters have created, for this work, a fictitious society, thereby alienating themselves from life and thus from the quality they most stubbornly pursue, . . . Style, we are at fault.

We must cultivate in ourselves a sense of this overwhelming responsibility. We must learn to scorn the inevitable barbarity of art centers—whether in concert programs, in art galleries or in pretentious architecture. We must maintain our embarrassment and our confusion when we stand before ancient works of a homogeneous society—of an entire past that seems to sneer at us. We shall enter Notre-Dame not for pleasure but rather to feel ill at ease. . . .

Through this repeated suffering, instilled in our soul and body, and through the passionate desire to free ourselves from it, we could find again and seize the forgotten weapons to conquer *audience* within ourselves.

In scenic art a movement has already started in this direction. We have opened our eyes, aroused by the spectacles we were once forced to endure. We are shocked at the exploitation of our indolence and at the inferior social position into which we have, like cowards, pushed our theatre. We are disgusted to have left the most powerful elements of the *mise en scène* in the servile hands of just any one, although we are already in possession of forms, colors, light, and thousands of their marvelous combinations.

Our festivals, especially in Switzerland, have taught us that art must spring forth from the heart of *all of us* and must be represented by *all of us*. Sometimes we would even wish to offer these festivals no longer as . . . spectacles! The dignity of our dramatic instincts is awakening. It is high time, for *living* fiction is the glorious gate that opens the way to all the other arts. In living fiction we manifest our aesthetic conscience and our feeling of close solidarity. It alone can again confer upon us some measure of dignity vis-à-vis a work of art and guide us toward the mastery of *style*.

Through rhythm, the art that transfigures can unite our organism with the indisputable expression of our soul; but it seems to have run away. However, it is not the art itself that has gone astray, it is its shadow! On the contrary, music is actually quite close to us. Let us not resist it; let us surrender to it the passionate expression of our inner life; let us yield to its entreaties. Let us wholeheartedly deliver to it the rhythm of our body—which it seeks to idealize and to plunge into an aesthetic space of light and shadow, forms and colors, organized and enlivened by its creative inspiration.

When embarking upon the road of *living* art, who does not feel the law of aesthetic solidarity burn deep down in his soul, destroying forever his dilettantish passivity? Yes! This is precisely because art is so noble a medium of *collective* expression! One cannot counterfeit it with impunity. When the pen that must portray living characters trembles in our hand, an inner voice warns us: Beware! Style is the man!

Let us beware, indeed beware, of spurious writing and the advice of calligraphers who have, hitherto, made fools of us.

Let us *trust* our hand; what does it matter if, at first, the lines will be clumsy? They are ours and they *will have style because we are responsible for them and because art will live in us.*

# Eurhythmics and the Theatre

*Der Rhythmus, Ein Jahrbuch* 1 (1911)
*Les Feuillets,* no. 14 (1912)

As an aesthetic discipline of the body, eurhythmics will certainly have a great influence on the theatre. It is, therefore, interesting to investigate the nature of this influence.

The term *theatre* is meant to include here both the auditorium and the stage, the spectator as well as the performer. Let us begin with the stage, and, since music presides over eurhythmics, let us see what kind of music the performer uses for his bodily expression on the stage.

In our finest lyric drama, the singer is rightly considered the representative of the action; he sings the words and accompanies them with appropriate mime. Nevertheless, the true dramatic expression remains locked in the score and, for all his singing and acting, the performer cannot fully embody it. He vacillates painfully between two forms of musical expression: the music which expresses a purely inner conflict and, hence, eludes physical realization in space, and the music which, on the contrary, violently seeks external expression. But— because of its origin, which is symphonic like that of the inner music—the latter is no more productive than the inner music of patterns and rhythms capable of being physically expressed. There are no doubt exceptions, though more apparent than real; and certainly clever directing could considerably improve the results. Nevertheless, the outcome remains simply a juxtaposition of music and performer. An organic union is impossible, for modern dramatic music is after all only the specific and extreme development of an art which long ago lost contact with the living body.

Here is the cause of the inevitable falsity of our present-day lyric theatre.

We must therefore not blindly apply to the extraordinary but decaying art of music the principles of an incipient art form such as that for which eurhythmics is preparing the way. One may ask of what use eurhythmic exercises will be for our singers, since they seem to find so little direct application for them on the stage.

It is evident that by implementing rhythm naturally in the singers and thus revealing to them the purely aesthetic harmony of their organism, this discipline will have the best influence on their musicianship and on the sincerity and the appropriateness of their acting—which will show a restraint that is akin to style.* But this is a general consequence, more precisely musical and restrictive and belonging rather to education than to art. We can only mention it here, for we are dealing with rhythm of the body.

Although in the spoken drama the actor may not find the equivalent of the art to which eurhythmics has introduced him, he will discover a common and essential element! *Space.* The discipline of the rhythm will make him particularly sensitive to the dimensions of space, which correspond to the infinite variations of musical sequences. Instinctively he will try to realize these on the stage; and he must then be amazed to note the injustice done to him, that he, three-dimensional and living, is placed in the midst of dead disconnected paintings or backdrops and wings. In the lyric drama, moreover, he will sense the impossibility of an organic union between such a setting and himself. Another juxtaposition! He is caught between two contradictions: one is related to music, which he cannot physically interpret but must nonetheless visibly present on stage; the other concerns the scenic arrangement, which has no rapport or contact with his three-dimensional and moving body and therefore obstructs his rhythmic movement in space. The singer, who will thus become aware of the painful part he has to play, could insist upon his rights and, in *full knowledge of the cause,* collaborate on the dramatic and scenic reform in which we almost in spite of ourselves are already engaged. Eurhythmics—by providing the aesthetic education, more properly speaking, the education of the actor—will authorize him to do so. This will be of inestimable value.

The most real presence of all on the stage, even though invisible, is that of the author, the poet-musician. If he has experienced rhythmic movement and has felt deep within himself the spark of joy and beauty that is lit by true bodily realization of music, he will, like the singer, become conscious of the dissonant juxtaposition in our lyric drama and consequently in his own work. Henceforth he will, on the one hand, hear his music and, on the other, see its action on stage; he can no longer confuse these two. The rhythmic memories of his body will reawaken in him a harmony that he had seldom known and that he had been unable to create on the stage. An implicit understanding will soon be established between the author and his interpreter, the actor. Both *will have doubts* about

---

*The same holds true, of course, for the artistic sense of actors in plays. To simplify matters the author limits his treatise to the opera singer.

their work. But doubt is always the beginning of a search for truth. How will they find this truth, this harmony?

The author cannot deceive himself very long: the current means of dramatic expression (score, singer, staging) have developed unequally, each in its own way; the result has been anarchy. If one uses them as we find them today, he cannot make the slightest progress towards their harmonious collaboration. *We must change the direction!* The need is for conversion in the true sense of the word. Music, having gone its way alone for a long time, cannot be brought in contact with the living organism of the singer through arbitrary modifications; neither can this be done with the lifeless material of our stages through an equally arbitrary stylization. Conversion here means taking the *human body* resolutely as a point of departure for both music and settings—and this means no less than a change in the very conception of the drama, including all the consequences that will follow. A conversion is always accompanied by sacrifices. In this case they will be quite considerable. To begin with, it requires complete objectivity and absolute submission. The musician must retrace his steps and boldly study the body he has neglected for centuries. Naturally the living organism must come to his aid by making itself an instrument ever more supple, more willing, and more aware of its latent harmony. The contact has been lost; *eurhythmics is trying to rediscover it.* This is its chief importance for the theatre.

We have still to examine the influence of eurhythmics on the spectator. Perhaps this, along with the preceding steps, will lead us to a new conception of the stage.

We are perfectly justified in assuming that, in the near future, rhythmic discipline will not only be incorporated in the curriculum of our schools, but that it will also be sufficiently widespread among adults so that a fair number of spectators will understand it; some may even have participated in it. What will be their inner attitude towards the performance?

Hitherto, only quiet attention has been expected of the audience. To encourage this, comfortable seats in semi-darkness have been offered, favorable to a state of complete passivity—apparently the proper attitude for spectators. This amounts to saying that, here as elsewhere, we try to distinguish as much as possible between ourselves and the work of art; we have become eternal spectators!

*Eurhythmics will overthrow this passivity!*—Musical rhythm will penetrate all of us and say: *You yourself* are the work of art. And indeed, we will feel it then, and can never again forget it.

"It is yourself" *(Tat twam asi),* said the Brahmin to every "living creature." Feeling "ourselves" in every work of art henceforth, we shall ask: what has it made of *me?* Our attitude will have changed; instead of passively accepting, we shall actively participate and secure the right to revolt against any wrong done to us. To return to the theatre, which is our true concern, it is obvious that our productions constantly offend this sense of active participation. As we have just seen, those who feel this violence will quite naturally begin to revolt. They will begin to have doubts, as did the author and the performer, and like these, they will seek the truth *elsewhere*.

Surely, I am not exaggerating! The awakening of art in ourselves, in our organism, in our own flesh, will tell the death knell for a considerable part of our modern art, in particular for scenic art. But what will then replace that scenic art, so highly valued and of such importance that we seem unable to give it up?

The spectator likewise must submit to the change of direction, the conversion which the author and his interpreters can bring about. He, too, must begin with his own body, from which the living art must radiate and expand into space to bring it to life. It is this body that determines the proportion of settings and of lighting; it is this body that creates the work of art!

The transition will be slow and will demand, step by step, a firm belief in the truth that is now barely glimpsed. The festivals at Hellerau will certainly constitute the most significant, the most decisive step on the road to the victory of *living art*. Every year they will homogeneously combine the exercises of the institute, from the basic to the most advanced ones, in imposing dramatic experiments. They will be the festival of the participants! And the audience, invited to attend them, will feel deeply that these pupils of all age groups and stations of life are assembled there to *represent the audience,* to be, like the ancient chorus around the flame of the altar, the audience's direct and marvelous spokesmen for living art.

After so many centuries of isolation, the spectator may then exclaim, full of gratitude: Yes, it is myself!

Our theatre will be conquered for him.

So we can see that eurhythmics and the theatre in its present state are two separate concepts. By returning the human body to its place of honor and by excluding everything that does not emanate from it, eurhythmics has taken a positive step towards a complete reform of our scenic and dramatic conception.

But our theatres will continue to exist for a long time to come, and we can foresee that eurhythmics will not only continue to exercise a beneficial influence on the actor and to add style to his acting but will especially affect the *mise en scène*. Instead of offering a display of dead paintings on flat canvas, the scenic arrangement will increasingly approximate the three-dimensionality of the human body in order to enhance the three-dimensional effect in space. The result will be a thorough simplification and a notable reduction in those objects which can be shown only by painting. Light, no longer constrained to illuminate the painted canvas, can spread out into space, filling it with living color and infinite variations of an ever-changing atmosphere. It will no longer exclusively serve the scenic artist but . . . the dramatist! The illusion, which is attempted today through painted settings at the expense of the actor, we shall ultimately achieve, in accord with the author, to the most perfect advantage of the actor. It is not possible here to go into further details about the consequences of such a reform. Nevertheless it may be understood that, in delivering the *mise en scène* from the yoke of lifeless painting and the illusion it supposedly produced, in giving it thus the greatest flexibility and utmost liberty, we also set free the *imagination of the dramatist*. . . . The influence of this scenic reform upon the dramatic form itself cannot even remotely be estimated.

Eurhythmics, for its part, will preserve its essential scenic principle; that is to say, it will not tolerate anything about it that does not directly emanate from rhythm as expressed through the body. Eurhythmics will, in its normal development, create for itself a setting that inevitably emanates from the three-dimensional form of the human body and its movements idealized through music.

Then the all powerful light, subject to music, will join in the *mise en scène*—light which gives us plasticity, which fills the space with highlights and moving shadows, which flows in calm rays or bursts forth in colorful, vibrant flashes. The human bodies bathed in this vivifying atmosphere will recognize it and salute *Music in Space*.

For "Apollo was not only the god of music; he was also the god of light!"[19]

# The Origin and Beginnings of Eurhythmics

*Les Feuillets,* no. 5 (1911)
*Der Rhythmus, Ein Jahrbuch* 1 (1911)

The origin of any work is rooted in the personality of its author, not in external conditions. The latter play a minor part; they can impede or further the success and expansion of the work, but they cannot initiate it. Here, as elsewhere, personality is paramount.

The essential quality of eurhythmics lies in the fact that from the very first it has never gathered the elements of its *discipline* from without, but has grown, on the contrary, gradually from within, like a shrub that draws its sap from the nourishing soil into which it sinks its roots. By seeking the cause of this phenomenon in the personality of Jaques-Dalcroze, we shall undoubtedly arrive at a firmer and deeper understanding of his great work and of its origin.

Two distinct traits led him to seek an organic union between music and the human body. The two traits correspond precisely with his predominant gifts, his *educational genius* and, what I shall call his *genius for synthesis.*

Obviously, in making such a division, I analyze somewhat arbitrarily one of the most integrated and least analyzable personalities. I believe, however, that in this way I can come close to the truth; and we know that we must systematize in order to define the undefinable.

One of the most remarkable traits of Dalcroze's educational genius is that the master cannot regard his pupils simply *en bloc.* To him they are a group of entirely separate individuals, and he instinctively treats them as such. Consequently he develops a keen sense of observation, an eminently creative sense of observation. If almost as a corollary we add his absolute inability to crystallize or systematize anything, his desire for a free vista at all times in order to re-create *with his pupils* an ever renewed life, we shall then better understand the beginnings of eurhythmics—which were from the beginning so simple that they virtually defied definition, but which nevertheless currently evoke vivid interest in themselves, quite apart from any historic aspect.

By genius for synthesis I understand the compelling urge to combine all the expressive media of an integral artistic life. Dalcroze possesses the *gift for life* to a rare degree; one might say that isolated elements, whatever they may be, are of no value to him unless they participate in the concert of life. All the activities of this outstanding man of action have invariably been directed towards mutual subordination of the means of expression in the pursuit of a superior aim. He himself is scarcely aware of this; that is the secret of his irresistible influence.

Thus, on the one hand, his observations of individual students during his lessons, particularly his *solfeggio* lessons, were for him an inexhaustible source of precepts; on the other, there were his experiments in synthesis, such as his songs for children, in part mimed and dramatized, the charm and success of which are well known. And later, the practice songs composed for older students and the like. . . . The two traits, observation and synthesis, combined to give Dalcroze the evidence and the experience he needed for his first attempt at eurhythmics.

From an educational viewpoint, he asked his students in his *solfeggio* lessons to beat time, for he felt the advantage of a motion that would somehow bring them into direct contact with the music. In most of his pupils such gestures awakened a sense of control, even of beauty, and they proved to be more than a mere technical aid. As the educator-artist, Dalcroze noticed that under this discipline his pupils' bodies lost some of their passivity, as though to join in the motion of their hands and thus let the musical rhythm permeate them.

From the second viewpoint, that of synthesis, he noted during the performance of his children's songs the very special enjoyment of the child in combining the songs with appropriate movement and the felicitous effect of such movement on his body—quite apart from the pleasure the child always derives from any kind of make-believe. But the relationship between music and movement was revealed to the master particularly through the songs he composed for the students of the conservatory, songs which, unlike those for the younger children, were not necessarily a dramatized game. He discovered that the gestures and attitudes accompanied the music very well, but only in a simple juxtaposition; and that, no matter how precise these actions were, the movements and the music were not fused organically and indissolubly to form a single mode of expression. He observed how the students' bodies resisted even this simple juxtaposition, and he realized that in order to approach such organic fusion he would first have to bring the will to act in harmony with the slow reaction of the body, by means of a vigorous rhythmic training. . . . And those observations multiplied, until they seemed to force the master to find a solution for a problem he had as yet only vaguely formulated.

Indeed, the situation was growing dangerous. Certain calisthenic scenes led him to experiments in pure plasticity and external beauty, and to an imitation of works of art. His extraordinary facility, together with the youthful enthusiasm of his students, carried them inevitably towards the superficial delight of eye and ear, without the discipline required to control and modulate such pleasure. Anyone except Dalcroze would have set out to construct a merely pleasing system, and, imprudently, to develop the aspect of plasticity, while neglecting the indispensable foundation of *solfeggio* exercises for the body. *From such a misconception the master was saved by his educational genius!*

Eurhythmics, as we know it, developed through Dalcroze's treatment of his pupils as individuals. He would never have gained the prudence and the reverence in aesthetic matters that now guarantee the future of his art had he not been able to detect in each of his pupils a touch of "true humanity." They in turn would never have shown him the unshakable loyalty, so essential to a man of genius, unless each one of them had felt his teacher's concern for each of them as an individual. This very personal *interchange* helped the genius of Jaques-Dalcroze to find his way to success and victory.

If what I called Dalcroze's genius for synthesis thus furnished the experience necessary to attract his attention, it was nevertheless a *return to teaching* that helped him find an approach to bodily rhythm. The *solfeggio* exercises which formulated the problem gave him the key to its solutions.

The master and his pupils—they are henceforth inseparable—wondered whether, while beating time with their arms, it was somehow possible to mark the rhythm of the bars with their legs and feet. . . . They tried this, calling it "faire les pas."

It was the beginning of eurhythmics!

The work was done in unison. The master was doubtless an unequaled leader but on the other hand he accepted advice and suggestions from his pupils.—These beginning experiments deserve our sincere and profound admiration. Eventually a kind of primer was established; they tried to develop exercises for the body that would parallel those of the *solfeggio* for the voice, and those developed so satisfactorily that Jaques-Dalcroze requested permission of Mr. Held, the director of the Geneva Conservatory, to set up a special course in "faire les pas." Heretofore, the work had been done during spare hours without any official recognition. Permission was denied, and Dalcroze was accused of "adopting the attitude of a ballet master."

So in the fall of 1904 Dalcroze rented a small hall close to the Conservatory. There the heroic labor, the slow and tantalizing conquest of the unknown, continued during the hours left after attending to the official program. While

Geneva ignored, or tried to ignore, the great work germinating within its walls, a few young girls—pupils of Dalcroze—and their parents quietly and unknowingly prepared, on the basis of their own confidence and loyalty, the brilliant future of Hellerau.

In May of 1905, the results of the training permitted a public demonstration of the "steps" at Soleure on the occasion of the Swiss annual music festival. The considerable success of the demonstration and the reacton of teachers and musicians encouraged Dalcroze to submit again to the Board of the Geneva Conservatory a detailed memorandum in support of his request for the introduction of regular rhythmic courses.

The Board remained completely indifferent, and categorically refused the request. To enlighten the public Dalcroze gave—in September of that year—a long lecture, although without demonstration by pupils. As usual people listened to him with pleasure, but did they understand him?

His overwhelming desire to initiate regular courses finally induced the master to rent a suitable hall. And in this hall began the great year of discovery. . . .

An artist of genius confronts his finished work as though it were an enigma. He examines it; sometimes it responds. When this work is a complete whole, such as a painting, a statue, a symphony or a poem, the answer is clearer. When, however, the work is not presented to the public in such a definite form but must, on the contrary, develop slowly and gradually, through time's infinity, when, though finished as soon as it is begun, it will never be really complete because it is *living,* the enigma becomes agonizing. No matter how many questions the genius may ask, his work can only answer: "I represent the obedience to your eternal desire, to your profoundest aspiration. Go on striving and I shall continue to obey. The more sincere your wish, the nobler your aspiration, the more perfectly I shall be able to respond."

This was the situation of Jaques-Dalcroze and his pupils at the time when his regular course of eurhythmics was inauguarated.

The *solfeggio* method for the body had already been determined, then; but where would it lead? How could it be developed, and to what end? They did not know, and from day to day proceeded in their search for the unknown. It is not possible to give here details of their work in this wonderful year of exploration. Besides, how can one tell that story?

During this winter an incident occurred that had a fortunate influence on Dalcroze's work. An artist often suffers because he is unable to define and analyze ideas that crowd his mind. He needs a terminology. The biographies of great artists frequently demonstrate this fact. Monsieur Edouard Claparède, professor of psycho-physiology at the University of Geneva, who had a keen interest in what he had seen and understood of eurhythmics, had several discussion with Dalcroze. As a result he gave the master his indispensable terminology, and enabled him to base his educational and aesthetic experiments on scientific facts. We can imagine how eagerly such a teacher seized upon these data in order to transform them into useful experiences. He began to devote special attention to inhibition, to stimulus, to the *temps perdus,* to the imperative "Hop!" devised to keep the body ready to obey the most unexpected orders, and so on. . . . From these discussions he derived also what was certainly not a system, but his rational method of instruction and observation.

In the spring of 1906, an extended lecture-demonstration of eurhythmics and plasticity was arranged in a municipal auditorium. The audience was full of curiosity, but it had not the slightest notion of the significance of the event. Frequently the master had to leave the piano, step to the front of the platform, and beg the spectators not to consider the demonstration a theatrical performance . . . ; he had to remind them that this was a new educational experiment, an attempt to transfuse musical rhythm into the body. The event was successful, but without practical consequences.

In the summer of the same year, Dalcroze arranged his first advanced course over a period of two weeks; he intended to present the result of his studies. The participants expected to hear a lecture series illustrated by demonstrations of his pupils and, thus enlightened, to return home thoroughly versed in eurhythmics. What an error!

After five minutes the master gave us to understand that everyone had to come into the arena and undergo the great experience for himself. All refused to do so. What! Intelligence was not enough? The whole body had to participate? We had to expose ourselves to the ridiculous test! The situation was at once funny and serious. Very serious indeed! Because it was a question of "to be or not to be" for eurhythmics. Henceforth everyone *had* to comprehend that eurhythmics is a *personal experience* and not a method. It had at all costs to be a personal experience. Oh, the magic of a personality! A quarter of an hour later, ladies and gentlemen of all ages and nationalities, in street dresses and suits, performed the required physical activity, attentive and submissive to the master's orders . . . ! To the uninitiated they offered, of course, the most incomprehensible spectacle.

Similar courses were repeated in the summers of 1907, 1908, and 1909. They were increasingly better attended and more cosmopolitan, and ever more remarkable, because the studies of each winter had enriched the experience of the teacher and strengthened the methods of instruction. At the end of the advanced course in 1909, the first examination for a teacher's certificate took place. This became necessary because of abuses by certain people who, after attending a single advanced course of two weeks, went off to organize courses abroad—a program for which they naturally were utterly unprepared.

In addition to all his activities, Dalcroze arranged lecture tours and demonstrations with some of his best students. How can one describe the amount of work, of effort, of initiative; how can one measure the indomitable resistance and heroic courage shown by this fearless man during those five years! In Geneva where he was, after all, among friends, his work met only with indifference or even rejection; or, still more depressing, with the sterile and passing admiration of a few aesthetes. Only in Germany did he find an echo, and serious attention to his teaching. Efforts were made to keep him there, but he declined anything as yet that would tear him away from his own country.*

During these trying times a Dutch lady, Miss Nina Gorter, became the master's trusted ally and an ever more indispensable collaborator. Miss Gorter was a professor at one of the conservatories in Berlin. Quite early she had begun to put on the *children songs,* some of which she had translated into German. Fascinated by Dalcroze's genius, she gave up her secure position in Berlin and moved to Geneva two years before the introduction of eurhythmics. Thus she participated in the very birth of the work. In Basel, Paul Boepple, supported by the intelligent principal of the girls' school where he taught music, promptly adopted Dalcroze's concept of instruction and introduced eurhythmics from its very beginning. This incorruptible Kurvenal, a sensitive, generous and cultured man, was the very person to understand the master immediately and to follow him as fast as his work grew. His name, too, will remain linked with Dalcroze. There were other sincere friends but, alas, they could give only their devotion and enthusiasm to the genius of Jaques-Dalcroze.

After a triumphal demonstration of eurhythmics in Dresden in spring 1910, Herr Schmidt, founder of the suburban garden city of Hellerau and the manufacturing plant *Die Werkstätte*[20] proposed to Dalcroze that he organize and direct the musical life of this little town in-the-making. Dalcroze asked time for consideration and returned to Geneva.

Shortly thereafter, Dr. Wolf Dohrn, founder of *Der Werkbund,* who was likewise interested in the development of Hellerau, traveled to Geneva accompanied by his brother Harold. He came to offer Dalcroze a model institute to be built on a hill overlooking Hellerau, and to provide—together with the imposing establishment—funds necessary for the development and expansion of his work. In addition to pupils from many lands who would flock to this center of life, the master would have the opportunity to train the children and youth of that little garden city, to find, as it were, virgin soil better suited for his teaching than those young people already spoiled by the routine of our conventional schools. So Dr. Dohrn, smiling and respectful, held out his powerful hand to a great artist who until then had been obliged to rely only on himself in his struggle against impossible odds! He offered the tireless worker a most valuable reward, the means to continue his fruitful work successfully.

---

*Some German conservatories and schools have since adopted his teachings and engaged one or another of his best students as instructors; but this is not the place to talk about the present.

How could Dalcroze decline such an offer! After some negotiations essential to the security of the venture, he accepted and moved to Dresden.

This review of the origin and beginnings of eurhythmics has shown once again that, in order to *live*, a work must develop in accordance with the laws of life. Its flowering cannot be forced; only patient and persistent cultivation can help the roots to spread in the soil, at the same time assuring the growth and blossoming of the tree in full sunshine.

We have witnessed the struggles and worries inherent in a creative work. But we forget one factor. . . . With his beautiful gift of exuding Life, Jaques-Dalcroze combines the blessed talent of arousing Joy. His pupils know this well. Even during their darkest hours, for there are always dark hours, the flame of joy ignited by their master brightens their path and guides them. Their life is forever enlightened by that flame.

He who has inhaled deeply the air of the Dalcroze Institute, who has felt this unique atmosphere vibrate with brotherhood, mutual aid, and common effort toward an ideal eagerly pursued; and who can now imagine the master in front of the serene new building surrounded by his pupils and by the group of happy children from Hellerau—these human beings of different ages, nationalities, and social backgrounds, yet united in the same thought; he who can visualize all this cannot help exclaiming:

> By the magic is united
> What stern Custom parted wide,
> All mankind are brothers plighted
> Where thy gentle wings abide.[21]

# Eurhythmics and Light

(1912)

*Le Rhythm*, no. 34 (Dec. 1932)

From the Hellerau Festivals we expect, not a definite and hence premature solution of certain aesthetic problems, but rather a firm and precise indication of the direction we must take in order to progress year by year toward such a solution. Then evidently new problems will arise!

These considerations, as everything else, that concerns the Jaques-Dalcroze Institute are related to teaching. I may, therefore, be permitted to present here a brief outline of the principles of the institute and some thoughts on one of its essential aspects, to wit: the part to be played by light in a school dominated by musical rhythm.

Our senses are rarely equally developed. Within a single individual a kind of equilibrium is maintained with regard to the sum total of his powers: if one of the senses grows stronger, the other grows weaker, but it is clear that their total power, which characterizes a personality, remains unchanged. Accordingly, we can influence our senses only in their *reciprocal* relations: the sensory variations are infinite and they differentiate human beings far more than we are inclined to assume.

To apply to education, what means shall we find helpful if we wish to try to regulate the play of our senses? In our schools, where the pupil is taught what men before him have thought and discovered, the problem remains simple; we address ourselves exclusively to the intellectual and organizing faculty of the personality. But how are we to proceed if we have to apply *directly* to the pupil's senses themselves for the purpose of harmonizing their mutual value? Here, more than ever, the divergences in personality will be felt; for no mediators are possible between instruction and the senses. . . . To begin with, the personality must discover its own senses; it must become *conscious* of the reciprocal condition of its senses; only then can it try to bring them into harmonious action.

It is by appealing to our two most noble senses, hearing and sight, that we shall best arouse this awareness, which will then be reflected through the entire sensory system, revealing its defects and the lack of equilibrium.

Eurhythmics currently appears to be precisely the method for this training; through its medium the personality affirms its body and soul without possible dissimulation. In a modern state boarding school, for instance, the pupil finds it easy to assert himself fully except in what may be called the aesthetic will of his body. His sense of life is completely awakened without however penetrating to the source of sensory equilibrium, and his personality is left without a reliable touchstone to teach him how to find that equilibrium. Now, since we must judge the equilibrium of our senses by means of those senses themselves, only a temporary *modification* of what they are accustomed to feel can render them perceptive of their usual proportions. Music offers the perfect means for this because, living on a continuous modification of time values, it possesses a pedagogical power of the first order. Out of this power eurhythmics was born and we do not have to repeat here how the latter affects our entire organism through the art of modifying the time values. But the work of our self-discovery cannot stop at this point; our second principal sense, sight, appears to be only indirectly connected with music. A method must be found to touch this sense *directly* and as in music, by modifying the usual proportions.

This is the point where light will have to join the game! In what form? Daylight is not at our command. Although we can dim it (drapes, colored glass, etc.) we cannot control daylight *itself* and modify its proportions at will. We must, therefore, turn to artificial light created by ourselves, i.e., stage lighting. For our eyes, this light is to the simple light of the day what, for our ears, the art of sounds is to shouting. It will be the *aesthetic ruler* of brightness—capable of modifying its vibrations.

Thus we possess here two stylizing elements which will complement each other for the aesthetic education of our senses. Now, as we know, there exists an intimate relationship between music and light. The ancients sensing this recognized Apollo as the god of these two reunited elements. This relationship will permit us to use music and light *simultaneously* as a single art that will most powerfully affect our personality.

Yet, while we are perfectly familiar with the art of sounds, our *artistic* knowledge pertinent to the art of light is still rather rudimentary; we must therefore study light with the help, and under the control of, music! This utterly new study, whose importance for the future cannot be overrated, holds certainly great surprises for us. First of all, we shall learn that, merely "to make visible," is not light in this sense at all, and that, on the contrary, in order to be creative or plastic, light must be an atmosphere, a luminous atmosphere. Consequently a harmonious and infinitely variable balance between illumination and creative or plastic light will bring forth ... *luminous sound,* the precise adaptation of luminous vibrations in space to musical vibrations. Through systematic studies and investigations of light the Jaques-Dalcroze Institute will create in each student a new sense that may be called the *musico-luminous* sense which will permit him to search for a harmonious equilibrium of auditory and visual sensations and to find in this equilibrium a new source of inspiration.

This study will require considerable time! It is not necessarily a matter of discovering something beautiful. Just as the exercises of rhythm produce beauty only if it comes as their normal, organic, somehow intrinsic result, so the beauty of light, indissolubly associated with music, can be only a by-product, at the risk of remaining a decadent game. We must slowly learn that to see and to hear can be one and the same thing, and intuitively understand that the entire art form will henceforth be based on this essential experience.

But only music can guide us on the new path, for it alone possesses the power of evocation.

Accordingly, like the slaves in *A Thousand and One Nights,* we must respond by "listening and subservience," if possible, dutifully assisted by candid and submissive eyes.

After the Hellerau Festivals present the results of such a study they can offer to the public instructive suggestions to satisfy its desire for harmony and beauty. Every year marked progress will give evidence of scrupulous and persistent work which cannot fail to open, again and again, new perspectives of a development to the spectators.

# About the Costume for Eurhythmics

*Die Schulfeste der Bildungsanstalt Jaques-Dalcroze,* Jena, 1912

Warmly dedicated to the pupils of the Dalcroze Institute in Hellerau

"As little dressed as possible," the artists say.

"Why and by what right?"

Some people advocate a pliant dress, which reveals the lines of the body, while at the same time it shrouds them in expressive and light folds. Others demand color; still others would prefer a bit of freedom and imagination.

"And why all this and by what right?"

My neighbor in the rear of the house whispered to me during a class at the institute:

"These dreadful black tights! Don't you see how they *cut through the line?*"

"I see; but you, sir, do not see, for you merely observe and that is a wrong attitude here."

"Why?"

"Do you seriously believe that these men and women, these boys and girls have undressed in this manner just to please . . . your eyes?!"

Eurhythmics is known as the art that awakens in us the sense of bodily musical rhythm and thus allows us, through gradual realization of that rhythm in space, to become fully conscious of its beauty and to enjoy its salutary power. The experience, however, progresses outward from within. If a serious-minded pupil stepped in front of the mirror to execute a rhythmic exercise, he would realize at once that he made a gross mistake, that he took the wrong direction in trying to adopt from outside what he should approach from within. The mirror seizes his image and reflects it falsified. There is no possible relation between the student's experience during free exercises in space when he is following only his inner rhythm, and the image obligingly reflected in the mirror. Your eyes, sir, play here the part of the mirror, As incurable spectators, they seize the external form of Jaques-Dalcroze's students and reflect a falsified image. Surely, some of the students must be painfully aware of this, for more things occur here between the auditorium and the stage than are dreamt of in your spectator's philosophy.

A pupil comes to the Hellerau Institute not to study the aesthetic life of the *body,* but to awaken this life in his own body.

The visitor distorts his own judgment if, while attending a class, he does not attempt, above all, to detect this miraculous awakening—expressed by each personality differently and with innumerable nuances—this awakening which no other discipline can offer. And if he does not bow his head, deeply moved by such an effort, his sensual curiosity disturbs the class, and instead of being drawn closer to Dalcroze's work, he drifts farther away. Of course, in order to approach such a work one must oneself take some steps . . . and take them quietly and respectfully, sustained by an irresistible and purely human sympathy for the master *and his pupils.*[22]

Besides, sir, the tights you condemn so lightly were not invented in one stroke and imposed on the pupils of eurhythmics from the start. There is a story behind that; and here it is in all its simplicity.

Ten years ago at the beginning of eurhythmics in Geneva, Dalcroze's pupils—young girls—performed their exercises in the street clothes they wore to school. First, sandals were substituted, because "strong beats" could not be executed with our absurd modern footwear. Then a skirt was designed slightly shortened and wide enough to give the legs the necessary freedom of movement, and a kind of blouse was added, leaving neck and arms relatively uncovered. Soon this skirt was found to be inconvenient, and so puffed breeches (knicker-bockers), fastened under the knee, and heavy woolen pullovers were introduced. The rubbing of the material between the knees led to the idea of a different type of breeches, all in one piece but not tightly fitting. At this point a few coura-geous students removed their stockings but kept their sandals! Later on, the breeches were tightly fitted, leaving the knees uncovered; this permitted still more freedom of movement. Lastly, some discarded their sandals: that was the decisive step toward complete freedom! Soon all pupils had bare legs and feet; and shortly thereafter, for the inauguration of the institute in Dresden-Hellerau, the black tights in one slip-on piece were adopted. They provided a minimum of clothes for women and men alike; black was chosen to avoid the always diversifying effect of individual fancies and to give this simple costume, on the contrary, the generally impersonal, I might say, austere character so necessary for the exercise.

Recently a lady wrote on this subject to Jaques-Dalcroze as follows:

"The brief period of freedom from all those annoying clothes when one's limbs move to one's heart's desire, unfettered by the black tights, when one becomes conscious of strength and of space, of line and movement, according to the laws of nature, this brief period gives me a sense of being one with the great universe, of expressing life not according to human laws but rather according to divine commandment."

Maybe the "spectators" will find in these few words a judgment that brooks no challenge.

This gradual and noble emancipation from old habits implies, on the part of both parents and pupils, a confidence and a passionate concern for the great cause. The emancipation itself guarantees a serious contribution to the eurhythmic studies.

Take off your clothes, sir, courageously put on these dreadful black tights—which, alas, will break up the lines of your body—and try that notorious experiment? At the end of three or four classes that garment will no longer exist for you; it is merely a precaution necessary to aesthetic decency, giving you freedom of movement, that is all. Then—after the exercise has absorbed your strength, after you have fought against and overcome the resistance of your organism, and flung yourself free at last to express the intended rhythm visibly, full of joy—then turn your eyes to the rear of the house, where they will meet those of your former self. And you will pity the poor visitor, as do all those you are watching at this very moment.

By discarding your clothes in favor of the black school-tights, you have left behind likewise the dreary shell of a mere spectator, never to return to it.

So much about black tights.

The study of bodily rhythm makes one particularly sensitive to the dimensions of Space. The study of Space will therefore be part of the institute's curriculum. Space must here include simple and flat surfaces as well as obstacles, such as various stairs, platforms, ramps, walls, pillars, et al. designed to render the body more conscious of its balance and flexibility, of the infinite possibilities in its expressive power. But in so active a role, Space needs the appropriate light in order to reveal itself clearly to the body—and the body as partner of that light requires all the plastic resources of Space that will enable it to receive that light and give it full play. Obviously black absorbs light and does not reflect it. Consequently it is not suitable for the study of light; for this purpose the shade of the school tights must be somewhat modified. Gray, if it is selected with great care, seems to do the trick; it maintains the necessary neutrality for a serious study of the body; and together with a luminous light beam it can become quite expressive. The school tights therefore had to have two colors: black for simple rhythmic exercises without special lighting effects; and gray for exercises with specific lighting, work that will always be more or less unusual.

A minor subject in the study of rhythm will be what we might call the study of folds. Indeed the pupil who masters his musical expressiveness in space will feel the need to acquire a more thorough understanding of this basic plasticity by combining it with another component—the material that covers his form and follows his movements in a softened rhythm. And he needs this understanding not to please the eye, but to feel the effect of this union and the new richness it can give his *inner* rhythm. A simple white or gray tunic—perfectly cut and tailored, because the value of the study depends on the shape of that tunic—will be satisfactory. This would be the third costume of the school. It is worn over the black or gray tights and may be taken off rapidly when, in the course of a lesson, the nature of the assignment is changed. Thus the same exercise could be executed alternately, once without the tunic (that is to say without folds) and another time with tunic (with folds). This can provide a source of valuable data for both pupil and master; it may even inspire fresh nuances of expression.

There now remains the Dance as it naturally develops from eurhythmics— but which Dalcroze keeps clearly separated in his instruction.

In whatever form dance is envisioned, it contains an element of freedom and imagination which indeed sets it apart and which even seems to make it approximate a dramatic performance. The question of dressing for dance practice depends, as elsewhere, on the feeling of the pupils. If, in executing their task, the pupils feel better wearing school tights, they should definitely wear them; on the other hand, if, in a public demonstration for instance, they themselves feel that a light dress would give them greater confidence in communicating their enjoyment to the spectator, this would be the right solution. The question is simple, then, as long as dance and eurhythmics are not confused. But if they are, experience alone can teach us, and it is then a matter of taste *because eurhythmics will always be the decisive factor.*[23]

The question of selecting a costume for eurhythmics is now easily answered at the Hellerau Institute, for it is reduced to the following points: How must the pupils dress to gain the greatest benefit possible from the assignments they receive, and, furthermore, how must they dress to facilitate the institute's study of the lighting that has been designed for them?

The pupils are fully entitled to keep for their work the dress which their own experience has proved to be the most suitable and most proper for them. Moreover nothing in the world should force them to choose for a public demonstration what their unspoiled and very sure instinct, refined through their studies, would reject.

But, you may object, is this so highly regarded art of the Jaques-Dalcroze Institute not the extreme of egoism? Everyone goes there to cultivate and perfect, through rhythm, his own personality; visitors, though well received, are not invited; and apparently everything must happen behind closed doors. And yet, all of us long for the same blessing; all of us would like to have our modest share of it! In our era, when the sight of a body in free and harmonious movement is totally denied to us—just when this sight alone could enliven and renew our art, our literature, and our conception of life in general—must, at that very time, the only refuge remain closed to us, the only sanctuary where this sight could once again inspire us?

The objection is perfectly legitimate: we must all share in this invaluable blessing. The point is only whether the question is properly stated. Would it not be better to ask ourselves what we shall do and how to do it, to be able to accept what the Hellerau Institute can give us? This corresponds precisely to the question asked by the institute itself at this very moment: How can we communicate to the public that we so urgently wish to give it?—For if the public is not prepared, neither is the Institute, involved as it is in its intense educational activity. The problem is to establish that link that will connect the activity of the school with the activity and the very different habitual mentality of the public.

There is only one means of achieving that; on the one hand, to affirm categorically and definitely the educational character of the great venture—this must be the role of the Institute; on the other, to come to the Institute and its presentations with the sole intention of seeking educational assistance which only the institute can offer—this must be the role of the public.

And let the audience not be mistaken! It has one of the most beautiful roles; sympathy, unselfish and respectful, combined with a sincere desire for knowledge and understanding—this is the *indispensable* complement of every aesthetic activity. The institute, too, needs this sympathy.

Whereas thus, at the beginning of this article, the curious visitor felt himself to be justifiably mistreated, we can assert that an audience forewarned and more eager to understand and penetrate into the admirable work of Dalcroze than to look at beautiful things will always be welcomed with open arms. The festivals are arranged to bring about this union. After a year of strenuous labor the pupils feel the urge to show to themselves in some form the best results of their work at an official school festival. In addition they deeply need not admiration, but sympathy. They ardently desire to be able to communicate to others some of their own enjoyment; and they know well that they cannot do this unless the invited public tries *to understand* them: what they have received they wish to give.

The great educational task of the Institute must therefore be enlarged to embrace the public, so that the Institute becomes also the educator of the audience. It cannot, nor must it, show merely the present to the audience. Surcharged with the future, the institute must offer the audience *that future* in the living and necessarily imperfect symbol of the present. In this sense the festivals will become the grand lodestar directing our attention from year to year towards a higher and more desirable goal; they will be *life* itself, not its representation; they will be living, not merely representative; their influence can never be measured, for life defies all measures.

And the public will come to this place to be freshened with this invigorating breeze, and to express officially its sympathy and gratitude. Thus a fraternal bond will be solidly established.

You will perhaps ask what these considerations have to do with the question of costume. It indeed strange that a wholly material question should take on such great importance.

Nevertheless one must admit this and even loudly assert it!

The Institute will give the audience proof of its educational character not merely through the composition of its program but also by maintaining this very character in the performance it offers. The audience must sacrifice many of its desires, and so must the institute, at the risk of grave objections.

May the visitor incidentally not be afraid of the austerity of a body so costumed; so much marvelous beauty, so many exciting developments have already found their place in this school that the future, far from being darkened by that austerity, is seen through that very austerity, and *only* through it, to be quite radiant.

# Part Four

# Essays on the Art of the Theatre

# Introduction to Part Four

The essays included in this and the subsequent section were, with one exception, composed during the last decade of Appia's life. It is likely that they form the bulk of the material that Appia himself intended to include in the projected volume to which he occasionally referred, but which was not, apparently, ever actually assembled. We know little about this volume except Appia's statement to Craig in November 1918, when, after announcing his work on *The Work of Living Art,* he mentioned plans for a volume of essays and prefaces. Several years later he referred to the book again in passing: "One must therefore wait until I have assembled *new* elements, and above all until I have complemented *The Work of Living Art* with a second volume where the reader will find practical ideas and Social Practice." A year later (February 1923) he mentioned it once more: "I am working: a book, drawings."[1]

Walther Volbach (personal communication to R. Beacham, 1988) has considered the subject in detail, and his assessment is useful:

> References of this kind allow us to conclude that Appia did indeed plan to combine a series of his essays, written during the twenties, into a single volume. We do not, however, know which essays he would have chosen, or whether he would have included some from an earlier period. Would he have restricted his choice to those with an aesthetic program, or would he have chosen some dealing with autobiographical material? Did he complete any other essays beyond those we have?
>
> It is possible that, after Appia's death in 1928, some manuscripts and designs were lost. We may assume, moreover that some were destroyed by Geneviève, the daughter of his brother Paul. The young woman was mentally defective, and is known to have burned some of Appia's work.
>
> To give a specific listing of essays intended for a new book planned by a great artist is, under the circumstances, mere guesswork. It is difficult even to determine the central idea which Appia wished to pursue. Terms such as "Dramatization" recur, but it seems unlikely they would have served him as the "leitmotif" for a new book. The term "The Living Presence" is perhaps a better choice, and Appia may have intended to use it as the title of this last publication. I have discussed the problem with friends and relatives of Appia. We agreed on some points, but could reach no firm conclusions. Many years ago I made up a "table of contents"[2] for Appia's book, but no longer wish to push my choice. My advice therefore to

readers who are acquainted with Appia's life and art is that they simply judge for themselves
those essays which would best represent the ideas Appia would have wished to expound in his
last work.

This judicious analysis is lent support by Appia's own "Preface" (placed
at the beginning of this section), in which he states "the New Presence is the
touchstone." It is a term that occurs frequently in those essays included in part
5. Rather than undertake to paraphrase this (or any of the other complex concepts with which Appia deals in these writings—some of them bordering on the
ineffable), it seems far better to allow Appia's treatment to speak—however,
and in what manner it may—for itself.

The works selected for this, the first of the two sections devoted to these
predominantly late essays, are those of a more practical sort; the more aesthetic
and philosophical were reserved for the subsequent section. Not surprisingly,
perhaps, all but one of these "practical" essays have previously been published,
whereas only four (out of thirteen) of those in the latter section have.

"Comments on the Theatre," published in April 1908, is the only early
essay included in this selection. It is interesting chiefly for its comprehensive
reiteration of Appia's critical analysis of the state of theatrical art (in particular
his dismissal of current scenic practice), together with a review of his ideas for
fundamental reform. Written after Appia's first experience and initial espousal
of eurhythmics, but before he prepared his earliest designs for "rhythmic
spaces," or engaged in substantial practical work with Dalcroze, it shows the
influence that the subject was already exercising upon his thinking, through the
emphasis he places on the relationship between music and human rhythm. His
insistence that "the new scenic order will be based on the presence of the human
body, of the plastic and moving body," to which everything will be subordinated, foreshadows the great and innovative work to come. He also presents his
analysis of the differing role of "sign" and "expression" in dramatic art; a subject
that will figure strongly in his later theory.

With the exception of a preface prepared in 1918 for an anticipated English
edition of *Musik und die Inscenierung,* which did not in the end appear; "Actor,
Space, Light, Painting," written for a conference in 1919, is Appia's first extant
post-War essay. It also represents his return to productive work after a relatively
fallow period. During the War Appia was frequently unwell, and although he
mentioned plans for a book *(The Work of Living Art)* to Gordon Craig in 1915,
he did little work during the period apart from occasional collaboration with
Dalcroze at his Geneva institute. For the most part, Appia's illnesses were
probably more emotional than physical. He was prone to periods of deep depression (sometimes aggravated by drink), and mental fatigue.

For a while after the armistice in November 1918, Appia's spirits greatly
improved, and as he noted in another letter to Craig, written at the end of that

month, he was ready (at 57 years of age) to embark on important new work. However, he also identified certain characteristics in his personality, which cast light on his subsequent work, including the essays presented here:

> I vacillate, and have vacillated all my life between on the one hand, atavisms and influences which have not been of a type to elevate or free me; and on the other, from desires, the personal needs of an artist and creator, which pull me, and which *should* pull me onward and upward. But this continual struggle is tiring, and holds me back somewhat. It is also a sort of inner guarantee, almost a sort of force, because it absolutely prevents me from saying or producing anything except that which I consider to be the purest and the best. . . . That is also why my private creations and unpublished work are more than what I can offer or show to others.[3]

The short essay is a succinct exposition of Appia's hierarchy of scenic presentation, and gives due emphasis both to the role of the human body as a means of expression, and to the need to overcome the passivity of the audience. It also introduces a subject which will loom large in his future essays: "the cathedral of the future," a changeable space where a variety of aesthetic activity will take place "with or without an audience." Appia conceived of a theatre in which the traditional architecture, the activity, and the relationship between audience and performance would all be radically transformed. New works of scenic art would be presented in buildings capable of providing the venue for a great variety of as yet unimagined aesthetic events. It is interesting to note that four years later, Gordon Craig, to whom Appia had confided these ideas, predicted "the theatre must be a *hollow* space with roof and floor only: within this space must be erected for each new type of play a new temporary stage and auditorium." The idea was an essential part of his conception of the theatre of the future as well.[4]

In the following year (1920) Appia wrote the brief piece "Art Is an Attitude," which reiterated both his prediction that new forms of art would emerge, all inspired by the human body, and his desire to abolish the barrier between spectator and performer. In 1928 the authors of what became an important and influential book, *Twentieth Century Stage Decoration,* which attempted to survey and summarize "the state of the art," asserted, "It seems today that in the domain of art every manifestation born swiftly, full of hope, and with pretensions to a durability reaching to eternity, dies with equal swiftness. Appia and Craig already belong to the long past, Craig perhaps more so than Appia."[5] With no apparent sense of irony, they nevertheless sought and received a foreword—this previously unpublished essay—from Appia, who died shortly before the book appeared.

His suggestion that such new forms would consist of "moving, more or less dramatic symbols, agreed upon by all" was one which he would explore in greater depth in several later works including "Living Art or Dead Nature?,"[6] which was one of his most widely published pieces, attracting a good deal of favorable attention. Written for the catalogue of an exhibition on modern scene design, it proved a particularly accessible presentation of his argument for rejecting traditional settings and static dramaturgy in favor of more expressive and vibrant formats emanating from the active presence of the living actor. Its eloquent description of the concept of "rhythmic spaces," and of a theatre architecture derived from this idea, undoubtedly drew extensively upon his observations and experience at Hellerau; the analysis of "the Hall" is particularly evocative. Its implicit call to "break down the barriers" was a demand taken up subsequently by those who in recent decades have explored and expanded the definition and potential of an art which, as Appia predicted, has burst the bonds of orthodox theatre.

Such ideas were dealt with more thoroughly in an essay written a little later the same year (1921), expressly for the students at the Dalcroze Institute in Geneva. "Theatrical Production and Its Prospects in the Future" was Appia's most widely published essay. In addition to renewing his call for reform of theatrical production through the careful coordination of a hierarchy of expressive elements, it also tackled the question of producing works of spoken drama. The actor in such drama was usually involved in works that imitated reality, whether directly or in a stylized fashion, through what Appia termed *indication.* The actor's words and gestures, together with the scenic environment, were all aspects of this indicative mode, which he contrasted with the direct *expression,* of which music alone was the primary source. In the absence of music much of the expressive quality was sacrificed, as well as the suggestion of an appropriate "rhythmic space," generated by the actor as he moved under the control of the music.[7]

Appia believed that existing dramatic works could in part be redeemed. Whenever possible music should be introduced into the play so that, though unable to exercise its primary expressive function, it might nevertheless serve to support and round out the action, ennobling the drama by forging, if only in passing, that unity between itself and poetry, which Appia considered the basis for true dramatic art. Similarly, the art of acting should be refined by engaging the performer in rigorous training in musically coordinated movement; in fact, in eurhythmics. The body itself would become an instrument for artistic expression instead of mimetic impersonation.

Finally, Appia believed that dramatic works could be endowed with a measure of control and integrity by the use of staging to reflect and respond to an altered awareness and expectation on the part of the audience itself. An audience conditioned by realism expected theatrical art to provide the direct replication not only of details of manners and behavior as conveyed through action, but also of the drama's putative historic and geographic locales, as represented by the scenery. The "idealistic" vision, however, only requires those elements which intensify and convey most readily the work's expressive qualities. This approach, which was a prerequisite for what came to be called production "concepts," was predicated upon the potential that art has to raise the consciousness of the audience and release the imagination from the random demands and events of everyday life. Appia believed that, through a theatrical art freed from the burden of simulating the petty details that encumber and obscure the deeper values of life, audiences could in turn awaken and intensify their own capacity for self-awareness and the experience of profound emotion.

Thus, by carefully investigating the meaning which a given work could have for its audience, and using staging to refine and express that meaning, one might create dramatic works that—even in the absence of music—could aspire to the controlled, coordinated and unified condition that Appia insisted must be the basis for any autonomous theatrical art.[8] He went still further, to assert that once the audience came to regard the theatrical piece as an expression in effect of its own self, in which it was directly and actively involved; once the actor's training in music allowed him to use his body not as an instrument for imitation but as one capable of direct expression, the basis would have been provided for entirely new forms of art. In another essay written the same year, "The Gesture of Art," which is included in part 5 of this book, Appia wrote,

> Can we not imagine a work of art that is free of a dramatic fiction and yet is provided by the living body? . . . Dramatic art makes use of the living body but is not its direct expression. Evidently another art form expressive of the living body itself must exist . . . the new art form will therefore have movement like dramatic art but will probably have no other relation to it.

Such ideas would, indeed, engender new forms of theatrical art in the future, including much of modern dance and "performance art." In order to provide the venue for such new work—and the experimentation leading to it—to take place, new forms of theatre architecture would be required, and it was to this subject that Appia turned six months later in July 1922 in the essay "Monumentality." In it he emphasized that what he termed "people's theatre" should stimulate an audience to learn and participate through the informal and sociable nature of the building itself.[9] Even its exterior walls should be constructed to allow performance to move out of doors when appropriate. The stage itself must be capable of merging with the other portions of the building into a single architectural unit, and, if desired, the lateral walls of the auditorium should be removable to allow it to combine with the lobby and other public areas, encouraging the aesthetic and social activities to merge. This informality would in turn benefit the performance itself; the spatial arrangement could help overcome the passivity of the spectators by giving them the impression that their own bodies are helping to create and define the space. The proliferation in recent years of performing arts complexes, multi-media studios, workshop and laboratory theatres and arts centers may legitimately be considered a distant but organic outgrowth and continuation of Appia's work.

Appia's insights on the relationship between architecture and performance have been reiterated and explored by theatrical innovators ever since. As one of these, Richard Schechner, expressed it,

> Putting everyone together in one space is the architectural version of sunlight. It makes people share in the event; it makes them *responsible* for the event. . . . Performing in divided spaces leads to illusionism. . . . [F]ar from diminishing audience involvement, single space staging sharpens it by throwing each spectator on his own. . . . [Y]ou are free to move closer to something that calls you, further away from something that repulses you. All within the envelope of the single space which makes the experience more dangerous and more communal.[10]

Appia's ideas were taken up by a host of later practitioners, many of them highly influential in their own right. One of the first was Appia's own disciple, Jacques Copeau, who in 1920 rebuilt the stage of his theatre, the Vieux Colombier, in a manner which, although it did not fully embody the entire scope of Appia's suggestions for reforming theatrical space, was, nevertheless, a significant advance. "It was an open stage, having no proscenium arch, footlights, or front curtain to restrict its depth. The audience was to feel that it was in the same room with the actors, not seated in front of a picture."[11]

Similar experiments were carried out later by Jean Vilar in his Théâtre Populaire, and by Ludovico Ronconi at the Théâtre du Soleil. Antonin Artaud also envisaged a theatre consisting essentially of four plain walls, with the action taking place on a variety of levels all around the audience, while light and sound similarly enveloped performer and spectator alike. The list is open-ended, but must also include the work of Grotowski and his Polish Laboratory Theatre, which abandons traditional theatre architecture "to remove setting, costume, make up, music, lighting effects, and even the playhouse itself, [leaving] only the actor to find his basic relationship with the audience."[12]

Appia's vision of the evolution of theatrical space was strongly reflected in the work of Richard Schechner's "Performance Group," Joseph Chaikin's "Open Theatre," and the widely provocative productions of the "Living Theatre." All found that the new varieties of theatrical art of the sort called for in Appia's essays in turn dictated the spatial reforms that he saw as inevitable. Analysis of the practice and underlying theory of each of these groups, therefore, instantly reveals an affinity with Appia, as well as the prescience of his ideas, however obscure the line of conscious influence or direct indebtedness may be.

The final essay in this section, and one of the last essays Appia wrote, is "The Art of the Living Theatre." In it he returns to the concept that much of the expressive quality of theatrical production is subjective; the audience itself helps to create the *mise en scène*, through the active engagement of its own imagination and emotion. If such "living" collaboration between audience and artists were to occur, it was vital to enlarge and open up the public's imagination and to make it receptive to new possibilities in popular art. Appia was concerned that the restrictive social conditions of the twentieth century and the growing pressure of technology were a serious challenge to human sensitivity and must be vigorously opposed. The burden upon the individual—now increasingly passive, demoralized and exhausted, as well as painfully isolated from his fellow-man—threatened to destroy the vitality of art and weaken society at the moment when the regeneration of both was critically important.

Direct participation must come to replace the morbid collecting and curating of individual impressions; the audience's compulsive desire to gaze upon images of itself was inimical to "living art." What was necessary were new types of activity which could integrate life, making connections between different modes of experience and different individuals: multiple art forms that could forge links from the individual's body and emotions to the larger body and concerns of the community. The achievement of such links could be accomplished only through a change in awareness and attitude on the part of the public, which must understand that new art forms represented not merely "technical development on the part of the stage director, but an inner and very profound evolution expected of the spectator himself." It was this subject that provided the essential theme of the visionary essays comprising the subsequent section of this volume.

# Preface to the Edition
# of My Essays in One Volume

## (1926)

The collection of these "Essays" in a single volume is not accidental. To judge a structure, one must gain a perspective that in a way is never attainable. One is therefore forced to proceed like the blind, move from detail to detail, and at last try to form an idea of the whole. This very idea, however, will remain quite speculative and inconsistent unless a certain criterion is available, an undisputed touchstone that permits the qualification and evaluation of various recorded manifestations, so that they may find a common principle that gives them reality by placing them in the correct perspective.

The New Presence is this touchstone. Without it, it would have been fruitless to begin the struggle; it is our Ariadne thread, both the point of departure and that of arrival. We must always return to it to find a reliable guide, a firm standard for our tests. Besides, how can we lose sight of this Presence which, in each of us, is precisely the individual we appreciate in others?

If the author anticipates, it is because he must inform the reader about the nature of this volume. It contains an investigation of topics chosen from among the most typical and congenial aspects of our modern life. Some are treated only by way of example, but these may also serve to induce application of their method to other subjects. It is important to know how we attack a theme; everyone may then select his objective as he pleases. The results obtained by a touchstone aim serve two purposes. They guarantee us the value of a metal and, at the same time, assure us of the stone's power of testing. The author must admit that he has lingered above all on the latter, for he is more anxious to stress the authority and blessings of the New Presence than to prove its value justified in the instances he examines.

Thus a golden thread holds together these essays and justifies their somewhat incongruous character. For the reader, it will be easy to find here a connection with any other topic familiar to him and to feel the solid quality of the bond.

We had to start with dramatic art in order to assert the possible and desirable existence of a Living Art. If we have animated one of the fine arts, sculpture, painting, or architecture, we should have shown a complete disregard for their specific nature, and living art would have become merely their caricature, as a "living tableau" caricatures painting or a so-called "plastic" group caricatures sculpture. The fine arts are motionless and are pledged to remain so. Cancel that pledge, and they tumble into anarchy, destroying each other. A real clock keeping time in the painted belfry of a picture invalidates both the clock and the picture. The same is true of a statue, because the slightest movement of a finger would annul the finger as a piece of sculpture and with it the entire statue. Hence we cannot animate that which owes its very existence to immobility. Dramatic art is the only artistic manifestation to make use of animated life. It was therefore necessary to take dramatic art as our point of departure and then leave it in order to widen considerably the significance of the term *animated life,* which finally became the title of the first section.

Yet we have stated that theatre is only one of the applications of Living Art. By taking it as point of departure, we have proceeded like a mechanic who, in reconstructing a machine, is guided only by gears three-fourths destroyed or damaged. With the help of a single vertebra, a zoologist approximately reconstructs an extinct animal. We can in the same manner recreate an integral art through one of the functions of the living and moving body; and so the possibility of the Living Art can no longer be denied! Its presence, even when unsuspected, is latent in all of us; under our clothes we begin to feel our body. From here it is but a step to consider it as a means of expression in itself. To free the body a technical effort was indispensable: Jaques-Dalcroze has given us his eurhythmics. Several attempts preceded it, as for instance, that of Isadora Duncan. Yet none of these had probed into the deep roots of our entire organism. They were merely a necessarily superficial transposition of the immobility of the fine arts into a movement which the use of music seemed to justify. And this perhaps with good reason, since music is *the* transposing art!

As a rule any art form and its technique go hand in hand, influencing each other in a continuous exchange. This cannot be true of Living Art, not only because it has been lost for a long time, but mainly because the technique of this art is mixed with its aim; our organism is at once the instrument and the work of art. This is assuredly an exceptional situation; and if dramatic art as hitherto presented as been the empirical art, Living Art has all the more reason to be empirical, since experience alone can inform us about the aesthetic capacities of our organism. Through experience we must begin to take full cognizance of the instrument, our body, and to perfect it before we attempt any artistic realization whatsoever. Working with a poorly prepared instrument would lead us to dire results and grave illusions. In a good number of cases eurhythmics has reached a degree of perfection which permits the advent of Living Art. How will this art develop? The future will tell us; for the moment it suffices to seek its existence at any price. But this raises a new question, that of knowing what influence this new art will have upon our public and private life, upon the fine arts, upon music and literature, and of recognizing its premonitory symptoms.

Here it is not a matter of vague feelings, of hazardous prophesies, or, especially, of any artificial construction. Never has the present so hermetically sealed off the near future. But since theatre has put us on the trail of a new art, Living Art, and then revealed its presence to us, it is evident that Living Art, which restores the lost dignity of our total organism, offers us a solid point of departure. With it we hold one of the essential forms of life. It implies the giving of oneself and thereby demands an attitude considered by thinkers of all times the sole liberator. I have called it "The New Presence." With it, we may proceed with confidence; though still a novice, it knows more than we and will denounce everything in our existence that would slur or contradict its high mission. It will always lead us back to humanity by showing us our place in humanity. The New Presence will ignore the barrier with which we unfortunately surround our personality, for it shows the general humanity in each one of our gestures, our emotions, our thoughts. When we speak of Them, it answers us "We," and its persistence is too gentle for us to resist.

The New Presence calls for the gift of the best of oneself, which it returns better yet and in a larger measure from those who accept this call. Its radiance is such that it forms, in every sense of the word, a new Being out of each one of us. Religions have sought to make of us exclusively moral beings. Art, which is a gesture, restores us to pure and simple human beings. All we have to do is to become conscious of it.

# Comments on the Theatre

*La Vie musicale* 1, no. 15/16 (1908)

*The aim of a work of art is to reveal some essential, salient character, consequently some important idea, more clearly and more completely than can real objects. It achieves this through a group of parts whose relationships it systematically modifies.*

H. A. Taine, *Philosophie de l'art,*
(Paris, 1881), 1: 41–42

## I

One evening in the theatre I had a seat next to two ladies who accompanied a school boy. Obviously the youngster was sitting for the first time in front of this large mysterious frame closed by a curtain, behind which unbelievable wonders were to appear. With a patronizing and determined tone these ladies tried to initiate their young friend: "You see, this is the curtain! Actually it is not a curtain but a painted canvas. This is the forestage, there are the boxes," and so on.

The orchestra burst forth; its sound made the poor boy tremble with delightful anticipation. "This is the overture, which is played at the beginning." In the child's features I could read something like: "Oh, all at once, music, stage, boxes, . . . and to be sitting here for the whole evening!" The indifference of those around is incomprehensible to him.

An agonizing pause until the curtain rises: "The curtain is opening; you see the scenery! There, on both sides are the wings; the backdrop is painted. It is night because the lights are blue. There is the tenor. Now comes the duet."

From time to time, these ladies exchanged views: "The dialogue is good,
is it not?—There, that is an understudy!"

Amazed and depressed, the young pupil looked around. An undefinable
disappointment began to take all animation from his face.

The theatre! To see beautiful and entertaining things as an apparent reality,
that is the child's conception of theatre. When he enters, the house seems unreal
to him; the reality for which he looks is behind the curtain. When our friend
left this house, which yesterday was still so full of promises, he must have
exclaimed: "And that is all!"[13]

Yes, my poor friend! and these ladies were right, but they should have talked
to you several months in advance, and, accordingly, on a different basis. The
idea of theatre, so engrossing, to youth in particular, is left to the hazards of a
repertory performance. And it is only in the tumult of intense excitement that
the child must try to get his bearings.*

The ladies would have been right in stating that theatre, like any other
work of art, must be "an ensemble of connected parts" whose "relations are
systematically modified." This occurs in the theatre superficially thus: a set of
contrivances is arranged by dramatists, sanctified by dint of their authority and
turned into a convention accepted by the audience. The ladies stated this clum-
sily, but after all, our scenic conventions of today are clumsy; therefore their
instinct did not delude them. But the child will never forget the deceptive words
that chased him so cruelly from the forest of his dreams, to set him on a solid
and clearly-marked road leading to theatrical aesthetics. Have we not, all of us,
had similar initiators . . . !

We still confuse theatre with spectacle. To be merely entertained, by looking at things presumably suitable for your entertainment, is a prehistoric stage
of that road we are talking about. There is no difference, except in quantity,
between a woman looking for hours out of her window and a Roman in a circus
of yore; the quality remains the same.**

A spectacle becomes a work of art only when its connected parts are
systematically "modified" in their relationships. This is characteristic of art.
Our pupil, unprepared, expected the stage to be an ensemble of parts connected
in the manner of "real objects," at least in appearance. Do we not relapse into
his error as soon as we abandon the conventionalization, so naively expressed

---

*Why not introduce a unit in education, the aim of which would be to explain the true idea of theatre
to children and thereby blunt its somewhat corrupting attraction in its present form.

**The film demonstrates in a palpable way how far the march backward can lead: instead of being
an invaluable means of instruction and observation, a pocket-edition of nature, such as the piano is
of music, the film wants to compete with the theatre.

by my honorable neighbors? Is not our judgment warped over and over by productions in the open air and on the realistic stage?

Some people demand a stylized setting (by which means and in which style?), others simplified scenery. Why? Then there are those who aim at increased elaboration, a quest for ever more precise social and historical reconstruction, creating a maximum of illusion. . . . Still others wish to rely exclusively on contrasts in light; some want to have a theatre of marionettes to avoid the trouble with actors;[14] others look for a theatre of colors, and so on and so forth . . . and all this to the exclusion of everything else. . . . Why?

The fact is that we have turned oddly talkative and confused since staging became a subject for discussion: what should we think of illusion? Where to stop? How to define it, if we do accept it as the purpose of staging? (A wag will answer us mischievously that illusion is to dramatic art what the *Musée Grevin*[15] is to the art of a Rodin. Let us not listen to him, for he surely exaggerates.) What about lighting? (The same disquieting character will at once whisper into our ears that to see the stage clearly does not yet mean genuine lighting, that owls see perfectly at night. And in a loud voice he will state: there is no light without shadow, no plasticity without shadow!)

A performance is an open-air theatre, a new decor by Jusseaume,[16] a laborious reconstruction of reality by Antoine, any sumptuous and incongruous concoction at Bayreuth, all are extolled in one breath as the *dernier cri* of scenic art. Upon monumental ruins, bushes are placed, sometimes set pieces, boards gaudily covered, even ramps. In this spurious frame a spurious tragedy is performed before a cosmopolitan crowd seated on stone tiers. . . . In our modern theatres, the seats for the audience are separated as far as possible from the acting area, and Bayreuth appears to us as the perfection: there, the frame of the stage is merely an immense keyhole (if you will excuse the expression), through which we witness, indiscreetly, mysteries not meant for us. In a place where stage and amphitheatre do form a single aesthetic unity, as in the theatre of antiquity, the presence of our sad, modern audience is barbaric nonsense. Just as barbaric as the manifest desire of a stage director to restore relations with "real objects," relations so marvelously "modified" in the Greek tragedy.

Let us pause here, however! In the theatre, this ensemble of connected parts includes light as well as actor and settings. "To modify systematically" relations between these parts implies that each one of them is under our control. Yet in daylight this control escapes us completely. Outdoors the production is thus deprived of one of its most powerful means of expression.* The aesthetic equilibrium between the parts is upset and all "systematic modifications" are weakened. The Greeks probably sensed this fact, which would explain certain of

---

*Needless to say that in art the hazards of the weather have no place.

these "modifications" that seem excessive to us. One of their aims was perhaps to adjust the manageable and modifiable parts to the intractable element (the light).

Here we are touching upon one of the vital problems related to *mise en scène,* light. It is important for us to render a precise account of it.

The unified dramatic work cannot escape Taine's definition. Therefore we have to find the means to make each part pliable and obedient. For the author this is already so in the printed piece, with or without music; there remains the *mise en scène,* with its elements in hierarchic order: the actor, the arrangement of the settings, the light, the scene painting itself.

Giving the actor the independence necessary for dramatic life and for a personal interpretation, we shall still keep enough authority over him to prevent his departing from this organically-established hierarchy. The three other elements are interdependent, but light has the advantage of being ideally flexible and perfectly controllable; hence it is, directly after the actor, foremost in rank among the means of expression.

The question is how to preserve in our indoor theatres the superiority of light over the other elements of the *mise en scène,* and how to replace its all-powerful expressiveness in outdoor theatres.

The problem concerns, as we shall see, the order of factors other than light—since, while completely controllable in our indoor stages, light quite escapes our control in outdoor theatres.

By analyzing the essential components of modern staging, their reciprocal effects, their simultaneous use as they operate at present, the influence of that simultaneous use on the actor's performance and on the very conception of dramatic action, we may understand why the supremacy of light is still ignored and we shall perhaps arrive at a different proposition on which to base the *mise en scène.*

This analysis will inevitably lead us to the dramatic work itself in its more or less close and legitimate relationship to the *mise en scène,* and enable us to determine its influence upon the elements of theatrical production.

Where music is an integral part of drama, it profoundly "modifies" the drama's timing, which entails, or should entail, an equally profound modification of the music drama in all its aspects. Besides beginning with the simple recitative, music permits expression to rise to an unbelievable intensity. This scope is in itself an aesthetic "modification" of the highest order.

From this point of view, music contains an invaluable stylistic power as regards the *mise en scène* and probably the only one which can definitely govern the production—i.e., strip the *mise en scène* of superfluous contrivances that are detrimental to those that do happen to be indispensable.

There is a mysterious relationship between music and light: "Apollo was not only the god of song but also of light."[17] Let us no longer separate what he has divinely united, let us try to obey him.

## II

Sound and light! two elements which, from an aesthetic viewpoint defy analysis. "Where other arts say: this indicates—music says: this is!"[18]

Where form and color try to express something, light says: I am; form and color exist exclusively through me.

How to reach these all-powerful elements; who will help us to unite them indissolubly?

Great musicians have never . . . paid attention to light; great painters and sculptors have never paid attention to music. What does it matter to us—one might say—since we have the technical means.

Yet it seems to me, on the contrary, that we too are guilty of similar indifference, and that it is important to make light visible to the musician's often inattentive eye and music more audible to the often faulty ear of the graphic artist. Only then can we begin our conquest of the *mise en scène*.

A profoundly inner motive alienates artist from the theatre. Will they permit a respectful layman to search for its origin?

"A lack of art?" Doubtless, and all of us suffer from it; but there is more to it.

The artist is accustomed to take seriously—that is, to appreciate "as an artist"—only works which necessitate a personal activity on his part, a specific contribution. We call this understanding a work of art. Yet our productions do their utmost to make this contribution unnecessary, even impossible. To be sure, through too indulgent a habit, we ourselves do have to establish, minute by minute, illusion in our settings. Yet . . . is this the personal activity so dear to the artist?

Indeed not! The very idea repels him. Yet the modern theatre demands nothing else of us, except really the most appalling passivity.

What can the artist make of such a work? He longs to act and is disgusted with the theatre because it thwarts his supreme desire, the aesthetic activity of the beholder.

If we wish to re-establish the union between light and sound—between the artist's vision and the musician's expression—it is imperative to find a scenic order that will satisfy the vital desire of the artist and to find a musical form that depends on this new order and is, at the same time, the expression of it.

Today, music, for its part, has gone off to develop its own virtuosity, uncontrolled and close to madness. Thus it alienates itself ever more from the innate rhythm of the human being, its creator.

So does the *mise en scène:* painting has become a virtuosity that pays little attention to the actor's presence.

Any reunion of these two art forms, as they now are proffered to us, can therefore not lead to harmony.

The artist must desire the life of sound—for his own sake. And the musician must feel the compelling need of an artistic physical realization of his work. From such relations, now become indispensable and consequently organic, a conciliatory art will blossom and expand.

Apollo will live among us again!

But at which point can sound and light converge in one and the same work of art? How can the desired union in the work of the future be brought about *a priori* and without the experience of the future?

Rhythm intimately unites the life of sound with the movements of our body. Here we already have a beacon, an important transposition. On the other hand, plastic forms are indispensable for the light to be expressive.* There remains the task of uniting the movements transmitted by rhythm to our body, which are the essence of music flung into space, with plastic forms revealed through light, which are the essence of light.

The center where sound waves, on the one hand (through rhythm), and light beams, on the other (through plasticity), converge, is the human body. This is the meaning of the term *conciliatory,* the temporary incarnation of the god of song and light.

With one hand Apollo assembles sound waves, with the other, light beams; then irresistibly he brings both hands, both these elements, together—bestowing upon them the full authority for their mutual interdependence.

The new scenic order will be based on the presence of the human body, of the plastic and moving body. Everything will be subordinated to it.

"When music reaches its noblest expression it becomes form (in space)."[19]

With this admirable statement Schiller became the harbinger of an art towards which we are striving. A century ago this great man hurled his prophetic "halt" at the world. Let us listen to him, trust him, and boldly state that all music that is not aimed at external form in space alienates itself from its "noblest expression."

It is high time indeed! Do we only maintain a memory of their separation where, incited by the voluptuousness of sounds, we have scorned the rougher road of their noblest expression . . . ?

Let us retrace our steps! Light will guide, even precede us, instead of throwing before us the ever darker shadow of our own egotism and passivity.

That brings us to the aesthetic development mentioned above—which be-

---

*For light alone and its unobstructed refraction we unfortunately possess only a frosted glass.

comes a unifying element in this renaissance. . . . The artist, attracted by light, which he knows well, as against sound, which he knows little, sees himself obliged "to do something" in order to achieve their union and to enjoy its fruit. The musician, tired at last of an unrewarding truancy, regains his balance and re-establishes contact with an art which has become unknown to him.

To the mutual advantage of both!

Instead of imitating the voluntary, inhuman, and unnatural isolation of the present-day musician, the artist will become conscious of the formal limitations of his own art; he will know that out there, beyond, he will encounter music. And the audience at our presentations will thank him for it. . . . Likewise the musician will meet the artist wherever he allows his imagination to tempt him to stray, if only it is outside his everyday domain.

All of us expect a problem to be seen in the right focus. And yet, everyone of us insists on wearing blinkers which, he thinks, protect him because they slyly conceal from him the growing dangers of the crossroad and the dead end in which he is caught.

In the following and last of my comments on the theatre I shall delineate the elements of a *mise en scène* based no longer on the display of dead pictures on vertical flats but on the plastic and moving presence of the human being. And I shall try, above all, to establish the influence of this new scenic art on the dramatic conception itself, prior to the production.

## III

> *Music, in itself, never expresses the phenomenon, solely the inner essence of the phenomenon.*
>
> Arthur Schopenhauer[20]

In the theatre "the phenomenon" means realism; the historic, geographic, and social symptom. It represents a type of a tree, a house, or a person. "The inner essence of the phenomenon" consists then in the phenomenon chosen by the author of the drama—of the elements that possess an eternal value.

The "sword motif" in *The Ring of the Nibelungs* could not express the sword proper, but, as it were, the fighting value of this weapon, with associated ideas and suggestions. Consequently, it is Wotan's resolution in front of Walhalla at the end of *The Rhinegold* that makes the motif sound again: the resolution to fight in the future and to give the weapon to his creatures (Siegmund). The "sword motif" expresses an inner mood. This is the inner essence of the phenomenon.

Any dramatic action is a combination of these two ideas, as Schopenhauer stated so well. And the secret of the *mise en scène* is to understand how these two dramatic elements can be visually realized, how they can somehow be blended on stage, in order to obtain a constant and perfect congruity with the dramatist's intention.

Yet does this intention not depend on the resources that the theatre, in turn, offers the dramatist?

Theatre is distinguished from the other arts by being either . . . a book (for some people this is its only existence!), or else and exclusively, it is a unified realization that requires the cooperation of several distinct minds, all subject to a single all-powerful direction.

But how to exact from one and the same man both dramatic genius and knowledge of current technical resources—resources favorable to the production? Here, as in other fields, a division of labor is evident. Like the painter who does not weave his canvas, the dramatist cannot acquire the skill needed for a reform of the *mise en scène*. Let us take the first step; the dramatist will soon join us in our anticipation of a flexible scenic art that is conscious of its flexibility.

The phenomenon is represented on the stage by painted scenery. Thus today we have hardly anything but the phenomenon, doubtless an important component of dramatic art, but one that should be subordinated to its superior. Moreover, present-day scenery has no contact with music; hence—digressing from music, the formative principle par excellence—it does not take us in the direction we seek. We have two dramatic forms: the spoken drama and the lyric drama. The first, deprived of the formative or "modifying" element, oscillates by necessity between an exasperated (and exasperating) realism and an idealism that tends toward the expression possible only to music. The second, the lyric drama, is by definition deprived of realism. Yet, it has forcibly seized realism, and embraces today fascinating but spurious works in which every word has to be understood if we are to justify the scenic realism. Thus, we cannot watch the stage throughout the evening because we must follow the libretto . . . in the darkness of the house. That is where confusion of vital principles lead us.*

As to settings, we have either the luxuriousness, stealthily borrowed from grand opera of former days, or the realism openly borrowed from modern legitimate plays. That is all.

And so the musician is left alone, with his dream unrealizable from the start. The dramatist, too—who does not wish to submit to the law of so binding and restricted a realism—remains alone, with merely latent possibilities for a flexible and profound dramatic idea. The stage director merely deletes whatever goes too far beyond realism. The dramatic conception has to bend in order to enter the rigid frame of realism, always offered as definitive. The triumph of the

---

*The fault is Richard Wagner's and the abuse made of his incomparable work.

"phenomenon," with or without music! For a long time even symphonic pieces have been based on the principle of the phenomenon. And this is a crime.

As a consequence, our painters—scene-painters—express their disgust about this state of affairs by turning with bowed head in the opposite direction. There are some who give us the "inner essence" to the exclusion of everything else, a fact that makes them unintelligible. Let us recognize their good intentions and profit from their instructive exaggerations, so that we may return to an aesthetic atmosphere with our plays, our music, and our theatre.

In the spoken drama, the formative element—in the absence of music—is the human body: a production will have style only to the extent that this can be derived from the body's plastic and living presence. However ingenious and clever a restoration may be, its aesthetic value will be measured solely by the degree to which its organization is based upon the body's indispensable presence. Everything else will be a dead "phenomenon," because it is not admitted. We are seriously affected by this moribund phenomenon.

In the lyric drama, equilibrium depends exclusively on music—I mean on the integral score. Music fluctuates (like the spoken drama but with a far broader scope) between notions appealing only to our intellect; let us call them Signs; and the direct appeal, the essence of music, Expression.

To show the entire square of San Marco for a scene played in a corner of the Procuratie Palaces[21] is to give supreme reign to the Sign. So are lilies of the valley painted at the bottom of a wing, to indicate spring; meticulously shaped trees beyond the acting area, to make clear that the performer is in a forest; an accumulation of ropes and nautical properties intended to express the idea of the sea; rustic properties, bourgeois knickknacks and the like—none to be used by the actor. This is the rubbish of modern production, which assumes an audience rather slow to grasp, whereas a word from the actor indicating the setting would suffice to orient the audience. It reminds one of a certain cuisine which, in misguided taste, drowns everything in a sauce; or, for that matter, a wit who keeps repeating his last pun to keep us laughing.

We have become accustomed to this lack of concern for the audience, and for that reason theatre is in disrepute. A dilettante who has no feeling for art paints tree trunks brown when seen against the full light of noon, for he knows they are brown. Our *mise en scène* proceeds on the same assumption, not as regards painting—the ingenious virtuosity of our scenic painters is well known—but indeed as regards its purpose. In the future we no longer wish to see on stage objects as we know they are, but as we feel them to be. Then the dramatist, finally in possession of a medium for expressing things as we sense them, will have free play.

In the preceding comments we have recorded the supremacy of light. If painting excellently represents Signs on the stage, light proclaims the reign of Expression. With the help of light we can pour living colors through space, render the picture flexible, control the Sign, this dead indication of something specific, and thus immerse the actor in an atmosphere designed for him.

The prodigious development of scenic painting, and with it scenic realism are the outcome of an escape—or at least the illusion of an escape from the austere limitations of the *mise en scène*. But these limitations are, on the contrary, our safeguards. Forcing us to "modify the mutual relationship of the parts," to quote Taine, they guarantee the theatre the quality of a work of art.

To give up a great part of the illusion created by painting evidently involves a change in our taste. This seems to me the most interesting point of the question I should like to discuss, namely, the influence of the *mise en scène* on the author's creative work, on his dramatic conception itself, on the motives he selects to develop, out of which to write a play. For realism in the theatre is in the end monotony, inaction, and above all, death of imagination. Besides, it is childish. A conflict of passions must not be presented to us as it would appear in everyday life, but rather in its inner reality; otherwise theatre is not an art and cannot be justified as such.

Is it the fault of our authors if they cannot conceive theatre in any other form than a realistic one? Even Richard Wagner's conception was realistic so far as production was concerned. For him, as for others, illusion had to be created. And whatever happened on the stage happened there in precisely the same manner for both the actor and the audience.

In the last analysis this is, after all, what characterizes the principle of realism.

With a new scenic order the author will know that the performance of his work can obtain "modification of relations" equal to those he wishes to work out in his dramatic idea, in order to save it from mere realism, render it expressive, and transport it into the realm of art. Then, assured of the stage director's cooperation and understanding, he will feel that his imagination has been set free.

It is impossible to measure the scope of such a reform and the influence exercised on an audience by a theatre that requires each spectator to be personally involved in the performance—the very character of aesthetic pleasure—instead of delivering him to inertia.

Purely technical considerations have no place here. In a comparable study of our current productions I shall attempt to press the problem still further by means of examples.

If through these comments I have succeeded in fulfilling the reader's desire—a desire for which he perhaps has tried to find a formula—my purpose is achieved.

Music alone can guide us over the new path, but, like the slaves in *A Thousand and One Nights,* we must "be responsive and loyal to it."

# Actor, Space, Light, Painting

(1919)

*Journal de Genève*, 22 January 1954
*Théâtre populaire*, no. 5, Jan.–Feb. 1954[22]

To judge dramatic art and its scenic evolution today, it is imperative to realize above all that there exists an interchange between the basic conception of the author and the means of production on which he can count. Of course it would be more precise to say that this exchange *ought* to exist, for at present, alas, the decisive influence is too one-sided; our modern conception of theatre and of dramatic production compels the author to limit his vision. Therefore it is important that we know all about the scenic element, which so tyrannically curbs an author's imagination.

The art of production is the art of projecting into Space what the author himself could project only in Time. The time element is implicitly contained in any text, with or without music. Let us examine what our scenic production offers the dramatic actor, in particular in Latin countries, where a conservatism that is sometimes salutary and protective can become a real danger when it concerns the living art.

The first factor in staging is the interpreter, the actor. The actor carries the action. Without him there is no action, hence no drama. Everything must be subordinated, so it seems, to this element—which takes first rank hierarchically. Again, the body is alive, moving and plastic; it has three dimensions. Space and objects meant for the body must scrupulously take this fact into account. The general arrangement of the stage comes directly after the actor in the hierarchy; it is on the basis of this arrangement that the actor makes contact with, and takes on reality in, scenic space.

So we already have two essential elements; the actor and the spatial arrangement of the stage, which must conform to his plastic form, his three dimensions.

What else is there:

Light!

Our stage is normally a dim and undefined space. It is evident that we must first of all see it, and see it clearly, But such illumination is no more than a preliminary condition, as would be the mere presence of the actor. Like the actor, light must become active; and in order to give it the rank of a means of dramatic expression, it must be put to the service of . . . the actor, who is its hierarchic superior, and to the service of the actor's dramatic and plastic expression.

Let us assume that we have created a space truly suitable for the actor; it will then be the obligation of light to conform equally to both the space and the actor. We shall see the obstacle which our modern *mise en scène* sets in the way of this achievement. Light has an almost miraculous flexibility. It possesses all degrees of clarity, all possibilities of color, all the variations of a palette. It can produce shadows and distribute the harmony of its vibrations in space as music does. In light we possess all the expressive power of space, if this space is placed at the service of the actor.

Here is our normally established hierarchy: the actor presenting the drama, three-dimensional space at the service of the actor's plastic form, light, giving life to both.

But—for you guessed it, there is a but—what about painting? What do we understand by painting in terms of scenic art?

A collection of painted drops and cutouts arranged on the stage vertically, more or less parallel and in depth. These drops are overlaid with painted light, painted shadows, painted objects, forms, and architecture. All this, of course, on a flat surface, for that is the very nature of painting. The third dimension is insidiously replaced by an illusory sequence in depth. But in the dim space of the stage, this beautiful painting has to be lighted. . . .

Let us suppose that an art lover places sculptures in the midst of sumptuous frescoes. If he illuminates the frescoes well, what happens to the sculptures? And vice versa. . . .

Our staging method has reversed the hierarchic order; under the pretext of offering us many features difficult or impossible to realize in three dimensions, it has developed scenic painting to the limits of absurdity and has disgracefully subordinated to it the living body of the actor. Thus light illuminates the drops (for they have to be well seen) without a thought for the actor, who suffers the deepest humiliation of moving between painted flats, set up on a horizontal floor.

All modern experiments in scenic reform touch upon this essential problem, namely on the manner of giving full power to light—and through it integral plastic significance to the actor and the scenic space. If our hierarchy is then an irrevocable reality—and this cannot be disputed—it is the inferior element, painting, that must be, if not sacrificed, at least subordinated to the other three factors that are superior to it.

But by what means?

Do not forget that secondly we deal here only with the *mise en scène*. What we are trying to do is gradually to re-establish an equitable reciprocity between author and production. We return therefore to the author and, through him, to the dramatic conception itself. It is the future of drama that we must prepare.

For a long time our stage directors have sacrificed the actor's physical and living presence to the dead illusion of painting. It is obvious that under such tyranny the human body could not develop its means of expression in a normal manner.

Today the return to the human body as a means of expression of the first order is an idea that dominates the mind, that stimulates the imagination, and that shows the way for experiments that are very diverse and no doubt very unequal in value, but which are all directed toward the same reform. Everyone of us has probably noticed on the one hand that a performer always tends, somehow implicitly, to draw closer to the spectator; and on the other hand has felt (some more deeply and passionately than others) a certain tendency in the spectator to reach out towards the performer. Yet our productions have forced us into a passivity so despicable that we have carefully concealed it in the darkness of the house. Now, with the present effort of the human body to rediscover itself, so to speak, our emotion promises to become a beginning of fraternal collaboration. We wish that we, ourselves, were the body we are observing: the social instinct is awakened in us, although we have coldly suppressed it in the past; and the division that separates stage and house becomes merely a painful barbarity stemming from our own egoism.

We have here reached the crucial point of dramatic reform. This point must be proclaimed boldly: The dramatic author will never liberate his vision as long as he considers it necessarily attached to a line of demarcation between play and spectator. Sometimes this division may be desirable, but it must never be the rule. The obvious conclusion is that the customary arrangement of our theatres must slowly evolve toward a more liberal conception of dramatic art. Sooner or later we shall arrive at what will simply be called the House: a kind of cathedral of the future which in a vast, free and changeable space will welcome the most diverse manifestations of our social and artistic life and will be the preeminent place for dramatic art to flourish, with or without an audience.[23]

# Art Is an Attitude

Walter René Fuerst and Samuel J. Hume,
*Twentieth-Century Stage Decoration* (London, 1928)[24]


This attitude should belong to all humanity. Instead, we have surrendered it to the creator of a work of art, making it thus the specific and personal property of the artist. A history of art has, therefore, become a chronological enumeration of art forms and their various techniques. There is music, architecture, sculpture, painting—as if art were necessarily hewn stones, sounds, colors—nay, even words. Our museums, concerts, and libraries seem to confirm this. Less than twenty years ago these institutions appeared to represent art, to be its depositories and its glorious trustees.

*This is no longer true today.*

At last we have left our spectator's seat and are ready to fight with all our strength for our right to participate. We seek art and want to find it within ourselves. Breaking the barriers, we dash up the steps that separate us from the platform, and unflinchingly we descend into the arena.

The inception of any work dedicated to the theatre requires this affirmative attitude.

This involves, of course, all our mind and body! To be "part of art" we must, like a neophyte, search for the point where the work of art and our whole personality will converge. In matters of the theatre this truly new gesture places the key to the scenic problem in our hands.

Here is the solution of which we may justly be proud. After all, what can our body do with painted canvas, why should it be impeded by such a setting once it has chosen to present itself? On the other hand, what can we exact of a setting to enhance the new artistic function of the body? Let us look into the situation.

Sport and the conquest of space have made us conscious of the effective-ness of our body: we who are responsible for our body are able to extend this responsibility to the space through which we pass, to the ground upon which we confer so burning a reality. How can we then continue to remain placidly in our seats, watching bodies like ours become degraded menials in space before us? For on the stage of our theatres the supreme object of the arts, the living body, our own body, is still violated and debased by the settings.

Thus, posed in its true light, the problem of *mise en scène* is solved. All that remains is to determine the technical results of this evolution and their influence upon our social life.

Let us assume two opposite poles: on one side, pure dramatic art, devoid of any alloy, on the other, any spectacle presented solely to please the eye.

The more dramatic art approaches spectacle for its own sake, the more it will reduce its dramatic value and, vice versa, spectacle loses in splendor as well as in variety as it tends toward the dramatic.

What is left to dramatic art when it is deprived of the delights permitted the merely pictorial art? The actor's living body! But this living body has three dimensions and it moves. The setting painted on drops has two dimensions and presents fictitious objects, highlights, and shadows. The actor, a *living* reality unaffected by these painted lights and shadows, is unable to come into an organic relation with painted objects. Lighting necessary to bring out the paint-ing is not meant for the actor and yet it falls on him. Lighting meant for the actor weakens the painting and distorts its pictorial aspect.

These obvious contradictions compel us to establish a rational hierarchy among the means of scenic expression.

*The actor* rightfully occupies the first place. Next comes *the spatial ar-rangement,* i.e., the general disposition of the setting as it is related to the actor's dimensions and mobility. Then follows the all-powerful *lighting.* The last place belongs to *painted scenery,* whose role is definitely subordinated to the three other elements.

Color is involved not with painting alone, since it involves the actor, the spatial arrangement, and the light; light by definition.

This hierarchy imposes upon the stage director a series of conclusions independent of his imagination and free choice. The setting, in particular its lines and rigidity, must oppose the living forms of the actor, for it is precisely in resisting these forms and their mobility that space acquires life and contrib-utes to a harmonious presentation.

These principles cannot be crystallized, they are not dogmatic; on the contrary, they are flexible to be adjusted to the various intentions of the drama-tist. There is, however, a law that will always dominate: the incontestable supremacy of the actor on the stage. To him everything must be offered, every-thing sacrificed. This law should not be broken unless a particular play clearly supports or demands such a weighty decision. This will never be to the honor of the dramatist or his audience.

I began this introduction with the statement that we want to "participate," that we have recovered our body which was lost for centuries and that we have experienced a new responsibility, a feeling of solidarity like the sudden revelation of a categorical imperative. *We have ceased to be spectators!* We have begun to dislike this role which, in any case, was never much esteemed. Therefore we seek a change, and our old formulas drift away in all directions.

The dance, the animated plastic art, is part of a vague repertoire that tends to overlap sports. Music, spoken words, spectacles, simplification or stylization, splendor and excess, alternate with and permeate one another. This anarchy is disturbing, because we sense its outcome: the issue will *depend on us,* on an aesthetic resolution arrived at organically, gradually, and smoothly.

Since we wish to "participate," we intend to be free; so we have become free! This is absolutely true! Let us strive to use our liberty nobly.

The time will come when the professionals of the theatre and the plays written for them will be completely obsolete—a time, when a liberated humanity will sing of its joys and pains, its thoughts, works, struggles, defeats, and triumphs. It will sing of them in moving, more or less dramatic symbols agreed upon by all. And the only spectators will be those whom age and infirmity will group around us in common and keen sympathy.

Then we shall be artists, *living* artists, because this is what we desire to be.

I welcome this time with all my heart.

# Living Art or Dead Nature?

(1921)

*Wendigen,* no. 9/10 (1922)
*Bottega di Poesia,* 1923
*Theatre Annual* 2 (1943)
*Players Magazine,* no. 4 (1962)

The evolution of dramatic art is in full swing; so much so that this evolution resembles a state of anarchy. More than ever we feel the need to come to an understanding on the subject of the theatre and to search together for the principle that can help us emerge from the confusion and inconsistency and can guide us toward a style we are striving for, but have not quite been able as yet to formulate. A theatre exhibition[25] therefore answers a legitimate desire, and we can only gratefully acknowledge the efforts made in this direction.

Immediately, however, a question arises: can theatre be exhibited? And if so, what elements does it offer for a complete demonstration? For this is precisely what we are seeking.

In the first place, dramatic art must have a building dedicated to its use. Architecture, unfortunately, cannot be exhibited. The art of mass and weight cannot be expressed by a model or a design, since these speak only to professionals. Anyone entering an exhibit of architecture, after leaving one of painting, will feel, for instance, that while the painting was well exhibited, the architecture was not, and that one thus passed from a tangible and complete reality (the painting) to a conventional linear abstraction which expressed nothing. Furthermore, since the significance of architecture lies exclusively in its service to the human being, it seems to have no place in an exhibit where it can appear only on reduced scale. Our exhibits of theatre architecture therefore have only a limited practical purpose and cannot convince the layman. The diverse arrangements of house and stage, the electrical and technical equipment with its possibilities are likewise shown in abstract reductions and elude three-quarters of the visitors. Turning now to exhibits of settings, we find again that space permits only the reduced scale of models and more or less colored designs. If we add to them designs of costumes which in an immobile sketch do not tell the quality of the fabric or the effect of the material on the actors in motion, we have everything the theatre can provide for exhibitions. Lacking only are documents, the playscripts and scores, photographs or pictures and, to complete the list, the musical instruments of the modern orchestra.

Is it really this we look for in the theatre and demand of it? Is dramatic art merely a conglomeration of such inanimate objects? Let us assume the best, that we could exhibit actual stages with people in settings appropriate to their size: would this be theatre? Movement is what sets dramatic art in motion (this is the correct phrase!), just as the conductor's downbeat brings with it the entire symphony, which does not until then exist in the orchestra alone, not even in embryo. For our eyes the essence of theatre is movement. Yet can this be exhibited? Of course! But this requires much time, very much time. . . .

Dramatic art—the theatre we want to exhibit—begins with movement. Everything preceding movement is no doubt useful and very interesting material but not indispensable and, hence, cannot represent the theatre.

We have then, on the one hand, the building, the stage equipment, the settings and costumes—on the other, living and moving beings, the actors, whose presence is the *sine qua non* of theatre. Dramatic art is above all the art of life, and this life can be expressed, if need be, without a building or decorative elements, for undetermined space and time suffice for this art.

What then drives us again and again to display our explorations in this seemingly so arbitrary field of scenic material?

Formerly the *mise en scène* consisted entirely of painted scenery on vertical canvases, cut in pieces and so placed as to provide a perspective view. The stage director's task was limited to arranging the groups and the movements of the performers within all this vertical painting while taking into account the conflict between the two-dimensional flats and the three-dimensional actors. The extraordinary development of scenic painting must be attributed to the increasing luxury of opera and ballet; it was enough like the conventional singing and dancing, stereotyped in never-changing formulas, so that the spectator accepted it without noticing too much the technical nonsense thus imposed upon him. However, theatrical verisimilitude and realism have upset our habits. To begin with we demanded of scenic painting historic, geographic, and social indications required by a test that was far closer to reality than heretofore. Soon the action itself became realistic and scenic painting could not correspond with the actors' playing. The issue of two or three dimensions became ever more imperative; on one hand, the director, out of long habit, still retained scenic painting, but on the other he called wholeheartedly for the plasticity (practibility) that painting denied him. As a result, the playwrights greatly limited their choice of locale in order to place their action in a frame that could easily be represented on the stage. That is where we were when dance—undoubtedly under the powerful influence of sport—gradually emancipated itself. The living and moving body has asserted itself, and it has done so, as a matter of utmost importance, outside of the psychological verisimilitude of a definite dramatic action. It assumed for itself the rank of expressive means. From that day on, scenic painting began to expire. Alas, it dies rather slowly, for our taste at least, but irrevocably; and aesthetic truth as represented by the living body has finally triumphed.

For all those who have a serious interest in theatre, the actor and his action, and the rhythmically moving three-dimensional dancer now dictate the scenic apparatus, including the arrangement of the house and the theatre building as a whole. We are free at last!

We now have only to prove our freedom by deeds; and that is the very reason for theatre exhibitions. Through them we intend to demonstrate the supremacy of the actor's living body over the inanimate setting—of living art over dead nature. The question remains whether the means we employ are sufficiently conclusive. Let us first of all consider the visitor, for here as elsewhere, we shall find both laymen and professionals, and our demonstration must be thorough enough to attract the craftsman and brilliant enough to persuade the layman. Can these two aims be reconciled?

Though movement by itself is independent of all surroundings, it is nevertheless desirable to provide it with an uneven space of different levels that enhance the episodes and bring out all the fine details; in other words to set obstacles against that movement. To this end the author and through him the actor must rely on the absolute flexibility of the inanimate material. Here we then face obligations entirely different from those which scenic painting disgracefully imposed upon us. For movement emanates from a three-dimensional body, and it seems clear that if we wish to serve that body, we must definitely reject painting on vertical flats or, at least, reduce it to a few pieces. Since space so conceived depends exclusively on the movement of the actor, our plans will be designed for the actor alone. The actor cannot determine anything without the dramatist. Therefore, the normal hierarchy will be author, actor, space. But mind you, this hierarchy is organic: the author cannot deal with space except through the actor! Because we neglected this fundamental technical truth we sank into anarchy in matters of staging. Here we touch therefore upon the core of the question.

Most drawings of settings and models in our exhibitions concentrate on plays already known and seek to realize a picture that has issued directly from the author's or the scenic designer's imagination without passing through the actor, as the hierarchy demands. Surely, the actor has been granted sympathetic consideration and accorded some place; his presumed action is roughly provided for, and the pieces with which the three-dimensional living actor must come in direct contact are even made plastic and practicable. Then a childish attempt is made to combine somehow the reality of such contact with the vertical fragments of a beautiful painting. The total picture, however, is always considered self-sufficient. The actor is condescendingly given a place in it, though he is unquestionably a nuisance there. Sometimes exhibited designs do not even show the settings as they really are, i.e., in a patchwork of two and three dimensions, but as they would be without this painful dilemma! The drawing of a setting should always give the observer an exact impression of its reality as it will look on stage, without hypocritical modifications (particularly with reference to the stage floor and the lower part of the flats). Otherwise the drawing is a fraud and contributes appreciably to clouding of the visitor's judgment.

The result of our normal hierarchy is that an exhibition of settings will no longer consist of sketches and models representing painting, but simply of spatial projects adapted to the actor's living and mobile presence, which in turn is placed under the command of the dramatic author. This hierarchic principle must be confirmed in the composition and integrity of the design. But since the significance—hence the expression—of these spaces depends on the actor's mobile presence, simple sketches or models of them will keenly impress one as being incomplete and arouse the visitor's's desire for the presence of the living body which alone has motivated them. Without this feature, a theatre exhibition will not be convincing to the public at large and will miss its point; for it will appeal only to those of the professionals who can, in their imagination, animate the empty and lifeless settings. Therefore the settings must include their natural complement; this complement is movement.

It follows that a complete theatre exhibition must show, on the one hand, the spaces designed for movement; on the other, the movement that inspired and shaped these spaces. The one without the other remains fragmentary. But movement on one side and space on the other are still not theatre. Their very encounter and fusion ignites the spark that kindles stage life and spreads its fire. This alone can be convincing to all. Moreover, movement without space can hardly be imagined, and so we would have two concurrent exhibitions: the rooms allocated to architecture, to technical equipment, to settings and models, and to costumes, and then the large halls for variable compositions of three-dimensional space arranged on the scale of the human body. The first rooms would be open all the time; the others accessible during the hours of live demonstrations and performances by actors, singers, and dancers.

Let us look at these large halls for a moment! They will justify and explain the very appreciable sacrifices made in the rooms for designs and models. The visitor, surprised at the exhibit of lifeless spaces, feels the salutary need for them to be filled, and this sense of emptiness is for him the beginning of wisdom!

He must be made to experience this.[26] Then, when the movements of the demonstrators give life to these spaces and when the two elements fuse into a living synthesis before the visitor's eyes, his doubt and the old prejudice will be dispelled. By himself alone he would probably not have thought the union possible; he had to witness it with his own eyes. We, the professionals, must provide him with the means for his experience.

In my book *The Work of Living Art* I examined the structure necessary for space if it is to associate with the forms and movements of the living being, and I came to the conclusion that space does not share the life of the body by adopting its form, but on the contrary, by opposing it. To achieve this, spatial composition uses only a small number of lines. They are the horizontal, the vertical, the oblique (ramp) and combinations thereof, such as—for example—a staircase that offers the body a kind of support that no other combination can claim. This simplicity permits easy handling of the material. There will be pieces of different sizes carefully constructed so that they can be combined and joined to form staircases, platforms, and ramps, supported, if necessary, by pillars evenly set at right angles; perpendicular drapes, screens, etc.; quite an intricate set of pieces based on rectilinear forms as opposed to the rounded shape of the body and the curved lines of its movements. Such pieces can be shifted manually by an intelligent and well-trained stage hand. Let us add that the demonstration will be all the more conclusive if color and costume are uniform, giving emphasis to space and movements alone, without distracting the eye by basically minor elements. The pieces are covered with canvas; the costumes are simple, either black tights leaving neck, arms, legs, and feet uncovered and bare (this is the rehearsal dress for Dalcroze's eurhythmics) or a short tunic over the tights. In these demonstrations light falls exclusively from above in order to show clearly the forms of the body in motion and the three-dimensional character of the setting.[27] Never footlights! Experience has shown it advisable (as a rule) to soften and to diffuse the light by means of muslin, tinged with golden yellow. These three-dimensional pieces are shifted before the spectator's eyes; we need no curtain, since we wish to demonstrate, not to hide. The entire arrangement follows that in the Jaques-Dalcroze Institute. On the last days of the exhibition actual performances can be attempted, while the necessary simplicity is always maintained. One might even venture to produce plays whose style was not too inconsistent with the adopted principle.

Halls devised for such synthesis will be a place for experimentation, for the art of the *mise en scène* will never cease to be empirical. They will also become a touchstone for dramatic art; in them playwrights will make valuable discoveries. The exhibition of such experiments will certainly induce them to participate, and from here to a fruitful understanding with the spectators is only a step! The theatre exhibition will have turned into a living organism! Space does not permit me here to expound on such a subject, but before I close my treatise, let me mention some facts which are indispensable to the reform of dramatic art and which I have already delineated in *The Work of Living Art.*

To enter the domain of art, our movements must modify their time pattern. The transposition cannot proceed arbitrarily; it must indeed originate from a principle whose guidance we can accept. Today only music can so serve us, since it is indubitably the expression of our soul and consequently born of our innermost will. It is therefore indispensable to transfuse the elements of music into our organism through rhythm. Jaques-Dalcroze, as is well known, has discovered the method of doing this. Seeking no other inspiration but itself, his eurhythmics proceeds from the inner being outward. The beauty of its exercises is but a natural result, and therefore eurhythmics alone can establish the aesthetic equilibrium of our whole being. Trained in this discipline, our body becomes a marvelous instrument of infinite possibilities. In contact with it, space comes to life and takes part in the living proportions of movement: the visible union is thus achieved.

I shall be asked what relationship there is between this phenomenon and our modern theatre. Our very attempt to reform the *mise en scène* calls in question again the whole problem of dramatic art, for it is clear that the two are closely interrelated. One of the current mistakes is the desire to reform the one without changing the other, and even to apply new principles to plays totally unsuited for them. Furthermore, have not many of our directors used these new principles as the sole pretext to stage a play they would otherwise never have considered! The emancipation of the body has freed us as far as the performance is concerned, but not yet as regards dramatic art itself. Overwhelmed by the weight of the past, we waver, not daring to shake it off completely, and we are bewildered by the new possibilities which have outstripped the dramatist. The expressive value of the staircase, for instance, has been recognized, and certain stage directors use it indiscriminately in every production.[28] Recently even an entire Roman orgy has been staged on a staircase, a place poorly adapted for sensual pleasure!

Ours is a period of transition and to dominate it we must be clearly conscious of this. Today we know that movements, forms, lines, light, and colors are at our disposal. The dogmas of the old staging have been upset, but we do not yet realize how heavily they have weighed upon the very conception of our theatrical production and have constantly suggested or imposed upon it the same forms.

The fateful frame of our stages insists on dominating our imagination; so much so, that a performance without spectators appears to us senseless, as though the artistic life of the living body must necessarily be exhibited! The quite arbitrary convention of our auditoriums and stages, facing each other, has consistently imposed that notion upon us!

Pondering this matter, one will observe that everything in the development of modern life tends towards a change in the theatre; in our very conception of it. In this case at least, the moving pictures exercise a wholesome influence. It is wrong therefore to assign the same buildings to both the current dramatic repertoire and to new experiments. Their rigid frame, working by suggestion, greatly hampers our efforts to free ourselves. So let us give up these theatres to their dying past, and let us build basic structures designed simply to serve as a shell for the space in which we shall work.

There will be no stage, no amphitheatre, only a bare and empty hall, which waits . . . ; everywhere clear spaces to store the set pieces; and complete lighting equipment. So much for the technical phase. For the other, actors, singers, dancers, rhythmicists, writers, musicians, and artists, all people of good will, offering their talents to the new task without prejudice for their individual professions; they will cooperate to benefit the common cause and will direct, suggest, or perform each according to his talent. When we feel strong enough to give a convincing demonstration, it will be easy to improvise tiers of seats for a public anxious to learn, and this public will naturally be willing to contribute advice and support. Gradually we shall come to conceive—with the public's help, no doubt—new productions linked together, and to expand or limit temporarily the importance or the scope of one means of expression in favor of another. This field of experimentation will become a kind of nursery for dramatic art whose development will no longer be thwarted by any unwarranted convention. Productions may well be anticipated in which the public takes part whether in music or in action and where only the old or infirm remain in their seats inactive or silent. Then art will live among us!

It is this art for which all our theatre exhibitions must prepare; toward it all our efforts must be directed, in whatever field they may be exercised. Then we shall learn that, in its noblest form, art is a gesture of mutual subordination, surpassing by far our narrow personal aspirations.

The influence of an institute of this sort cannot be measured; it will reach across our entire culture, regulating and vitalizing it. The painter, the sculptor, and the poet will not attempt to express in their works what living art alone can realize. And the playwrights and artists participating in our demonstrations will beware of borrowing from the fine arts and literature themes incompatible with movement. The public's taste will be purified; this will enlighten its judgment and enable it to collaborate still further and more efficaciously in the great task. This is a dream for the future! However, nothing prevents that dream from coming true one day if we begin forthwith to prepare its advent. Theatre exhibitions are taking on an avant-garde character, and the writers rather than the stage directors still suffer under the weight of a dead tradition and an old routine. Indeed, as I have said, the conception of theatre must be set free. Our dramatists are as yet unaware of their freedom and continue to regard the theatre with suspicion or to submit to it passively. How can they be induced to change their attitude? The duty to convince them falls upon us, the stage directors, and our projects must all bear witness to a blissful emancipation.

# Theatrical Production and Its Prospects in the Future

## (1921)

*Il Covegno* 2, nos. 4–6 (1923)
*Theatre Arts Monthly* 16, no. 8 (Aug. 1932) (abbreviated form)
*Theatre Arts Anthology,* New York, 1950 (abbreviated form)
*Cahiers de la Compagnie Madeleine Renaud, Jean-Louis Barrault* 3, no. 10
(1955)

Dedicated to the pupils of the Jaques-Dalcroze Institute (1921)

For many of us, theatrical production is no doubt a sharply circumscribed term. It implies the idea of the theatre as an established institution, and we place our curiosity and the yearnings of our imagination in this somewhat rigid frame. Thus the question of production embraces the sum total of art, care, and intelligence applied to the realization of a dramatic work on the stage, and is the concern of the scene designer, the stage director, and finally the actors.

From personal experience or hearsay we are all familiar with the current experiments in this—I believe very special—field, and we are gathered here to discuss the importance of these experiments, their history and their prospects in the future. I say "we," for this topic involves mutuality. And if I alone were chosen to be the speaker I would consider this lecture no less drawn from the experiences and aspirations of each of my listeners.[29] My role is merely to coordinate these manifold impressions, so that we may fairly evaluate the known facts and orient ourselves about their possible development if not their inevitable evolution.

It is really superfluous to seek a definition of the term production. Words would add nothing to what we already know about it, at least nothing useful or, above all, inspiring.

May I be permitted, though, to preface this talk with a kind of warning.

Just as we would choose our seat in the theatre, so I must here first insist that we agree on our basic position.

Usually, when speaking of a well known phenomenon like the theatre, one begins by expounding and analyzing the obvious factors and then leaves them to be developed at will. In this case I must take the opposite route, lest the power of our habits give the words a meaning they do not or should no longer have, and we become entangled in unsolvable misunderstandings. Here is my approach:

I feel obliged to ask you to erase from your memory and so from your imagination everything you know about, and have seen, in the theatre, including the pleasure of being seated comfortably in an orchestra chair in front of the opening curtain! I go even further and urge you to follow me: We must make a clean sweep and forget the house, the stage, even the entire building which encloses them.

The title of this talk must not suggest anything fixed. I repeat: we have made a clean sweep!

Only under those conditions can we take up each one of the elements of staging as such, outside of the stage itself. Then, by reuniting them outside of every fixed or conventional frame, we shall probe into the relationship under which this union can be achieved.

Here is creation in its proper meaning. And without any irreverence we commence with these words: "And the earth was without form and void; and darkness was upon the face of the deep." May my kind listeners however fear no dizziness and trust in me: I am pulling the curtain!

When an author has completed his play, what is the element he feels to be essential to its performance? The actors, unquestionably. Without actors there can be no action, hence no performance, hence no play—except on our bookshelves. The first step in the realization of his play therefore concerns the actor. In space which is "without form and void" the actor represents the three dimensions; he is plastic and so he occupies, accordingly, a fragment of space upon which he imposes his form. But the actor is not a statue; being plastic, he is also alive, and his life is expressed by movement; he occupies space not only by his volume, but also by his movement. His body, alone in unlimited space, measures that space by means of gestures and movements or, more precisely, he thus appropriates a fragment of that space, he circumscribes and conditions it. Remove him, and space becomes again indefinite and elusive. In this sense his body creates space.

It remains for us to command time in a like manner. The movements of the body have a time duration. We speak of "going fast, going slowly." Measuring space then involves measuring time. The living being has taken possession of reality. But all this is still arbitrary; movements are not regulated and their time pattern remains uncertain: a will must in turn subdue and measure them. From our point of view this governing mind is the playwright; he is the evocative force; in his hands the actor is a compass for space, a pendulum for time. The author regulates space and time; that is his formal power (I use the word in the sense of external form). An organic hierarchy results from these facts, which we may name as follows: the author, the actor, (scenic) space. You will observe that I have not mentioned time. And indeed, if the presence of the actor affects space, which the author can only measure through him, time remains in the hands of the author. In other words, the author imposes directly on the actor the time duration of his role, but must depend on the actor to realize that duration in space. This would seem to be self-evident. We shall see, however, that our theatrical anarchy of today is due to our ignorance in this respect.

How can this transfusion of time and its projection into space be achieved?

Let us start from the base of our hierarchy, i.e., the author and his written text. This text is of a certain length and is divided into scenes, each of which has its respective length. Does the author possess any means of specifying the time value of his text definitely enough to impose it on the actor? He has not; the duration of speech is indeterminate; speech may be uttered slowly or rapidly; it may be broken, and so on. These variations occur during a lapse of time that is difficult to span: excessive slowness may destroy the chain of ideas, excessive speed may make them unintelligible; yet between these extremes, there is a wide margin. The author may insert directives into his text for its delivery. We may make use of the metronome for that purpose, but these notes are not part of the text proper, not an integral part of it, and, thank goodness, the metronome cannot be carried onstage! Furthermore, the actor cannot precisely conform to the annotation, nor to the metronome. In short, the author, who ought to control time, does not control it at all; speech does not furnish him the means for such control.

Allow me at this point to recall that tonight we are talking about a purely technical problem that is concerned not with the manner of composing a play but solely with the original material in the hands of the author; thus not with the choice of a situation and the words to express it but with words in general, whatever their specific meaning, just as musical notes are discussed apart from all musical composition.

I hope this is well understood.

The written word in itself does not determine the time element needed for its delivery. The duration of a word is approximate and left to the actor's own free will. . . . Thus the actor, lacking precise time values, projects onstage only a vague space, since space is in accord with time. This reign of willfullness is the hallmark of our modern theatre. The director, the designer, electrician, technician et al., . . . they all work only approximately together, a procedure intolerable in any other art form. The author's will should be the law, yet we know he does not hold all the strings in his hands. Too often he merely prevents them from becoming too entangled.

Theatrical art is said to be extremely complex. That is true. And in view of this fact let us draw a comparison and take as an example the conductor-composer of a symphonic poem with chorus and soloists. For the presentation of this work he is unencumbered by the stage, but he encounters the awesome complexity of orchestra and voices. His composition is written; the singers, all the diverse instruments and musicians of the orchestra are assembled; the score is placed on his stand. He opens it at the first page, lifts his baton, and the integrated rehearsal of his work begins. The singers, having studied their parts in advance, are thoroughly acquainted with them, and so are the orchestra members. This is comparable to the study of roles by the actors in a play and the preparatory work by the designers of settings.

The composer, his hands raised, glances over all the participants to make sure that all are looking at him. Indeed they all are. Then and only then does he give the down beat and do they begin to play their various instruments, and to sing their roles, as an ensemble which, I repeat, is integrated.

Why must he interrupt so often? Because they do not play or sing exactly what he wrote and determined beforehand or they have not properly caught the explicit meaning of the graphic signs he has used, or still more because these signs have not yet awakened the sense of the form and expression implicit in those signs.

Sometimes the conductor, pencil in hand, rushes to the desk of an instrument and adds to its score a new conventional sign which will facilitate the playing.

This is the rehearsal procedure for the conductor-composer. You will note that here the hierarchy suffers no interruption or interference. No tenors direct the orchestra or argue with the conductor, no harpist meddles in the business of the soprano soloist.

The composer is the sole master of the rehearsal. He is the only one to whom the participants listen, or the work will not be performed. And if it is properly executed, the composer alone has decreed it, and he alone sees to it that his will is enforced. His tyranny is absolute; all the participants know it; they can take it or leave it. Why? The orchestra score is set down on paper just like the dramatist's manuscript. The conventional musical signs are equivalent to the letters of the alphabet, and the composer appears to be just as much present as a human being as is the author of a play. Where is the difference? Let us go further and assume the composer is dead, so that the conductor has only the score from which to execute the will of the departed composer. What is it that distinguishes him so decidedly from the director who stages a play of a deceased author? After all the book of a play and the score of a symphony are merely two aspects of conventional writing.

The answer to this question is of the utmost importance, and if I may, I will draw your attention to it. Since we are dealing with conventional signs, it must be that the two cases of signs are totally different. We spoke of the approximate and often indeterminate nature of duration in a written text; the letters of the alphabet and the series of words made of them do not possess, by themselves—or in themselves—the power to establish the definite duration of a speech. The conventional signs of the musical notation have this power. It is in fact their *raison d'être;* if they lacked it, they would not represent music, for music is an art of precision. The conductor of an orchestra possesses in the score, and independently of his own will, the necessary means of translating those signs into the performance in time duration, or a series of time durations, perfectly and definitely determined beforehand. If the participants do not obey, they are no longer executing the score! Where is the dramatist's dominating baton? And even if he had one, who or what would make it authoritative? His text? Does this text contain any directions for the baton? And if the actors, the director et al. are absent-minded or recalcitrant, has this text the power to bring them into line again? And is the piece ruined by the clumsiness of the young leading man or of the painter? Alas! Here is the kingdom of whims. A wrong note, a missed cue, and the music ceases to be what the score says. Have the innumerable stupidities during a stage rehearsal the same effect? What is it then that gives the score this tyrannical influence, this sort of categorical imperative which makes everyone feel that here the question is "to be or not to be?"

Time! Yes! Time is determined in the score but not in the written play. The baton transmits the rhythm of time to the participants. How can this be done for the spoken word? The written score protects those rhythms from any attack. We must admit that the difference between the written work of the dramatist and the written work of the musician is great, so great in fact that the two do not seem to belong in the same category. And yet they both claim to be works of art. Is this claim justifed? The work of art is the result of an ensemble of technical means under the command of a single artist. The artist must grasp in his hands alone, and control by his will alone, the technical means which he considers the prerequisites for his purposes. The value of his work depends on this. To be an artist means, after all, to conceive and to execute a work of art. If this involves a division of labor, the division is only apparent, not real; the artist must always and in everything be the master. The work he offers to the audience is his own work; otherwise it has no place in the realm of art. The musician controls his composition all the way, even in its performance. This essential privilege is denied the dramatic author. The work he offers to the audience is not entirely his own; he does not control his work and cannot, therefore, be an artist. Whatever influence and authority he may have is not implicit in his text.

Let us repeat once more: The musician controls time; the dramatist can merely place his work within time; hence the capricious character of his work. The stage offering him a space not measured by him remains foreign to his manuscript. During the performance the author is well aware of his impotence; he feels it still more painfully when he talks to a painter or a musician during an intermission. . . .

We have now reached not the crux of the problem but rather its true beginning. It would be a waste of time to be concerned with theatrical production if we did not desire to produce a work of art. Its fascination lies, in fact, in that aim. The stage, we all feel, should stir the responsive faculties of the same order as those which a work of art arouses in us. Perhaps we are resigned, but our desire remains nevertheless alive, and we are moved deep within our heart—on our own account—when once, just for a minute, a living performance is presented to us which may have a claim to beauty. I appeal to those who have experienced this emotion and the painful reaction which they suffered. We are deprived (let us be fair, we have deprived ourselves) of the foremost of all arts, the Art of Life. So much so, that the term a "work of art" has come to mean something immobile. . . . Yet movement is such an essential factor of our existence that it must not be excluded from art. Still we curtail art in this respect. In a gymnasium, for instance, movement is sometimes beautiful; yet the casual occasion from which it springs is fortuitous and does not aim at art. In the theatre there are examples that have such an aim; they are rare to be sure, but they may give us hope for beauty in the future; provided, however, that those few examples do not remain isolated.

The problem of staging may thus be categorically stated: how can the dramatic author become an artist, and who can furnish him the means to reach this goal, since he is unable to provide them himself?

We can give an answer only if we no longer conceive of the dramatist's work as divided in two parts: on the one hand, the manuscript, on the other, the stage. The task is difficult; but we shall fulfill it. Let us recall the musician's work and its performance in a concert. The same integrated performance must be obtained for the dramatist.

When we hear a symphonic poem we feel that in its direction and execution there is an element of personal inalienable life completely missing in the lifeless works of art. We owe the dramatist a palette; this palette is alive no doubt and its life seems elusive. Yet the dramatist must hold it in his hand, shield it, and draw upon it at will; at his will alone. The task is to capture the mobility of life for his own use. Space alone is like a canvas beside an empty palette. The canvas needs colors—and, to life, color is movement, that is to say, time. Our

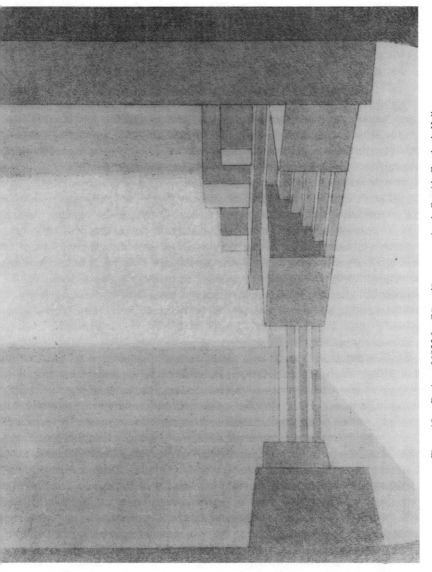

Figure 19.  Design of 1925 for *Götterdämmerung*, Act 1, Outside Gunther's Hall

artist-to-be will be able to choose with his brush the time-durations of movement and to project them on his canvas, i.e., into space. We have seen that the metronome is an artificial device—not an integral part of the text. Today the musical score is the only text known to us which implicitly contains these time values. At the moment we have no other source. Then let us give it to the dramatist; nothing could be more precious to him. With a score space is assured him, for no one lacks space. What he does not yet possess is a method of uniting the two elements. The performance of his drama must achieve this union.

Music has set the dramatist free, but what is its relationship to staging? We said movement. Do its time patterns correspond to the habitual movements of the actor? Not at all, and there's the rub! An agreement acceptable to all concerned must bring them together. The actor's movements indicate his emotions but do not express them. Our forefinger indicating a command does not in itself express driving ambition; nor does a frown express long silent suffering. The actor observes these signs in himself and others and applies them as well as he can to his role; it is part of developing his characterization. Words likewise are indications, symptoms; the phrase "to love" has never expressed what we feel when we love. We may love all our life without ever saying a word about it. We may even be loved and know nothing about it at all (Arvers[30] at least assures us so!). Such is the time value of words: it has no relation to that of our feelings. Our gestures go deeper, but their duration, like that of words, is not necessarily that of our feelings. A thrust with a dagger does not express the long-lasting hatred that leads to this action; it merely demonstrates the hatred. In our daily life we possess no means for a direct expression and therefore we infer indirectly the feelings of which the external life is merely the symptom. Without music the actor is then a bearer of symptoms, nothing more. All the art of a Racine and a Bartet[31] does not suffice to express the character and the predicament of Bérénice. No doubt one or the other, the actor or the playwright, will go beyond what we see and hear in real life. Yet this is only an increase in quantity. One might even say that Racine has forced the events to assume a form in which he could offer the dramatic indications of symptoms. Hence our emotion and also the satisfaction which the actress playing Bérénice must experience; she has time to show these feelings! This may mean a great deal; qualitatively it means very little. For the author of a spoken drama, time serves to augment the symptoms. In this sense he does employ it a little, and the higher the plane on which he places his play, the greater will be his freedom to make use of time.

If music controls time, it must have good reasons and sufficient justification for so doing; otherwise, how could music dare violate so pervasive an element as time? We ourselves are this justification. Shall we accuse an art we ourselves have invented and developed of violence? We ourselves commit that act of violence, and we are driven to it by the overwhelming desire to express ourselves to ourselves. We gladly admit that music expresses what our words and gestures are incapable of expressing. For this purpose we give it every liberty in advance.

What use does music make of time in relation to us? The dramatist enlarges the time-durations in order to focus in them the indications he needs to communicate with us. Music has nothing to enlarge, to prolong; it simply expresses— and its expression takes on the suitable form and time value without previous deliberation. The musician's soul is poured into it and that is its guide. But from the moment this innermost secret is put on paper, music takes command, the musician renouncing it. Music reveals to the listener the form and intensity of his inner life in proportions which he accepts because he is familiar with their origin (we know the deadly boredom we feel if we do not accept them!).

Music can be a remarkable medium between the dramatist's manuscript and the stage. More than that: by controlling the continuity of time-durations, music determines likewise the relative intensities, i.e., their dramatic value. The performer who sings his role no longer needs to interpret it; music does that for him; music imposes its own eloquence upon him. The performer no longer has to grope for his intonation; music imposes it upon him; he need no longer try on his own to bring out a certain passage; music is responsible for this. The performer's silences are indicated to him by the music, which knows above all how to fill those moments! In short, music takes command of the entire drama, projecting only so much of it as is necessary to motivate and sustain its expression. Thus music becomes the supreme regulator of the integral dramatic work; it holds the balance. The hierarchy with which we began contained only three terms: author, actor, scenic space. Music adds the fourth. In fact, by taking over time, music finds its proper place between the author and the performer.

Because of our clean sweep, which led, I admit, to a barren environment, we were able to grasp the essential elements of dramatic art and to place them separately before us. We can now approach the modern theatre without fear of any misunderstandings.

The emancipation of the art of staging is of recent date, so recent indeed that custom still clings to the most progressive experiments. On one and the same stage, simplified modern settings are frequently seen to follow those of the old-fashioned opera. Thus we are in a period of transition; we live in the past as well as the future, and the present fluctuates between the two, often in a void! We notice however that the reforms are applied chiefly to the spoken drama while the musical drama has preserved more or less intact the scenic tradition of the opera. This is a curious fact, but we have an explanation for it. The author of the spoken drama has begun to realize his unfavorable position and the arbitrary staging of his works, and he is trying to restore the place he had in the past and to secure it in the present; having thrown off the yoke of literary traditions, he wants to be free of the scenic shackles as well and thus to replace the pre-established arrangement which his text does not now supply.

Musical drama, on the other hand, seems to us merely a continuation of opera, and we see no need to change its method of staging which has been derived from opera itself. To use the singing voice in presenting a dramatic action appears to us too much like opera to merit a different scenic form. Wagner, for instance, used music; hence his dramas are operas, and so we give them the same kind of settings we give those of Meyerbeer![32] We lump them together with a production style that has no possible organic relation to their scores. In so doing we cut off the flow of musical expression and prevent it from being projected into space. On the one hand we have the orchestra and the singers; on the other, the painted scenery. Under such a system the poet-musician is a dethroned monarch deprived of his authority, though we continue to pay homage to him. His position is painfully abnormally, and our splendid orchestras, our magnificent soloists, only underline this irony. Everything is lavished on the score; nothing on the stage. Our performances of Wagnerian music dramas are merely concerts in which singers move about without motivation while changing dioramas are presented to our eyes.[33] The orchestra stops playing, the voices stop singing; the concert is over, the curtain closes, the diorama disappears: so ends one of those unfortunate exhibitions. Sometimes the music seems to be performed in one hall and the production in another. Music is for us an art for the concert, an art for the ear alone.

Plato proposed that the state be based upon music. How, people will say, could conditions of social life ever be established on the performance of a symphony, let alone an opera! Is the piano not a plague, are our music schools not obsolete institutions? This is all the word music arouses in us: not at all surprising, since opera has developed an absurd, degenerated scenic art for our eyes, and since this art, for its part, has for so long relegated operatic music to an inferior rank. We do not know what music really is. Unfortunately it reciprocates; for it deserted our organism long ago to appeal only to our ears, and we know with what impudence! We have had no wish to include it in our integral life and music in turn is no longer interested in our enfeebled body. How then could the actor function as its interpreter? Music does not even reach him! Yet, I maintain that the vocal cords do not direct the production: hence our directors of lyric drama must lack the most fundamental notions of that art form. In this field everything still needs to be done. We have the grammar but do not consult it; so we speak pidgin English.

Let us return for a moment to the literary play! It attempts to provide what music alone could grant it, and with sure instinct it gives the actor sovereignty. Painted scenery is out; all the scenic material is at last put at the disposal of the living body. It was high time! But the remarkable thing is that music has entered the realm of the spoken drama! With the same stroke that made the three-dimensional presence of the actor supreme, we discarded the setting. A void has resulted, and we resort to music to fill it. Music returns to the actor by the back door. Their close technical kinship cannot escape the author or the director, but they both upset the hierarchy, because they take the word as point of departure. Thus music plays a secondary role; it supports or rounds out the action. Who among us has not felt a shock, unique in its way, when in a play the sounds of music suddenly rang out? Pure, undisguised truth seemed then gently to appear to strip the actor of the tinsel that covered him, of the nonessentials that stifled him.

Truth seemed to whisper: "You allow me to make this brief revelation. So be it! However, I could say more, much more!" And if the spoken word is superimposed upon music, we feel at once how powerless words are. Music always tells the truth; when it lies it says so—but words! Thus, a scene into which music enters, no matter what it may be, is immediately ennobled; fortunately, we have the decency to employ discretion. Such indiscreet melodramas as *L'Arlésienne* or *Manfred* have become embarrassing to us.[34] One does not let a goddess enter just any home with impunity!

This somewhat surreptitious use of music is characteristic also in the need it reveals. Weary of the uninterrupted music of the lyric drama, nevertheless we yearn for its presence; we feel how its expressive power brings the actor's soul far closer to ours. We do not know as yet its stylizing force in space, but we surmise it a little, as does the actor. During the brief moment when the incidental music is heard, his gestures are modified, he feels the divine element penetrate his body, and he would be insensitive if he remained unaffected. This is a step in the right direction; music has a foot in the door. If, for instance, a scene in which music plays its invisible role has been practiced without music, the first rehearsal with music will demonstrate that the entire scene has to be reshaped from a new angle. The capricious nature of the preceding rehearsals has found its master.

The play without music will still live for a long time, perhaps forever; and its staging, vitiated by dead traditions, will be revived through contact with a less specialized art, and will adopt from it new elements at random. But the art of staging can be an art only when music is its source. This does not mean that a spoken drama could not sometimes be performed excellently; it means rather that the degree of excellence remains a matter of chance.

We have now reached two conclusions: the first concerns the source of the play, that is the author; the second, the means of presentation, that is the actor. If the author is to master his art, as any artist must, he should be a musician. If the actor is to dominate space and make it tractable to his moving and plastic body, he must first receive music from the author. We may add that forms in space (including light) will become expressive, that is to say living, only when they are subordinated to the actor (not directly to the author, as we already know). Each of us can ponder these principles. It is no longer a matter of taste, rather of established facts. Those to whom music is an art in concert form will perhaps not like those facts; others who know music is the art of rhythm, order, and general harmony of the Universe, will find their assumptions confirmed by these technical facts. Technique can not err; its laws and their combinations are beyond our understanding. If we disregard these laws it is we who err.

As to dramatic art, we have deceived ourselves for a long time; we have split it up and have clung to that part which, strictly speaking, can exist without the stage. Thus for many, dramatic art rests on the shelves of their library! In that case, of course, it is superfluous to build theatres, to fill newspaper columns with reviews and to cover our kiosks with theatre bills. Let us read plays, and then close the book and think of something else!

Permit me yet to add a few remarks about the dramatic author, the author-musician as he has now become—and about the relation of the actor to the stage. This will enable each of us to devise, in his own way, a production based on the new scheme. I mentioned in passing that in order to accept music, one need not be a musician, one simply has to acknowledge its absolute power, which is indisputable. Furthermore, although we were not always aware of it, our life today tends towards a bodily eurhythmics which is bound to influence profoundly the forms of our thought and the nature of our feeling.

To take music as the source of drama does not imply that musical sounds themselves must be the origin of a dramatic idea, but merely that the object of the music should also be the object of that idea. It does mean the internalization of dramatic feeling, inspired by the assurance that music has the means of expressing the inner life without restraint, and does not have to leave anything to media which can merely indicate the inner life. Such assurance must be the basis of a unified dramatic action. A sculptor can do nothing with the most marvelous block of marble if he has no chisel and hammer. In art the process is the first inspiration of the artist. If he lacks the means to express his vision in three dimensions, he will become a painter or engraver; he will not draw his inspiration from the three dimensions. If the dramatic artist knows he can express to the fullest the conflicts of our inner life (I say express, not merely indicate), that knowledge will inspire in him an action very different from the one suggested by words alone. And if in addition he can rely, as we have seen, upon the externalization of those conflicts in a corresponding space, his whole dramatic vision will be transformed.

Music does not express the phenomenon, but only the inner essence of the phenomenon, writes Schopenhauer; thus it expresses nothing related to his story, geography, social conditions and conventions; no real objects at all. Of all these matters music expresses only the Idea. Human passions are eternal and eternally the same: music proclaims this. The more the passions that the dramatist tries to express are stripped of the fleeting quality of our existence, the more he will find music his benevolent ally. It cannot be disputed that this is the hallmark of art.

Let us proceed to the actor! We have seen that musical expression profoundly modifies the external form of our gestures, i.e., their successive time-durations, and that the actor, therefore, need no longer interpret his part; but present it clearly as it has been entrusted to him. The actor's value will be his compliance; music transfigures him, renders him unable to resist. The bearer of an inner action obviously behaves differently from the interpreter of an action dictated by external contingencies. He first submits to, then accepts, the modifications that are the requirements of art, and in so doing he discovers the secret of his own beauty. Convinced of his wonderful metamorphosis, he tries to find in space whatever can support and enhance his superior mode of living. And thus the actor will dominate the scenery!

We come now to the scenic technique itself, and the conclusions we draw from it will cause you some surprises. I hope they will be pleasant! There is no need now to go all the way back to the Deluge. Our final problem is to animate space through music by the actor who is himself transformed and transfigured by musical dimensions.

First we had to make a clean sweep. Now we shall take the opposite approach and begin with the stage as it is in our conventional theatre, yet without losing sight of this study's purpose nor crowding our treatise with superfluous technical details.

The floor of our stage resembles a portable and transformable shelf in a library. The proscenium arch facing the spectator takes up about half of the total height of the whole stage apparatus, so that the floor is a flat surface suspended between two more or less empty spaces. One often says that "the boards (the floor boards of the stage) represent the world." It would be more appropriate to apply this term to the entire stage house from the roof to the basement. The spectator sees only a fragment of the entire stage. The principal element of our staging is, as we know, the painted setting, cut in pieces and arranged in sections, one behind another, to afford perspective. And since the parts of this setting must constantly make room for others, these canvas pieces are suspended in the flies or are stored in the basement so that they can easily be lowered or raised to the stage. The stage floor is divided into small, equal segments that can be opened to let the canvas pieces rise from the basement or let those onstage disappear there. The intermediate position of the floor makes this mobility possible. Yet many stages still have a rigid apparatus whose only flexibility lies in the height of the stage granted for the hanging pieces and in the trap doors, which are often quite large.

However, in recent theatre buildings the stage floor has been given a minimum of rigidity without the use of movable platforms; the floor can be lowered or raised, as a whole or in part.[35] Certain stage floors even have a built-in turntable whose diameter is slightly larger than the proscenium opening, on which several settings are mounted at the same time and are rotated so as to appear one after another within the proscenium frame. Thus a play with several settings can be prepared entirely in advance and may unfold in front of the audience like a picture book.[36] With our system of painted flats the maximum flexibility of the floor remains valuable and desirable.

Upstage the setting is enclosed by a full painted backdrop, and the flies moreover can be masked by a canvas piece forming a ceiling at a more or less right angle to the vertical flats or wing pieces. The same arrangement on both sides and upstage. The setting then resembles a sort of fly-cage. . . . The practicable pieces alone are three-dimensional; they are placed before or between the vertical flats for the use of the actors; the term "practicable" applies to everything that is plastic and hence conforms with the plasticity of the human body. What is impracticable in these practicables, alas, is the task of bringing them into accord with the fictitious painted setting. No device can conceal this incongruity.

There remains lighting. Because the stage space is dark, it is imperative to illuminate and illuminate well the painted canvases. Such painting presents shadows and highlights simulating some plasticity; shadows as well as highlights must be visible, so they have to be illuminated! There are two kinds of light for a painted setting: one is fixed on canvas by fictitious painting; the other, installed to make the painting visible. The painted light cannot strike the actor, though it concerns him; the real light hits him, though it concerns only the painting! And in such an environment we place the living, plastic and moving body of the actor. A light that is not designed for him strikes him, and on the other hand he moves in front of painted light! He is visible, but that is all. There is still the lower area to be lighted, otherwise the painting would be only partially visible. This is the task of the footlights, but they too hit the actor. Controlling all this fine lighting is like playing an organ or piano, which can be directed and varied as a whole or in part.

On occasion the painting receives light by transparent means; for this effect the canvas must be painted and prepared accordingly. (In Bayreuth the fire descending from the rock of the Walkyrie in the first scene of act 3 of *Siegfried* grows ever more menacing; this is done by progressively showing through the backdrop the parts of the mountain, which represent the stream of fire painted on a transparency.)

After light comes color. A painting is free to use whatever color suits it, whereas the best equipped theatres have scarcely more than three or four colors on tinted glass for their light effects. Everything else is haphazard.

That is the scenic material available in our repertory theatres. It is difficult to imagine a more contradictory combination, and it is a miracle that we obtain with it the visual effects we are accustomed to. Yet whenever the curtain opens on a setting without actors or whenever the picture remains empty for a moment, the overall effect is usually acceptable. The painting, well lighted, fulfills its purpose; its fictitious relief and perspective create an illusion, and the cut-out canvas pieces cleverly arranged are combined advantageously. And since it is the actor who draws our eyes to the bottom of the picture, in his absence we are quite willing to be lenient toward the inevitable and clumsy contact of the perpendicular painting with the horizontal stage floor. We let our eyes wander elsewhere. If in an art gallery, where we have just admired beautiful frescoes or marvelous tapestries, a group of people should appear, circulate, or sit down to talk or sing in front of those pieces, and we were told to consider the subjects represented in these paintings or embroideries as related to those people, we would question the good sense of our guide. But who would dare accuse our stage directors of foolishness?

This is the irreconcilable inconsistency to which we must apply our first attempts at a reform. We shall then notice that by altering one of the production elements we distort all others. If light were to be directed on the actor alone, the painting would suffer so much that it might as well be eliminated; the same would be true of the stage floor and its practicable pieces. The least effort in favor of the actor would tend everywhere to oust the painter. But the actor cannot be eliminated! What is the solution to such a dilemma? This is the whole problem: either the actor or the painting! And the current reform is primarily concerned with the extent of the environment and the number of objects that may be represented by painting without too much detriment to the actor: for after all something, some location, must be shown.

Those among my listeners who remember only productions of drawing-room comedies are probably astonished. With few exceptions the rooms in which their action occurred were in tune with their sets of furniture and with the presence of the actor. And since facial expression plays a major role in this type of play, the footlights do not disturb them. Perhaps so; but does this mean that every dramatic action must take place in an enclosed space broken up by doors and windows? And what is to be done if a garden is called for in one of those plays? Well, you will say, we know that trees cannot be transported onto the stage and, in the last analysis, the actor takes priority. Quite so! The theatre is therefore a place for conversation, and it matters little where the people talk, provided they can be clearly seen and heard. Then why have the stage at all and its artifices; why separate the auditorium from the stage? Why not have a simple place well lit and acoustically good? Expenses would be so reduced that theatres could be built in all corners of the city. The theatre would become the last asylum for conversation.

Figure 20. Design of 1922 for *Hamlet*, Act 1, Scene 1

Nothing can be said against this; it means the deliberate selection of one form of dramatic art and the espousing of it to the exclusion of the others. It might happen in the future, and this very clear division of work would be justified; for the majority, however, it will seem insufficient. Rightly or wrongly, the majority, like all majorities, will consider the whole range of passions too complex to find an outlet and expression in simple conversations; for the majority considers space a thing in itself whose influence is not to be denied, let alone scorned. It also believes that we possess yet other, more powerful means for the expression of our inner life because not all the manifestations of life are reflected in words; and lastly, that dramatic art must express these manifestations of life as an integral whole. So let us admit that the drawing room comedy poses no scenic problem, and let us look at the situation from a somewhat broader view.

Reform was applied first to lighting, while everything else remained unaltered, and the footlights became the scapegoat. They affect the lower part of the setting where the actors move; thus the footlights make them perfectly visible; no facial play escapes us. We call this "seeing well"!—Facial expression does not occur in isolation; on the contrary, it is correlated to the bearing of the head, to each one of our gestures and our attitudes. This general mobility must not only be visible; it must also be as expressive as possible; the plastic effect is therefore one of the conditions of expression, and this plasticity results always and everywhere from contrasting shadows and highlights except, of course, when we touch an object, but unfortunately we do not touch the actors!

The actor, already immersed in the general illumination that suppresses shadows, finds himself in addition struck by light from below which definitely destroys any last trace of shadow that might remain. It is like a drawing room replete with chandeliers and brackets, the floor of which is brightly lit. People will cut a poor figure in such a room and seem suspended between heaven and earth. Such is the actor's relation to the footlights. Without plasticity his whole body resembles a flat painting. So everything is done to reduce the actor to two dimensions! Yet the mobility of his features is in three dimensions! If you suppress the plasticity of his body, you must replace it with something else; just as the photographer, who has the lens focused on his subject's eyes, must retouch the resulting exaggerated detail of the other features. The actor makes up his face according to his particular role and that face moves us! But the eyes cannot be made up. Thus we have painted features around the eyes which maintain their natural expression, even though blinded by too bright a light.

This is, I repeat, what we call "seeing"! And we dare to invoke the theatrical perspective to find an excuse for this criminal treason against humanity! Eager to see all of the actor, we end by seeing very little of him. The example of the footlights has confirmed the fact that what we call "seeing" is childish nonsense. Like children, we want to hold an object instead of looking at it, and when we have it in our hand we no longer see it. Step by step, the use of footlights was considerably reduced. The patrons protested; their cherished habits had been interfered with. It seems they could not "distinguish very clearly." But the monkey was not the one who held the lantern.

The scenic painter presumed, therefore, that he could easily bungle his job without being caught; in fact, his traditional virtuosity had the worst of it. Today color remains his sole resource, if we except line wherever it can harmonize with the stage floor (which at last has become genuinely practicable). The scene painter, in the common sense of the word, is but the virtuoso of an instrument that has been cast onto the junkheap. For a while he will still survive because of traditional inertia, then he will disappear like the artist of historical and narrative paintings.

Let us state again: lighting has determined the entire stage reform, and come to the support of the actor. Thus we were forced after all to regard him as the very first element in the hierarchy of representation; the fragile wavering setting, as I have described it to you, cannot hold its own against him.

The actor's authority has initiated a period of normal hierarchy. We are still groping, to be sure, but this time we are on solid ground. We still lack the technique but no longer the principle. Heroic efforts by Pitoëff, Gordon Craig, Stanislavsky, and Copeau[37] prove this. For each of them, in his own way and his own particular field, ranks living man first among all the other elements!

The ground is firm, but it is also immense; and here our stage directors sometimes go astray. They throw out the baby with the bath, as the Germans say, and often nothing of importance remains . . . which is far from being bad; it is better to add with care than to stifle with nonessentials. The remarkable thing is that the reform was initiated in the theatres for plays, dances and pantomime. In dance and pantomime, the human body is then the medium of expression with music and without speech; in plays, it is the interpreter of the spoken action without music. On the one hand, music reigns supreme; on the other, the visual action of the drama is elevated to become the equal of speech. The two extremes adopted the hierarchy. The other art forms, however, remained more or less in the old tradition. When we leave a production of Pitoëff to attend *The Walkyrie,* we tumble from extreme modernity into the most abject routine. Where indeed the governing element must dominate, we deny it authority, except—listen well—where the dramatic action is subordinated to bodily expression. Nothing is more instructive.

The conclusion to be drawn is that music is not yet recognized as the basic regulating element, unique in its kind of power, while the actor has gained a supremacy not justified by the spoken word alone because the word cannot regulate. If we therefore instinctively ascribe the rediscovered hierarchy to bodily expression we do so probably because this hierarchy must directly derive from our living body in order to be installed as final law. In short, despite

Wagner and his imitators, the lyric drama does not furnish us the foundation we expected of it, and music will triumph in the theatre only through the intermediary of bodily feeling—exclusive, for the time being at least, of the dramatic element, which we at first regarded as the indispensable source of inspiration.

Bodily feeling all by itself belongs to sport and gymnastics. To give it the character of art we must modify it. We know that music alone can do this, and so, in the end, we are once again face to face with music and the living body, but this time in full knowledge of the cause and with no preoccupation except to unite them forever in a harmony whose exalted significance and happy future we already anticipate.

So considered, the relationship of music to bodily art is of the utmost concern (I call upon your instructors to testify in this matter), for obviously a reciprocal subordination demands sacrifices. I cannot deal with this question here, but intend to do so in a lecture especially devoted to it. I shall likewise bring up the disturbing problem of an organism so saturated with music that it can free itself from music's tutelage!

The union of body and music is primarily a question of procedure; we shall see then whether that union does not considerably broaden the very Idea of theatre. All of us know, I am sure, the value of the Jaques-Dalcroze method! No, let us not call it a method! This is a shabby word for something so beautiful! Let us just say eurhythmics, please! The advantage of eurhythmics over any other procedure is that it does not seek beauty; beauty rather is its principle. Everything considered, it is therefore not a professional training (I hope our dear professionals bear me no grudge). It is a human discipline which establishes in us a harmonious equilibrium through the medium of our body. It affects our whole being and thus corresponds with musical art which affirms the correlated unity of soul and body through harmony and rhythm, the expression both of our soul and of its concrete existence.

Here, it seems, we have the perfect procedure to prepare our body to express music on stage and thus gradually to establish the elements of a revived theatrical art. But . . . why in the theatre whose progress is so slow, exposed as it is to so many obstacles irrelevant to art? And the stage separates the performers so pitifully from the audience! Great ideas always have a personal origin and in the beginning are championed by a small number of courageous personalities! The masses have no will of their own; they must be guided to it: a forest is no substitute for a signpost. Please, will you not be the signpost?

To return to our theme, why should staging be the exclusive prerogative of theatre? Does our body really need to tread the boards? Must it really exhibit itself? Without barring the well-intentioned spectator who is anxious to learn,

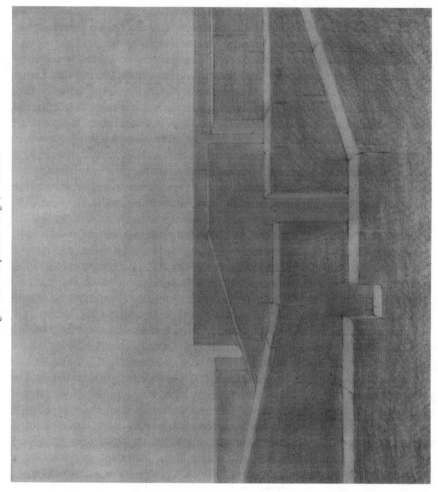

Figure 21.   Rhythmic Design, "Scherzo"

let us not regard him as indispensable for living art, for which we alone are responsible after all. We always imagine "we are going to perform" when we prepare the proper space for our plastic movements. This is wrong. "To perform" is indeed something quite different! Do I have to tell you this? All of us feel it; perhaps you are not yet conscious of it. For you "to perform" means to add to and for your body artificial and arbitrary elements in space which are alien to it and frequently degrading. Here you are in the very school to learn how to avoid those appendages. Here you learn precisely not "to perform." On the other hand, surely nothing prevents you from taking hold of space and subordinating it to the proportions and harmony you have established in yourselves. If you obtain satisfactory or remarkable results, you will not wish to exclude those who do not enjoy such great privileges. This will not be theatre at all. Quite the contrary, it is definitely its negation; for your wish to share your enjoyment opens the curtain wide and makes you step across the footlights once and for all!

There is no reason for me to continue and elaborate on a subject you know better than I. You are the first to know your possibilities and your true limitations; the very first, above all, to wish to maintain them!—Let me close, not without emotion, to be sure, with the following words:

The future of our theatre is based on living art. You are the fortunate representatives of this art. Its future lies in your hands. The wonderful renaissance of dramatic art depends upon your efforts and your integrity!

# Monumentality

(1922)

*Revue d'esthetique,* Oct.–Dec. 1953

When we arrive in Florence, is our attitude different from the one we have when we enter a museum? How can we not see that regardless of all the great impressions we receive, such an attitude leaves the soul empty.[38] Even before we reach these real places, which after all are perfectly concrete, we transfer them into the past. Then, what are they doing here under our very eyes in the present? What business is it of ours to go visit them if we deny them reality?

"These great witnesses of the past," so the saying goes. Now, come on! Does it never occur to us that they are great witnesses of the present as well? Why don't we even think of that? Do we believe that by scanning the *Baedeker,*[39] or taking home photographs of all those stones and those canvases, we become part of this present?

Our conception of art remains that of the collector and historian. Little does it matter that architecture cannot be confined to halls open only at certain hours; we are more than willing to create such halls in our imagination. Who dares say that he brings back a living and harmonious synthesis of Italy? On the one hand we stuff ourselves with what we call art; on the other we somehow enjoy, or are interested in, watching the Italian people. Who would think of establishing any relationship between the crowd in the Via Calzaioli and the square of the Signoria or the campanile of Giotto . . . ? Where then do we locate the notion of the present that is nevertheless so evident? In ourselves? Can we seriously feel capable of establishing the least trace of harmony between the Signoria[40] and ourselves? If this is the case, why do we need so many commentaries, explanations and data? Ruskin[41] fully sensed this! Yet he deceived himself with a supreme illusion when he tried to evoke from the shadows of the past a real present, to extricate from these stones some degree of contemporary affirmation. Alas, these stones, do they not, on the contrary, cry out to us in their tragic neglect? Do we not feel that they will never be there for our happiness?

We laugh at the caricature of *Madame Bucholz in Italy*[42] and do not suspect that it is the caricature of all of us. There is a difference in quantity, but certainly not in quality. The artists—in particular the German artists—who came to Rome a century ago were more sincere than we. They resolutely divided Italy into two parts: the works of art and the Italian people. Since, at that time, life had still preserved something picturesque, the separation was less noticeable than it is today. Yet it certainly caused Goethe considerable suffering. He was the prototype of active life; for him poetry was the upshot of "circumstances," his most striking flashes of intuition were all related to the moment and the day; everywhere and always he sought to establish organically the best possible living synthesis. How could the human problem of the monumentality in art not have filled Goethe with anguish? In his time and in his native country the problem did not reveal itself in the same way as it does to us. For the Germans of his day, Italy represented a revelation to which one willingly surrendered for cultural enjoyment. It provided, moreover, the only possibility of awareness of one's own artistic insignificance. Today the arts of reproduction and the railroads have enlightened us; the historians, literati, artists, guides, and the *Baedeker* carry us smoothly into the center of the Italian "Museum." Thus we arrive in Italy loaded with baggage that hampers each of our steps, impairs each of our impulses. Then we return home, and when we unpack our presumed riches we are quite surprised to find nothing new in our suitcases! Pardon me, I am mistaken: all the documents we took along are pressed into a tight bundle, and an empty space is left. Our daily life will never fill it. And yet that void is waiting for Life. We took everything, brought back everything, except Life! And so the sincere souls—quite a rare species—return disappointed. Why be surprised? Are they not like Faust pressing Helena in his arms and noticing that he embraces merely the dress without the body which would fill it and give life to it? It is as in the Louvre in winter, when we have walked through a large museum peopled by the needy who go there to get warm.

The intellectual has been compared to an old-fashioned purse in which the gold is kept only in one corner by a ring, while the other part of the purse hangs loose and empty like Helena's dress; Faust represents, of course, the hypertrophic brain full of gold. By this token, all of us are intellectuals when confronted with a work of art. We wander through the galleries of paintings, the halls of sculptures, like puppets made of matchsticks afflicted with hydrocephalus. And we push our unconscious insolence to the point of surveying the architecture with this lifeless body—an architecture conceived for the living body! Our display cases properly shelter the Greek amphora, but where is the wine to fill them? Where are the lips to touch them?

Everyone knows that nine-tenths of Italian architecture is veneer. The model of this type is in Florence; Santa Maria del Fiore is but a huge cardboard box topped by an admirable cupola that is doubtless rather surprised at the peculiar pedestal forced upon it. Let us enter: the cardboard has given way to architecture, a sinister kind if you like, but certainly architecture. Naturally the interior of a Catholic church clearly implies human actions that cannot be truly consummated in a cardboard environment, since the human body has three dimensions, freely expressed. Veneer, on the other hand, would suffice for anything two-dimensional. We should frequently have two buildings before our eyes for comparison: the cathedral of Florence and the Parthenon. Any commentary would then be superfluous. As long as the human race exists, the Parthenon will never be an anachronism; for it sprang from the living body that will always be recognized in it. But what shall we do with buildings distorted from the very outset by an artificial and nonviable culture or else designed so exclusively for a single period of mankind that their survival in the ensuing periods is achieved only by corruption? He who considers the cathedral of Florence beautiful is a collector; he who feels at ease in the square of the Signoria is a barbarian. The Parthenon is not beautiful, it is living; and life does not require an epithet. I select these examples because they are well known and particularly conclusive.

And sculpture? Those who despise museums would like to set it up in the streets and crowd our public buildings and private homes with it. Why should sculpture be there, and what would it do there? Are we in the least concerned about sculpture? And even if we tried to care about it, where would we find the criterion for our judgment? Architecture cannot be measured with the same yardstick. Where shall we look for it? Alas, we have lost it.

And painting? Since it remains immobile, it too belongs to the monumentality of art. To make painting portable, we have divided it into sections of flat surfaces; and, in the absence of architecture, to enclose them, we have set these fragments in gilded frames. Then we assemble them against walls, likewise flat surfaces without even frescoes . . . and we gaze upon this beautiful arrangement! In our own homes this absurdity is still conceivable, for even under the most favorable conditions, our daily existence itself is segmented, detached, and uprooted. But in our museums? And yet, let us not speak ill of them; indeed they save us. Our museums whisper into the ears of those who can hear their judicious voices: "Now don't fuss so much; after all, we spare you the obligation of being utterly deceitful; perhaps we are even the only ones who speak the truth. Whatever you do not dare admit, even in a low voice, we shout over the roofs in your behalf and with your sanction!" Yes, to disavow our museums would mean to be blind and deaf, to consent to an even greater decadence. Fortunate the painting, the sculpture that finds a refuge in our galleries. And woe the architecture whose splendor, once it is dead, corrupts the active Life or deludes it with its decomposed organisms.

Lately a famed foreign architect confided to me the agonies of his profession. "You see," he told me, "the freedom from want which my country enjoys permits me to build for the future; but, unfortunately, this does not imply predicting this future with any certainty. You can discard your scenery, your temporary frames which are no longer suitable. I pile up stones; and if I err in my forecasting, these stones stand there nevertheless to testify to my error and to warp the public conception. Every work of art that does not directly correspond to the need of the living becomes eventually corruptive. This is my conviction and I shall go still further. I am of the opinion that monumental art, as we know it, has finished its life; it is no longer alive, only vestigial. We are entering a new era in which art will demand that we live in it, and we, in turn, shall require art to live in us. When this magnificent reciprocity has been definitely established, when it has become almost so automatic that we can no longer conceive art without it, a monumental art form will probably develop as the supreme expression of this reciprocity. It can be assumed that, after a period of great development, this art form, like those of the past, will run the risk of stultification. However, since this new monumentality will have been the work of artists conscious of their responsibility—which has hitherto not been the case except in Greece—their creations will in all likelihood bear the imprint of this awareness, and so will enjoy a certain immunity: their reality will no longer be historical like that of our buildings, but will always preserve enough positive and contemporaneous vitality to guide taste instead of paralyzing and corrupting it. Now you understand why every new assignment means a new anguish for me!"

I asked my speaker what he meant by sense of responsibility among Greek artists, especially their architects. "They did not search," he answered, "for their inspiration in doctrines, in personal tendencies towards mysticism or sensuality, in a taste for pomp and luxury, or even in the desire merely to please and obey their superiors. They candidly began with the living human body, convinced that the architect must serve the body, be justified by the body. Therefore their buildings are immortal! The architects felt their responsibility towards the body. Art will never endure unless it derives from a sense of close human solidarity. The Greek temples and theatres are typical examples of this. The Romans created theirs with the fundamental triviality of the Latin race. Our own cathedrals remain the last majestic echo of the principle of solidarity; their presence in the midst of our dwellings is like a silent challenge. It is significant that today one speaks of the cathedral of the future. The survival of these imposing buildings keeps alive our memory of their basic function and challenges us to restore this function anew at a time when we desperately aspire to join together."

I asked my interlocutor what he thinks of the monumentality in Paris. "That is precisely what I was going to tell you; I see that our thoughts run the same way! Paris enjoys such a corrosive gastric juice that it dissolves, absorbs, and transforms the toughest elements into living substance. The problem of monumentality does not seem to exist in Paris. Errors like the Trocadero, for instance, are recognized as errors and thereby become a part of life. This sounds like a miracle, and I might be inclined to believe that the monumental unity of this city—a unity said to be incomparable—stems from its power to assimilate its monumentality. Furthermore, the Parisian knows, above all else, how to live; and if the tower of Saint-Jaques is dead he envelops it with such an intensity of daily living that he actually breathes into it a semblance of life. We should remember also his need for ceremonies and his genius for creating names. For the Parisian any name belonging to the city of Paris takes on the value of a type; his innate sense of form permits him to force upon the whole world any proper name of his city as though it were the name of a person worthy of consideration. If we translate, for instance, the name 'Tuileries' into German, making it 'Ziegeleien' (brick or tile-works) we suddenly notice its vulgar meaning and realize that Paris has compelled all of us nevertheless to connect this name with images of power and lustre. One way or another, Paris invariably knows how to link its monuments to a living presence, even those monuments which would seem to be the most exclusively historic ones. Its bustling and flexible life struggles against disintegration and slows it down. Paris will no longer be Paris when it weakens to the point of abandoning this struggle, whose wonderful secret it holds.

"Every city has two or three proper names conveying somehow a typical character, but I know some very important ones whose various names are antonyms, as it were, for example Munich and Dresden. The type formed only locally and by custom must not be confused with the type existing in and by itself. If all the street names in Munich were altered, its burghers would be bewildered but the image of the city would in no way be changed. Munich is justly considered a unique city; yet its originality comes from the kind of life one leads there. The Münchner has not been able to give its buildings the stamp of his personal life. Therefore we have, on the one hand, the Münchners and their typical way of life, and on the other, the buildings of their city. There is no lasting contact between them, and the inhabitant's existence is marked more by the continuity of his actions than by the setting in which he moves. A Parisian, by contrast, cannot talk about the slightest happenings of his existence, of his day, of his plans, without intermingling his talk with names of streets and neighborhoods. For him, this is not only a matter of contact but almost of identity. Therefore, he finds himself lost wherever contact is missing. To live in the Via Tornabuoni in Florence means simply to live in this street and to enjoy the beautiful name it bears, but the street and its name no longer have any contact with the current Florentine life. To live in the Quartier Saint-Georges in Paris, on the other hand, means living in a very specifically contemporary world, apart from any historic or monumental considerations. There is no doubt that this makes the Parisian the worst of tourists: he wants the active and palpable life, and he wants to live it himself. The tourist, however, is only a spectator wrapped up in his own atmosphere wherever he happens to be. He lives only through reactions—as the expression of his face sadly proves, for one cannot react continuously as a tourist's existence apparently necessitates."

To engage my architect further I asked him another question. "If you were free to act as you please, what kind of building would you erect?"

He jumped up as if thrust by a spring: "To begin with, I would not consult myself! I would try—as I have always done—to fathom the life of my contemporaries, to discover their drives, their successes, their defeats. Like a professor I would carefully examine the implements used by the student for his work. I would seek to remove the useless or misleading ones without arousing his suspicion and put within his reach instead those which he needs. Should it become imperative, I would guide his hand a little, but I always prefer not to put any intermediary between the work and the hand holding the tool. Wait, I have not finished, and I know what you are going to ask. You would like to know the form of my buildings. I repeat, I would not begin with me but with them. Formerly the social classes, the trades, and the profession rarely overlapped; the needs of each group were clearly circumscribed. One remained in one's place, and the cut of a garment or the plan of a house revealed one's social standing. Monumentality prevailed, and uncertainty was impossible; the outline was provided and the architect's imagination had to work within it. However, a limitation voluntarily accepted is always a factor of freedom; hence that imagination produced the maximum possible, as we all know.

"We mistakenly believe ourselves still free, and consequently continue to accept limitations which were overthrown long ago. Thus we resemble a court clerk whose papers have been irremediably mixed up and who, in order to keep up appearances, continues to file them in little piles in an obsolete cabinet without further checking them. In the schools of architecture, we learn how to build the different cardboard boxes in this nest of drawers as if each of the labels corresponded to documents that should be filed there. But our documents are mixed up or exist no longer. What are we to do now? Here begins the tremendous responsibility of the modern architect—and his crime, if he ignores this responsibility.

"Our court clerk kept a filing cabinet in order to maintain his reputation for accuracy. We do the same. In spite of the change in our social and private life, we hold on tenaciously to an outmoded classification. This is only too evident. You will tell me that compromise is necessary in certain fields, and that it may help restore the sinner to virtue by letting him cling to a semblance of methodical procedure which eventually may lead to some sort of resolution. I do not believe so; a delusion is short-lived, no matter what one may say. In this case, the maintenance of the delusion renders any normal evolution impossible. Our activities are no longer so differentiated as they were formerly. By keeping each one within too restricted a framework we distort them all; the restraint they must endure in order to be kept, in appearance at least, within the compartment forced upon them, makes their evolution unhealthy. The unhealthiness of our architecture and that of our activities go hand in hand.

"Our disbelief in the influence of buildings upon the activities of those for whom they are designed causes the gravest harm to those activities. Thus you see what the architect's responsibilities are. On the one hand, he is bound to follow the course of social evolution; on the other, to affect that evolution by suggestion, which means he must often be ahead of it. His inspiration must derive from an intuitive understanding of all aspects of society, which presumes quite a rare degree and extent of culture. Yet our schools of architecture are not concerned with this at all. Modern architectural studies should consist of two sections: pure technique, and a general survey of contemporary civilization and culture, with the aim of stimulating the intuition expected of architects. This second part would be completely international, embracing the experiments made in all countries. Their timeliness, their success, and their future would be discussed. Toward the end of the studies, the two sections might well be combined in one course in which practical conclusions would be attempted. If a final competitive examination is planned for the courses, one of the first subjects I would suggest to the students would be a meeting place for a city of about 50,000 inhabitants. The social and geographical character of this city would have to be precisely stated, so the student could clearly perceive everything which these given data leave to his own judgment and to his initiative as a living person. I have no doubt about the first practical result of such studies. Permit me to point it out again!

"The idea of monumentality, which we have extended to include sculpture and painting, can and must be further enlarged. But for this purpose it must be carefully defined so as to apply almost exclusively to the present. We shall see why.

"Every work is monumental which relies on duration rather than on immediate suitability; consequently monumental works are planned to stimulate the admiration of men rather than earning their gratitude. This idea has a certain manifest application in all human activities. The music of a patriotic festival is monumental when the composer sacrifices the effect desirable at the moment to the abstract existence of a score which, to his mind, must survive the forever fleeting performance. The score by Gustave Doret[43] for the winegrowers' festival in Vevey is a typical example. In this sense we have no music as yet appropriate to such grand celebrations; hitherto none of our musicians was ready to sacrifice his fame and profits for the initiation of what we might call an outdoor style—that is, a style for great crowds, a style that can never be reduced in order to make it popular, and whose rigid annotations (as musicians know well) would be understood only by professionals. A committee is monumental when it sacrifices to its pretentious existence the particular efficient and recognized initiative of a manager who must act alone. A theatre is monumental when its construction consumes all available funds, leaving nothing for the staging of good productions, which were after all, the sole purpose for the building and should have been the first consideration. The diploma is monumental when it is granted on the basis of an examination which is known to be no test of the true capabilities of a student. Monumental is the deluxe edition of a work which because of its character must be handy and easily accessible to all; or a bookbinding that makes the common use of a volume impossible. Again and above all, we create the monumental when we give a definite plan to a building that is supposed to lend itself, on the contrary, to continuous transformations and thus to conform in space to the development of works whose nature is to remain resilient and indefinite.

"I have intentionally emphasized the depreciatory meaning of this term, since we have too frequently forgotten this meaning and make the monumental exclusively synonymous with grandeur and solemn beauty. However, the principle of duration and persistence inherent in it is not always to be rejected. For example the written and transmissible notation of Shakespeare's dramas is monumental! The persistence of Christianity through the centuries is monumental, but what would we now do without it? The score of *The Ring of the Nibelungs,* which Wagner wanted to burn after his third draft, is monumental. I have already mentioned the salutary and inspiring monumentality of our cathedrals.

"Perhaps you notice that the term can be applied in an opposite way, for instance, a structure that anticipates the future and for which certain demands of the present are ignored by the architect because he considers them short-lived compared with the great aspirations he foresees in the near future; such a structure has the right to monumentality. I can now resume my definition (actually too partial to the negative and reprehensible side) of this great principle by asserting that in any field every positive realization of an idea is monumental whenever it corresponds no longer, or not yet, to strictly contemporary needs. Its presence, as we have just seen, can have a regrettable, even corrupting influence—or on the contrary, a stimulating, prophetic or merely foreshadowing effect, through the strength it accumulates and holds in reserve. The crux of the matter is then to be able to distinguish—and, for the architect, the task is exceedingly delicate.

"Let us assume, for example, that he receives a commission to build a people's theatre. For many of us this term will evoke the picture of a modest building at low cost. If we turn then to details, the house will have to be furnished with cheap seats and the stage equipped for inexpensive productions. What do you think of that? . . ."

"Sorry, this is too obvious," I replied, "but having some ideas of my own on this subject I am all the more anxious to learn yours!"

"I doubt," my speaker answered, "that our aims are very different. It may be, however, that you have not had the courage to follow them to their final consequences or, at least, to accept those consequences. And here the principle of monumentality is going to support us as much by prohibiting certain arbitrary fancies as by sanctioning daring ventures which we would perhaps not have dreamed of without it.

"First allow me to be a little pedantic. Language—French especially—is painfully slow in following our rapid evolution; to be sure, it has not foreseen the evolution, and, therefore, we must constantly and precisely define the new meanings which we are obliged to give to old words. 'People's theatre,' though it seems a simple term, contains two ideas, both of which are about to undergo a complete change. Dramatic art has burst the frame that held it rigid for so long, and the very idea of theatre has so enlarged that it gives us vertigo and a slight feeling of anarchy. The idea of 'people' too is no longer circumscribed and now resembles a sort of amorphous and tentacled nebulous shape.

"Do we understand by 'people's theatre' a place for performances accessible to every purse? Or rather a stage under a more or less despotic censorship either with a prudent and conservative aim, or, contrariwise, a radically progressive one? Would such a theatre have to exclude works difficult and expensive to mount?

"These considerations do not even come close to the problem as it currently presents itself; therefore, my use of the phrase 'people's theatre' is a misnomer. There can no longer be a 'people's theatre' for these two words have become meaningless; they denote a 'monumental' form of the past. Unable to seize precisely the demands of the present, we have to realize an idea of the future, which naturally will appear 'monumental' until the social and artistic evolution justifies and rejoins it, discovering in it a ground already prepared.

"Yet my project would be unanimously rejected if I did not take the present into account. Here a question of accommodation arises, which even verges on what we call cunning . . . : in my project I must play down the elements of the future which it does not include but which it must suggest. On the other hand, I must somewhat artificially emphasize those elements that concern the reforms already considered desirable. This see-saw game need not make sense to anyone but myself. But how can I achieve, under such delicate and complex conditions, a harmony that has nothing arbitrary in it? How can I create the impression of a necessity which in itself creates conviction, which can influence public opinion and guide the taste toward the future, the very future I have to foresee and for which I have to prepare? Where can I begin? Which direction do I take? This is when I return to our two types of buildings—the Florentine cathedral and the Greek temple! How can we hesitate? It is quite obvious that the Greeks have given us the direction forever. Let us then begin, like the Greeks, with the living man and reconsider the proposition in these words: the people and the theatre!

"Strangely enough, with this new phrase a more precise definition is not necessary. By beginning with the people we have defined it; by subordinating the idea of theatre to the people we have made ourselves masters of this idea. My task as architect will then begin with a search to discover what kind of theatrical auditorium is needed by a modern community, and, on the other hand, what mission this auditorium has to suggest to the community. The School of Fine Arts did not teach me this, and I must still find out everything.

"Before anything else, we must first recognize that a modern community is no longer passive. The theatre, as it has been understood, is a school of passivity for the spectator; consequently it can no longer suit a modern audience. What part of the theatre encourages audience passivity? Unquestionably the actors. The position given to the actor exercises a direct influence upon the spectator, and we must first change this position. Its most typical aspect is the actor's remoteness from the audience, stressed inside the house by the foot-lights, outside by separate entrances and, in general, by a way of life that is far removed from the spectator's own. The audience, for its part, lazily perpetuates the habit of paying for and choosing its seat, then of expecting the actor to do everything else. However, these conditions are an anachronism, and the actor, as well as the audience, can no longer consent to such humiliating relations.

"Between the two is the play, the production, whose existence hitherto has of course depended on this activity of the actor and this passivity of the spectator. Yet the concept of a production has gradually changed since the once-legitimate conditions of its existence have been transformed. The actor now tries to bridge the distance separating him from the audience in order to fulfill his desire for activity, which is easier for him than it is for the audience, because the actor is active by definition. Since a work depends on the dramatic author and the stage director, these two persons have aided the actor in many ways to make possible, even desirable, a new rapport between actor and audience.

"Returning now to the original name of the building, I have been asked to design a people's theatre. We shall note that the architect should collaborate with the actor, the author, the stage director, and the audience in order to furnish each of them with the maximum stimulus possible to draw them more closely together. It is only a step from this anticipation to an acceptable fusion in the future! The structure must anticipate this union but not overtly. . . .

"As you see, my task is becoming clear: its monumental side is to antici-pate, without revealing the coming fusion of the actors and spectators in a collective action; its immediate and expedient side is to prepare for this magnifi-cent future by arrangements that stimulate the audience to activity and permit the actor to progress further and further towards meeting the audience. We have seen that everyone is quite willing to understand and to support us if we use a little diplomacy. Our role is thus that of a pedagogue, for it is obvious to me that a modern architect must be an educator."

"Allow me yet another question, please," I added. "What structural material would you prefer for such a building?"

"Here you touch upon a delicate matter of architectural aesthetics," my visitor answered, "for you are aware that this aesthetics is based on the principle of gravity. As long as only bricks or stones were used, it was easy to express this principle by reserving the brick for unimportant buildings. Today our materials are numerous, so perfected, so well suited to compromises, simulations and every impudence, that it is very difficult to preserve even an appearance of purity and simplicity in architecture. But it would be wrong to be intransigent on this point. Aesthetic principles are like anything else; life determines their application; they must not direct our life. When the aspirations of our Christian culture turned towards renunciation and mysticism, the architect progressively dematerialized his stone. As the principle of gravity yielded to the affirmation of inner life, he expressed this renunciation of the tangible world by deriving his triumph from religious ideas rather than architectural principles. Gothic art therefore gradually developed into an art form that overcame stone, which is earthbound by nature, and pushed it heavenward. Never perhaps has life governed an aesthetic principle more strongly. But the result, however unnatural it may be, is of indisputable beauty. Let us not forget that our life creates the principles of art. If, in an era of perfect and happy equilibrium, life was able to draw a new aesthetics—that is to say, Greek art—from paralyzing traditions, this art owed that feat entirely to the equilibrium, and so do we. Why do we demand such a creation in our muddy, confusing and seething period of transition? If we imitate, our work will be dated and inorganic; if we search for some sort of style in our sick imagination, detailed from our active life, we shall merely create a monstrosity, for a monstrosity in any life is that which departs from the norm of this life. Thus we would be surrounded by monstrosity if modern technique had not come to our aid. And that is where I should like to lead you. Whatever one may think, this technique has developed with a sense of timeliness even where the means would seem to have multiplied unreasonably. Like opponents arming themselves with everything they can find before an imminent strife, modern scientists and technicians augment their arsenal, looking toward a period that they foresee as bound to be exacting and perilous. I do not speak of war machines here—a subject unfortunately all too obvious— but of the generally extraordinary development of modern technique in all fields.

"But to return to architecture, this technique gives the architect what he needs to adjust himself to the boldness as well as to the vacillation of a confused and bewildered period or, on the contrary, to dominate them as an informed pedagogue. I have chosen the latter part, and, since everything is relative in pedagogy, I approach the question of the building material not from an aesthetic principle alone but also from a principle of social aesthetics similar to that which guides us in the education of our children.

"My 'people's theatre' will be conceived with the aim of stimulating people to meet and to enjoy a sociable atmosphere in a building dedicated to this purpose. For me the theatre will be the pretext for this task, but for the people it will be the bait! Do you see? I shall therefore take good care of this bait, by arranging the instructional installations in such a manner that they appear to be part of the theatre, not merely to be associated with it. I shall still try to give them as great an importance as my double-dealing can grant them. Lastly, I shall keep in mind all the various possibilities of enlargement and transformation which modern technique can accomplish. The auditorium of the theatre will not be placed in the center, for the back and the sides of the stage house must be provisioned, allowing eventually for performances given more or less out of doors. To this end gardens planted with shrubs instead of trees will keep the space available without revealing its subsequent usage. Although apparently rigid, the proscenium may be widened and narrowed at will or may even completely disappear in the walls and the ceiling, allowing the stage to merge with the house in a single architectural unit. The space reserved for the orchestra pit will easily be covered and the auditorium seats, arranged in the shape of an amphitheatre, may be turned over to form a horizontal floor on the stage level. Consequently the stage floor will be placed (in sections) on hydraulic elevators. There will be neither galleries nor boxes on the sides; behind the auditorium, in the rear of the house, I shall probably place two large deep galleries, arranged in tiers, which may eventually be connected to each other and the house proper by stairs running along their entire width. These galleries, whose admission price is not intended to be different (in fact, there will be one admission price for the entire house) will serve as an approach to the terraces through side and rear doors. House and stage will receive a good deal of daylight and may thus be used at any hour of the day. At night the illumination will not be furnished by visible sources (chandeliers, etc.) but will merely pervade the space; modern technique has lately given us the means for this indirect lighting. Confidentially, I shall also retain the possibility of opening all or part of the lateral walls of the auditorium (and, as I mentioned, of the stage) to combine these two areas with the lobby and promenade hall, the terraces and gardens, thus creating an atmosphere of maximum sociability which will quite naturally encourage performers and patrons to mingle during intermissions. The decoration in general will be beautiful in line and color but still have no high-relief and as little fabric as feasible, for good acoustics comes before anything else even in the lobby and promenade hall.

"The building material used must be fully revealed in the construction; the aesthetic principle of balance in gravity will not be expressed in it. Strictly speaking, my building will be architectural only in its function; its monumentality will then remain at a minimum in the present as well as in the future. This is desirable. The people must obtain the keen, unforgettable impression that they, their living bodies, are creating the space and delimiting it. The living body must feel free to modify at will this existing space and its confines. The crucial part of the problem thus consists in preserving absolutely ideal flexibility in a structure, which, nevertheless, must arouse a sense of strength and permanence. I am convinced the solution is feasible.[44]

"It would be interesting to pursue this project and observe its use as our so-called 'people's theatre'; to envision the things which will take place there, the performances and entertainment to be given, the festivals and quite various events which such a creation in space could inspire, to discover how and why the premises will have to be changed; lastly, to guess the name that will be given this whole structure as the most appropriate to its functions at all times. Yet, though the architect has the duty to foresee all this, his official authority does not go so far; the work of his intuition, of his personal initiative as a pedagogue is completed with the building. Thereafter, the architect becomes simply a collaborator of the authors, actors, and the public, subordinating himself to them. He will always have to be consulted no doubt, but the center of gravity has moved; he has delivered his work; it is the others' turn to prove themselves deserving owners."

My visitor spoke these last words with solemn ardor and deep emotion. I myself was greatly affected; I had followed him with growing, almost feverish passion, full of admiration for his noble reserve, and grateful for all he led me to sense behind his words. This simple written report cannot, of course, convey the intense life in his voice, his look and gesture. But my reader will certainly have supplied this lack with understanding, especially if he is interested in our subject and knows its importance and timeliness.

To summarize: for the artist the centuries of unconscious and carefree work are past. If once he could be certain that he would remain one with his contemporaries, he is certain no longer, has not been for a long time. In our day Life forges ahead; it goes beyond the work of art in such haste that it has no time to turn around to ascertain whether the artist is following. Moreover, it shows no desire to do so, for it has lost the complete confidence it once had in him. But the artist needs a point of departure. If he persists today in finding it in himself, he will remain lost in the rear guard, and Life will outrun him ever more. How can he complain? Has not his blind pride led him into this impasse?

"Art for art's sake"—we now have it and know all about it! But what nonsense! Does one ever say "Life for Life's sake"? Would this mean anything at all? We have "dropped" the artists, left them sulking like naughty children while we went on alone. As soon as they stop sulking we shall gladly welcome them back; until then, they must learn through hard experience and we will not help them find themselves by purchasing their paintings and statuettes, by accepting their old-fashioned and thoughtless designs or their fickle music. Quite the contrary! Their only salvation lies in a sincere confession of their failings. Then Life, active Life, will extend its hand and, returning to purely human feelings, the artists will have to agree that this Life alone can offer them solid ground on which to place their springboard. The work of art is an artifice; if active Life does not furnish it enduring substance, the work is scattered and lost in space and absorbed like the pyrotechnician's rocket in the dark sky. Therefore the artist is forced to turn to Life!

Conservatism, like any form of laziness, fears the effort, the unknown, the potential sacrifices, the inevitable shocks, and thus holds us where we are. The modern artist is well aware that his art must be reformed. An intelligent artist can no longer doubt that a picture in its frame has become a childish thing. A musician composing a symphony now surely senses that the ground on which his feet are resting is not the same as ours. All this makes them suffer, poor fellows, but instead of seeking the source of Life in Life itself, they persist in trying to discover it in the clouds from whence we forced it down some time ago!

The spectacle of Life, however, is not the active Life. This Life has still to be lived, and the artist recoils from this. . . . Surely, we are often enough still incorrigible spectators; yet the artist goes much further! He wishes to remain a spectator of spectators; he takes them as his models! No circle could be more vicious!—Oh, if the artist were only willing! But there we are, he is not; hence, it is now up to us to force him. And with this assertion I should like to close.

We must carry the responsibilities that the artist declines to accept. We must unceasingly prove to him that we can do it, that we are worthy of the task; and for this reason we must refuse to be eternal spectators as well as to be ourselves the spectacle.

Let the artist come to live our Life; otherwise our door remains closed to him. We have no need of what he can offer us. It is our turn to give! Let him know this and be satisfied! There will be no cause for him to regret it, nor for us to regret having compelled him.

# The Art of the Living Theatre

## A Lecture for Zurich[45]

### (1925)

In a production of *The Misanthrope*, the drawing room of Célimène was indicated by simple hangings; only the costumes, considerably simplified, and the equally inconspicuous furniture indicated the period of Molière. This was done in order to de-emphasize the historical milieu of so purely human a plot, and by the same token to make the characters stand out.

My neighbor, visibly shocked, grumbled: "How queer of Célimène to furnish her house in this manner!" This seems to me the perfect attitude of a realistic spectator, i.e., one who likes to see the place of action exactly as everyone transported there would find it. Very cultured people share this opinion. It is therefore important to look for the origin, the deep source of this attitude, before condemning it. After all, it may perhaps be justified, and scenic idealism may not be everybody's taste.

First of all is the *mise en scène* a work, an art in itself, whose conception can be worked out before it is ever applied? Does it exist independently so that it merely has to be adapted to each new play? Certainly not; if this were the case, we would not even discuss it. In short, staging is the method employed by theatre people for visibly presenting a dramatic action. It is not even a technique regularly adopted; rather, it is conditioned by the dramatic action; without this action, staging is an idea that makes no sense; properly speaking, it is nothing—nothing at all.

Yet our definition involves an unknown factor, our eyes, whose variable requirements cannot be entirely or implicitly predicted by the text (with or without music); in other words, staging includes elements needed for the visible presentation of a piece, yet not contained on its printed pages. Consequently, although the dramatic action is the prerequisite for the production, our eyes nevertheless determine the staging and always create it anew. In this sense we may assert that we ourselves are the *mise en scène* and that without us the work remains a written piece. We are therefore responsible for the production, and since we do not intend to let it disturb us, . . . we have the right to criticize its precise appropriateness.

Thus the question assumes a new aspect. In the first place we must know who we are in relation to the dramatic text. We ourselves, not the play, must be examined first. This viewpoint may seem new, yet it is as old as the world. What is surprising is that our attention must be called to it.

When we use a microscope we regulate the position of the lenses according to our vision and not according to the nature of the objects we wish to examine. The same holds true for the theatre. The play is a given factor; it is up to us to adapt ourselves. Staging is precisely this adaptation.

The world we see does not always strike our eyes in the same manner. We can regard it as a spectacle outside of ourselves: this we call, "to look at." Or it pervades us involuntarily and blends with our inner life, where it exercises on our unconscious a somewhat tyrannical influence, which in turn is modified by our mood of the moment. Our entire view of things and beings fluctuates between these two extremes: one is the objective or realistic way of observing; the other, the subjective or idealistic, which feels through seeing. If therefore, according to our definition above, we are, and wish to be, the creative producers of such and such a play, we must begin by questioning ourselves about the aim we pursue in the theatre and what we expect of it when we enter the auditorium. Do we ask dramatic art or the dramatist to present life to use as a show we merely observe—as the scientist observes nature—or do we wish to identify ourselves in the theatre with the characters and thus recognize ourselves in them? Does dramatic emotion consist of curiosity and its result, which is gratification, or rather of sympathy and its result, which is a stirring of the soul?

Perhaps we do not yet suspect it, but the entire problem of staging is here formulated, and its resolution depends on us. I shall go even further and maintain that our dramatic art altogether depends on the spectator, that is to say, on the quality of his vision.

Is the audience everywhere the same? Is it an entity, and does our internationalism also standardize our dramatic art? It might seem so if the play alone is considered, but we have seen that the latter is not the first concern of staging, for this is in fact determined by us, not by the play. The taste for an imaginary world of any sort is common to all mankind. Those who are timorous or who despise the theatre satisfy their taste by reading, by the fine arts, or in a thousand other ways held respectable and moral, the true import of which escapes their undeveloped consciences. Honest men admit their irrepressible urge to forget themselves in order to be enriched by witnessing a performance not offered in daily life, passions and sufferings they do not have to experience, happiness and triumphs that carry them beyond everyday living. In short, through fiction animated and presented by beings like themselves.

But dramatic enjoyment is a matter of reaction: a Russian reacts differently from an Italian; a Parisian differently from a Scandinavian. The production they want and which they have to create themselves, as we have seen, will therefore be different for each of them. The interest shown by a European in a performance of the Far East has nothing in common with that experienced by the natives. A Spaniard views a *corrida* with other eyes than does a Scot; a Norwegian reacts to a drama of Ibsen differently from a Florentine. Internationalism has not yet changed the genius of the races or the influence of the climate, but fortunately this has nothing to do with artistic productivity. Contrary to all appearances, internationalism, industrial by its very nature, does not touch artistic creation although no doubt it facilitates its diffusion.

Thus if on the one hand we are the spectators, the creators of the *mise en scène*, there is on the other the genius peculiar to each race that determines the form of the production—the presentational form, as we shall call it. And since this form in turn inspires and determines the form which the dramatist will choose, the chain seems to be unbroken. Actually, however, this is not so. Theatre people know the sheep-like habits of their audience and use them as an excuse. Without grumbling we endure the continuous violence those habits do to our good sense, to our taste, to our need for harmony and sound aesthetic propriety, hence to our dignity. We tolerate on stage what our art exhibitions, our concerts, and our lectures would never dare present without provoking explosive revolt. Even more: we permit the imposition of a dramatic and scenic art which is completely at variance with our heritage and our own genius. How can we know who we are in relation to the theatre and what we require of it? How can the dramatist and the stage director know and gratify our true wishes? We have placed ourselves outside the question and lost the right to criticize, since we do not even know what we want.

Internationalism in the theatre means the death of dramatic art. We have said that it cannot touch the work of art; but it is drying up the source, and the responsibility for this decline falls entirely upon us the spectators. Do we not have the right to protest? Courage to do so would not fail us if we had the slightest notion of the claims we could make! As things stand now, the dramatists look in vain to us for suggestions indispensable to them. For lack of these, they fling themselves into destructive internationalism.

To summarize: the *mise en scène* is nothing in itself. The spectator creates it and, in so doing, inspires and determines the dramatic production. Consequently, to deal with the *mise en scène* means to observe ourselves in this respect and to try to discover, in our heart, the origin of our taste for dramatic art and the form suited to bring this art into accord with our deep atavisms and the genius of our race.

Our point of departure is thus clearly indicated and circumscribed. To begin with ourselves undeniably assures us a more beautiful voyage and wider horizons than we could have if the curtain, wings, border, lights, and spotlights of our stages were the sole guides and cicerones . . . !

I have talked of realistic and idealistic vision. If we wish to define the two concepts solely from the viewpoint of staging, we must above all state that the realistic vision does not proceed directly from the text of the piece (with or without music); whereas the idealistic vision is exclusively inspired by that text. I shall explain.

The author gives the dramatic action a historic and geographic environment or, if it is pure fantasy, he indicates its surroundings suggestively. The objective realist, considering these notations independent and self-sufficient, relies on them alone, and he expects the stage director to adhere to them. When those settings have been realized, he places the dramatic action in them, convinced that the right harmony between the two elements—the play and the production— is as automatically established as in real life. The subjective idealist proceeds in the opposite direction. For him only the text of the play counts; all indications outside of it are approached cautiously, and his staging is inspired primarily by the text itself. Not until this has occurred does he consider the scenic annotations and appraise their possibility. For the realist, the only scenic possibility is the exact historic and geographic reproduction of the author's choice of location. For the idealist, it is a matter of degree. The realist places the dramatic text somewhat crudely in the reality of a pre-existent environment. The idealist surrounds the text with the scenic elements needed to illuminate it and discards all those which are superfluous, and thus would lessen the intensity of the text. I repeat: for the idealist reality lies in the text of the play; for the realist it is in the pre-established environment. In the theatre the realistic conception separates man from his milieu; the idealistic conception views the milieu exclusively in its close relations to the inner life of the characters. For the realist the drama of Parsifal occurs in Spain; for the idealist it is within ourselves.

Yet someone will perhaps ask me, why not pay greater respect to the express wishes of the author? Does he not know better than we what is needed for the visible presentation of his text, and does not the idealist arbitrarily usurp his place? This issue is extremely important, for it concerns our responsibility towards the theatre. Today the dramatist must reckon with the fact that the great majority of our patrons are realists. His concept is closely linked with our vision, just as the teacher's way of expression is linked with his pupil's reaction; and so strong are the ties that even if the dramatist conceives his work without concern for the realist's view, he reverses himself as soon as he decides to have his work produced. He violates his dream to satisfy us and, alas, he finds on our stages accomplices only too compliant with his cowardice or his technical ignorance; they leave him no choice: all stage equipment is devised for a realistic scenic art, i.e., an art form with no direct and profound correlation to the text of the play.

But is it really an art? Can we dare talk of a scenic art without tongue in cheek?

Taine informs us that "the aim of a work of art is to reveal some essential, salient character, consequently some important idea, more clearly and more completely than can real objects. It achieves this through a group of parts whose relationships it systematically modifies."[46] Are our painted settings a voluntary and systematic modification on our part? Do we not, on the contrary, desire a realization that is still more accurate? Does not the technique of the scenic painter actually aspire to reduce these vexatious modifications as much as possible, and to give us the illusion of reality? But to give the illusion of reality is to negate art. Dramatic art, in its very nature, is a modification of real life, a systematic concentration such as our daily existence is unable to offer us. Hence nobody will ever doubt that it is an art. Only the *mise en scène* is still looked upon with suspicion and subjected to endless arguments. To have tried to make of it an independent art form is a grave aesthetic error; and yet we continue to hold onto the technical aspects of settings instead of letting the play itself guide us. Naturally this does not satisfy our eyes. So much for the audience.

What about the author of the drama?

This unhappy creature is aware of the inflexible rigidity of our stages; he also knows our unbelievable tolerance of this condition and the distortion it has wrought upon our taste. The struggle seems to him too unequal; to reform the stage would be relatively easy, but how can one count on the assent of an equally reformed audience? Above all, how can one make that audience accept such reform not as a mere technical development on the part of the stage director but as an inner and very profound evolution expected of the spectator himself?

At the beginning, I said that we are the *mise en scène*. Thus our staging remains in an inferior state because we are too warped to be able to formulate our wishes and, like children, we accept what we have as inevitable.

However, for some twenty years we have possessed an incomparable criterion for judging the quality of our taste in matters of performance and to enlighten us about the nature of dramatic art: the film. Nothing, absolutely nothing stands in its way; and it is generally agreed that there is no chance of competing with the wonders it can offer our eyes. What is it then that makes the theatre so radically different from the film, even when the word is accurately synchronized with the image which, incidentally, is hardly desirable. Of course, it is the presence of the actors in flesh and blood, a presence that brings about an immediate emotional response. In everything else the film possesses means in comparison to which our most precise and sumptuous productions are mere child's play. Why then require of the theatre that which it cannot give and which is so freely offered elsewhere?

Art lives on sacrifice. Painting forgoes plasticity and living light; sculpture, color; pure music, space; architecture, the expression in time-sequence that is the exclusive secret of music; even the poet refrains from appealing directly to our eyes. Is dramatic art alone to give up nothing? Its fleeting existence, at any rate, ought to warn us. But no, time and again we demand of it an illusion that is alien to it, instead of the one it has all the power to give us, namely the great and divine illusion of life, the life of our body and soul, the only illusion of value and the only one acceptable to art. Here as anywhere else, Man is the measure of all things, as Protagoras states. Thus Man, his body and his soul, will be the "measure" of the environment required by his presence on stage. And everything not measured against him or of no concern to him must be rejected; that is the dross which still encumbers the theatre and to often conceals the incomparable treasure of our human nature[. . . . ][47]

The artist who specifically chooses the living body and soul of the actor as a means to express his own self makes himself dependent on the technical method of this living body and soul, and in art, technical requirements are irreducible. The technique of the dramatist is concerned therefore at once with the actual presence of the living body and with its expression of emotions. The one pertains directly to the presentational form; the other, to the conception of the drama. On the one hand, the author must be able to rely on a suitable arrangement of space in which the characters of his play will move; on the other, he is aesthetically bound not to select a story whose scenic environment would overshadow the presence of the living actor. Now, both of these obligations primarily concern the spectator. It is not enough for the stage director to follow the dramatist, and the dramatist to agree to the sacrifices demanded by the dramatic work. These sacrifices must also have our consent, the consent of the audience. Since the majority of spectators are not inclined to consent, the conclusion must be drawn that there are obstacles that prevent them from doing so; it is important to know these.

Certainly we all have within ourselves a very secret, very deep feeling for that which constitutes dramatic art. Our life nourishes it and defines it accurately; we may say our soul is a theatre that has no peer. All of us recall moments in the theatre which made us tremble with such happiness that we were moved to tears. Schopenhauer, the philosopher artist, assures us that the source of the purest tears lies in the compassion our own suffering arouses in us after it is over. As an example he gives Ulysses at Alcinous' palace where, at a banquet honoring the unknown guest, a bard recites Ulysses' adventures without suspecting that he is extolling them in the presence of the hero himself. Ulysses slowly covers his face and sobs in his cloak.[48]

Schopenhauer could not have chosen a better example; it is so eloquent that one must believe in it. In purest essence dramatic feeling would thus be the result of an encounter between the theatre within ourselves and the one in which we are the spectators. Let us emphasize, however, that here the dramatic themes need not be identical with our own; sufferings or joys we have never felt, can create in us emotions of the same quality as those we know from experience. I shall even go further; the mere fact that we see our inner life presented in a form that is free of those petty nonessentials that invariably cheapen our life is enough to stimulate emotion about our human condition. This is what Schopenhauer had in mind. The tragedy of our existence lies not so much in our circumstances as, quite often, in our incapacity to intensify our feelings and lift them to the heights of exaltation. In this sense dramatic art is a releasing force. And we would betray this art by dragging into it the contingencies and humiliating influences of the environment in which we struggle. . . .

The mirror of manners it is called! What nonsense! Where in all of Molière's Paris would one have found an Alceste or even The Affected Young Ladies as he presents them in such farcical synthesis? Manners can serve as a pretext or simply as a frame to be shattered by the genius who touches it with his fingers. Shakespeare understood this well and did not burden his dramas with the tinsel with which we still deck them out. For him the weakness of a character faced with the necessity to act was not to be found only in Denmark.

The result of all this is that we take an adverse attitude toward our enjoyment of drama when we encumber our stages with arbitrary and accidental elements, precisely those from which we would like to escape in the theatre. (And let us say in passing that modern life is too rich in purely visual impressions for us to dare invoke it as an excuse.) Some imagination, hence some faith, faith in ourselves, in our merit and our nobility would suffice to impress the exploiters of our indolence and our negligence. Whoever takes the initiative will see how fast the already tottering structure of our traditional staging will collapse, and with it very likely three-quarters of our dramatic production. How can we measure the significance of this blessing?

Once we have secured an inner conviction, we need only compare it with the realities surrounding us; in other words, test it. So far, I have carefully avoided giving examples from the theatre as it exists; they would have diverted the attention and extended the length of my argument. But now the issue is clear: we are undoubtedly sufficiently informed so that we may learn to recognize the enemy.

Part Five

# The Aesthetic and Prophetic Essays

# Introduction to Part Five

Throughout his creative life, Appia insisted that no art, least of all that of the theatre, could be adequately described or evaluated without constant reference to its ethical and social function: to the manner in which it grew out of, and, in turn, expanded the lives of those in contact with it. This constant principle, which always provided the touchstone of Appia's work—its point of vital connection with a reality from which predominantly theoretical investigations might otherwise have estranged it—took on increased significance in his last years. As the condition and prospects of conventional theatre (even one reformed along the lines he had himself set out) interested him less, the potential role of new, hitherto unknown or only dimly conceived developments took ever greater hold upon his imagination. Technical advances, new art forms, new architecture and performance places, as well as a radically altered awareness of the nature and potential of art to enhance and fulfill man's life—Appia's thought reached out prophetically, and seems to encompass it all.

Like other artists of the period, Appia responded to the vastly altered conditions of a society whose social, political, spiritual, aesthetic and psychological bearings had been violently disorientated by the World War. Supremely sensitive and prescient as he was, he became one of those whose "antennae" perceived with dreadful clarity the factors which have contributed to the continuing crisis in so many areas of twentieth-century culture. Although he analyzed the nature of the crisis and sought solutions primarily within the field of art, he insisted that, properly understood and redefined, art had vast implications for achieving a happier condition *generally* for modern man.

Appia's prophetic analysis, and many of the ideas he advanced for confronting the dilemma of art in modern culture—ideas expressed in their most concentrated form in the essays in this section—became widely relevant as society and its art grew increasingly preoccupied with a perceived state of alienation and social division, a breakdown of communal values and relations, and a pervading sense of existential isolation. The therapeutic response to these conditions were to a significant degree anticipated and outlined by Appia. "Art will never endure unless it derives from a sense of close human solidarity," he had asserted in the essay "Monumentality"; the task was to develop the new art forms that could encompass and express this solidarity. These could only be dimly perceived as yet; indeed Appia called the realm of such new art "the Great Unknown," while pointing out (in the same essay) that "dramatic art has burst the frame that has held it rigid for so long, and the very idea of theatre has so enlarged that it gives us vertigo and a slight feeling of anarchy."

In light of this perception, it is not surprising that the essays brought together in this section that comprises the core of Appia's final aesthetic writings are only marginally concerned with the theatre: he had, he believed, left it far behind. His concern now is with "the New Presence," which he defines as a condition of reciprocity between life and art, and, in turn, between artist and public. Indeed, above all else, the note heard throughout these works emphasizes that the passive role of the public (variously characterized as consumer, spectator, collector, voyeur, etc.) must at all costs be transformed into one of active engagement with the work of art. Moreover "Living Art" would, ideally, abolish the distinction between artist and public altogether: all would join in creating and, in the process, *becoming* the work of art themselves.

Before dismissing such notions too readily (or cynically) as the naïve musings of an aging but still innocent dreamer, one should consider how widely Appia's early and articulate call for new forms of art, for a new relationship with the audience, and above all for a greatly enlarged conception of the role and extent of art within society, has found echoes in our era. The performance groups, environmental and laboratory theatres, happenings, improvisation, and other experiments of recent years, all taking shape in a variety of new forms and formats, were distantly perceived and predicted through his evocation of "study sites," communal and collaborative art, and new modes of creative activity, "with or without an audience." The connections may inevitably have become tenuous, but they are there.

Of course, many of the ideas that Appia explored and espoused after the War had been evident in his earlier work, particularly that undertaken at Hellerau. The yin-yang sign so prominently displayed in the pediment of Appia's great theatre had not been placed there for purely decorative effect, but to symbolize the idealism and vision immanent in the activity taking place beneath it. As Wolf Dohrn had stated at the dedication ceremony, those devoting themselves to eurhythmics hoped that it might replace "both the unproductive intellectualism and the joyless athletic training of the age with a new system dedicated to the spiritual development of the body, or, if you prefer, to the physicalization of mental and spiritual exercises." He hoped further that at Hellerau "we shall witness how its people will present celebrations and festivals, for themselves and others, of a type that no other place can offer, because nowhere else will there exist a population so widely and equally educated and invigorated by such a sense of community."[1]

These concerns, further developed and given greater urgency by the cataclysm of the War, provided the basis for much of Appia's subsequent agenda: more advanced formulations of these same ideas occur repeatedly in the essays. Hellerau was to be universalized; or, more accurately perhaps, society was to be transformed to embrace and protect its ideals. A dangerous and endangered world was to be made safe both by and for eurhythmics.[2]

However, the original impulse and inspiration for the ideal of a broad physical and spiritual renewal of humanity through movement and music was far older than its most recent incarnation in the eurhythmics of Dalcroze. Motivated as he was in part by a desire to re-create the ancient Greek *orchesis*—to express inner emotion through the union of music and movement in dance—his work, and its subsequent refinement by Appia, was one more expression of a Greek-inspired movement for artistic reform that had long been evident and influential in European culture. Indeed, many years earlier, Friedrich Nietzsche had seen the potential for such reform in Wagner's music itself, noting that music demanded "her equal sister, gymnastics, for her necessary embodiment in the real world of the visible" and that the new type of dance thus formulated would act as "judge over the whole deceitful contemporary world of show and appearance."[3]

The radical proposals and criticisms that Appia puts forward in these essays must therefore be seen not as the isolated, semimystical musings of an eccentric visionary, but, in their broader cultural and historical context, as the latest (and arguably a most advanced) attempt to reform society in the light of ancient precepts and models: an endeavor that has characterized many of the most innovative and far-reaching developments in Western arts and letters since the Renaissance. Appia draws on this context and this tradition constantly in his writing, sometimes explicitly; more often, as an informing subtext and implicit commentary. His work is "revolutionary" in the truest sense: it seeks to *return* society to a former and happier state.

It is also useful to bear in mind the personal circumstances under which Appia wrote the essays. During much of the period, his health—both mental and physical—was precarious. In 1919 he had to leave his home on the banks of Lake Geneva, for a healthier, more elevated site. The following year, he was taken under the care of his friend Jean Mercier in Geneva, and in September 1921, he voluntarily went into a psychiatric clinic near Bern, for treatment of chronic depression aggravated by alcohol. Although soon greatly improved in body and mind, he remained there, intermittently, until the following October of 1922. It was during this period that Appia, doubtlessly benefiting from a sense of relative security and personal serenity, composed many of his late essays including "Theatrical Experiences and Personal Investigations," "Living Art or Dead Nature?," "Theatrical Production and Its Prospects in the Future," "A Dangerous Problem," "New Forms," "The Gesture of Art," *"Port-Royal,"* "Monumentality," "The Intermediary," "The Theme," "Picturesqueness," and "Mechanization." They are suffused with touches of "local color" derived from his circumstances at the time.

"Reflections on Space and Time" was written somewhat earlier. It would be little more than a fragment but for the fact that, however brief, it is complete in itself. Essentially a logical exercise, it is quite different in style and tone from the other more discursive essays, permeated as they are with example, anecdote, and—whatever their shifts in mood and diction—the pervasive sense of a personal voice. It presents instead, a highly concise and abstract statement of the basic principles supporting Appia's theory of the "work of living art," which are described and illustrated far more extensively in several subsequent essays.

"A Dangerous Problem," by contrast, is far richer and its ideas more resonant. In it he returns to concepts which had long been evident in his work, to develop and explore them further. Foremost is the belief, mentioned earlier, that (once reformed) contemporary art, like its Greek antecedents, can provide the most vital and immediate expression of the human spirit. Directly echoing countless assertions by the Greek philosophers,[4] he states that "music expresses the reactions of our soul." A little later he evokes Plato to suggest the process by which such initially personal expression is linked to the well-being of the larger community; first, through the enrichment of the individual's capacity for perception and self-awareness, and then, the imagination enlarged, through the development of compassion, empathy, and a sense of shared life with others. In describing this transition he makes use too of the Platonic notion of ideal form, which because of the decadence of modern music, must again be derived from the idea of the body itself. The body alone can inspire music's revival—its "return to basics"—and through it, the renewal of society.

Appia designated "New Forms" a fable, and as such, it should be allowed to speak for itself. If a subtext is useful in grasping its meaning, "Man Is the Measure of All Things" is the one that seems most appropriate.

"The Gesture of Art" takes up the theme once more of society's salvation through art, and the need, if that is to take place, to transform the role of the individual from onlooker to that of active participant. In the process, a sense of reciprocity both between the individual and the work of art towards which he "gestures," as well as between that individual and the larger community of which he is part, will be engendered and nurtured. In the second half of the essay, Appia turns his attention more specifically towards theatrical art, and again evokes the concept of a "living art," which uses the body not in its costumed and fictive *role,* to convey stories, but as a means of direct expression akin to music which, in turn, must motivate it. "Evidently another art form expressive of the living body itself must exist. The body is alive only because it moves; this new art form will therefore have movement like dramatic art, but will probably have no other relation to it."

Appia does not further specify this new art (beyond emphasizing that its redemptive social value requires that it be open to all to take part), but he identifies eurhythmics as its embryonic form. Although eurhythmics did indirectly engender theories, movements and schools which in aggregate resulted in the diverse species of modern dance, it is unlikely that any of these latter manifestations could fully embody Appia's ideal. Yet, like Artaud's concept of the "theatre of cruelty," Appia's vision of "living art" has profound importance as a provocative *idea,* and has exercised real force upon the artistic imagination (and thereby upon tangible works of the imagination), even though the thing itself remains elusive and unrealized.

The essay on Sainte-Beuve's *Port-Royal* seems odd, both because of the relative absence of the aesthetic themes reiterated in Appia's other essays of the period, and because, unusually, he adopts the somewhat unlikely role of literary critic. The object of his critique, moreover, seems a curious choice. Sainte-Beuve is most widely remembered today (certainly to English readers) because of Marcel Proust's masterful *attack* upon him, an unfinished mixture of fiction and criticism. Proust's work (1908) condemned Sainte-Beuve (who enjoyed a formidable if somewhat middle-brow reputation amongst nineteenth-century readers), as the personification of a false view of literature. Sainte-Beuve's evaluation was condescending and often philistine, utterly conventional in its moral outlook, and so blinkered that often he quite failed to recognize writers of real genius, while lavishing praise upon mediocrities.

It has been suggested that Proust's critique was essentially an exercise in self-therapy,[5] and rather the same impulse may lie beneath Appia's far more positive assessment. He probably found the criticism of modern life and values in *Port-Royal* compatible with his own state of mind at the time: he was, after all, in total seclusion in a sanatorium. In the essay, he writes, "For how many of us is the aim clear, the necessity for the effort evident, the lever within reach—yet the decision does not come! Lives glide away in sterile contemplation of the window dressing which we have so rightly called good intentions." At the very time he composed this essay, he wrote in a similar vein of himself, "it always seems to me that one has done nothing, and, above all, that one hasn't known how to do well, what one has done. The awareness of all the possibilities is somewhat distressing, but also rather pleasant."[6]

The ideal of a "retreat," which he espouses in the essay and finds in the example of life at Port-Royal, must inevitably have been colored and conditioned by the immediate circumstances of his life at the time, and by his conviction that he should use his sojourn to conceive and fashion these essays in which he placed such importance: "We must compensate the cloister for the privilege it grants us, not let this benefit simply fall regularly into our lap. The sounds of our meditations will pass beyond the walls and, quite possibly, we shall be amazed at the echoes they will arouse." Only near the end of the essay does he apply the insights of his analysis of the example of Port-Royal to more specific and contemporary issues of art and society.[7] They provide him with another point of access and analogy for explaining and promoting the elements of the aesthetic manifesto and program of reform, which have been dealt with more directly in his other essays. Thus, by a somewhat wayward and unlikely route, he comes to rest in familiar areas once more.

"The Intermediary" is also tinged by autobiographical material. Appia draws upon his own earlier relationships with individuals who significantly affected his development, to describe how, by indirection and example, such people may exercise deep and beneficent influence upon a younger person. The role also places a profound responsibility upon the "teacher," and Appia describes the type of preparation, selection, and control one must exercise to "transmit" the truest and most valuable expression of oneself. Here, therefore, in another area of human exchange, Appia is concerned with the same concept and gesture of reciprocity encountered elsewhere in the essays. The goal, once more, must be to "become an integral part of mankind." From all accounts (from those whose lives he touched), Appia himself came close to being the ideal intermediary evoked in this essay.[8]

"The Theme" is an important and cogent essay, not because initially its ideas are particularly new, but because Appia expresses certain of his now familiar themes in a readily accessible and persuasive manner. Again he calls for the direct experience of art in place of a morbid desire to collect and display it. His analysis of music, which is central to such an altered attitude, although sophisticated, is straightforward and articulate.

Appia then goes on to sound certain notes which have a very "modern" tone to them. He points out how destructive it is (particularly in presenting art to children) to burden pictures or music with narrative or interpretative ballast that only encumbers and retards the direct experience of their innate emotional and sensual expressiveness. Children, he asserts, *know* better; it is only adults, conditioned by the extraneous demands which an uneasy society makes upon art and artists, who lose the ability to respond to aesthetic encounters openly and without preconditions. His conclusion, that "art cannot and must not be explained" finds recent resonance in, for example, the call by Susan Sontag for a change of attitude in her essay "Against Interpretation": "By reducing the work of art to its content and then interpreting that, one tames the work of art. Interpretation makes art manageable, conformable. . . . [It] is the revenge of the intellect upon art." Half a century after Appia it still sounded disturbingly iconoclastic.[9]

The same idea dominates the short study "The Child and Dramatic Art," which Appia evidently fashioned as a simplified and less developed argument for consumption through the medium of a popular magazine. It adds nothing new, except in the latter part which applies his conclusions to the practical question of the costumes children wear (or ought not to wear) for games of make-believe. Such a practice conditions children at an impressionable age to think of art as representation—something to be viewed—rather than a direct emanation of imaginative and emotional expression: "living art."

The idea of solidarity, which had been an important component of Appia's aesthetic creed for many years, is dealt with comprehensively in "Picturesqueness." He points out that once art and artists have become separated from their ancient and exalted task of directly expressing humanity's collective spirit, they become alienated, esoteric, and ultimately, irrelevant. If the modern world is to recover and repossess its art it must return to the original source of all aesthetic endeavor: the human body. In the meantime, the primal impulse of art has been displaced by a decadent preoccupation with sentimental and materialistic concerns: art as souvenir of the past, or as mere commodity. Such deprivation from the vital spiritual nourishment which art alone can provide is unhealthy: and Appia concludes in a polemical tone, by citing contemporary examples to illustrate the point.

Somewhat similar concerns inform "Mechanization," which is arguably the most political of Appia's essays. In a strikingly prescient passage he notes the peril inherent in scientific development: "We shall go as far as our faculties will permit, and catastrophes warn us of the limits that are dangerous to pass. But the moral problem implied in mechanization . . . is concerned exclusively with our conception of life and its solution depends on our free will." Technical advances have brought a particular burden of responsibility to ensure that the power of science is used ethically and with great restraint. He sees a disturbing correlation between the notion of "art for art's sake" and that of "science for the sake of science": the power of the imagination can be used well or villainously in either sphere and only an abiding sense of "the New Presence" can determine the outcome for society's good.

This, Appia explains once more, derives from a sense of solidarity and reciprocity between the individual and the larger community; an attitude to be engendered and put into practice through new forms of art. "Our modern weakness is the result of our consistently passive attitude as spectators and, in particular, as spectators of works of art." The basis for such art will be the human body, set in motion by music, to express our collective selves. Such expression must, he insists, be guarded and exercised with great responsibility, "lest mechanization, escaping our control, gain the upper hand; and God knows how far it might draw us if we let it go." The massed, carefully coordinated and highly dramatic ranks of moving bodies which characterized the Nazi rallies a decade later, provide a chilling example of the misuse Appia warned against.

In "The Former Attitude" Appia identifies sports as one relatively harmless example of how the dishonesty of art, and its failure to link up with human reality, compels society to find other more honest expressions of itself, even if they fall short of providing an ideally sensitive and creative alternative. "Sport . . . is sometimes disagreeable or rough, but nobody will dispute that it offers us the pleasure of frankness not found elsewhere." Its integrity is derived from the human body itself. The gradual alienation of society from its art means that it has entered a period of transition and experiment, and Appia states that his purpose in composing these essays has been to "clarify the question a little," while suggesting the technical basis for future investigations. Modern painting, music and dramatic art have lost their way, and without recourse to basic principles of the type Appia has identified, art will become nothing more than a "series of experiments in a vivisecting room, more cynical than anything imaginable." The subsequent history of twentieth-century art does not lack examples to verify his prediction.

"Man Is the Measure of All Things" provides a logical and succinct summary of the analysis and principles variously identified and presented in the earlier essays, whether through parable, polemic, or prophecy. It adds nothing to them except admirable clarity and eloquence.

In considering Appia's essays, one is conscious in the end not only of their remarkable foresight, but equally, and with some sadness, of the extent to which aesthetic evolution and reform have failed for the most part to advance very much beyond his ideas or indeed, to solve some of the problems that he first identified and described so long ago. Perhaps this is inevitable, given that he began in the 1890s by seeking to reform the theatre, and ended his life calling for the transformation of society itself.

Theatrical art in the first decades of this century developed very rapidly—though sometimes randomly—through a spectacular range of innovative and experimental work. The dislocation of traditional theatre—particularly the displacement of its scenic basis, which was due large if indirectly to the efforts of Appia—left a vacuum, which a great variety of new aesthetic forms rushed to fill, some more substantially than others. In the resulting confusion of ideas, styles and techniques, Appia's influence is more easily identified and traced in terms of the guidelines and principles his work provided than through any particular individual, movement, or school.

In terms of practice in the conventional theatre, his contribution was nevertheless decisive. As Jacques Copeau acknowledged, "It is he who has brought us back to the great and eternal principles. . . . We are at peace. We can work with the drama, with the actors, instead of worrying eternally about more or less original decorative formulas, without searching for new processes, new and startling methods; a search which leads us away from the main point."[10]

Appia's more visionary calls for social reform and "living art" have had a mixed response, having at best identified an agenda and basic principles, while providing a stirring manifesto reminding us of the potential of art's high office in contrast to its sometimes degraded contemporary role. Appia has sometimes been called a mystic and a dreamer, but he was never that. The gift of his genius was to formulate distant, difficult, but attainable goals. His theories and the changes in attitude and practice he demanded were rarely immediately conven-ient, but they were nearly always desirable, and never impossible. Above all (and as a contribution separate from the question of the worthiness of particular elements of the reforms he conceived), Appia's certain and uncompromising assertion that the subject was not peripheral, but lay at the center of human endeavor and achievement, remains a source of admiration and inspiration. From it we may still experience what Gordon Craig termed "that strange joy which is desperate and tragic because of your peculiar *powerlessness and power*." He was, as Craig better than others could judge, "the very noblest expression of the modern theatre."[11]

Figure 22.   Adolphe Appia, circa 1923

# Reflections on Space and Time

Written about 1920, appeared in *Aujourd'hui* 3, no. 17 (May 1958)

Where Space and Time meet, there is Line.

Since we cannot conceive Line except in connection with Movement, it is movement that brings about the meeting of Space and Time.

From the aesthetic point of view we have only bodily movement and in it we realize and symbolize cosmic Movement. Any other movement is mechanical and does not belong to aesthetic life.

We have two ways of conceiving Space. One is Line, which occupies no other Space than the distance between two points. This physical ideality enables Space to unite with Time.

The other way is Space outside of ourselves—which manifests itself either in a material in which we simply trace lines with our movements, or in obstacles that "stop" the lines we are tracing.

In this kind of Space (space outside of ourselves), lines traced by other beings in our presence must also be included.

Pure Movement (the ideal line) is not supposed to meet obstacles; consequently, Space outside of it exists only when the line is traced.

But obstacles, other lines than our own, and the like constitute a Reality that influences our movements and in a way removes their ideality.

This creates an infinite variety in the quality of Space and in the quality of Time, in the power of the first and the power of the second. The more our Movements (Lines) are influenced by Space, the less is the power of Time. The more Time rules (in music for instance), the less perceptible is the quality of Space outside of ourselves. Thus the two elements (Space and Time) are rarely found in perfect equilibrium (the ideal) and always one of them must be subordinated to the other.

Movements, executed together, deprive the Line of its independence, emphasize the power of Space, and, in addition, constitute an aesthetic Social element. This is its great value, a value of exact appropriateness which consequently will constantly vary. And therein lies the great importance of eurhythmics.

The Sensation of Space has thus two sources: our Sensations as expressed in lines, and the influences from outside as they appear in forms, resistance, obstacles, and lines of others to which we must mutually subordinate.

We may conclude from all this that the Art of Movement is, in fact, the art of balancing in Duration (Time) the variable proportions of the two kinds of sensation of Space.

It is the art of an appropriateness in the proportion of Time and Space.

# A Dangerous Problem

## (1921)

During his first drawing lesson a rather gifted pupil observes almost passionately the professor's gesture that indicates with a deft touch how to transfer his subject to a sheet of paper. For this beginner the simplification is a direct and comforting revelation. When he takes the pencil, his hand will not obey him with the same facility, but he does not mind; what matters is that he has seen and now knows. Then in a rough sketch he attempts to execute the detailed forms of the model.

Why does the word "sacrifice, sacrifice" so often return in the professor's talk? The pupil must become quite accustomed to it, and, above all, understand it well! At the very beginning art may seem to him to have an element of pleasant freedom that humors his negligence and indolence. Memories of an exhibition come back to him; he thought he saw in it what he imagined to be a lack of care or ability and, since his sketch is taking on the same aspect, he is willing to listen to it. Yet a single stroke by his professor troubles him anew. So, art is not altogether freedom; the simplification is obtained, but its quality still eludes him. Trying to copy his model, he relapses into childish details; when he tries to avoid this, the arbitrary character of his work becomes as clear to him as daylight. Sacrifice, sacrifice . . . ; but what? Is it to be the conscious design? The "polish"? If he is honest, this is all he can understand and he begins to ponder. Does one sacrifice in order to simplify matters? Possibly; though he does not believe it.

New corrections make him think; they emphasize certain details while, with one stroke, they annul others, which he thought were quite good. This is vexatious; yet he cannot deny that in spite of everything his drawing has improved. Once again he applies himself and, again, a slash destroys some of his best touches. The rough sketch is completed, and, during the second lesson, he begins to add shading to it. Then everything seems to start all over again. Why should he not place the shadows as he sees them in the recesses of the model? He sees them so clearly; just as he sees the highlights of the relief! It is easy to say sacrifice, but as for him, he relies on his eyes, which sacrifice nothing and have no right to. Or have they?

He watches his professor's face; has he a choice? But this would be against the truth; nature leaves us no choice. Here is the truth, and it has to be seized as it presents itself. The problem certainly becomes serious, if one tries to remain honest.

"You see poorly, my friend; you do not know how to see."—He! With his good eyesight? Come on! And he continues desperately to "see poorly." Hence the result suits his good eyesight but not what his eyes see. This is strange! Thus his eyes are not what he thought them to be; they could be mistaken?— "Definitely, my friend; and they are not only mistaken, but they fool you. You must teach them how to see. Do you really believe that nature will accept your sheet of paper without resistance? You must fight against resistance and overcome that resistance. You must subdue nature. You see nature before you; learn also to see it within yourself. It is a question of taking possession; otherwise, how do you expect to express it with charcoal on a sheet of paper!"—"Then it must not be copied respectfully?"—"Undoubtedly, but it is yourself whom you must respect."

With these words the second lesson ends and the pupil goes home burdened with his drawing board and with something else, too. To sacrifice. . . . He begins to have a dim notion of this sacrifice and why it is expected of him. This is quite evident. His sheet of paper is not nature; this is already a sacrifice! Then? He remembers how the most accurate parts of his design would indeed be the least in accordance with his model. Is virtue in art of a different order?— This preoccupation takes hold of him to the point of modifying his behavior. He observes, observes; his affection for everything around him becomes an agony; he begins to talk to objects: "But tell me now who you are?"—and the object invariably remains the same, separated from him before his eyes, the gate to his soul. He begins to listen: "Well, take me," says the object. The dialogue is established. At last . . . he stretches out his hands: he has understood! Now he seizes the object and returns to his drawing board. That's it: he wants now to give what he has thus taken. This is the sacrifice. Oh, he understands!

The appointed hour arrives, and, at the studio, the professor is very calm. "It is easy for him to be calm! He knows; that makes it easy enough. But I. . . ." The student's hands touch the drawing board to set it up; he perceives they have become respectful; and they hold the charcoal very firmly. And the model, still the same, is in front of him. He cries to it from the depth of his soul: "Yes! I want to seize you. Just wait!" The heart speaks; the hand obeys poorly. Is the study of drawing then teaching the hand to obey the heart? This sequence of phenomena, if it will ever take place, fills the student with admiration for

Everything. "Life is admirable; let us express it! I want to express my admiration for life!"

The student becomes a disciple: the artist is born! Sacrifice—this too is a study and the longest one; for it is not the concern of the object. Oh, no! The student loves the object too much to require of it anything like that! It is he who is going to make the sacrifice.

With certain new lines the young artist feels as if he divides himself. It seems to him as though this new line had been drawn on his sheet by the model itself; hence there is a great likeness; and yet he saw it differently. Who guided his hand? He continues; the hand obeys with less and less trouble. Oh, that's it; now it is *he* who draws, no longer merely his hand; he is the giver. The source, the origin, by Jove, is not before him, it is very deep within him! From this depth a mysterious impetus brings it to his hand; his eyes, those good eyes of his, have to make a complete journey; from the casting to his hand they must pass through his inner self. This then is art? "Yes, art is this *road;* what you put on your paper afterwards is a work *of* art, the result of this journey. No more, but surely no less. Through your work you attest to the reality of this noble endeavor. Art is a testimony and yours is the privilege of being able to testify."

To be an artist! The sweet melody singing inside him readily follows the impulses of the soul; the harmony is strict, it expresses responsibility. To be an artist means to respect the *road,* then to respect one's brothers to whom one wished to show it. He will never forget this; the melody and its solemn harmony will never cease! He is an artist.

The object of this artist was the model; in short, the entire outer world, but reflected in his soul. His work was the expression of this reflection and his hand its artisan. Art, therefore, is not, as its name indicates, a mere contrivance; it is a spiritual process. The working of a painter, for instance, is the act of obedience, and everybody obeys in his own particular manner; the painter, with his hand; another artist, probably differently, depending on the specific art, i.e., the *road.* Is this not the most direct approach? For, after all, the painter draws things, and though they may be unconventional, they are the only ones he has; consequently they must contain his testimony in its entirety. They themselves are his work.

And the poet? Would we know, without his writings, what fills his soul, and would we see his vision? Yet the signs of writing are conventional; the characters of a language we do not know remain totally mute signs; our eyes see them, that is all. The *road* is thus different from that of the painter, and yet it is no less art. Art is indeed the *road* but not exclusively this or that road. In this regard human nature is quite rich; it varies its methods. Those of our arts which offer their testimony by means of expressive signs we call fine arts. Their road ends with these signs, although, if they are not always accepted by the spectator, they do not require of him an intellectual rearrangement, since they themselves

Figure 23.    Rhythmic Design

are the work of art. No so with writing. Here we have an art that can communicate solely through conventional signs; poetry.

Music too. An orchestral score is no more intelligible to the uninitiated than are the letters of a foreign language. Do the two art forms travel the same *road*? Words are the poet's only gift; they suffice and can even be read silently (at least for a time, for true poetry is evidently always resonant and animates the features of the person possessed by it. We identify it with its notation because we no longer *live it*.) Poetry would therefore have this feature in common with music: its notation concerns only our memory; and one can perfectly imagine a state of culture where all music would be performed by heart. Hence the conventional signs are not the ones, after all, which, on the one hand, approximate music and poetry, and on the other distinguish them. We must probe deeper.

The sound of words will not do without their signification, and their enunciation is a phenomenon quite different from musical waves. The beauty of a verse is somehow inseparable from its meaning, whereas musical sounds are independent. We do not look for any signification in musical sounds, neither do we expect them to have any; they simply are. Articulated *sounds have a meaning;* their sonority in itself is not poetry; poetry makes a detour. We certainly hear the sounds, but if we do not let them pass through our understanding they are nothing at all. How different are the two roads? In the poetic design the meaning of words is, by intention, the manner of transferring the object to paper. In music sounds and their multiple combinations are in their design *already* the vision with which the artist triumphed over nature and over the object before he puts it on paper.

Returning to our student of the fine arts, we can boldly suggest that, having understood the *road*, he made . . . music!

I would like to make myself clear. Music is the direct expression, for instance, without the intermediary of the design. Its technique precedes its conventional notations and does not really need them to exist. The designer, however, has nothing but his design and the poet is no poet without the signification of words that make up his design; and that signification is not a *direct* expression. But I must, of course, specify one point! I spoke about the vision of the artist. What is the vision of the musician? Never a plaster model or any other object of the outer world!

But music does not express the world around us; though through a sacrilegious act of violence certain musicians use it as analogy. Music is unable to express the Parthenon, yet very well able to express its *Idea;* indeed it alone has the power to do so. The poet, on the other hand, knows how to explain it to us, to make us understand it, to convey to us its sovereign beauty; yet he cannot by his words penetrate the Idea of this immortal building.

An art—music—that can express only the idea of the phenomena takes its source where the ideas are formed.

Our student rightly understood that he must express on paper the idea of the model, but this idea must then recover its accidental form. And he has before his eyes the particular model that his design will represent, purified, it is true, but the *road* from his eyes to the charcoal (not from the model to the paper!).

In order to express the Idea of the Parthenon, music by no means goes to Greece, and the musician will perhaps entitle his composition: *Andante Sostenuto*.

Let us say, briefly, music expresses the reactions of our soul, for the creation of an Idea is the result of a reaction. In music we are thus not merely the creators of an expression but also and above all, the creators (conscious or not) of the object of this expression. In its entire range—from its origin to its tonal manifestation—music is a Creation of our personality. Since the Idea strips the phenomenon, i.e., our personality, of its mere contingencies, by expressing ourselves in music, we express the human soul of which we are only one of the representatives.

Such is—pardon me—such should always be the dignity of the musician. Whether the musician afterwards believes himself free to risk his throne is another question, yet whether or not he wants it and accepts it, royalty is there, and its attributes are the musical sounds. There is, therefore, a responsibility; a king is not an ordinary citizen; *noblesse oblige*.

The object of music is our reactions in their eternal form, that is, in the guise of the Idea. Music expresses this guise, which is its very nature, and all of us know it. Nevertheless a musician is a distinct individual, he has a name, and during his brief life, his whole existence represents the transient outcome of ancestral and traditional heredity combined with the entirely personal contribution of his own mind. If the reactions are thrust upon him, their quality is his responsibility.

As a consequence, the musician is under the obligation of watching himself infinitely more seriously than any other artist.

A teacher cannot play the saint in school and the rake at home.

The fact that music does not have the precise signification that the word has does not mean it can defy honesty. Quite the contrary! Here the musician must indeed prove his *noblesse;* to abuse a situation so unbelievably privileged would be dastardly. The instrument, the scepter and its power, is in his hand. He can play on it or make a game of it; but then his hand is not worthy of it; his work is despicable and relapses into the reactions of a mind inferior to such a power.

The personality of the musician is always preeminent even when it escapes any censure. For the personality the question is not one of using the means, the Techniques, but rather of the object implied in such means, and that object is for him the life of his soul.

If musical technique could express the personality of Mr. So-and-So, we its listeners would be free to choose and could deny it access and contact as we do elsewhere. But if Mr. So-and-So uses music, he makes us partners of his expression; for this reason his despicableness becomes revolting. Why, then, do we not revolt more often but instead remain in our reserved seats? Is it because we paid for them? Perhaps so. We want something for our money, whether it is bad or not. Thus our senses are dulled; we suspect, alas, that we would do as badly, and that lulls our conscience. As the public, so the music. It is our task to judge it.

Plato based the State on music. What did he mean by it? Piano concerts, soloists and choruses? Did public life become an opera for the divine Plato? Yet this is all that currently remains of music for us.—Music is the art of arranging time in a harmonious form, which is therefore superior to our daily accidental experience of time. And its object is we ourselves; music is a transfiguration of our life; it lifts the niveau of our life within the reach of the Idea, and so makes us conscious of our supreme function. But its formal power extends much further still. Time alone means nothing to us who exist in space. If, therefore, a Plato gave music sovereignty over the State, he did so because he considered it capable of seizing our essential being, and because he understood—he, the creator of Ideas—that by dominating and regulating time and its order, music could do the same for space, the two ideas depending on one another.

Not the sounds but the rhythm regulates space. There is no doubt that we ennoble our *social* life if we base it on a rhythm born of the superior elements of humanity and on a rhythm common to all individuals of this society. Does this mean that each of our gestures has to take on this form? Certainly not; and if the great legislator considered only the State, he did so because he knew well that a lasting refinement must be based on a community, not on the individual. Music, as we have seen, does not express *a* human soul but *the* human soul. The idea of music is humanity as a whole. Even more! One speaks frequently of the rhythm of the universe; we notice that our universe follows rhythmic waves; the term and the Idea implied in it have been adopted by science. To follow merely our animal rhythm, no matter how one may envision it, would be to forswear ourselves. Perhaps this is the reason why man has created music and given himself up to it.

That music has become for us only a play of sounds is just a historical phenomenon; in music, our creation soars high above history.

And yet we have dwelt on the historical phenomenon alone!

Thus we write histories of . . . music. Let us rather write the history of our abuses of music; we owe this to music.

Music, as we understand it today, is a fragmentary isolated occupation, a luxury of our piecemeal culture which we have pushed to an extreme like all luxuries. We call this its development. For Plato music does not mean to create sounds or to perform them, but to live in them and the life of sounds is not a concert but a mental attitude which we may occasionally express in formal performances as a dedication. Then perhaps we shall understand the Parthenon rising above the palace and the huts of the city.

"Sacrifice, sacrifice," said our professor of design. Sacrifice to the gods? Perhaps; but we look no longer for the white bull to gild his horns. We must sacrifice ourselves to the gods; the gilding and the white purity depend on our intentions.

Art places its means of redemption in the hands of all of us. But art lives on sacrifice. We pay homage to art not by driving separately each one of our arts to madness and solitary depravity.

Gottfried Keller[12] tells us of the aberrations of a provincial small business-man who tries to play the wit. When traveling he writes ridiculous letters to his wife and compels her to answer him in the same vein in order to publish later all this rubbish under a pretentious title. Yet he carefully includes in every letter a separate sheet with notes about his store and his petty affairs. Do we not do likewise? Are our concerts not too often an immature and false exaltation of a very dull inner life? Let us not exaggerate anything.

Music expresses our reactions, but not the quality of reactions of every listener. All of us react, but we do not react in the same manner! If the composer is sincere—Beethoven seems to be the perfect type, and his music was probably not powerful enough to relieve him—well, if the composer is sincere he will offer us precisely his *quality* of reaction. It may be ours too, and perhaps he will also take us with him into a superior sphere of quality and thus make us happy, if not always appreciative enough! This is legitimate and is one of the prerogatives of art. But the composer can also *imagine* the manner in which others than he himself will react: his music will then be dramatic. Let us seriously ponder this matter. Is not all music dramatic for us the listeners? Surely, since it expresses somebody else's reactions; yet for the composer it will be so only if he himself assumes the part of fictitious characters; to express oneself is always lyric. The pleasure we seek in the theatre arises from comparison; we have but our own persona as a measure for judging a character suggested by the actor; if he moves us, we indeed cry about ourselves.

Schopenhauer asserts that our best tears derive from the compassion we experience when we think of our own sufferings. He gives us certainly an eloquent example with Ulysses sobbing in the folds of his cloak when a stranger recites his misfortunes.[13] We have the same experience in a concert; we are moved by the recital of our own joys and sorrows. Very likely the rhapsodist glorified Ulysses' wanderings by his song; so does the composer glorify our secret life, and we do not reproach him for that!

This is one end of the line. Let us go directly to the other; then we shall see what we find between the two extremes. The composer, we said, created a dramatic work if he imagines the reactions of fictitious characters. The great charm of truly dramatic music lies for us listeners in the fact of a double dramatization: first that of the characters, and then that of the author in his characters. Listening to Tristan proclaiming his suffering we are deeply shaken by this suffering in itself; then our emotion is transferred to the author; such are Wagner's feelings about the anguish of this man! Our admiration for Wagner, which was first for him as a technician, suddenly deepens and becomes impressively human. It takes but one step from here to find ourselves, and our tears (who does not shed them in this third act!) are for three characters reunited in a wondrous combination: Tristan, Wagner and ourselves.

Here is another example. Wagner longed to present to, and express for us conclusively, the external world as it is reflected in the mind of a genius, at once candid and thoughtful. Did he *choose* Hans Sachs and Nuremberg to accomplish this?[14] It is doubtful. How conscious his choice was will forever remain a mystery. Thus the life and the insignificant reactions of these good citizens come back to us transfigured by their passage through the soul of Sachs. For this music drama Wagner wrote a complete and very brilliant prelude, contrary to his habit in that period. By placing Sachs as it were on the platform—a little like Prometheus rising from his rock—Wagner tells us "Here was a man as I wanted him to be."[15]

The great master made the resources of the most lavish music serve this intention, and whenever we hear this music it seems to us as though he would have liked to go still further and higher. As in *Tristan,* we make the miraculous synthesis of admiring Sachs, being carried away by admiration for Wagner and very happy to be invited to all this. Dramatic music has every right to such exaltation, but under one condition: we must understand the cause. In a concert, the prelude to *The Mastersingers* remains a plain monstrosity.

Between the lyricism of pure music in which alone the composer opens his heart, and the other extreme represented by dramatic art, there is a rather wide field. We shall call it imagination. Here the composer oscillates between a purely personal lyricism and an objectivity in accord with a subject. One can see that this is a paradise for applying titles! There the musician invites us for a walk, and our enjoyment, as on every walk, will depend on our strength, and, above all, on how we react to the view of the country shown us; and since the musician makes the walk more delightful for us, his company is all the more appreciated. There again, the composer can carry us much further and can give us wings. . . .

The exaltation we called childish may well be something else after all; and since technical means play a great role in art perhaps they can enlighten us. That the so-called "modern" orchestra is an incomparable phenomenon, everyone knows, and often only too well! It places in the musician's hands the most formidable tool that an artist has ever dared brandish and permits him to drop it upon us, the weak anvil. Its extravagant development stems unquestionably from the inner wealth of some rare geniuses who created the organ through which their faculties would function. Wagner, to whom we owe the ultimate evolution of this power in his time, had two very distinct reasons for creating this organ. The first was his temperament! Let us admit it, who among us can follow him therein? He obeyed this temperament without the shadow of a scruple. The other reason is the entirely inner action he wanted to reveal to us (for the first time) and to express fully, leaving nothing unsaid. Without his temperament and its resulting music we would pay no attention to this action; with it we have been inevitably induced to mistake the musical letter for the dramatic spirit. Here we are guilty, but excusably so.

Then, grasping the hammer of the Bayreuth giant, we try to use it as he does. But there is the rub: our temperament is not his, and our object could not be the same since we have not understood it. *From this very moment we have violated music.* Wagner outraged us: a giant confronting deaf pygmies, he had to knock us down in order to be heard. Those who came after him were, I believe, not much greater giants than we, and yet, armed with the same tool, they have done us equal violence, but certainly without the mitigating conditions of a Wagner. Let us state it plainly: this was a crime against music as well as against the public. We are far from being relieved of our emotion, and our nervous system will still be affected by it for a long time.

To please these ailing people, one must first revive and then charm them. We know which musicians undertook this. However, to charm a sick person does not suffice; he must also be healed, and his affected nerves are in need of a tonic, not of being shamelessly titillated or unscrupulously doped. The Wagner-tool has become old hat; a hammer must be sought that will hit hard and yet not crush the anvil. Materialism has found it in the modern mechanics. Its handle fits our hand only too well, and its metal is quite brilliant. The anvil submits to it willingly, and everything seems to work better. Still the shoddy products of the mechanician leave our soul isolated and uncontrolled. Already thoroughly mechanized by a civilization of words, not of ideas, our soul seems to find in this music the authentic proof of its decadence. We navigate haphazardly between this beautiful method and the traditional ruins. Our musical exaltation is thus immature after all, since we push to its extremes an expression that is out of date and to its paroxysm an art unworthy of the name. But we are all aware of this and seek to fill the accusing void. Which element of our celebrated civilization should we select for this purpose? Upon my word, our hand admittedly was fortunate: we have chosen our own body! The unconscious sometimes has an advantage, indeed nearly always! We are unable to utter the word *music* any longer without feeling it underneath our clothes.

The fact is fortunately undeniable. Music, exasperated, profaned and turning to folly and licentiousness (at least it would so be turned), applies to our body for protection. But this body, long enslaved and consequently debilitated, finds itself surprised at the new role it is asked to play. It sharpens its point of honor, props itself on its two feet to support a companion in distress, and this effort gives it such new and unfamiliar power that the two protagonists find themselves now quite erect and face to face with one another. Music, however, is still terribly frightened: at no price does it wish to return to its deplorable ways and its horrible loneliness; the body finds music to its liking and will not hear of ever parting with it again. Their health is fragile. One does not pass from a pitiable condition to the warm atmosphere of an *entente cordiale* without losing a few feathers. Prolonged neglect has left the body weak, long abuses have left music disorganized, yet, nevertheless, more robust. Since they will go on together as brothers, since they *must* do so, the stronger will lead the other, but with all precautions and sensitive consideration due a convalescent! The body will readily agree and respond to it with complete submission. Music enlightened through its own failures must give up the elements that caused its decline; besides, how can the body, gripped by amnesia, follow music in such a helter-skelter? This splendid intimacy will owe its nobility to reciprocal *sacrifice.*

There is that word cowardly—again. Yes, certainly; for we are concerned here with to be or not to be, to have been or to be no more. Nothing less! One sacrifices oneself justly for a cause. Is the cause of music not as good as any other?

Let us be honest! The musician can never restore the strength of his companion, the body, by consistently walking on stilts. Let us strain the voice no longer! The sacrifice is tragic for the musician who holds the dangerous tool in his hand and knows how to use it. Let him put it down and cover his comrade with solicitude! He must no longer strike: he must walk in step.

In writing these pages with the most respectful sympathy I never took my eyes from the musician, and I dare hope he will not take this amiss.

# New Forms: A Fable

## (1921)

"This is all very well, but it won't change my mind," said my neighbor, and not one of the guests felt like smiling. Evidently times have changed greatly. Experience is valid only for one person, as the saying goes. However, if all have the experience together, it should serve also . . . at least, so we believe, and we stop at this wonderful verb: to serve. To serve what? To illustrate his thought, my neighbor arranges objects that are in front of him, such as ashtrays, cigarettes, liqueur glasses; he does this with a sure hand that clearly expresses his way of thinking. *Confident* of our experiment, we try to apply it to others who likewise have objects on the table. They, too, arrange them as they please and with the same idea in mind. Will the parties agree? There is but little chance. Let us start all over! And for this little social game the candlelight continues to burn at our expense. It is an accepted custom to match our pawns by placing one against another.—Experience serves only one.—After all, did we create it?

Let us change the locale. This is the salon of Madame, decorated by an artist, one of her friends. The lines are simple and nice; the corners are well defined; there is no crowding. Small frescoes transport us to charming country places, vaguely animated by even more charming figures. Everything is orderly, well arranged; chairs, well spaced, rest on their legs; tables carry few objects, not yet those for tea, the smell of which will soon penetrate the room. A few flowers isolated in their crystal vases rise from stem to petal; daylight shines through the half-open bay window.—The mistress of the house, unobtrusively but admirably dressed (by her friend, the artist), is expecting her guests, a book in her hand, some letters nearby. Everything here is well prepared for a refined gathering, for discreet, orderly conversation. No intruder is likely to appear. The atmosphere could not be more propitious for all that adorns life and gives it a natural dignity. Would this charming lady possess "the art of evoking happy moments"?—Here are her guests. The milieu surrounds them with pleasant comfort without making it too difficult for them to adjust. They sit down and talk. A perfect arrangement for a fastidious party. Let us go on. . . .

We are now in the foyer of a concert hall constructed according to the most modern acoustical research. In the lobbies the purpose of this place is expressed in severe sobriety that demands silence. In the hall proper our eyes are not attracted by any specific detail. The high beautiful walls seem to wait; the platform has the aspect of a grandiose altar also awaiting the spark to set flames rising toward the sky as a token of gratitude. The plainness of the seats inspires activity rather than indolence. The audience is about to enter.

Let us go on. . . .

On his birthday Albert received a fine book in which the styles of architecture are analyzed and shown in large illustrations. Abacus and entasis no longer hold secrets for him; *he knows what they are*. The earlier movements are followed by the periods of the Henrys and the Louis. Lastly, modern art, well represented, initiates the pupil into the search for freedom characteristic of his generation. Free, free . . . no longer to stagnate in antiquated styles, but to imitate nature in its great variety, to delight in new forms!—Oh, how well he understands this drive towards full vitality!—To encourage him, he is permitted to transform his room according to his ideas. In his feverish ardor, Albert wants to change everything, including the form of the walls, doors, and windows. He almost reproaches the daylight for not obeying his orders, not satisfying his modern ideas. But where to put his books? He conceives extraordinary shelves for them. And his notebooks? He will trace on their covers daring designs, which—at the very least—will be unlike anything known. It remains for this youngster only to write with sympathetic ink on lotus leaves with a hummingbird feather.—What are the ideas he will thus inscribe? Well, he has not even thought of that; no, indeed, he wishes to be free at last!—

A week later, Albert falls ill. During his convalescence in his transformed room he totters on his poor little weakened legs; his trembling hands make the lotus leaves tremble and his tired eyes search for a spot, a single spot to rest a while. . . .—

And there is the sun! Oh, how beautiful it is, how good!—

A corner of a public promenade; great and perfectly-spaced trees contrast their upright trunks with the crowd that has come to see the unveiling of a monument.—Prior to that event, artists had met all the requirements and, fascinated by the task, had spent many days seeking a conviction capable of creating an image, a will strong enough to give it precise expression. Stimulated by joy and agony, they went through the fire of a hard-won realization: their work is to be an entirely new manifestation of contemporary thought; never, perhaps, will this idea be expressed again with as much audacity and sincerity.—The die is cast. The work, chosen by a jury, is slowly raised toward the sky in the natural setting provided for it. Today it is open to the view of all. It must be shown and its modesty is of no interest to anyone.—

It is in the corner of the promenade, under majestic tree trunks. Harmony is achieved; the deep desire of the artist has found its form. And we, concerned largely with ourselves, walk in front of it.—Let us go on. . . .

Let us climb a mountain. At the top is a sanatorium built and equipped according to the most modern requirements. There nothing is overlooked to fight sickness. Verandas, bathing facilities, scales, impeccable linen, modern kitchens. The entire establishment resembles a white and constantly scrubbed plate. Strict discipline is imposed on its attendants. Everything works smoothly.—

Yet mark: there are eyes and their glances. These windows of the soul have been forgotten. The other windows are open wide, and the sun streams in.

My friend has come from Bayreuth and in what condition! He rushes to a music store; buys scores; rents a good, a very good piano; takes theory lessons more seriously than before; learns all about the orchestra and the handling of voices. . . . All this is for the one great feat of understanding Wagner. He neglects nothing to achieve his aim. How he admires the incomparable master!

My friend is quite talented and profits from his studies; he becomes familiar with orchestra scores. He will be able to compose and orchestrate like Wagner, thus plunging his audience into the same irresistible passionate surge!—He succeeds. His pastiche is ingenuous, the very image of his model! This modern orchestra, what a medium of expression!

Freedom, freedom. . . .

The painter has to express the very vibration of things, movement included, and even more than that. The painter is free, oh so free! to express several movements at a time. This is the principle in a studio.

Opposite lives sculptor Y. He believes that a plastic form should emerge from formless surroundings; life will spring from contrasts, a life denied to the definite form without support by the indefinite form. This is self-evident, and only thus will art, finally liberated, express life as it defines our time.

Farther off, architect Z knows that a façade is homogeneous, and that its unity must not be violated by the material used in its construction. His idea is to cast it like lead in a mold. He even succeeds in this, and his art, finally freed from an unpleasant feeling of heaviness, rises in a single unit of unrecognizable origin. It is the victory of mind over matter and consequently a precise expression of our contemporary evolution.

I climb up the stairs to rest at my friend A's (alias "Mr. Awning, *canvas*," for the outsider; "Staircase" for intimates). A large studio with pleated heavy drapes, hung effectively, and expectant . . . ! My friend A lives in three dimensions: he always speaks about them, always reminds you that your body likewise has three dimensions and then adds that it is alive and therefore moving. — Letting myself drop on his couch—which of course *resists*—I am fully conscious of my three dimensions.[16] Don't you see, he tells me, that bodily feeling emancipates us from ourselves, makes us free at last? Our entire contemporary culture leads toward this redeeming evolution . . . !

I know that tune; and, exhausted with freedom, I leave him!

Free, Free! From what? This refrain rings in my ear like the whim of a fool. For heaven's sake, from what do they all want to be liberated? From themselves: they are already, to the utmost! From others? They talk only about their fellow man and are bored when they are away from him. At home again, I search within myself for new forms and for the freedom that justifies all these efforts . . . and I find the soul unchanged, the heart always the same and, on the outside, three cumbersome dimensions. Once it occurred to me to perfume by dog when he came home smelling badly. The poor creature sniffed every place, in every corner of all the surroundings . . . everywhere he smelled eau de cologne. Because of our modern bathrooms we need no longer smell badly. Would we look then for new forms to put us on the wrong scent? It may be possible, though unkind to all.

I dozed in my chair, my head heavy, my heart aching.—Toepfer in Doctor Festus[17] gives the mayor "his grand normal dream." This evening, I believe, I had mine.

Atmospheric waves drew all of us into cosmic space; breathing was hard, yet holding on to each other, we had to follow the others. The silence was absolute, beyond terror. For us who were uprooted without the shadow of any firm spot to cling to, one hope still remained; this could not be eternity, for we were still measuring time; therefore a change had to come sooner or later.—Indeed we finally arrived at a finite space; our feet rested on ground similar to our earth. Oh! any enslavement rather than this moral storm! We would not shrink from any meanness. Penned up like sheep, we felt dominated. From our own planet, we had preserved only a soothing feeling of fatalism and a minimum of self-control had been gained. Hope? No. Despair? Not despair either. There was suddenly dead calm.—

Unfamiliar sounds, clear but unintelligible, came close. Perhaps our fate had been decided. If we could only understand! The sounds were harsher now; we understood, it was our language!—

"These are from Earth. For the interrogation let us create *their* atmosphere."

Walls went up; a place appeared. As we sensed limits in the infinite, our eyes regained their normal expression, our thoughts their normal flow. The proportions were not ours, but they were proportions; we could adapt them to our size with a little effort that was not unpleasant, after the inconceivable terror of an infinite, of a probable eternity. Enclosed, we became ourselves again. Glory was lacking, but it was *human.*—The atmosphere became heavier, forms more specific. What would the interrogation be like? —As the passing of time in a film is cut off by scissors, so our time was abruptly cut off.

"You are a writer?" (This was addressed to my neighbor.)

"Yes, sir."

"Here is a sheet of paper, will you fill it with your thoughts?"

There was no reply. Ink and pen were close by; no writer can work without them. My neighbor began his task. He seemed to scratch his head as in Daudet's story,[18] and—trembling—to set down what his nails found there. After a moment his nails found nothing more, and the sheet remained almost empty.

"Is this all?"

"I believe this is all, sir."

"In that case, henceforth, this is all you will need."

And the invisible one handed the unfortunate writer a cutout the size of a postage stamp.

"Do not exceed these dimensions."

"No, sir."

That was all for him. And so he withdrew silently, because to ask for anything more did not seem appropriate.

"And you?" (Fortunately another neighbor; this gave me time.)

"I am a teacher, sir, our schools are marvelous and. . . ."

"Here is a child, instruct him."

"Yes, sir."

Where was the child? It was only necessary to speak.

My neighbor spoke, and, accordingly, a childlike form appeared in the mist, and approached the teacher. His words, however, soon failed to hold the phantom child's attention, and he found himself addressing empty space.

"This is all?"

"Sir, the child is not here!"

"For you he is here. In the future address your lesson only to him."

"Yes, sir."

And my neighbor, a mechanical doll in his arms, disappeared. With each disappearance we became more tense.

"You are a woman of the world, madame?" (Silence.) "And you pretend to have artistic interests?"

"Oh! Yes, sir."

"Here are materials to paint with, to create sculpture, to compose music, to write poetry, to plan a villa. Begin." (Embarrassed silence.)

"No answer?"

"But, sir, I . . . I do not . . . I do not know . . . this. . . ."

"You know how to converse?"

"Oh! Sir, yes, indeed."

"Do so.—Is that all?"

"But, I . . . I do not know, sir, I. . . ."

"Really.—There is your salon, madame."

And my new neighbor disappeared inside four cheerless walls within which was a spinning wheel.

Evil possibilities, indeed; but what to do when confronted with such a voice? I forgot to mention, this voice was not commanding, or offensive at all; its timbre was merely irresistible, like light.

"What are you?"

"A musician, sir; the modern orchestra is a medium of incomparable expression . . . and I. . . ."

"You feel a need for expression?"

"Yes, sir."

"The atmosphere here is favorable, it records inner creativity. Will you for a moment concentrate on what you have to express."

"Oh! with great pleasure!" (Long silence.)

"You have found something?"

"But, sir, my desire is boundless. . . ."

"Nobody questions that. Here is your instrument. It should suit you."

Our symphonist collapsed, a piccolo flute in his fingers. A telltale calm remained. How to escape it? We were immersed in it. . . .

"You are a physician?"

"Yes, sir."

"Here is a patient who suffers much. Relieve him and try to cure him."

"Yes, sir."

Long silence. Groaning was heard.

"You have succeeded?"

"Not yet, not yet, sir."

The groaning increased.

"Sir, have patience, I beg of you, I have just *verified*. . . ."

"Yes, I can see it. Here is your patient, and beware from now on of approaching any other."

"Yes, sir."

And the physician withdrew, holding his own image by the nose.

For a moment I felt someone behind me trying to come forward. I eagerly stepped aside.

"Sir, I am a philanthropist; I love my brethren, and I try to make myself useful."

"Very well. Here are several people. Make them happy!"

"Yes, sir, I shall try."

In an outburst of love he started by embracing them. The unhappy people did not notice him. He inquired about their circumstances; they began to talk among themselves. He put money in their hands, but the pieces slipped through their fingers. With explanatory gestures he built for them small, simple, yet practical houses, then hastily he scheduled meetings and concerts for them; he tried to lead them. Suddenly he found himself alone.

"You have succeeded?"

"Sir, they are not here! . . ."

"And you, where are you?"

"Here, sir."

"So I see. Stay here and do not pester them, do you understand?"

Silence. Withdrawal.—The eyes of the interrogator became visible, at least to me. His glance. . . . Oh! his glance! If I could only understand it. . . . I thought I could.

And then there was a long line of people and a series of other deceptive experiences, shamefully endured. Several people, nevertheless, were in a very good position; others were apparently sustained in their difficulties by the support of helpful witnesses. Then a sound of wings was heard.

Just when I had decided to speak, still another person advanced slowly, silently.

"I know; you are searching."

"Yes, sir, I am searching."

The majestic glance deepened still further; it released a radiant fire that moved gently in my direction. Immersed in this warm clarity, he disappeared; only the light remained. Here I am, the last, I thought; what shall I say? Again the glance sent off a bright beam. Irresistibly drawn toward it, I stepped forward.

"I think . . . I think I understand, sir. Only . . . I do not know."

"Continue not to know unless you are *with them.*"


At that moment I woke up in my chair, stretched out at ease. The evening had advanced; embers in the fireplace twinkled maliciously, like eyes.

Returning from a world that spoke, I found it pleasant to put them back in their place: "All right, so what? What holds you back?"—A little blue flame sprang up long enough to hiss in my ear: "That was salty, was it not?"—Then it retreated into the frosted glimmer. I grasped the tongs but did not go through with my gesture. After all, why deny it. To be sure, it was salty! Saltier than our tears, saltier than the whole ocean. . . .

# The Gesture of Art

## (1921)

### Preface

The purpose of this treatise is to reveal the secret working of a single existence, just as it developed, and to do this in a form that is not biographical nor even chronological. Its aim is to demonstrate, once again, that the deepest values in life come from ideas that are the result not of reasoning but of a series of forceful experiences. For the sake of greater clarity I first intended to include some designs, visible testimonies of my development, but I had to abandon this idea, for the designs have already been published in my preceding book, *The Work of Living Art*. Nevertheless I hope that even without such support, the reader can grasp how and in what form the gesture of art has appeared to me and taken possession of my artistic conscience. For, though I prefer to explain this gesture within the frame of my own artistic activities—and this constitutes the bio- graphical character of my study—it should not be concluded that I limit the field only to the experiences to which I happen to be accustomed. Quite the contrary! With this explicit reservation I dare hope for tolerance for an experiment that might easily be misunderstood.

The passionate ardor that inspired this study will perhaps be felt in these pages.

### I. The Onlooker

There are those who die as they are born: *Onlookers* of the external world. The unconscious appraisal that the child makes of his environment continues for them the limit of their ability to adapt themselves. Once they have reached that limit they stop, then decline and disappear. They depart; the door of their theatre box is closed again, and the performance goes on, totally indifferent to their absence and to the carriage that takes them elsewhere. These people can be very active and useful. Some store up in writing everything that comes under their observations. This may be considerable, but it is booty. They have taken; they have given nothing. This baggage remains behind in the theatre box; at the most they take along their opera glasses for other shows . . . certainly no longer for this one. Until the end, they consider themselves instruments of observation. Forever *onlookers,* they are not surprised to see the same spectacle unfold behind them as in front of them, to their right as well as to their left, because for them life is a panorama of which they are the center; they move only in order to grasp the details better. When they do move, the panorama changes its aspect, no doubt; but this is of little concern to them, as long as they are offered a full view of it and a seat in the center.

They are immobile in spite of all this movement.

The position of *onlooker,* which these immobile individuals maintain from birth to death, reveals itself in many ways of course. It might provide a pleasant theme for conversation, since everyone could contribute his own observations and experience. Yet this writer does not regard the subject as pleasant; rather he thinks that with it he approaches the crucial point of our existence. He believes that the goal of life is an attitude, that the approaching of this attitude is of prime importance, and that all other problems have no importance, very likely no significance, except in relation to this attitude.

I spoke of an approach. There is consequently a distance to traverse, a road to follow. What can they be?

In my preceding study, *The Work of Living Art,* I quoted a passage from Schopenhauer, the philosopher-artist, who boldly asserts that all outstanding men have stated, or tried to state, "the same thing" in the specific area of intellect, knowledge or art in which they happen to be active. It is impossible not to subscribe to this idea, which, though paradoxical in appearance and in form, is so deeply human in reality. From this truly frank and suggestive view-point all activities and their consequences are symbols since, above and beyond their intelligible and definite meaning, they express the same desire, the same urge for some "thing"—which is unknown, perhaps, but which nevertheless can be expressed only through our aspirations and our actions. Schopenhauer must have sensed the power of his idea, for it is quite evident that no cultured person considers that his own works exist in themselves and for themselves alone: all agree that they are symbolic. Since we live in action, our only means of approaching the attitude which must be the goal of our existence, of understanding the space we must cross, and of finding the road we must follow is clearly through symbols based on activity. Our mind is such that it gains more time and covers more space by employing the tool we call symbol than by any other tool imaginable.

To interpret a symbol, that is to say, to purge it from the incidentals that are part of it and give it its form, it will suffice to recognize the precise difference between the incidentals and their eternal content. (In philosophy: the phenomenon and the inner meaning of the phenomenon.)

In every field of activity the inner essence of the phenomenon can be identified only with our own self. Humanity is the one immortal thing we can perceive: whatever is only related to it is nonessential, whatever is inextricably connected with it is eternal. Time and space, for instance, are related to our mode of living. We feel painfully dependent on them, but merely dependent; our personality does not identify with them. Compelled to adopt their restrictive forms, we accept them and *know* that in so doing we depart from another center of gravity. Will the new center be one in which the centrifugal force which now restricts us must renounce its isolating power?

Art, philosophy, natural sciences, and those sciences concerned with the more specialized and direct knowledge of man and with the influence we can exercise on him or to which we can ourselves submit—all these are, it seems, superior activities. Next we place the more or less manual, intellectually passive occupations. At the lowest level we discover idleness, a search for happiness where it cannot be found, but in our sense an activity nevertheless. When we now try to separate the inner essence from these various activities, we have to admit that their classification is probably illusory and that their degree of involvement (indicated by the results each obtains) or their degree of clarity (indicated by their expression of the hidden essence) do not depend on their place in society or what title society gives them.

Let us therefore begin by examining these diverse activities in order to measure the extent of the nonessentials they contain.

The study of nature, in all its aspects, appears to us dominated by phenomena. The aim of both the man of science and the man who applies that science is to observe, ever more extensively and more meticulously, these phenomena, the laws that govern them, their mutual influence, and the conclusions that can be drawn from such observation. Imagination and intuition undoubtedly carry scientists beyond such observation and enable them to ascertain phenomena before their existence can be verified. Therefore the study of nature can concern only the phenomenon, unless as an intellectual game it falls into the domain of philosophical speculation.

Psychology and its branches, the desirable or harmful applications of it (pedagogy, politics, etc.), inquire into the human phenomenon. This is primarily an experimental activity, though the experiments are made with our fellow men. Statistics (in the widest sense of the term) is its proper field even in its applications, since these are an integral part of observation itself and must therefore be statistical. The teacher stands before his pupils, the leader of men before individuals or assemblies. Their objects are perhaps less diverse than are those of the scientist, but they are certainly quite different from his objects; for in these fields, the observer is of the same species as what he observes! He is an ant observing other ants.

Art occupies a place apart; it always has done so and for good reasons. If, everywhere else, the phenomenon and observation of it tend to become confused, even in their use in art, the phenomenon is always subordinated; acoustics are never confused with a symphony, nor colors with a painting. In art, the phenomenon is not central, as it is in other fields, but it is instead replaced by a central concern seemingly unrelated to the phenomenon.

Although manual workers are overshadowed by the scientists and industrialists, their product remains much closer to its maker; and this closeness tends to bring together the work of the artisan and that of the artist. The knowledge of his craft is certainly a prerequisite for the artisan. But in applying it he begins to probe into the same unknown as does the artist; the phenomenon and the purpose beyond the phenomenon are no longer confused. What makes the artisan so valuable is not his exclusive use of the phenomenon but a superior aim that he is able to conceive.

The statement about the artisan reminds us that a certain amount of manual work is involved also in science and in its application. Perhaps it is arbitrary to discriminate between the true artisan and the man who works in the same manner in behalf of science and industry. Therefore it is vital to define properly their essential difference, which derives from their aims. The role of the technician is to facilitate the functioning of phenomena as much as possible. His aim always concerns the certain phenomena and is exclusively directed toward promoting them. The artisan has no such obligation; he has the perfect right to select the combinations of his material, that is, of the phenomena he employs. In this regard his profession is free in comparison to the totally dependent profession of the man of science and its branches. We ordinarily abuse the term "free" in referring to a profession. The free man is the one who is in full command of his work, including its *purpose,* not he who spends his days as he pleases! A workman confined to extremely hard labor, who may introduce into his work an element of discretion that belongs to him alone, is in a far better position than the scientist whose research would be paralyzed by the least deviation of this kind . . . !

This brief account has doubtless made us aware of the new problem facing us. Existing classifications of work and their implied meaning have little value; still less, the social standing which these classifications suggest. Every category of work will have to be thoroughly scrutinized anew, until the ultimate differentiation is found that can provide a new scale of values.

As we consider the various activities of man solely from the viewpoint we have already suggested, we discern two ways to consider phenomena and, more important, two different ways to utilize them. One would seem to correspond to the attitude of the *onlooker,* the title of this chapter. Here, we approach the

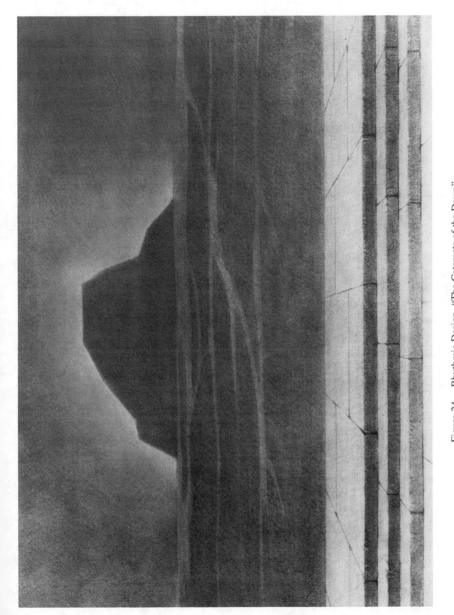

Figure 24.  Rhythmic Design, "The Cataracts of the Dawn"

phenomenon by scrupulously respecting what it does; we can make use of it, whether for purely scientific ends (knowledge), or for a utilitarian aim (technique), by humbly trying to understand it. Intuition may be of precious help in this attempt, but the intuition still must be strictly based on observation of the phenomenon after the fact, if it is used at all.

The other attitude seeks a new element (or new challenge) independent of the phenomenon and governing it. This element is not concerned with utilitarian or scientific ends, and, consequently, our exploration of it may be stopped or taken up wherever we wish. It is an element outside the center of that panorama displayed exclusively for us as spectators. The search for this element breaks this tenacious charm of *onlooking* and almost violently installs a new order. This does not imply as yet the superiority of either attitude. We already understand that the two attitudes can collide with each other at certain points, indeed can even somehow penetrate one another a little, and this must make us cautious. For he who remains an *onlooker* of life until he dies lives on a much lower level than the one who seeks and finds another approach to activity.

It is characteristic of a panoramic view that it unfolds before us, and that we see nothing whatever except the spectacle *presented* to us. We may change places but our attitude remains the same; as a result, only our reaction to the sight of the outer world makes us conscious of ourselves. If we close our eyes nothing remains. Some distinguished men have held such an attitude but they rightly surmised that there must be something else. Intellectually they even probed into this (philosophy is relentless in this regard), but whichever direction they took, they succeeded only in pushing their own horizon farther away. In a complacent euphemism they called this "enlarging," but very few were able to maintain the illusion until death.

Art is the force that works upon the dual function of our personality; this is its very essence. Its aim is to remove us from the spectator's position, to pull us away from an altogether unfavorable relationship and to free us permanently from a paralyzing centrifugal force. If we only would let it act!

I have mentioned art alone, with no reference to the individual artist and his work. Using the telephone is not an activity, but meditating on a work of art and letting it sink in *is* an activity, or definitely ought to be. Now we have on the one hand, the artist—the creator of the work; and on the other, the person for whom the work is conceived. This distinction is a bit arbitrary. The artist creates as much for himself as for the beholder; yet if the latter achieves a healthy division only by approaching the artist as closely as possible, the artist in turn will obtain freedom only by resolutely going to meet the beholder. The activities of the two differ, but their aim is the same, as we shall see.

Many artists use sound, form, color, nay, even words as the electrician uses electric current. They are manufacturers. For many amateurs, on the other hand, the work of art merely embellishes the panorama they enjoy. They are consumers. Art really has nothing to do with either of these two groups who are but one step away from the idler. The idler, though, may escape from his predicament, whereas the manufacturers of art and their consumers, believing they can escape the emptiness of their life through their activities, deceive themselves to the very end.

The essence of art must therefore be found in the division of our personality, and its aim is to free us from paralysis, not at once but in a gradual yet almost miraculous evolution. Consequently wherever such total or partial division of our personality occurs, the *presence* of art is manifest whether an actual so-called "work of art" is present or not. And whenever we firmly desire to escape the centrifugal force that isolates us as individuals, we are headed in the direction of art.

Art is therefore not a work; art is above all, a *decision* to follow a deliberate course. Who would prevent us from believing that this decision is applicable to all human activity?*

Let us return to more concrete ideas. Everyone is aware of the high regard, usually mixed with a bit of envy, which is enjoyed by man called "an artist." We can also note our satisfaction upon discovering that an artisan "brings art" to his craft. If in other professions we do not always use the term "art" to designate this particular contribution—because our ideas in this connection are still confused—we nevertheless experience in many cases the same pleasant surprise. In all activities a division between objectivity and the entirely personal contribution can bring about the desired effect, to stimulate our involvement. This is everywhere the result of a decision, I should like to say of a conversion (in the real meaning of the term), but we are not ready for that, or not yet anyway.** Let us be satisfied with a "decision," a potential force which, when it grows, will surely become capable of the great acts of liberation.

However, if we agree that art is not in itself a work, then we are obliged to distinguish between art and other activity. This brings us back to the statement that the decision peculiar to art can actually be made in every human activity. An artist, therefore, is not merely the creator of what we refer to as an art work; but, on the contrary, any of us may become artists. We all have the means of stimulating this latent force in ourselves. Our decision must be unselfish; this is precisely what makes it valuable.

But disinterestedness does not work in a void. Its etymology implies leaving the center that has been of interest to *us alone*. Thus we leave ourselves and

---

*For instance a psychologist who is willing to take this direction unquestionably reveals the presence of art. In leaving the exclusive domain of science and its branches he becomes a philanthropist. And philanthropy in its purest form is undoubtedly an expression of art.

**It is, of course, noticeable in education. A true educator is always an artist.

enter the panorama in order to become part of it. Here duality operates; to detach oneself from something does not mean to obliterate it; rather, to give it less attention. Art—that is to say the decision, its peculiar feature—allows us to see ourselves reflected in the spectacle of life. And since the object of the picture that best epitomizes and magnifies it is the human being, our likeness, we can take mankind as a mirror in which we *recognize* ourselves. In this sense, art causes us to recognize ourselves in our fellow-men, and having achieved this in art, strengthen the decision to apply the same process to all other activities. All the higher religions are directed toward this end. Their value depends primarily on the extent of the sacrifice and the determination they demand of us.

This is all very well, perhaps we may say, but it does not alter the fact that the work of art and its creator exist and that artistic activity is, after all, usually far more narrowly defined. Of course, but you will have noticed that so far, I have avoided the term artistic. To me it seems to restrict the idea of art and probably it is the cause of so much confusion on this point. Today it seems to mean merely the application of a general principle, and only a particular kind of application at that. This adjective, artistic, never quite satisfies us; we sense its vagueness, and, almost involuntarily we even sense that it suggests some inferiority. Does it not sound somewhat weak? Do we confine art to this single definition because we are afraid to admit how much it is absent from our daily life? If so, we can leave the responsibility for this definition to the artists whose profession it is, as we believe—thus remaining separate from them, and, above all, separate from their works. The isolated position of the artist misleads us; we forget that his activity is a symbol, like all others. We stand *before* a work of art as before a cast-off object, which we have only to contemplate. Here the misunderstanding begins. But artistic creation necessarily carries the seed of this misunderstanding, which exposes the artists to all the dangers of a chronic decadence. Why? Because the artists stand alone. We refuse to collaborate with them, we who ought to be their models. And so, far from being willing to identify ourselves with them, we are not anxious for them to identify with us. We place the artistic creation before us like a painting on an easel; yet this is the activity which preeminently, almost by definition, seeks to move us out of the center and to unite us with our fellow men. Still, this is not surprising. Did we not treat the teaching of Jesus in the same manner? Who would dare deny it?

Everywhere and always we take the symbol for its divine reality. If I am not mistaken, this is called materialism, or, at least, it is the mental attitude that leads to the shallowest materialization of our existence. The years that have passed have proven it, and the condition in which they have left us is not unrelated to this fact. "Thou shalt not make for thyself any graven images." We have done just that; and we have idolized and served them hypocritically. This has been our vaunted idealism, our purified Christianity, our refined art. This is what has become of our love for our neighbor. Like barbarians we have lived and are still living in a forum of debased material symbols before which we parade unceasingly. To them we address our prayers, but they have hearts of stone and do not hear us.

I have lingered on the subject of the spectators, of those whose attitudes are negative. Let us now consider him who has experienced the duality achieved through art and who is willing to yield to it completely in order to be free—the creator of a work of art. Today his situation is tragic. Since the artist, removed from the center, faces himself as well as mankind, he seeks fervently to tie these two visions together, so closely that they blend into one. That is his aim, even though he may not always be conscious of it or, at least, not always capable of expressing it. He wishes to reflect mankind and to find himself in it. He has the means to accomplish this, but for a long time mankind has avoided the efforts. Worn out by the struggle, at last he renounces the *living* mirror and creates an artificial glass that reflects his own image. There is no doubt whatever that he is aware of the distortion; it disturbs him and he strives to reduce the discomfort, as the photographer tries to reduce exaggerated perspective. But to no avail: the *living* mirror alone is able to receive his life and to give it back transfigured. The glass merely reflects a distorted image; the expression of his face remains lifeless. How could such a tool ever kindle the fire in the eye? For this one must be reflected in the eyes of others, not be miserably forced always to assume one and the same image. The artist, beaten, grimaces at his own image. We have too many examples of this to doubt it.

But what about us? What have we done to allow us to judge him? Nothing! Precisely nothing! We let the artist who looked for us lose his way in the deserted expanse of the panorama. Everything must be *offered* to us while we remain unresponding in the center.

Everywhere art is the liberating force. It *is* life, freed from whatever paralyzes or arbitrarily colors it. Undeniably it is influenced by its geographic and historic background and these are perhaps formidable influences. Yet such influences, far from contradicting our assertion, only make it clearer. Though art needs some support from circumstances (I might almost say, a certain amount of circumstantial matter is necessary in a positive and complete work) it can nevertheless always affirm its independence in a symbol which transcends all such contingencies. A Japanese offers the symbol of his freedom as eloquently on a thin small sheet in Indian ink as a Rubens does on huge multicolored canvases. In three chords played on the piano the composer can convey his independence as clearly as he could by means of a large modern orchestra. The *actual* presence of the symbol does not depend on the quantity or relative quality of the elements used by the artist; therefore art is independent of milieu. Here as elsewhere, we confuse the phenomenon with its inner meaning. The specific means of which one or another artist avails himself is no more part of art than is the potter's clay. Art begins at the point where the potter introduces into his work the expression, no matter how modestly this is done, of his freedom. And the child, adding ornaments of his own imagination to the sketch that he copies shows as much or as little of the presence of art as an engineer who expresses the whole mechanism of a tremendous utilitarian construction in a personal, nontechnical manner.

Does this mean that the development and perfection of technique are unimportant? Certainly not! Our concern is only to distinguish clearly between the actual presence, as we call it, and the incidental form given it by the artist. Freedom can indeed assert itself alone; but it is a vessel, and we feel the need to fill it and thus to occupy the space and time it puts at our disposal. Here the form of the symbol enters the game, and we have seen that this does not depend exclusively on the creative artist but that all of us are responsible for it. Now, when we criticize the form and ignore the divine presence that breathed life into it and gave it a sense of solidarity, we degrade the symbol and, by the same token, all artistic activity. It would be just as bad, however, to be content with the mere presence of art and otherwise to attend to our own business.

Thus we find ourselves in a vague and poorly defined sphere of activity. Time and again lured by the form alone, we anxiously return to the center, in our opinion the most favorable viewpoint for contemplation. Then, however, we become conscious of our responsibility and disturbed, we abandon once more this ominous center to become wandering adventurers. But the artist does not seek us in this vague sphere, so we never meet him. Many do not mind this, and therefore give up a happiness which they cannot imagine and thus do not desire.

Others, inadequately prepared, suffer because they feel the injustice of this separation. Still others despair; they understand the importance of gaining a duality, and yet they search in vain for their reflected image. Two more steps and they would discover it. But like some neurasthenics, they stop at a line across the road incapable of reaching the goal of their aspirations. How much do certain faces, seen in exhibitions, concerts, or on the street, betray this troubled condition, which no pretense can hide! They have brought learning and refined taste into their life—everything except the ability to give themselves, and therefore they are always in quest of themselves.

At this point I may be asked what the gift of oneself can actually be, a gift so earnestly sought by the artist. The very question both defines our attitude and condemns it. One possible example will perhaps bring us closer to the solution of the question itself.

When we talk about art—that is, about art works—the observer cannot help noticing that the work is almost invariably regarded as existing in itself and as having always so existed in a pre-established harmony. The *blank page* is forgotten. Yes, the blank page! No matter whether the page is of paper, marble, or canvas, does it ever occur to us *clearly* that, before the work is complete, it is merely inexpressive material awaiting the artist who is entirely responsible for the new creation?

Everything has yet to be done, absolutely everything: form, color combination, the grouping of words and sounds. Nowhere can the artist find anything, anything at all, with which they can be compared. He faces a blank page! All the others—the artisan, the scientist, the historian, the psychologist—all of them have beside their relatively untouched page a second, well-documented page. Their labor is a work of intuition, applied to already available material; often it is only a compilation, a combination, an intellectual speculation arrived at by means of ready-made components. The artist, however, has before him only a single page, totally empty. The components that the visible world seems to offer him so liberally provide him with no data. A landscape, a moving body, or any similar subject chosen by the artist obviously has not the power to project itself into the domain of art. It can even be maintained that the subject resists interpretation and that there is always a struggle between the artist and nature. The waiting blank page expresses this struggle; it does not possess the sensitive compliance of the photographic film. The artist knows that he has to use force, for the external world no more contains the seed of a picture, a statue, a poem, or a building, than acoustics, the seed of a symphony. The subject which is only *represented* by the art work has nothing to do with the latter's quality as a work of art. Accordingly, the artistic interpretation belongs to a mode of existence different from the material reality and, in this sense, every work of art is the symbol of a victory over nature.

The scientist strives to wrest her secrets from nature; the artist has the power to bend nature to his will; and it is his will, not nature, that is expressed in the work of art. The tyrant gives orders, and the slave executes them; otherwise the slave has nothing in common with those orders. The artist is the tyrant and nature is his slave. No freer profession can be imagined.

The artist's first impulse is to express the happiness he feels in his freedom! But freedom is primarily a state of mind, a mode of being; it is above all the result of a victory. If the artist yields to his surroundings, his work will present merely a slavish or fanciful reproduction. Many weaken! Yet fortunately there are some who can not yield. Then the blank page acquires a wondrous and tragic value. Then, too, begins the arduous conquest. And here the miraculous duality of art sets to work: the artist hears an echo to his victory cry; he has compelled the external world to serve him as a sounding board, as an obedient surface that can reflect his own image to him, the creative artist. And now it is he, the conqueror, who will be able to *give*! But to whom?

Oh, the wondrous and tragic value of the blank page! This untouched, yet demanding space has been the cause of the sacred intimacy without which the work of art is stillborn. The artist is powerless when he faces the outer world alone; he imitates and compiles, and he cries out in his agony. From our modern art galleries, our concerts, and many other events rises this monotonous and pitiable cry; we come to dread it or to meet it with cynicism. The artist who conquers is able to create something that resembles himself, thus establishing a kind of contact. But, alas! now he feels the pain of his new solitude; he sees himself honestly now, and not in the artificial mirror of his arbitrary fancy and his search for technique. Yet he misses looking into the eyes of others. The image of himself provides the indispensable condition for his art, but not yet the *object* of his deep desire, the ultimate affirmation offered in a look from another that will say to him, "It is I!" Though his own reflected image is a force, it expresses his agony and exasperates him. Deprived of that other look, the artist then cries out in his agony. We have compelled him to do so.

The simple artistic recording of the world around us that characterizes our modern works of art is an ephemeral product that is really neither science nor art; its appearance of objectivity does hardly set it free. The most it can give us is a cry that has no response.—By contrast, whatever form the artist gives his cry of anguish before the image of himself, the outcry is a true work of art, though as painful for the artist as for us.

Not without apprehension does the writer here touch the domain of the inexpressible. Yet, as he stated at the beginning of this study, only the symbolic form is capable of guiding inspiration to the mysterious depths of the unconscious. The reader may therefore forgive him for having adopted this form and for seeking under the veneer of words the invisible realities that escape rational analysis.

## II. The Reflected Image

In his chapter on tears, Schopenhauer, the philosopher-artist previously quoted, assures us that our purest tears have their source in the compassion incited by our own suffering, and are therefore caused by a tender look into our own heart. As an example he offers Ulysses who, listening to the recitation of his adventures, covered his face and sobbed freely. The example is indeed eloquent; everyone recognizes himself in it. Since tears are sweet whenever they do not flow at the time of our suffering but are only its echo, we have for a long time felt the need to evoke them artificially and in a manner that leaves us free to indulge in them at will, without the compulsion of reality.

This is the origin of dramatic art and the source of the emotion we demand of it. Our many old tribulations, and our joys as well, are reflected in the characters of the play, and they come back to us in a plausible form in which we *recognize* ourselves. This reappearance moves us and transforms our real emotions into a symbol that bestows upon them an everlasting value. Those emotions are therefore mixed with admiration. We extend the scope of our feelings in the theatre; it is incontestable that our aesthetic enjoyment there results from the momentary communion with all our fellow men. Thus dramatic art brings about the liberating duality; however, it does so artificially. The image of ourselves is presented to us *without* our actual assistance, and to go on with our example, everyone when leaving the theatre feels a painful shock upon again encountering the spectacle of real life. We were able to cry about fictitious joys and tribulations and now we feel ourselves shut off from real joys and sorrows. Confronted by fiction, we first exclaimed: "It is I, yes I"—then at last: "It is we, *ourselves*!" Yet we refuse this identification when we are faced with reality, and therefore, we cannot be liberated. We shall not enter the "Kingdom of Heaven."

The creative artist goes through a rather similar experience. He cries out his agony and thus presents it to us in a spectacular form. Increasingly insistent, he expects an echo. Unquestionably the realization of his work comforts him; he feels a tenderness akin to love. . . . He admires his work and identifies himself with it! But if his experience is confined to this, the work remains a monologue, even though it may be quite beautiful, and impressive. We can see and hear it with great sympathy, but if we are not actually moved by it, we perpetuate the seclusion of the artist and his work. If an artist reads these lines, he will understand me.

No, the artist feels that he must not dwell on private and entirely personal admiration; his dignity is at stake. "Certainly it is my image"—he will say— "But is it not theirs, too—those who are indispensable to me?" . . . He wants to present the mirror which has reflected his own image to others so that they, too, may recognize themselves in it. He wants to free himself from it.

As we have seen, we refuse this offer.

The reflected image is then the artist's last resort. It shows the quality of work he will produce until his work is completely liberated. Dramatic art is an artificial example of such a reflected image. We should understand its lesson, a negative lesson, it is true. Our passive attitude prevents us from going beyond that single example and thereby gaining a new insight. We erect a permanent symbol, like a statue, in order to idolize it, as if Dionysus were made of marble.

It follows that artists are not free, that their creations have no meaning for us and that art does not count in our life. Many are willing to put up with this state of affairs, but I am not speaking to them.

These pages sound like an indictment, yet their aim is constructive. We cannot build with dilapidated material. The ground must be cleared; debris provides a poor foundation, and I should like to get down to bedrock before erecting the new building.—To this end let us assess our position.

To consider life a panorama with ourselves in the center appeared to us a sterile and comparatively negative attitude. We then sought an attitude different from cold passivity, one that would take us beyond the reach of the centrifugal force that works to exclude us from life. The symbol helps us find such an attitude by expressing in a concrete form a reality that otherwise would escape our understanding. To interpret a symbol, it will therefore be enough to strip it of those incidentals that make it a definite, i.e., concrete object, and thus discover its eternal meaning, which would have been inaccessible to us without its help. We have found also that the more we *take part in* life, the higher is the level on which our actions operate, and the more disinterested they become. Consequently, activities that call upon us merely to describe the phenomena of life (and to study in detail their possible and useful combinations without authorizing us to interfere personally in the true nature of these phenomena in order to modify them according to our needs) are essentially inferior to those activities in which the phenomena are subordinated to the demands of our free will. This distinction authorizes us to establish the measure of nonessentials that characterize this or that occupation and assign it its place not in society, but in humanity itself. So we shall establish a new evaluation of activities based on this measurement.

Art seems to be something relating the eternal essence of things to the representation of them; it is a principle, not a work. Since it forces us to give up the attitude of the passive spectator, the negative position in the center, we have likened it to the resolution taken toward this end and compared it with a *decision*. Indeed, art liberates us. Whenever we are determined to ensure its call, art will appear. It is independent of what we call the work of art; the latter is only a particular manifestation of art and of extremely varied value. The new table of evaluation must be applied to it as it is to any other activity, for nonessentials can become as tyrannical and harmful here as elsewhere. It is even probable, as we have already stated, that art may reveal itself in all human activities, *according to our attitude and the decision involved.* This will determine the worth of a personality on all rungs of the social ladder and in this new currency a person of the highest reputation may not be worthy of tying the sandals of a shopkeeper.

However, the artist occupies an exceptional position, since his decision (the presence of art) is already implicitly involved in the very origin of his work; the remarkable privileges he enjoys are therefore justified. While we remained in the center, we expected the spectacle of life to be *offered* to us; whereas the artist felt the need to offer it to us lest his activity remain meaningless. His decision is unselfishness itself. Art is a free impulse and the work of art is its crowning result. Yet if the artist can ever hope to become one with his fellow-man, the latter must anticipate him: this is the gesture of art *for all.* The work of art is as much the concern of the audience as it is of the artist himself; and the gesture of art is the prerequisite of the artist's existence for which we are responsible.

Religions acknowledge and recommend such a gesture. We have seen that the teaching of Jesus may be regarded as a unique doctrine and model in this respect; in it, art is firmly supported. Without the gesture of art and the attitude it implies, our role in life remains an optical illusion. Having received nothing and given nothing, we disappear, empty-handed.

This survey has so far omitted that typical artificial example, dramatic art. It is a burning issue; everyone is sensitive to this art form and must come to terms with it. Here we are at the very core of the problem and nothing could better convince us of our responsibility. And this, it seems, is precisely what we dread.—Let us face it boldly!

A play is written to be performed. The purely literary drama is nonsense. If it can exist without production, why build costly temples and make so much fuss about it? The answer will be that a majority of literary people disapprove of such temples. Perhaps, and in so doing they show an enlightened taste. However, this is less a matter of taste than of principle. Never to attend the theatre because it is poor is quite all right, but to condemn production as such, under the pretext that reading a play is more fascinating, is to commit an amateurish blunder. The musician analyzes an orchestra score better when he reads it in silence, but he will never consider this reading, this analysis, an independent thing existing by itself. The reason for this doubtless is that the combination of sound and rhythm conveys no significance to our intellect, whereas the grouping of words allows an intellectual understanding that gives therefore the illusion of a complete work, a purely literary work.* Nevertheless, the fact remains that dramatic art, because of its origin, is an art form which appeals to the eye as much as to the ear.

The deliberate neglect of this fact has thrown us into an anarchy in respect to dramatic art. The performance of a work is the only normal form of dramatic art. Currently performance of a drama requires the stage and the actor, on the one hand; on the other, the house and the audience. Since this study deals exclusively with the human aspect of performance, technical questions do not belong here. Thus there remain the spectators and the actors who in our theatres are distinctly separated from one another. The spectators are completely passive, an attitude encouraged because everything is presented to them. To entertain the spectators, the actors agree to imitate the external reactions caused by the impact of the characters and the situations. This fictitious game makes sense only if we recognize ourselves in it, and that is what we call verisimilitude.

There is then, on the one hand, a spectator who momentarily forgets his own surroundings to embrace those presented to him by the actors; on the other, there are the actors shedding their own personality to assume imaginary, but psychologically believable, characters. Fiction can go no further! Not content with its hold on the stage, it obliges the audience and the actors to lose temporar-

---

*In my previous book, *The Work of Living Art*, dramatic art has been thoroughly treated. Here I cannot possibly present more than a summary and this solely from the viewpoint of this new study.

ily what gave dignity to their life, namely, the vivid and active consciousness of their own personality.* At the end of the performance everyone takes on again the trappings of his own personality. This slipping in and out of character contributes much to enjoyment of the theatre, and is perhaps comparable to the pleasure which alcohol or any similar drug gives us: it is at the same time exciting and stupefying; it stimulates our emotions and lulls our common sense to sleep. Intermission always finds us in a morbid mood; we drag our body here and there hardly knowing where our soul is. Our pretense notwithstanding, it would be interesting to surprise and fix in photographs our facial expressions at this moment. There is a good reason for keeping our foyers so sumptuous; nobody would wish to spend an intermission in his study.

All this is in itself normal. Dramatic art would be ineffective if a portion of our daily life became entangled in it; the whole must be entirely imaginary. Theatre is the only art form that compels us at such a price to abandon our own self in order to recognize ourselves. The dramatist and his interpreters lull us into a hypnotic sleep to keep us in passive subservience; and, since it is a pleasure to forget ourselves as long as we are permitted to find ourselves again whenever we desire, we do so willingly in the theatre.

And the actor?—There is no doubt whatever that he feels the greatest satisfaction. In spite of the difficulties and serious shortcomings involved in a theatrical career, all actors love the theatre and give up acting only regretfully and late in life. Such constant abdication of one's self is too strong an opiate to be given up early! For actors, the sleep is not hypnotic and passive; on the contrary, it is the semblance of an activity pushed to the point of exaltation. We must not overlook the fact that, for the actor, the fiction extends well beyond the duration of the performance; he has to study his roles, develop and rehearse them, and thus to maintain himself in an imaginary atmosphere during a great part of his life. In addition, actors *offer us* the result of their labor. Is this not the outstanding feature of their profession? Other artists do so too, but with a significant difference; they offer it through their creations, not through the medium of their own person. Their works are their mouthpiece; whereas the actor speaks to us directly, with his whole personality, his body and soul. For this reason the work of dramatic art is the only one whose existence depends not only on the creator, but on the performers as well. Its material is *alive*. Colors, marble, words, and sounds do not live and do not directly arouse our interest *in humanity*. The actor arouses it, for himself, his own person, and the crime we all commit is that we reject him.

Thus even this very complex art form shares the fate of all others; it requires of us a disinterestedness that we are not willing to assume. Here however, our conduct is more reprehensible than in other arts because here the very

---

*If a real accident happens to disturb the performance, all feel the shock of embarrassment.

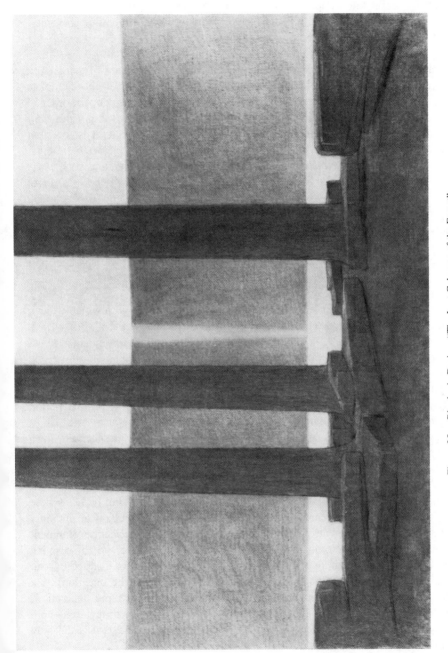

Figure 25. Rhythmic Design, "The Last Columns of the Forest"

existence of our fellow men is at stake; elsewhere, the artist, for all his suffering and our failure to support him, at least preserves his personality intact and perfectly free.—Dramatic art, therefore, always poses a problem of humanity, and we are right to fear it.

It is, as we have stated, the only art form that avails itself of the human being, the *living* being, to convey its work. It does so by means of actors. But is this the only form in which the living being may express itself in a complete work of art? Must our body necessarily assume a dramatic fiction in order to enter the realm of art? How about the statue and the painting? Is not this very body their most noble and perfect subject? They immobilize it, it is true, but perhaps the immobility is not an indispensable condition for the aesthetic presence of the body. Actors are not immobile! Can we not imagine a work of art that is free of a dramatic fiction and yet is presented by the *living* body? Cannot the beauty of this body—which fortunately nobody will dare deny, though many disavow it—have a value of its own, an independent existence in the realm of art without being immobilized for that purpose? If this is the case, dramatic art may be merely an application, quite possibly a wrong one, of the body's aesthetic life, which in my previous book I called *living art,* and we have the right to seek for the human body a different and very likely less damaging application.

The specific aim of dramatic art is to offer us an image with which we can identify. As we have seen elsewhere, such an encounter is the aim of all art. Now, only the actors' external appearance substantiates their resemblance to us, for the rest is dramatic fiction as opposed to our own real experiences. Yet the actors' external appearance is considerably modified by their costumes and completely governed by the imaginary world the costume represents. The costumed body then is merely the bearer of the fiction; it depends on that fiction and can indulge in nothing alien to it. In this sense dramatic art *makes use of* the living body but is not its direct expression. Evidently another art form expressive of the living body itself must exist. The body is alive only because it moves; this new art form will therefore have movement like dramatic art but will probably have no other relation to it.

But, one might ask, why speak of movements of the living body? Where can all that lead? Movement not directly utilitarian is accepted, if at all, only in sports and there because we assume that it will help our physical development and the balance of our faculties. Otherwise, we would never go to so much trouble. We call anything that has no practical value a luxury or distraction, and this includes anything that might free us temporarily from the one thing that seems honorable to us: practical activity. Theatre is the supreme distraction, since it forces others to engage in our activity for us. So defined, theatre is both sleep and its dreams. Instead of lying in bed we sit in a chair; that is the only difference.

In the theatre we remain outside the dramatic dream, i.e., in the auditorium, not on stage; therefore, this dream must be presented to us through a fiction in which we can recognize ourselves. In living art this will no longer be necessary; liberated from materialism and its conventions, which we had to accept in order to find them believable, we shall identify ourselves with both the actor and the audience that judges him, and it is unlikely that we shall fail to recognize ourselves in our own person! This will give us complete freedom, since everything will be plausible to ourselves. The actors have always moved on stage in accordance with the requirements of verisimilitude; their movements did not express the dramatic action but simply interpreted it for our eyes. Another principle will now be substituted for the verisimilitude that hitherto dominated and conditioned all dramatic art, a principle no longer drawn from external reality but from our inner life, the life of our soul. Our concern for verisimilitude will be replaced by our concern for the superior truth that constitutes and expresses our personality. Movement is an external factor, fusing time and space. We need, therefore, a principle that will prescribe our movement in its time pattern and in space without being subject *to external reality*. If it dictated duration (timing) alone, we would not have space, and vice versa. Hence it is imperative to discover this principle in movement itself.

Except for dramatic art, our arts of space (architecture, sculpture, painting) are immobile; for them, a time element does not exist. As for our arts of time—but which are they after all?

The spoken word and the printed word have a certain, though arbitrary, time value; we may read or talk fast or slowly. Literature indeed *does not express* time; its timing depends on our whim and its role in space has nothing to do with the space it takes on the printed page. Literature depends, moreover, on the meaning of words, and in this sense, it obviously does not belong in the fine arts.

Music is produced and expressed in time, but only in time. Since it has the power to determine precisely the successive time elements, it is the art of time *par excellence*. If a way is found to unite music with space, we shall have the principle we are seeking.* Movement is akin to music through its participation in time; our movements have time value, but as in speech, this time value remains arbitrary as long as it is not definitely ruled by art. Music has the necessary authority, for music is not merely an uninterrupted sequence. There is a pause, the sequence is resumed, and again a pause; thus, the time durations successively used by music are variable and susceptible to infinite combinations. Dominated and determined by the composer, they establish the phenomenon called *Rhythm*. Our body gives us basic examples of rhythm in the heart

---

* See *The Work of Living Art* for an explanation of this problem.

beat, in breathing and in walking. All rhythms are slow or fast, and they correspond to the circulation of our blood, to our movement over the ground, or in space. By applying musical rhythm to the movements of our body, by subjecting them to this rhythm, we transfer the sense of time into our organism *by means of an art,* and thus find the principle that directs and dominates our motions. For music is not the expression of the visible world, of nonessential phenomena we want to avoid; it springs from our innermost life. Since rhythm gives form to music, it is rhythm alone that, through the medium of our moving body *and solely through this body,* can give time its realization in space. Obviously lifeless and mechanical movements contribute nothing to the secret life thus revealed by music. Our body—alive and therefore moving—is for us the meeting place of time and space in the realm of art. And music possesses the indispensable authority to bring about this legitimate union, which results in a kind of metamorphosis.

There is another aspect to the problem. Dramatic art is subject to verisimilitude: for our eyes the actors' movements have significance only as a result of this principle. Although one of the objects of dramatic art is the conflicts of our inner life, the actor can present such conflicts solely in an external visible form which is understandable and familiar to us; here, there can be no question of expression. All of us know and feel that our gestures and attitudes merely approximate the inner fluctuations of our emotions and that, without speech, they remain ambiguous. Consequently verisimilitude unites time and space only in a juxtaposition which is incomplete, unequal, and subject to very diverse interpretations. We are therefore mistaken in calling it a principle; it is instead simply a requirement of dramatic art. The actor's mobility carries in itself the stamp of arbitrariness, a factor responsible for his influence upon the audience. In setting ourselves free from the requirement of verisimilitude, we abandon what has until now been the actor's principle, movements. Therefore, a new principle must be found, and since our body needs no spectator at all to assert itself in a work of *living* art, we must seek in ourselves the approval formerly accorded the actor by the audience.

We are our own audience; our verisimilitude is within our own self, and the movements expressing it will be dictated by music, the direct expression of our soul. We shall then give the complex and pretentious spectacles in our theatres a deeper meaning. By means of music we will preserve only the inner core of all phenomena, for music never expresses anything else. Even its visible realization through our moving body will no longer be subjected to arbitrariness, because our own conscience will be its sole judge. The incorruptible spectator, now both judge and participant and no longer mere observer, will be the conscience that will hold us to the dictates of music. To keep a jealous watch over this conscience will be our main effort. This is the new task which will now occupy us. But first let us summarize the preceding pages.

Art, more completely than any other human creation, serves to release the duality which characterizes our highest activity. The gesture of art means to *offer oneself*. The artist wants to identify us with his work; we must, therefore, first offer ourselves to him so that he in turn may be able to give us an image in which we can see ourselves. Without such meeting of minds, the artist remains alone reflecting only himself; his work is a monologue. We, for our part, remain alone as passive spectators of our world. The work of art is then merely an exhibition for us; we have contributed nothing to it and hence are incapable of identifying ourselves with it. Thus, centrifugal force soon eliminates us.

This is the situation in the fine arts. Dramatic art, however, is an art form whose very existence is based exclusively on duality, but, alas, in a fictitious combination! This results in a grave danger for the audience as well as for the performers. The pleasure provided by the theatre impairs the spectator's consciousness of reality and tends to make him unfit for meaningful reactions. The mania for de-emphasizing his personality forces the actor into an existence that prevents him from leading a social life, or even a dignified private life. Nevertheless, since he gives himself, body and soul, his attitude is infinitely more respectable than that of the spectator.

Today, dramatic art is the only one of our arts in which the *living* being presents himself to us. Should we then decline the effective assistance of *life* in a work of art because of the dangers it involves? The theatre, of course, errs in deluding us about the part we assume in the work of art, and also in another way, as we have seen. Therefore, to escape this danger, we must find for the *living* body, i.e., the movement in the work of art, a purpose other than verisimilitude, one that exclusively governs and characterizes theatre art. Here music, through the medium of rhythm, proves to be all-powerful. Under the command of rhythm, our body can become truly expressive, not by whimsical movement, but, on the contrary, by movement that is the expression of our deepest emotions. Since verisimilitude, which after all depends merely on the opinion of the audience, is not requisite for this art form, theatre art can exist by itself with our innermost conscience as its sole spectator. The beauty of the human body will no longer be imprisoned in an immobile symbol (as in painting and sculpture), but *will live* in both time and space. Because of the ideal quality of musical expression, its ideal use of time, the human body will shed the realistic accessories which now smother our life.

*Under the command of music, movement makes our body conscious of the inner meaning of phenomena.*

In a previous book, *The Work of Living Art*, inspired by a certain statement by Taine, I have probed at great length into the reason why music alone is capable of giving our movements the character of a work of art. Here I shall confine myself to a brief account of this matter. Taine wrote as follows: "The aim of a work of art is to reveal some essential, salient character, consequently some important idea, more clearly and more completely than can real objects. It achieves this through a group of parts whose relationships it systematically modifies."[19]

Music offers a maximum of such modification. As a matter of fact, the art of sound needs a group of time values unavailable in our daily life. The expression of our inner life, the object of music, takes no account whatever of the form we spontaneously give to our gestures and attitudes in real life. Besides, these gestures are far from *expressing* our feelings; at best, they are able to hint at them. The entire drama of our existence takes place within ourselves and in a different time pattern. For instance, a quick frown signals that we suffer, but our suffering may last for hours; so we have not expressed it. Music seizes this inner duration and modifies it freely according to independent laws. Rhythm and the expression stimulating it can impose themselves upon our body and dictate its movements. The result is a "group of parts linked together" whose value has been "modified" by music. Anything but music would lead to arbitrary modifications that would have no value or justification in the work of art. Music alone has the power "to modify systematically." We can, therefore, trust in it without reservation; we surely must do so out of respect for our body, this incomparable instrument that we have ignored too long.

Our trust in music is founded on a thorough study of the relationship that can be established between it and our body. This implies a particular flexibility that permits our submission gradually to become automatic, and subsequently to awaken our aesthetic conscience, which the preliminary, absorbing studies left dormant. The judgment of our aesthetic conscience will continually test our complete surrender. Music will imbue our body with its boundless rhythm and thus endow and enrich it with new life. For a long time our soul has responded to music, but only as an echo; although it has recognized itself in music it has been unable to express its joy in this recognition. The meeting has remained locked within our conscience. Now this echo takes visible form, our body proclaims it! We recognize ourselves—and this time with body and soul; rhythm resounds no longer in the vacuum of empty space. Musical expression remains no longer a captive of sound alone; henceforth both boldly burst forth toward the light; their identity is consummated.

The union of the body with music, which makes them virtually identical, poses not only an aesthetic problem but a moral one as well. If *the imaginary world* of the theatre has already shown us that we have certain responsibilities, the *reality* of our body along with the modifications imposed upon it by the music presents us with an ultimatum. The answer to the ultimatum and its repercussions on our diverse activities, on art forms, on our whole existence, will conclude this treatise.

## III. Identity

The power of a symbol lies in its universality. The symbol establishes the relationship between the limited example it represents and the eternal truths which we could not express without such a symbol. It is our tangible and ever-present proof of these truths. Despite its limitations, it recalls an origin that stands free and above the accidental and inescapable contingencies of life. The practical value of the symbol seems greater than the value of reasoning; for the latter can be applied only to objects that can be intelligibly expressed. The symbol is concerned with realities of which our soul is conscious and often overflowing, yet which it is unable to describe. It is therefore natural that art should be the highest and most important of our functions in this world; the symbol is the justification of art; it is its very nature.

The intellectual device, which the symbol is after all, and the aesthetic device of art tend to merge. The first transforms all the manifestations of human life in order to relate them to a single principle; the latter expresses our inner life in a form in which everyone can recognize himself. These two devices can truly unite only when both derive from our entire existence and not from the fictitious artifices of the theatre. Then we feel the deep bonds that unite us with nature and mankind; we are induced to make the "gesture of art," to anticipate the artist, by trying to identify ourselves with his work. The visible reality of the life around us is a supreme symbol, but we will discover no essence beneath it if we remain mere spectators. Art says to us, "It is you; recognize yourself in all things!" and we recognize ourselves *in it*, the symbol of all things. Another step remains to be taken; the last sanctuary, the *"tat twam asi"* (it is yourself) must be entered! Once more, for the last time, we must be liberated and must *dominate* our liberator, dominate art! Only then shall we have the power to offer ourselves to art and be worthy of serving it as a model.

Richard Wagner closed his music drama *Parsifal* with these words: "Wondrous work of mercy! Salvation to the savior!" At the end of his life the master understood that symbol in whatever form it appears is free to express itself only in proportion to its dependence on men, that by seeing beyond it we bestow power and freedom upon it; the symbol must obtain these from *us*.

Art, we have said, involves making a decision which results in a certain attitude. Our own impulse determines the work of art, which is but one of its results. A work of art can exist without our effective assistance; but it is then a monologue, and the exhibition hall is its dismal loudspeaker. If we would accept our task, if we would follow the artistic impulse, we must abandon the dangerous passivity of the passive spectator and take part in the concert of life, because the artist and his work will enable us to become the living witnesses of the fruitful decision. Through us the work of art will take its place among the most eloquent manifestations of our culture instead of being merely its fortuitous ornament. In a concrete form it will lift high the abstract symbols of religion. Has it not always done so in periods of cultural flowering? And do we not feel that this is its proper function?

What we admire in classic Greek art is probably not what the ancient Greeks saw in it. We try to find in this art form a model for us; the Greeks were the model. The artist transfigured the model into a truthful synthesis, something like a painter who attempts to typify a large family in a single portrait; each member would recognize himself in it together with all the other members. Before a Greek statue we are before a people. Undoubtedly the Greek experienced a serene joy in identifying himself with the collective image created by the sculptor. For him the sight of a statue was not an expression of desire; it was only the blissful evidence of a fact. We may doubt that he admired a beautiful young man more than the Beauty that the young man represented. On their bowls the Greeks inscribed, "This is a beautiful thing," but the image was not a portrait. That would have degraded the meaning of the inscription. Their works will never serve us as a model. Their artists had a great collective model before their eyes. Their art is an *example*. The clear eye and well-poised body of the athlete are not models but indeed examples: under such and such conditions the human body acquires this form. Trying to copy the form without taking into account the conditions that helped create it shows mistaken judgment.

Through the brilliant work of Jaques-Dalcroze, musical rhythm made its appearance in Geneva about twenty years ago. Experiences gathered during these years have demonstrated that the study of eurhythmics (called rhythmic gymnastics at first) can easily be combined with other educational activities, and that even people quite busy otherwise can find the time to devote a few hours every week to these exercises and to discover through them an unexpected source of emotional balance, of joy and enthusiasm. The practice of eurhythmics should continue as a life-long, salutary habit. Eventually it establishes a harmony superior to that of our ordinary existence, relieving us temporarily from our concern about the harmony of that existence. We give our whole being to eurhythmics, and it is returned to us simplified and ennobled. After practice of this discipline we acquire a better standard for things in real life; we are less sensitive to passing conditions of minor importance and more aware and respectful of essential and lasting values. Eurhythmics teaches us to see things from a distance. The desirability of such an influence cannot be disputed. Especially in our day, when the dizzy progress of applied science aims at placing the machine above the individual, eurhythmics, since it is lived, teaches us irrefutably the supremacy of our total being. Appealing to our deepest emotion, it meets with our wholehearted *assent*.

Previously I stated that the work of *living* art, the art created by our own body, is the only one that needs no spectator. Although this seems to contradict solidarity, one of the essential features of eurhythmics, actually, it is the confirmation and corollary of that solidarity. To gain a semblance of understanding on the part of the public, the creator in the static arts exhibits his work; otherwise he cannot hope for contact. As a rule, the work itself expresses only this desire; alas, not its realization. Our body, alone and left to its own devices, has no social existence; it is neither the work of art nor its spectator. It is waiting; its expansive force remains shrouded and dormant. But when conquered by music, the body suddenly sheds the veil of nonessentials that individualized and isolated it; becoming *social,* it strives to unite with others like it. All it has to do then is to find conditions favorable for such joint activity. And here, just as when the body found itself actually alone, the presence of a spectator is unnecessary and very likely not even desirable. When alone, the body already sensed its inner kinship; when united with others, it has the greater fortune of blending its own expression with theirs. This is a social communion in the name of beauty, or conversely, the beauty of the body sanctified by social communion. An activity more *alive* and more deeply symbolic can hardly be imagined. Other activities are a fragmentary application of our faculties and thus represent only a symbol of limited power.

What will be the influence of this supreme symbol on the other arts and other activities in general?

The dangerous position of *onlooker* separates us from the outer world. We use our faculties to understand what is *offered* to them and assimilate it as we please, calling this "cultivating the mind." The possibility of an exchange never occurs to us. We think we are very generous in being open-minded and curious to know. Those who adopt this attitude to a high degree enjoy general esteem, particularly if they juggle with the ideas they have acquired, thus giving the illusion that these ideas serve some purpose. Nature, more humane, sometimes does extract profitable results from such ideas, making these men the instruments of a superior force. But unfortunately this is not always the case, and, too often, one wishes the juggler had remained merely an entertainer. The play of ideas is admired; the act of serious thinking fills us with respect. Why? We do not know. The mania for mental labor is not very different from any other mania; we exalt some and scorn others, and no matter how utilitarian we would like to be, often an utterly superfluous labor appears valuable to us simply because it is exclusively mental.

The more we cultivate and consolidate our distinctly personal traits, the more we isolate ourselves. The one and only method of participating effectively in the concert of life is based on the intense search for points of contact, for affinities. All attempts in this direction are therefore highly respectable. Here again the normal scale of values must be reversed, for everywhere objectivity is proof of superiority; and there is no greater objectivity than to deny oneself in order to approach others. If intellectual fervor, which is the basis of all individualism and the reason for so much superfluous toil, is not dangerous, it has, at any rate, nothing in common with unselfishness, in spite of the beautiful appearance of its zeal and hard labor. Since our life is a great symbol, we always feel the need to transform the lasting truths into a symbolic form that we can seize for practical use. Hence the religions; hence our art forms; but hence also our responsibility for their symbols and our guilt if we distort them. "Style is the man!" A symbol is the expression formed by us of a reality that cannot be expressed without this assistance. Thus if there is in our life an activity whose object is style, or, if style is the man, whose object is ourselves, we would be extremely wrong to neglect it.

Eurhythmics is an act of devotion. Many practicing it have felt so, including the author, who writes with emotion these words drawn from his own experience. He believes in the power of unselfishness. He knows that principles like laws do not change mankind and that another way must be found because the source of all progress is within ourselves. He believes, furthermore, that humanity is lost if it insists on placing the body in opposition to the soul and in living in such rigid dualism. Death teaches us that the body decays, but what do we know about it? Are our eyes with their limitations infallible? We console ourselves with the immortality of our soul. What do we know about this and what can it mean? Are not our feelings and hopes concerned exclusively with our worldly mode of life? Can eternity make sense for us? Let us find a different subject! Faith in life is the master of death but not faith in the life of the spectator! When the spectacle is over, what is left for him? This is the reason for the importance of our attitude: in offering ourselves to mankind we serve life and we master death.

Music pulled out of its isolation, the body set free from its solitude, the plastic sense brought to *life,* the architectural surroundings at the service of the body and its movements; finally and above all, the desire to realize *together* this harmonious synthesis; this is indeed a beautiful program! And it is clear why we refused to serve the artist as a model: we had nothing to offer him! Now he will ask us. He is very well aware of the boundaries of the work of *living* art and understands that his lifeless work of synthesis must begin at these very limits. He will capture the almost flowing infinity of movements in a definite form from which he can exclude all the imperfections inherent in everything that *lives.* His work will be a perfect whole. His model will be not our moving bodies but the modifications of them effected by musical rhythm. The artist himself has sensed them; he has observed the identity of those modifications in the moving bodies of his brothers. His own work, *the work of lifeless synthesis, will henceforth not express the fleeting reality of the movement but its decisive influence on our organism and the repercussions from this influence on our whole life.*

The artist will apply this attitude to everything around him and the style, deeply felt, will bring life to him, to us, his models, and even to inanimate nature. His work, which previously was merely contemplative, will be *living,* in the precise sense of the term, in spite of its immobility. And we shall recognize in it the new way to sense and perceive the external world, our fellow men, and ourselves, which *living* art has revealed to us. These modifications, the characteristics of the new work of art, will have made conscious in us the principle of identity which, as we know, is the principle of freedom.

The gesture of art will have found its symbol.

# After Reading *Port-Royal* by Sainte-Beuve

## (1921)

### Dedicated to René Martin[20]

When, years ago, Dr. Louis Appia was asked why he took an interest in the Salvation Army and the endeavors of these people, the laconic old gentleman usually answered: "If you want to know the camel, go to Africa."[21]

Here the question does not concern camels but, perhaps, Africa whose climate appears not at all unattractive during the winter months. Will the kind reader accompany me? Our guide is a not unimportant man, so his austere appearance should not deceive us. He knows more things and more joyous things about Africa than he cares to have us believe; if his shell is rough, it protects his heart much better against the cold. We shall begin, if you like with a select itinerary.

The value of reading lies exclusively in the associations of ideas it evokes; and the reviewer's merit consists in pointing out the greatest number of such associations and in stating them with precision. He thus determines for the reader the scope of the work, and moreover enriches it insofar as his own discoveries surpass those of the reader. For a valuable book the choice of a critic is, therefore, of great importance, since he is able to give us the work more completely than we could absorb it unaided. A good critic, for his part, associates himself with the author and can become inseparable from him. Alexandre Vinet's[22] criticism is known for its irresistible charm. This incomparable thinker, this marvelous writer begins by observing—or rather by pondering his subject, and even where he disapproves, a deep sympathy underlies his fervor; he is a Christian.

His attention, however, does not dwell long on the flower and fruit; he cannot savor them fully before digging down to the roots; first the man is considered, and then the work. He may not explain the work through the man, but he always feels a warm sympathy for the author. What impartiality he thus obtains and from what height he exercises it! For us, his look falls from very high; for himself, his hands deferentially dig into the soil; like a cautious gardener he examines the roots, slowly and at the same time ardently.

The unprepared reader is therefore quite surprised when he has to read several pages apparently dealing neither with the book nor with the author. Vinet sets his course; he knows what he is going to tell us and understands clearly what we need to know beforehand to understand him well. For those who are familiar with his manner of introducing a subject, such preambles hold the solemn interest of a musical prelude through which the poet-musician invites his listeners to become acquainted with the themes of pure humanity which he will later present on the stage in the accidental guise of specific characters. We approach the author and his work in a mood of contemplation and respect, very conducive to a fair appreciation of them; Vinet has carried us to the heart of the topic before even mentioning it. This is not affectation on his part, but necessity. Above all else he wants us to love the author. He is a Christian. It is no longer a question of our own taste; the topic has grown and absorbed us. This is probably why every reading of Vinet is ennobling.

*Port-Royal* indeed fulfills its title; it is a royal subject! Under the pen of Sainte-Beuve[23] it receives a truly royal treatment; it is as if this artist has cast a magnificent ingot. Sainte-Beuve takes pains to assure us of this and, in fact, we do not doubt it. Yet he does not possess the high degree of heat needed to remove the dross. This requires the fiery spirit of a Vinet; and under his religious hands the ingot is purified and becomes a work of art. It can be asserted that to possess *Port-Royal* means to have had it pass through the sovereign manipulation of a Vinet. Thus if *Port-Royal* seems created to arouse infinite associations, what will it be when offered to us in its full splendor! With these two writers we possess it in all its aspects. With and without nonessentials—one might almost say: on earth and in heaven.

Associations have a suggestive power of the first order; and under the influence of these readings our thought takes such an audacious flight that it sometimes requires an effort to return to its point of departure, to recognize and verify it. We seem to have taken the flight with no impulse but our own. Gratitude is added to our increased resources; we are no longer alone in the grand adventure; we bear the responsibilities together. Each one of the personalities who have created Port-Royal or who adhere to it, each event, each episode of this noble venture is ours in History and in Eternity. We can associate ourselves with them, oppose them, compare ourselves with them, and simultaneously do so with other ventures and other aspirations. One time we shall approach *Port-Royal* by considering the whole with its unavoidable nonessentials; another time, the pure Idea will emerge alone. We shall have surpassed the phenomenon and shall feel ourselves in the ideal atmosphere where associations are the most abundant. It is from this widened viewpoint, this dominant height, that I wish to speak here about my own reading of this book.

*Port-Royal* is a complete whole viewed from any angle; this is a characteristic of all great works. Yet some episodes are more evocative than others. The members of the Arnauld family,[24] joined in the same isolation, are one example. Here are the words by which Sainte-Beuve brings this home to us:

> For imagine all the love, all the prayer, all the exaltation which poured out, not only on holy days, but every day, every monotonous hour of that contrite, contemplative life, and in overflowing, transformed themselves into compassion, charity, and self-sacrifice for all. Imagine what must necessarily have radiated from and among all these hearts—mothers, grandmothers, daughters, granddaughters, sisters, sons, nephews, and brothers, among all these human beings united in a single feeling of repentant trust, immolation and adoration! See them all somehow in our mind lined up before us kneeling at the morning lamp in the outer sanctuary that they use, and under these vaults which they make resound night and day; imagine—try to imagine—this inexpressible and invisible communication of thoughts, of feelings, through song, through an emanating radiance, through all that is the purest and most ethereal, the communication of the eternal soul under the eye of God; and then ask yourself whether in all the blessed future times there will ever be a more beautiful sight on earth![25]

Thus there was a force sufficient to move, one after another, persons of the same blood and high status, upon whom were lavished all the resources of a stimulating intellectual life, a brilliant and remarkable society, an outstanding activity befitting their equally outstanding talents—a force powerful enough actually to induce these individuals to leave all this, gradually to unite in the same thought, and moreover to sustain the common effort to the very end! Something that we might expect in a single person is thus found in an entire family within the same period of time. Still, such a union can be understood and has no doubt occurred, occasioned by some great cause, by some act of violence, by a defense or a liberation where there was a mutual feeling of solidarity and responsibility and agreement about the strategy of attack and the means to be employed in the strife.

But here—! The strategy of attack was retreat; the means were self-effacement and renunciation; the aim—Ah! There we are! The aim was still liberation. For this reason they had to defend themselves and consequently to use violence. Against whom? Against themselves! For whom? For their fellow men. These truly exceptional human beings understood by what means they had to begin to gain the right to devote themselves to others. One, humbly and alone, set the example; the others followed in the same way. United, therefore, each of them knew the road that led him to the other. It was not necessary to name him; they went to him whose need was greatest, and they helped one another in silence without examination or questions. They fortified each other implicitly for the preservation of the common effort and its influence. Sainte-Beuve felt all this in his innermost heart and stated it in Lausanne. Fortunate the students who heard him!

Although, historically speaking, these successive actions of the Arnauld family were, in their essential power, the outcome of a dogmatic faith, and as such were only of the time and the period, their significance extends so far beyond those religious circumstances that they acquire the value of a type and a symbol. All of us need an initial impetus; and this will always result from a conflict provoked by given circumstances in a specific situation. These circumstances stem from the influence of a period. But the effort is everlasting; only the lever varies. Let us then hold fast to the effort. The Arnauld family gives us the example of a series of efforts; their aim was noble and great. Whatever the lever, such souls could not have made a thoughtless choice even if they had had such a choice. Their echo still rings pure, and with good reason.

We speak of the religion of effort. Effort is not even a means; how could it be a religion! Effort is a condition, a manner of living. A sybarite strives all his life to increase and vary his sensations. Is this a religion? Only by the goal it sets for itself can effort take on some resemblance to religion. That goal avails itself of a lever that remains accidental. One takes what is within his reach; the goal alone matters. It would be better to speak by *example;* it is not a religion but, perhaps, has the power of religion.

The passer-by, who asks you to walk in front of him before he informs you about a matter of distance, requests an example that is a point of comparison. In a demonstration the words "for example" invariably please the listener, for they enable him to compare.

If the members of the Arnauld family came, one after another, to assemble at Port-Royal,[26] it means that one among them, then others in turn, provided a point of comparison. With what did they compare life in Port-Royal? Surely with that around them, more or less their own life. However, the incentive for such a determination must lie deeper. The atmosphere their souls breathed was transient; their souls were not. At Port-Royal one did not become attached to transient time; time could lead you there but could not hold you there. But when these people placed themselves beyond time, this did not mean that they ignored those who were still in it. On the contrary, they strove to conquer time within themselves in order to overcome its sting and free others from its grip. Thus their effort called for a decision.

For how many of us is the aim clear, the necessity for the effort evident, the lever with reach—yet the decision does not come! Lives glide away in sterile contemplation of the window dressing that we have so rightly called good intentions. Their mere appearance seems meritorious to us; we flatter ourselves that we are well oriented, as if the pointing of the compass would suffice to bring us into port.

For the Arnaulds the port alone counted, so once the decision was made the rest automatically followed! When they were kneeling, all of them experienced exactly the same thing. Any potential distinction among them was completely wiped out; they felt and knew that all of them had reached the same shore by the same route; the decision, the effort, the arrival. Henceforth they would live in a superior sphere of ideas from whence they could offer a purified and truly redeeming assistance.

Why are there personalities whose counsel is so highly sought after though not always followed? Strangely, they are the ones who attend most to the details of things, and yet their manner of dealing with them shows detachment and inspires resolution and courage. These details are the lever. Experience is said to serve only the individual, but these beings would ardently like to have it serve all, and they often succeed in this. Like the master who gives technical hints at just the right moment to facilitate the apprentice's effort, they attach importance to inspiring a simple movement of the soul; they know every inch of the road.

Was the period of Port-Royal particularly favorable, and did it offer a more powerful lever than any other? I do not think so. The contrast between the high seas and the haven will, always and everywhere, remain unaltered. The particular circumstances must not deceive us on this point. The question was not to abandon Paris for the Val de Chevreuse. Often the antipodes are closer than we suspect. Are they not to be seen in two glances encountered in the same street? The influence of the situation and the gossip it blows into our ears do not even touch the question. The choice of the lever remains our task. Our growing materialism tries to paralyze us and, like Mephistopheles, it wishes forever evil, yet forever creates something good by maintaining, against its will, the equilibrium it would like to destroy. As it piles up block upon block, the spiritual life fortifies itself in direct proportion to the strength of its adversary. The spirit alone will always be a multimillionaire. The stockbrokers of civilization, faced by the unshakable markets of culture, sense this only too well for their liking. They overlook no means to fool us, but the spirit is not made of paper or metal; its worth is permanent; it is undisturbed by the fluctuations of the stock exchange. We can, therefore, not invoke the contemporary situation to explain our amnesia and our lack of initiative. At the most we must accuse our eyes of nearsightedness which, for the mind, is an infirmity. To evaluate an object, one must get up, go to it and around it, for *living* things have three dimensions, possibly even four. Printing and its derivatives have merely two; they offend our soul, and we allow this. How many of us really know high relief, let alone statuary in the full round! We illume our study with evenly diffused light for we want to see everything. Both highlights and shadows are missing; the relief is dead. Flatness is a term of contempt; yet our life is flat. How can we bring out its highlights, enliven its contours? Perhaps by changing the light. To see everything is not to see well; shadows are often more revealing than lighted areas. One speaks of light that blinds.

Does not our thirst for conquest for conquest's sake resemble a continuously burning magnesium flare, and our modern life the beautiful result obtained by such illumination? Retouching will not alter anything; we lead a retouched existence that is certainly not very glorious since we see it as a necessity. Broad daylight is also light, but to retouch it is to create a falsehood. Our objective ought to be changed as well as our films. The entire procedure must be rectified. But we prefer constant pain to an extraction and we know it.

Broad daylight is the conscience of the soul, and by conscience I do not mean the voice of remorse, but that of simple statement. Our magnesium-like conscience is so bad that we invariably feel guilty if any daylight is mixed with it. Why? Does not the sun reveal to us much beauty and does this not compensate for the inherent imperfections in everything *living*!

For the Arnaulds, dogma was the chaff, the imperfection inseparable from life. We shall have others like them, no doubt, but this example should give us support, even inspire indulgence towards ourselves. When a country we might have visited is beautifully described we regret having missed it. Our churches teach us the most famous remorse, in its purified, transfigured form. We should decide to go out into broad daylight and to go there without fear and without reproach. Who would blame us? Once there, we should see clearly an accomplishment which, I assume, would be a blessing.

The happy man is radiant; he is not the sun but at least he reflects it, and many a *camera obscura* would be readily satisfied with such reflected light if this were offered to it. Port-Royal had swamps that had to be cleared. This was no secret, and after the swamps, there was always something else to be done. Broad daylight guided this work, so that it could proceed with certainty and without ceasing. We too shall hardly be idle. Sweat is good; it both indicates and maintains health. Are we afraid of health too? Everyone knows why sanatoriums multiply. An Italian once boasted to me of the larger number of policemen in the streets of Rome; he saw this as a sign of security. Our fine public health and its too numerous guarantees is like that. Our money slips away through two outlets: killing and curing; one to be free and the other to enjoy that freedom. There is a third outlet, alas, the one that makes the cure so urgent. The organization is perfect, so the weakness perhaps lies in the assumptions beneath it.

To hear the voice of our conscience, that is, to be fully conscious of our state of mind, broad daylight is not enough, however. Silence, and with it contemplation, is needed. Yet, every hour of the day we seem to want anything but silence. Does this not indicate our guilt?

Our civilization resembles the hole in which the ostrich hides its head. We no longer see anything but ruffled feathers. Is our life so intense? Rather, it is crowded. The fire that is always cut off from the flue produces more smoke than flames; congestion occurs at the obstruction and it does not draw well. One must "give the fire air." Many desire this and could accomplish it, but they are content to envy those who enjoy this boon and refuse to follow them. "You are highly privileged," they say! Charles Dickens tells of two quite well-to-do ladies whose library is their pride and main concern. A friend returning from Italy relates her impressions of the trip. The ladies sigh: Oh, if they too could run away! But then, there are the books.—Only a forceful action could rescue them. Such an action is within the reach of a number of us; it would resemble an extraction without insensibility. It is childish to wait for a violent toothache. The Arnauld family, much to its glory, did not wait.

Once the fact is recognized, the decision made, the goal glimpsed, there remains the choice of a lever. It is perhaps, even probably, at hand. If our "library" is not portable, we must abandon it. Heavy luggage hampers the journey and may discourage the traveler; with it, alas, we would carry along the too familiar microbes; the atmosphere would remain filled with them, and our cure would be doubtful. We thus arrive at a bare fact, a clear choice. The Idea becomes a reality; either Paris or Port-Royal, the one febrile and overtaxed, the other austere and profound.

Let us not forget that Port-Royal itself is a creation not built all at once in expectation of the Idea that it might embody. Rather the Idea came to take possession of it and to give it a soul. The stones will always be there to shield the Idea, but it is not conversely so; we know of temples still waiting for their faithful. The theatre at Bayreuth did not wait for *Parsifal,* nor did the Parthenon wait for the Greek genius. Our own modern buildings all too often expect of us the kind of existence that will harmonize with their unnecessarily simplified lines. An Empire bed is not a better stimulant for dreams of glory than is a white bedstead for maiden images. The dreams must come before their settings.

We have compared the dogma of Port-Royal to the lever that lifts the soul and carries it to its shelter. This dogma is based on an idea of reform; it was the historic symbol of that idea. Our lever could well be similar and our Port-Royal the place to work it out and give it a persuasive eloquence through our example. Meditation is the retreat of the soul, and the soul supports the body. Our dogma, therefore, must enlighten the place of retreat, which will become the symbol of that dogma. The dogma will specify the place and consequently give it the necessary proportions. Retreat does not imply rest for the body; retiring is not a negative gesture. This gesture, on the contrary, implies a change; rest is only expectation; anything at all may follow it. The retreat must have a result; it must demonstrate the soundness of our decision. It will be an example.

Our lives are embedded in public life, but this life is always shifting, and we are often fixed in it less firmly, less finally than we assume. And though our burdens and responsibilities remain the same, we can carry them in different ways. The arbitrary part, of which we remain the sole judge, is what constitutes our liberty. It is our contribution to the art of living and gives our actions their specific value. The painting of a fresco is not the gesture of art, but the decision to do so is that gesture. The art of living is, above all else, the decision to undertake it; the rest is the work of art as distinct from the art itself.

It has been said, perhaps rashly, that the function creates the organ. In social life, this assertion is incontestably correct. Today's society has made a retreat a necessity. The organ must be created. Who has not sighed when visiting the cloister of a monastery! Does this sort of nostalgia derive from the desire to become a monk? Not very likely; we know too well what it would cost. Yet retreat, so perfectly represented in the arches of the cloister, fills us with envy. This is not the empty quietness of the sanatorium; we fill these silent stones with thoughts. The cloister is suggestive; we see the best of ourselves in it and deplore our inability to offer anything similar to the noble being we sense within us. Thus the organ to be created would be a cloister without its iron rules. It must be still more; oh, we know this well! The hour belongs no longer to deep solitude. We have learned to condemn those who shake the dust from their feet; we want the door to the reception-room left wide open. Formerly the rule of the monastery was to overcome the obstacle through humble submission to its austere principles. Today the obstacle has changed; it is, to the contrary, to stay in contact with external life, a sacrifice that creates difficulties for our monkish egos. For if the remedy is to be radical, it can be gained only at this price. The effort will go toward directing the actions we must take; our hands must be stretched out, not coldly folded in the sleeves of a frock. We must compensate the cloister for the privilege it grants us, not let this benefit simply fall regularly into our lap. The sounds of our meditations will pass beyond the walls and, quite possibly, we shall be amazed at the echoes they will arouse.

I now approach with some apprehension the practical realities. It may be observed how carefully I have traversed the ground to this point. Now we are here. Some experiments with lay congregations in houses of retreat, in phalansteries,[27] have been made under various pretexts. Some offered the individual an orientation or even a specific frame of reference; others brought together, temporarily, personalities already established in a definite direction who felt the need for mutually fortifying themselves in their resolutions; still others were assembled around a leader, an initiator, a reformer, an artist, or merely around an Idea or a suggestive work. Religious feeling, artistic convictions, the desire for synthesis or simplification, for health, for agricultural communal life: all have by turns served as levers for these interesting attempts. The idea is therefore not new, and in this respect the ideal remains the same: to meditate profoundly in order to act more forcefully. This will be the goal of all the Port-Royals. Thus it is above all a question of opportunity; and probably a number of such enterprises failed; or at least stimulated no response or continuity, because the circumstances had not been taken into account. Desire is not enough; our desire must remain in direct and vital communication with all human beings.

The duties imposed by solidarity took a dogmatic form with the Arnaulds. It was the opportunity of their day. Ours is quite different. Our dogmas are broader, and with them, our duties. General submission to the same spiritual law would violate our individualism, which has become legitimate, and would weaken us accordingly. Therefore our "rule" must be more flexible. Without rule, however, a retreat would not be effectual. Hence, we must pause to deal with the first step.

Port-Royal was not created by a collective movement, but by individual personalities. This is characteristic of it and of all forceful actions; for even a collective movement needs a leader, who will differ according to the milieu and the circumstances. Each of our rallying centers will therefore have a leader.

Philanthropy and religious feeling frequently go hand in hand and often paralyze one another. Their universality concerns the masses rather than individuals, and if they have any given duration, it is at the expense of personal influence, and especially to the exclusion of individualities who cannot yield to such leveling. The aim of philanthropy and religion is humanitarian but not social. Both are more concerned with physical and moral well-being than with the integral development of the life forces which, on the contrary, they would rather deaden. In saying this I do not mean to belittle them, but to assign them a place distinct from the retreat which we are seeking.

Here it is the personality of the leader that would be of importance, regardless of the philanthropic or religious feelings that might inspire or sustain such a personality. Yet only these feelings possess universality; all the others are specialized. Almost all human activities have men as their Representatives (in Emerson's sense);[28] although by dint of their character rather than of their knowledge or competence. The virtuoso is possessed by his technique; the Representative dominates it, hence his influence. The profession of some of these Representatives itself implies a kind of communion; the degree of the Representative's power determines the success and vitality of the association.

The artisans' guilds in the Middle Ages were excellent examples of this kind of association; so were the workshops of artists in the Italian Renaissance. Here, however, emulation played a major role and could degenerate into jealousy. The artist would then retire, perhaps to the advantage of art but not of the *life of art*. The genius grew still more inimitable; he blazed a trail with his work, but he himself did not travel over it. Very likely it had to be this way; no price is too high for the life of a genius. Yet these violent conflicts are no longer fashionable; our modern life is so fluid and changeable that it does not offer the artist obstacles severe enough to test his strength and to prove his full measure. The struggle today is of a different kind; the contest has changed. X-rays penetrate our ivory towers. The retreat is within man, no longer outside; for himself unquestionably, *but also for his fellow men.*

We know the prestige of certain personalities; we yield to their charm and submit to their influence. Unfortunately our life is noisy and crowded, preventing us from hearing their melody in its harmony and purity. We grasp mere fragments whose combination escapes us and, though fascinated, we fail to experience the total effect. This is vexing for us, and perhaps even more so for the singer who would like to give himself fully. As in an opera, we select arias unmindful of the whole. Here the forces are lost; on the one hand, silence and concentration are lacking, on the other, the echo that stimulates, inspires, and enriches. Our social acoustics are defective. Could we not lay wires as one does in over-resonant halls to guide the sound waves? We espouse so many things that we retain nothing, at lest nothing complete; it is like a telephone system with only one piece of apparatus. Our respect for the Personality remains really too platonic. Devotion is not necessarily an action; one should also know how to receive.

Perhaps our Retreat ought to be an attitude of expectation, of silence and of attention—not of attention to all voices, only to some. The smaller their number, the better we could understand them. It is important to *select* our Retreat and to hold on to the choice we have made. Our lives are in this respect like museums or collections—one more object in their showcase, one more book on t heir shelves appear to us a sign of culture, whereas the opposite is the case. The artist will always prefer to lighten his design instead of adding a single useless item. We do not live in abundance, but in a superfluity that suffocates us.

In art sacrifice is the rule, and it results from a strict choice. We no longer want to sacrifice anything; we want to know everything or, at least, as much as possible. "He has traveled much, read much, what did he not attempt, he has only friends, etc., etc." These are our ideals.

The Germans have a word that has no equivalent in French; they call somebody who shows himself to be an artist in his attitude towards life *einen Lebens-künstler.*[29] He knows how to make his choice, to hold on to it, to examine its content and to adjust himself so well that he has created a new life for himself, a life wisely limited that will *suffice him.* Such a man is distinguished by the precision of his ideas, the originality and clarity of his thought associations, the somehow pre-established harmony he can give these thought associations, and by the conversationalist's pleasant gift of linking quietly and securely what is said to him with a few established ideas. In his company the shadows vanish; the problems present themselves clearly and are often unexpectedly resolved; he has simplified life for you.

Such personalities are radiant, but their radiance comes from a single source; hence the amazing plasticity of their vision. They animate everything, because they themselves are *alive*. When we leave them we take with us an inner happiness in being alive. They can instill this happiness in us because they possess it themselves and we wish we could place ourselves under their radiance over and over again. And why not? There are many opportunities to do so. Nay, even more; we have received, could we not also give? Are these people too perfect to receive anything? A bedside book . . . such personalities should always, like a good book, be at our bedside, at the bedside of our reflections, our dreams. During conversation they have imposed nothing upon us; they have always assumed the role of a sounding board. Their presence has been ingenuous. It is up to us to prolong it throughout our days. Alas, in order to pursue other stimuli, to enrich our experience, so we think, we pass by the only experience that is valuable. Why erase its imprint or let it be crushed by the steam roller that lies in wait for us at every street corner? We need the Retreat!

As for the *Lebens-künstler*, does he lack anything? We never think about that. If he has sacrificed so much, we think, it was for his own well-being. Why fuss about it! We have no time, we say; so many things are required of us, and, unable to give, we do not even know how to receive. These superior beings know isolation. Solitude maintains strength; isolation can make such strength painful. Probably it is with no little effort that they try to disguise this. They are happy, no doubt, but their happiness could well choke them sometimes if nobody is willing to share the strain of it. Such homeopathic doses as we demand of them certainly do not suffice to keep them at their proper level. Thus we long for the Retreat, yet without really wanting to obtain it.

If the actual presence, the living Personality, possesses beyond words means of action not unknown to us, a book also holds invisible powers and thus substitutes for the spell of the Presence, incomparable as that is, a kind of security which the fortuitous contingencies of reality cannot offer. A book we like gives us total peace from the moment we first take it in our hand. It is our friend, steadfast and yet forever new, for we never approach it twice in the same mood. We say to it: "This is you," and it answers: "It is I"—a dialogue that contains a world of rejoicing. Let us interrupt for a moment this continuous dialogue, so full of serenity. This book has a firm hold on us, yet we feel free. When we put it on its shelf we do not give it up. To this Retreat, at least, we can devote ourselves; consequently, it is the best known. There are people incapable of such devotion, but, more importantly, there are people who wish nothing else.

How can one make these latter desire a communal Retreat if their minds are more accessible to books than to the living Personality? Here again, the choice requires a solitude that our modern life is far from granting us, or at least so we believe. We wish to keep *au courant*; that is, we do not want to dwell on anything. This is the reality of the well-informed person. Does a guide know Rome?

Now if we place to one side both the living Retreat, as I shall call it, which only the actual Personality in flesh and blood can offer us, and the book Retreat which is of the spirit alone, there still remains another more or less prolonged Retreat. To find this is a practical matter that may be solved by everyone according to his taste and means. This third retreat is in man himself; it will therefore be a twofold Retreat, but one does not come without the other.

It is good to buy a Sandow apparatus,[30] but to leave it in the closet makes both the expenditure and the equipment useless.

To reach the Retreat, in our own home or elsewhere, means of course to make a plan and to make it a *complete* one. We must decide what we are to take along, and, more important, what we are going to leave behind. Some self-analysis may help determine our course. To begin with, we shall try to find out why we need a retreat. Surely it is the dissipation of our strength that causes us to desire this. Let us find out, therefore, whether this weakening stems from our condition and the sort of work that is unavoidable, or, rather, from our indecision. Having determined this, let us search in the back of our memory for the elements of humanity, of culture, of living personalities of art, of thought, etc., that have strengthened and enriched us and which, specifically, have given us simplicity. Let us faithfully assemble them; they will be the companions of our solitude and we shall be theirs. But the selection must be very exclusive! A friend may perhaps wish to follow us, to aid us with his living Presence. Let us keep only those worries that we absolutely must take along. Then let us put on the insignia of the order to bring us into harmony with the silence of the cloister, with its peaceful arches. Finally let us accept the monastic rules as just what is necessary for our ultimate satisfaction. . . . Then we shall know the whole case history and, I imagine, we will not need any doctor.

Thus armed and prepared we shall, not without solemnity, enter the sanctuary of reflection, where it is hardly possible to remain entirely passive for very long. The *choice* we have made will result in a salutary simplification. Our abated sensations, our pacified thoughts, will gain such prominence that we shall scarcely know them, and very likely we shall long to express this new clarity. We shall wish to impart it to others and shall discover that the Retreat by no means isolates, separates us from our brethren, but, on the contrary, brings us closer to them in an ever more cordial sympathy. Enjoying a privilege, we feel its responsibilities and wish to establish a contact impossible under the pressures of our daily lives. At first we were concerned only with ourselves, but then a new choice arose, for, strangely, one must be alone to feel the urge to give. Amidst the crowd we were constantly demanding.

At Port-Royal this is the experience of everyone! The nature of our talent is immaterial; what counts is deeds, writings, bold works or indeed even silent persistent patience, whose eloquence will not be ineffective. For *we shall act!* The Retreat is a supreme laboratory; it must produce a treasure. Let us therefore not regret the sacrifices imposed upon us. How much have these self-denials, often so difficult to bear, given us!

Then, when we return to life in the community, we shall wear the tonsure as a halo and, in difficult hours, we shall deferentially lift our hand to it in joyful assurance. Retreat is within man himself. Life may definitely deny us the cloister, but will it ever deny us the moments of concentration, these sanctuaries where we have placed the best of ourselves that will always be the best of our fellow men?

To be rich, must we not *choose* our treasures, keep only these and keep them alive?

# The Intermediary

## (1922)

Who has not observed a nurse glancing around before she leaves a sickroom? For an instant and no doubt unconsciously, she identifies herself with the patient who is under her care. She pictures to herself his weakness and above all his condition of dependency. She makes whatever slight changes are necessary to place everything he needs well within his reach. She asks no tiring questions; a kind instinct suffices.

When the invalid recovers from his illness and wonders why he cherishes his memory of the hospital so greatly and why life in good health usually does not offer anything comparable, this silent friendly understanding comes to his mind: somebody had identified herself with him, had understood and actually experienced his own needs not through reflection but through *sensation;* there had been a complete union.

A mountain guide, certain friends, certain books or works of art, and so forth share, when the opportunity arises, this role of a higher humanity. They are intermediaries and as such their presence and our memory of it are dear to us. But their strength lies in their neutrality; the nurse is not the doctor, the guide is not Cervin.[31] Everywhere machine belts are necessary; without them the generator does not function and the machine remains inactive. The belts in themselves are nothing, not even a dormant force, but, adjusted to the right distance, they connect two separate parts of a machine. The nurse and the guide understand this excellently. The distance is not always the same; only the generator is fixed, and the machine varies. Hence an adjustment has to be made; to produce something the two parts must be within reach of each other. I am not a mechanic, but I can hardly imagine a machine that does not obey the principle of the transmission of power.

In all probability the same is true of human beings. At any rate there is nothing to suggest that it is not; everywhere transmission of power is evident;

in the tiniest of our organs as well as in the largest of our institutions. We prove this when we speak of the latter figuratively as of a social organism. Hierarchy, indispensable to social life, is, after all, only a series of transmissions. If one of the conveyor belts is too short or—as is unfortunately more often the case— too long, the "order" does not reach the wheels; they are in perfect condition, but they do not move. Sometimes it even seems we are content with the mere presence of the necessary machines and we do not inquire much about their operation through exact contacts and proper distances.

Is not our personal life too entirely dependent on the accuracy of transmissions? The most superficial self-analysis will show that, wherever we are troubled mentally, we have to look for a flaw in transmission. Of course it is not always the fault of the intermediary; often we do not fully realize the contact he offers.

An English artist inspired by eurhythmics designed sketches for a fresco in which all the figures turn indifferently away from those who extend their arms toward them, and stretch their arms, in turn, toward other figures, and so forth. Its eloquence is so poignant that the artist did not even have to give the picture a title! We avail ourselves of all the electricity we can, except the great electric power of mankind. Machines are the object of all our attention; while living organisms must get along without engineers. Thus, these living machines creak in every joint and do not produce one hundredth of their potential power; very few produce even an acceptable average. Yet their performance is sanctified and accepted as fated. The mechanic keeps his eyes fixed on the manometer to make sure that his machine is producing at its maximum level. Who is the mechanic for our human society? The teacher! He is our hope; he really is the great engineer, but, since he deals with a living machine, his title does not come up as yet to his rank. He who observes, governs, and supervises the heartbeat of our children cannot help being a great artist, and he can make himself the only person worthy of this title, because he alone realizes that our ruins cannot be rebuilt with rubble.

The monument of a Rousseau, of a Pestalozzi[32] frequently represents these men touching the shoulder of a child with one hand while indicating an object in the distance with the other. These gestures signify the core of teaching by expressing its fundamental principle, namely transmission. The ex-libris of a pedagogical association could even adopt the picture of machine belts joining separate flywheels, if the idea of machinery were not repulsive to us in describing a function so supremely alive. In any case the symbol should be precisely defined and should be augmented by a mechanic paying full attention to the adjustment of these belts. One might object that modern education is the opposite of transmission, since it aims at discovering the sources of knowledge within the child himself. But, indeed, a motor has not the same function as the producing apparatus; it merely makes possible a number of unspecified operations and can adapt itself to any machine by transmission. It is a force applied with meticulous care to a mechanical whole, whose purpose is unknown to it. The comparison can be carried much farther; the force that would remain latent without conveyor belts represents knowledge accumulated during centuries of mankind's awareness. Thus, the task of the teacher is based primarily on correct adaptation; and mechanics know how delicate this task is, how much conscientiousness it requires.

Here then is the child brought in contact with all the knowledge that preceded his birth! His organism grasps whatever he can assimilate, and his feeble powers are stimulated in this considerable task by an ingenious intermediary, the teacher. This lasts for several years. The adolescent has become so accustomed to the motor that he believes he manages it by his own power; and, aided by ambition, he often attains a rare degree of perfection in his effort. This very perfection raises for him a grave and troublesome question, that of a division of effort, for he feels he cannot go much further in his development without specialization. He begins to understand the importance of the motor and wants to fit it in the best possible way to the new form of his studies. He therefore shifts the transmission belts so that they reach only part of his producing machine. This is a critical moment. Heretofore he had been almost unaware of this force, because it was transmitted to his entire being. Now a considerable part of his self will remain without direction; its movement is left to its own decision under its own responsibility.

The released forces have certain accepted protective devices, but the pupil, suddenly a student, must discover his own. Yet his extraordinary freedom, too quickly acquired, does not induce him to look for these protectors; so he often simply does not find them or, at least, not those he wants, or those which are indispensable to him. The more he specializes in his studies, the more he feels an emptiness otherwise—in spite of the rare joys of his emancipation.

In this dangerous period the influence of a professor can be powerful and salutary. It is regrettable that our Latin customs did not adopt the *informal* close relationship between professor and student, once so felicitous a part of German university life. To see in his home and in private life the man whose professorial dignity sets him apart during his specialized instruction is an initiation virtually imperative for the maturing young man. Here he can observe—for good or ill—the influence of specialization on his professor too. He learns how his chosen field supports or curtails the general development of an individual, and what degree of harmony can, and must, be established between knowledge and one's duties toward family and society. If the professor is a man of superior quality, he will be able to convince the student, merely through his example and almost unintentionally, that there is a solidarity uniting all branches of knowledge. He will protect the young mind from immature judgments, the hasty solutions of dogmatism that weaken him as a whole being by causing him to denigrate everything outside his own province. His studies will then not isolate the student, limit his horizon, his thoughts, and conversations through a surrender of things outside his field to the arbitrary misapprehensions of youth. Instead, his studies will teach him the discernment and appreciation that will enable him to adapt all that life will offer him to his own nature and character.

It is clearly a fact that the student does not know how to bring his studies into a consistent relationship with his personal life, so rich at his age; this carries him to certain excesses in his habits and ideas. They are the same, as a rule, and are little in accord with the student's better aspirations. Here the intermediary is more indispensable than ever. He must place everything the novice may need within his reach in a form which may be grasped. The pressures the student will undergo are so strong that it is not enough merely to caution him and then abandon him to the path of least resistance. To make his choice he will have the greatest number of alternatives at his disposal, excluding only those which might confuse him. The countless temptations of a large city will then lose their corrupting influence; he will yield to them only so far as he can without compromising himself.

In his autobiographical writings, Goethe bears witness to this process of adjustment with its ups and downs, its creative periods of intense activity and periods of incubation. This wonderful genius unites each twist and turn of his mind, each change in his feelings, the smallest everyday experience, with what he already knows or divines. His life remains a lesson perhaps unique of its kind, if one can read what he confides to us and guess what he keeps to himself. Goethe is *biographic;* he never tires of telling us this, and none of his writings can really be understood without this clue. He assures us that his verses are all written for an "occasion"; it is clear to anyone who knows him that the same is true of his prose. As artist he conceals a world of impressions and feelings under his preoccupation with his work and with its more or less technical aspects, and in the same manner he conceals under a literary disguise (such as dramas, etc.) his knowledge of the mechanism of the universe, of society and the individual. In this sense it may be said that every sentence of Goethe contains his entire life. That life was extraordinarily rich not because of circumstances, but solely because of his own personality, and so each sentence is full of inexpressible meaning. Goethe is probably the ideal intermediary—even more through the manner in which he manipulates and assimilates all elements than through his actual teaching. He was conscious of this, which explains his casual treatment, the large number of notes, and the apparently careless form of several of his writings. *He lived*—and life has only one form, itself.

There is, perhaps, a genius of this kind in the French language, although I have my doubts. Concern for the written form eliminates too many things and exerts too profound an influence on the basic nature of our Latin life. Our thinking, moreover, is too often paralyzed by the weight of thought preceding us, to which we attach a disproportionate importance. The Latin race is not free. It lives and rests on the style of its past; there is a lack of simplicity in this regard. A French writer knows above all how to give his thought a "literary" form—otherwise we would not acknowledge him as a writer at all. Yet, what remarkable personalities might otherwise be demonstrated to us! And how much their mediation could help us! Here, there is a great deficiency. The phonograph lets us hear the voice of a singer who is a thousand miles away; but the printing press fails to let us *live* with those of our fellow men who could best assist us in our development and be the most helpful on our journey through life.

Our young men detest reading a biography because it is alien to the needs of their imagination and their independence. The experiences of another person are of no interest to them! Our autobiographies in general lack form—not the too famous "grand style" but what I would call vital form. They are a chronological listing of facts and impressions or, all too often, an overbearing and sterile self-analysis in which the author analyzes his own analysis and the suffering caused by it, proceeding to analyze the analysis he makes of the pain of analysis . . . and so forth.

All the writings of a great personality ought to be biographical in Goethe's sense, as Pierre Jeaneret says.[33] In most cases our unreasonable demands on form prevent this. In writing we try to make our impressions and experiences correspond closely to their immediate object, not suspecting at all that, in this way, we portray neither the object nor the person who observes or feels it. There is, on the one hand, the plant in an herbarium, carefully labeled; on the other, the botanist—but no fresh air, which alone can give them dimension and meaning. I think that in our writings we do not sufficiently reconnect each of our experiences or impressions of our fellow men. We hold fast to the phenomenon alone, not grasping the innermost essence that relates the phenomenon to all mankind.

In the stifling mass of present publications (without even considering purely technical or commercial writings), only the unpretentious books are of value, for it takes feeling to avoid pretension; one cannot remain separate from mankind. The author who views himself apart from his brethren will always produce a purely literary work, while the writer who can unite the beauty of words with the essence of humanity will be truly great. We do indeed have such men, but they are mostly men of the past; for our modern life is insulating and, hence, inhumane. The artist who now seeks to create something vital and not something mechanical is forced into seclusion. We use this term "mechanical" carelessly, since we still let ourselves fall under the influence of the machine; we produce mechanical thoughts and feelings in the belief that we are thereby timely and sincere. We always hide our soul under a costume! Racine's tragedies certainly lose nothing by being produced in their original period costume; as a matter of fact, we would come far closer to the admirable core of humanity if they were so produced. On the other hand, many scenes of Molière would profit from a performance in bathing suits. But what would remain of the majority of modern literary plays if we dressed them in the costume of Eve, our ancestor?

The only costume of eternal mankind is what I call "biographic" in Goethe's sense; for who, if he is sincere, would persist in making his environment the decisive influence on his inner life? Have our passions a color? Are not the books which would exalt and stimulate us to action those which keep accidental matters of a particular period subordinated? These are also the only books that could fulfill the beautiful task of an intermediary and, moreover, do so unintentionally, for intention is always destructive. The living intermediary is not made of intentions, but solely of individual realities. All the efforts of a teacher will come to naught unless he is lacking in pretension. Holy men did not heal through medicine prepared for some malady but through their mere presence as manifested in their prayers and sacrifices. The secret prayer of the teacher would be: "Oh, that I knew how to throw off all that is not part of *me!*" For he rightly feels that his weaknesses and faults are not he himself; this is the only optimism, incidentally, which a sound ethics must grant us.

Like the artist, the writer is not truthful when he is not himself. To talk of the objectivity of a Shakespeare is sacrilegious. The purely objective—even if it could be attained—would have no effect on us. A Flaubert interests us only because of the desire to be objective, which was his strongest wish, and in this sense he is biographical. Unfortunately, where this desire is not infectious, pathologically speaking, it remains negative, sterile, and of little value. But these are most frequently the very writings preferred by our youths in the belief that reading them will bring enrichment; as though they were outside of mankind! Whenever we do not recognize ourselves we are submitting to the machine, and there are many machines to deceive or destroy us. The intermediary is a responsible transmitter; he must choose, and we know that our degree of nobility and purity derives from our choice among the elements that make up our personality. If the law imposing this task of elimination is categorically imperative towards ourselves, how much more so will it be toward our fellow men. We willingly leave this sort of responsibility to those who have voluntarily made it their profession, and yet we forget that it is our profession not to consider ourselves alone in life.

How many of us through inertia or false humility have kept ourselves from becoming a set for transmission! The link of a chain that refuses to join the others leaves a gap and loses its *raison d'être*. We may polish and embellish this solitary link, but all the inlaid work and gilding will not give us continuity. Just as in certain games, the chain forms again behind us; having lost the right to unite with the living, we remain alone in their midst. How many disillusioned and yet eager looks do we not observe! They search in the circle for a space for themselves, but they must be swift and, if need be, violent to avail themselves of it.

Suppose a young musically gifted man decided to dedicate his life to music. For him, as for those who counsel him, this profession has a single aim, to compose musical works. If he is capable of teaching music and conducting concerts and operas, we think his goal has been more than achieved. The same is true of the other arts! The beginner considers the acquisition of technical skills his only preoccupation; he must master his metier. No doubt, but . . . to what end! A person enters an agricultural school in order to learn to cultivate a field; a locksmith learns to make locks, but what are the locks without doors? Or a house painter without a house to beautify? Where is the field, the deer, the house for the musician? Certainly not the array of sounds, nor the authority over an orchestra, nor even the intelligent teaching of music. All these are only means; the aim of the musician, I presume, is to express something. It may be wise to look into this matter. A music school, alas, does not give him the slightest help in this direction. All he learns there is to express himself like a parrot, with little concern for what he will think fit to convey to his audience later on. In all schools of art one learns to express the degree of his skill, so a *prix de Rome* has to look anxiously for a subject.

We are encumbered by "farmers" without fields and "locksmiths" without doors, a situation that would be pitiable were it not so cynical. In such a system the artist does not seem to belong to the living organism of mankind. He brandishes his tools, he menaces us with them—and we let him do this without even a frown; he has every right to laugh at us and he certainly does so.

In Oberammergau[34] the young peasant who is selected to play the part of Christ is consecrated to this honor at a tender age. Every effort is made to develop his best traits, to prevent the slightest errors, and to instruct him in his task. He is given a special place in school and as an adolescent he is treated with great esteem. He is groomed physically as well as mentally, so that if he had beautiful hair, he learned to show himself worthy of it.

Like the teacher and the clergyman, our young artists are destined for the highest duties; they have to express the very essence of life, give a transfigured image of it by means of a sensitive synthesis which requires the highest and most respectful concentration on its object. Their technical skill should be demonstrated only by subordinating itself to this object. What would we say of a farmer who wants to grow wheat on a tarred pavement? And even in the field is it not necessary to work hard, to break up the ground, to fertilize it, and to tend it jealously? It is not the *bal des quart'z 'arts* that produces the harvest.

To express the human soul is to reveal one's own. The artist's object, therefore, is the life of his soul; otherwise he creates an artifice or even less, since it is something of an end in itself, while all the virtuosity of the artist is but a frivolous and criminal game he plays with us as well as with himself. One speaks of the influence of art. What influence can a manifestation have, however brilliant, absorbing, or esteemed, if it is just an impudent falsehood? An overrated personality dazzles us with capabilities not integrated into his character; he takes the means for the end, and throws dust into our eyes. The venality of our public life seems to force the artist to seek recognition at any price, and often, God knows at what a price! Success excuses everything. "A name" is sometimes achieved by deplorable compromises. Nothing is considered odious if it makes money, or, apparently, if it contributes to one's artistic or literary reputation. Such is the dignity of the public of which we are a part.

Let us return to our young musician. After leaving the music school, he will compete his studies with a recognized master, whose personal contact, in addition to the purely technical instruction, could exercise a decisive influence on his future career. When I was twenty years old I had a music professor who would take me for a walk after the lesson, during which he avoided talking to me about music or, at least, merely inserted it quite naturally in his observations and opinions on other matters.[35] Yet, when I left him, I realized that everything he had said or shown me was related to music, either to compositions I had submitted to him, or to the attitude he considered indispensable to musical composition. Without seeming to, probably without intending to, he injected in each of our conversations a sense of responsibility: Whenever we separated, his look, his handshake seemed to say: "All right, you have the ability; but to what end will you use it?"

When I returned from these walks I had, of course, no desire to open my piano or to take up my music paper; instead I searched earnestly and eagerly for something to express. My professor had instilled in me this concern, this regard for my person and my art. He achieved this by bringing my inexperienced and as yet limited mind in continuous contact with a multitude of things of which I had never dreamed, by broadening my vision, by justifying and confirming my intuitive ideas, by pruning superfluous branches to let me see at a glance the slim trunks full of promise. Swedish gymnastic exercises had preceded our expeditions to lofty heights, but without these preliminary exercises I would probably have been unable to follow him into the rarified atmosphere. My professor had served as guide, as living intermediary; this was his conception of a music lesson. How can I ever forget it! He brought within reach everything that could enrich, ennoble, enlighten me and so well that the need to express myself became irresistible. Indeed, the issue was no longer to compose some "music." Whenever I took up my pencil or set my fingers on the keys, I had an almost physical feeling of devotion for music and for him who had revealed it to me. Such intimacy between professor and disciple gives a definite orientation. Like Schopenhauer, the disciple realizes that we all have only one and the same thing to express, and that art has the power for such expression. Art for art's sake, music for music's sake, means to turn disgracefully from this "thing" and to deprive us of that which alone can justify our attempts. In short, we and our art become superfluous, and hence harmful.

My professor would not have made himself understood had he said this in so many words. He knew well that, for a young mind, he could only serve as the transmission belt, not as the motor. We speak of the divine Plato; now, he is the intermediary *par excellence,* and in this role we call him divine! To take part in the concert of life, in the dance of the stars, we must voluntarily submit to the laws of gravitation. If we are carried along against our will, we remain obscure, poor, shapeless creatures, lacking force or radiance. For the majority of us, work is a material necessity, but should be a moral obligation as well, for how can we be attractive unless we flex our muscles? The individual's culture, so highly valued by certain people, is a capital that has to produce revenue, or death will remove it with us, rendering our life meaningless. Mankind is a motor of such accumulative force that, without continuous and persistent transmission, it runs the risk of destroying itself. We have perhaps experienced this. Everyone of us must be an intermediary. This is a beautiful role; a mother understands very well that she must be willing also to *accept* from her child, or her relationship with him, unreciprocated, will be barren. The division of labor is a necessity that does not involve departmentalizing our individual nature. Yet in many cases we think it does and we have based our social life on the principle of producer and consumer with no great concern about the accumulation resulting from ceaseless consumption without any outlet. The overcharged receiver bursts, scattering unproductive energy. In art, for instance, what an abundance is needed to attract our attention! Wagner said that the English "devour music" (*fressen Musik*). Never satiated, we devour everything that comes our way—a hodge-podge we could never possibly assimilate![36] The creative artist, quite aware of this, uses condiments at random, ignoring the most elementary rules of hygiene, for it all has to "pass," and indeed it does, thanks to the idleness which helps the digestion of the minority, who are called, ironically no doubt, the privileged. So assimilation becomes illusory, and vital forces are squandered; some give excessively not expecting anything in return, others swallow voraciously while unable to offer something themselves. We adjust our existence to accommodate it to one of those two ways of being and thus deepen the gap between individuals all the more.

Along the railroad tracks in the outskirts of Paris, there is a surprising multitude of little houses, and we wonder who can have chosen to build his home in such a location. The people are said to be retired small shopkeepers trying to divert themselves with the passing trains. Are there not shopkeepers, in retirement, as it were from the day of their birth, content to watch other people pass by? Their small houses certainly do not adorn the countryside, but this matters little to them, provided something is going on that they may observe. These people kill time watching others busy themselves. They would never make good guards for railroad crossings, for derailments would mean another distraction for them. They have made themselves onlookers of life, which is the dullest of spectacles if one does not take part in it; and thus they create the boredom they dread. Well-conceived charity begins with giving one's self: definitely so, because the only remedy against boredom, the worst of evils, is the gift we make of ourselves. Let us be charitable in this respect and everything will be for the best.

Only what we have taught do we know well. Perrichon[37] gives his daughter to the man to whom he has rendered a service. To make ourselves liked, let us consent to be helped, and if we wish to draw nearer to others, let us help them. This is the essence of all close family ties; this exchange created by indissoluble bonds and great obligations. It is the price we pay for harmony.

During a walk my professor drew my attention toward a recently-built loggia that enlarged the building to its advantage and led to a lawn that rose above the road. Its exquisite proportions and delicate arches delighted my eyes.

"What do you expect them to do with it?" objected my professor. "If you lived in this house, would you ever think of leaving from this side or even walking around here? Ponder it well; put yourself in the owner's place."

So I did, and at once the charm was broken. Of course, one does not step out of his house to expose himself to the view of passers-by; besides, facing north, the loggia darkened parts that were not blessed with too much light in the first place. Observing it more closely, I noticed that there were no furnishings, no matting, not a seat, and it made the villa look uninhabited, something I had previously not perceived.

"Do you remember the symphony we heard yesterday? You did not understand my aversion to the charming andante that followed the first movement. But who would think of singing like that after such intimate solemnity?"

We resumed the road to town; my eyes were opened, and my guide, intuition personified, took me by the arm.

"You told me that every day you write a kind of resumé of your experiences, unconcerned with the logical course of your impressions, or the form in which you put your notes on paper. Have you noted, when rereading them, whether an invisible thread ties these notes together?"

He touched upon something that, indeed, had greatly surprised me several days earlier. I had tried to arrange my notes and connect them with transitions. This robbed them of a life that I did not know they had, and that I did not even suspect.

"My friend, that life is the thread that connects the most incongruous items. Without it you have many contrasts, much variety, even an appearance of harmony. But they are artificial and would leave even a friend reading your page unimpressed."

So I gradually learned to recognize what Goethe calls "the spiritual link" and so I became a musician, thanks to a man who understood his responsibility and the dignity of his art. I could give many other examples.

"Why continue this exercise?" he told me while scanning some pages of a composition I had submitted to him. "How do you expect anyone to follow you? You can't even follow yourself."

God knows whether I was really proud of that passage and of my own stubbornness. Or another time: "Here you are too cautious; you will be accused of cowardice." Or another time: "Bravo! This bar supports all the rest. This is the key, I was quite afraid that you would spread the arch too wide." Or again: "You so crowd your garlands that the column which is, after all, your beautiful thought, can no longer be seen."

He had not merely a vivid, stimulating way of expressing himself; there was also a universality in his thinking and feeling, and everything, including his technical remarks, had three dimensions for him. I had become so accustomed to this that the language of others seemed flat to me, as if it were written out on paper, which it probably was. This remarkable man gave himself to me as he had slowly developed through the inner toil of total purification. Only so was he willing to offer himself, considering any other form unworthy to give to his fellow men, let alone his disciple. It is through example that one gives himself, that one becomes an effective intermediary, and in turn finds himself worthy to receive.

In later years a friend took the place of my professor. We made many trips together, often on foot. When refreshing our memories we would seldom mention places and roads by their geographical names. We, quite naturally, came to distinguish them by the ideas that occupied us when we were passing through them, and this was not at all a childish game. My friend was a very learned man.[38] A humanist and scientist, he had probed the most diverse matters and so our geographical vocabulary was singularly rich: a village was associated with Mohammed, a road with a discussion about potentialities, an inn with the rising sap. The power of the idea was a rock surrounded by rhododendrons where my friend, as though talking to himself, had disclosed to me certain procedures of Plato, the ideas, and his confidence in them as approved by experience.

Our entire relationship, which was a unique kinship of thought, thus revealed the living contours of our two minds by the light of a torch we kindled together. I therefore cannot possibly think in any other form: he molded me, and, proceeding with the utmost care, brought out or deepened only those aspects of my intelligence that he completely understood. By leaving alone the core of my personality, he fortified it, developed and electrified what I still did not know about it, adorning it with the charm and refinement peculiar to a supreme mind. The ideal intermediary, he gave to me with one hand while he was willing to receive with the other. Tremendously enriched through him I often felt that I, too, had given him much, so highly did I prize his slightest approval. Lucky the young man who finds such a friend on his way!

Why are friends of this kind so rare? Many persons are potential friends, but we must know how to recognize ourselves in our fellow men. Without this first step, what could we offer? Transmission is impossible without accurate adjustment to the particular situation. To know oneself well means to manage what one possesses. We are accustomed to spread ourselves too thin or deny ourselves too much; we either underrate or overrate ourselves. These exaggerations neutralize each other when we attempt to discover ourselves in another person; we are more impartial towards others than towards ourselves and, in this sense, we know them better. Would my friend have soliloquized for hours in my presence, had I not offered him his own self as interlocutor? And does not the charm of a friendly argument lie in the fact that objections and contradictions awaken in us the reverse of our own thought, providing the complement of our convictions? If not, why argue at all? To be right? This would be childish indeed.

By placing ourselves always apart from our fellow man, we impoverish both ourselves and him. Discussions are particularly gratifying when our partner, while giving himself, has accepted us. Discussions in which we meet as two indifferent people, if not adversaries, are utterly pointless. Indifference sterilizes, and hence causes suffering. Unfortunately, kindness and affection often closely resemble indifference; we think we must fill the pockets of the person arousing our sympathy, instead of merely looking in his eyes in order to accept his glance, to give him ours, and thus to feel the unique glance of mankind. The saint sharing his cloak with the beggar would undoubtedly have liked to give it all to him; but he felt a bond with the unfortunate. To put ourselves in the place of others remains hypocritical and deceitful unless we have recognized ourselves in them; otherwise the very idea is meaningless. A young peasant woman was struck by unbearable pains that made her breathing very difficult; during some of the attacks her husband held her in his arms, adjusting his breathing to hers and probably suffering more than she did each time he inhaled. One day I met him in his yard. He breathed so heavily that I thought he was ill. When I expressed my sympathy he merely answered,

"It is not I; it is she."

He was perhaps wrong, but he was right too! Certainly he had not learned that in a mirror.

To be sure, teachers will understand what I have attempted to express on these pages—they who breathe with their pupils and therefore guess what may disturb this vital function! They will surely forgive a layman for interfering in an art that is not his own. Precious memories and also a long experience, upheld by countless observations, have induced me to do this. Many of us have long been won over to the cause of the intermediary, some perhaps too consciously;

others, guided by spontaneous intuition, which does not alter their sincerity. But the division of labor, modern specialization, the exaggerated value we attribute to virtuosity in every field, all dispose us to specialize also in our personal relations. From the professional we expect only opinions concerning his domain; if he crosses this barrier, we are quick to believe he is mistaken. We think the same of a layman (what a sad word) when he meddles in the secrets of the studio. Our fears are justified, but perhaps we confuse too easily those who deeply feel the interrelationship of our sense and our minds with incompetent persons who naively juxtapose ideas and procedures they do not understand in an attempt to achieve a special technique of artistic, intellectual or scientific knowledge: a man of letters, for example, who attempts to express music through words, a musician who interprets a painting, an architect who thinks he can compose a symphony, a philosopher who wants to build, and the like. My professor did not at all confuse a *loggia* with an *andante*; he probed far deeper!

Harmony in our activities does not imply that they are interchangeable, nor that a technique taken in figurative meaning has a real analogy with another. Music must unite organically with poetry in order to express something precise, and no title it is given will make any difference. "To picture something" in a piece of pure music is painfully childish and heart-rending to the musician. The correlation of our senses is a different matter and concerns not the object of any art or knowledge but exclusively our whole attitude as human beings toward any object.

Péladan[39] demanded that the opera house at Bayreuth be perfumed during the flower-girls' scene. He confused analogy with sensorial association; the pungent perfume of someone who sat near us in a concert can well remind us of the concert, but it is absolutely irrelevant to the program. We might as well torture the entire audience during the second act of *Tosca;* the physical suffering would have nothing in common with the emotion that overcomes us in this scene.

Speech is virtually the only tool of the teacher as he faces his pupil. By speaking he suggests, and fortunately speech can escape technical confusion; it easily indicates the laws of correlation and harmony, and can associate ideas without running the risk of confusing or juxtaposing them. The obligation to select terms keeps prudence alert, and when it comes to a test, the exclusive use of appropriate technical terms draws a line of demarcation that is insurmountable and protective.

Talking to me about music, my professor took care not to introduce matters of design, just as an artist will never go to the piano or sing to explain the meaning of values in art. Such associations belong to speech exclusively. (Literature, not belonging to speech, has not the same freedom.)

An association of ideas unaccompanied by a commentary, on the other hand, is the most revealing. Then it is up to the pupil to bring the ideas together; the pleasure and consequently all the benefit will thus be his.

To know how to ask questions in order to obtain information and penetrate a subject requires a considerable degree of judgment. If we give a young man the necessary tools, he will only have to inquire about their use. Sparing him thus the needless trouble to look for them himself, we shall increase his zeal for work. Through spontaneous association he will come to forge for himself different tools for other tasks, and he will be able to verify the fact that their principle remains the same although their techniques change. This experience alone will give him the clue to his own life and to that of others: specialized by necessity, he will recognize, in other specialized fields, the same essential elements that govern his own. His partitions will no longer be airtight; a common idea will connect them all with mankind, even the narrowly restricted techniques of his own field.

Having profited from his benevolent intermediaries he will, in turn, find himself to be one; he will become an integral part of mankind, and this is the purpose of all education.

# The Theme

(1922)

Dedicated to Henri Bonifas[40]

I showed pictures to a small boy and made up a story for each them. Suddenly he interrupted me impatiently: "But, they are beautiful just as they are!" I stopped in confusion, and I have never forgotten the lesson.

In art this child's reaction is the beginning of wisdom; and it seems we do everything to prevent the child from arriving at this first step in aesthetic understanding. We suggest to him that religious feeling emanates from historic facts. The important events of history have their dates, and dates keep the great discoveries, the great works of art in the boy's memory; finally dates organize for him the efforts of thought. Thus the child's vision assumes a chronological form, which implies a sequence of facts, hence, a report; and the imagination grasps only what happens before and after; it cannot dwell on the period in between. Already a victim of fleeting time in his daily life, the child is now also unable to hold on to it in the past. And yet, it seems as though the past is the very place in the world, the only place where Time loses its tyrannical power, the only place where we could linger!

What listener has the courage to get up in the midst of a course on the history of art or of philosophy and state "that things are beautiful just as they are"? Where is the student of theology whose indignation is aroused when talked to of "the old covenant of Moses with respect to the tent of the tabernacle, or of Samuel choosing one of Josiah's sons"? The most wonderful testimonies of the divine Omnipresence we put in chronological order and carefully remove them from ourselves.

In explaining the pictures, I persistently tried to transfer into time duration what belongs exclusively to the Present. The child sensed this; I robbed him of the most precious gift, the prolonged sense of the Present. In art the error appears of less consequence than, for instance, in religion, where the tendency is criminal. Yet in religion too it has impoverished our life pitifully by making us blind. To see a work of art properly does not mean to see it as part of a sequence! It is here, before us; in order to present his lively vision to us the artist immobilizes it. Why do we put it back in time, that is to say, in a chronological story, invariably asking what it represents? The question manifests a need for anecdote; for we do not wish to leave it; like the Jews, we want a beginning and an ending! As a result we see immortality in an infinite time duration, whereas the Present alone can be immortal. A work of art is the triumph of the Present. You spend the morning before Michelangelo's *David*, it is there; you get up at midnight to see it again, it is always there, entirely indifferent to what you did and experienced during the day. Its only date is the minute of its completion; but from that mathematical point on, it escapes Time. To destroy it is to deliver it up anew to that great enemy, while our death means for us deliverance from it. Art is the triumph of life outside of Time.

Objection will be raised that music and poetry have a time duration; certainly, but they are arts precisely because they dominate Time, because they only use Time without submitting to it. A symphony lasting three-quarters of an hour is not three-quarters of an hour of art; rather it is a work of art haughtily borrowing a certain segment of Time in order to fill it with an expression that has nothing to do with the material reality of this time duration. (This we feel strongly in a concert when we are not bored!) Space is the only stable form in our universe; Time can modify but never annihilate Space, for without Space, Time does not exist.

Setting aside for a moment the arts of Time (music and poetry), let us consider those of Space (sculpture and painting) in order to examine the harm done to them by our anecdotic conception of art. To begin with, what about this conception, which is really rather queer in view of the immobility of these art forms? If the artists had wished to communicate to us the least fragment of a story, they would have found means to give it sequence. Since they have chosen immobility, they probably had good reasons to do so. For it would be a mistake to imagine that they would submit to a technical necessity; the artist is free, entirely free; his work and his technique are his free choice; and only the painter or sculptor has chosen immobility as his means of expression. All of life was at his command; he has made a choice and held on to it, with varying degrees of success, it is true. Did he do so to snub Time? No more than the musician; like the latter, the painter uses Time, only in a different way. An artist is by definition a violent person; therefore his is the kingdom of art, and art is essentially a conquest. Not to admit this is to be ignorant of art. I am convinced that to reach a work of art we must bear this knowledge foremost in our mind, perhaps even exclusively. Without it we do not have the key to that phenomenon, the touchstone of the entire culture.

Why did our prehistoric ancestor carve on his weapons and his dwellings images of an animal, the reindeer, the prerequisite for his existence? He did so to fix its image outside of Time, that means outside of the birth and death of that animal; to have this servant constantly in sight. With his drawing he defied Time; he made a work of art, which is an act of violence. And when he prolonged his shout, varying it until he produced a sequence of sounds, he made Time serve his will. In this sense the work of art is supremely arbitrary; its presence is and must be a defiance. To understand and appreciate it, we must lose ourselves in that mood of conquest which demands of us, whether or not we are artists, the highest degree of courage and independence. This is why art liberates us.

Thus, what I have called the anecdotic conception of art does not affect the work of art but ourselves. Through it we give testimony of a dependence incompatible with the artist's creation; instead of raising ourselves valiantly to the level of the work, we pull it down to us into the atmosphere of nonessential realities where it cannot live. So it resists and escapes us. Under such conditions we could look at a painting for a year without having seen it for a second; it is not where we think it is.

Nevertheless, without proving ourselves always worthy of its presence we do feel this presence a little. A work of art in our home is a refuge; to be sure, we do not reach it, and our days slip by in front of it; yet the sight of it maintains hope in us. We look at it with a sigh, a sigh of relief but also of regret, above all of gratitude. It makes us suffer certainly, yet we love this suffering, and there are moments when we come to dominate it; then joy alone remains, the joy of victory not over the work of art but over everything else: we have overcome the anecdote, annulled Time, our watch has stopped and will not run again until we return to what we call reality. The work of art is the dream of our waking life; to misapprehend this is like counting the hours of our sleep while we sleep, and this is just what we are doing every time we ask, "What does this represent?" This question does not belong in the realm of art; it is irrelevant to it and consequently never answered.

On the ceiling of the Sistine Chapel, the Creation of Man is not man's Creation. Can this beautiful man be God? A man creating the first man? The "Creation of Man" is the idea that preceded the fresco; with the fresco finished the title is vanquished and we contemplate its defeat: art has suppressed the anecdote of the "Creation"; that was its function, and Michelangelo is guilty of this violence; what we see is his creation, which has no other history than the history of his heroic conquest over Time; the anecdote is revived, not in a human mortal form, but as a transfiguration that escapes Time. Great as an artist may otherwise be, he stoops if he clings to Time.

But what about religious art? Art is art; whether it "ignores" a religious subject or any other is of little importance; its victory is what counts and without it art is suppressed by the subject.[41] Why did art reach its greatest flowering in the periods whose customs and general spiritual attitude provided the themes for art? Precisely because the artist did not have to worry about a subject: it was thrust upon him and overcoming it became automatic! Nobody should be preoccupied with Michelangelo's theme. Even a Rembrandt, at a time when the artist had a greater choice, took no account of subject. His *Pilgrims of Emmaus,* probably his most anecdotic canvas, tells no story; the painting dominates the biblical account and presents it to us more purified even than the most sober words could have done. This is not Jesus, nor hardly the disciples; moreover, the artist cannot show Him to us; he does not dwell on a personality, even though it be divine. Does a philosopher accept the content of his writing as his very thought?

Poetic art and music apparently escape the audacity of the painter and the sculptor. We believe the poet and the musician have something to tell, and only the form, the technical procedure, distinguishes them from the writer of prose. Technique dominates the work of the painter and sculptor so imperatively that it is easy to exclude from it the anecdotic idea that is always ready to deceive us. What then makes us imagine the musical work to be like the chronological tale, when the art of sounds is so different from literary expression that it obviously cannot adopt the latter's purpose? A tale is visibly presented to us (outside of real life) exclusively in the theatre, consequently in a duration, a form which, together with Space, employs Time. Pure music employs Time alone; this is its essential character. I have established and developed this principle in detail in my books and so I can merely sketch it briefly here. What distinguishes music from words, in this sense, is that, through their use as language words come quite close to our daily life and to the time during which this life flows, while music has only Time itself in common with life, without being at all bound to the use we ordinarily make of it, i.e., the forms we give to the duration of our existence. It can therefore be asserted that music only avails itself of Time without ever yielding to it, and that it thus creates an entirely ideal time duration which, although it is within real Time, remains independent of it. Music has nothing in common with poetry except the use of Time, which does not imply a tale, whereas the use of words by its very nature and even without plot is an account of feelings, impressions, thoughts, and observations.

The object of music seems not to be as clear to us as are the themes of poetry; the definitions of music are, therefore, numerous and contradictory. Some want to see in it only a collection of sounds like a collection of solid forms in architecture; others solely the expression of our sentiments and our passions, but in a general form which excludes the anecdote (words never express anything: they designate or suggest). Still others are inclined to see in it the account of these passions and constantly attempt to explain every piece of music! One definition seems to me undeniable and to be applicable to every kind of music. Schopenhauer wrote: "Music never expresses the phenomenon but only the inner essence of the phenomenon." The artist-philosopher touched upon the crucial point from which music should never deviate. With words we possess the language of the phenomenon. And whether, in poetry, we try to exalt that language until the words are deflected from their meaning, or whether we even create new words with the single aim of escaping the daily reality, the word remains still the strict outgrowth of the language and cannot be detached from it. The word is real no matter how it sounds or what it is; it cannot be elevated above the exigencies of rational exchange, which make up language, except by taking liberties with it. Therefore we did not place Poetry among the fine arts. (Goethe denied it this place too!) Music did not originate as a means of communication; its primitive forms—improvised singing, dance—are lyric and concern merely those who create them; a dancer takes part in the music he dances; a shepherd pours out his feelings over the mountains regardless of who may hear him. In this sense music is the only one of our arts that is spontaneous; the others are presented to us, music is within us. The testimony of music's invisible presence concerns exclusively the person who gives it; he gives his own self to himself. And if music were anecdotic, which it is not, it would still not be a tale, for a tale is addressed to someone.

It follows that if music is to specify its expression, i.e., to address itself to someone, it must turn to the poet. This cooperation assumes two forms that on occasion may be combined but which remain nevertheless distinct: the work of the lyric poet and that of the dramatic poet who uses music—the poet-musician. The shepherd singing an improvised text reveals to himself more or less clearly his desire to make specific purely musical expression. This can go so far that he passes unwittingly from pure lyric to dramatic art and to telling a story. The fact that music avails itself of Time inclines it to seek a theme but does not force it to do so. Like the painter, the musician can take advantage of the prejudices and convictions of his era to motivate the form he gives his composition, but he always dominates it (J. S. Bach). It is the use of Time that permits him to unite with the poet and to fluctuate between the pure and simple expression of the flow of emotions and the specification of the particular nature of that flow in a story sequence.

The life of music is infinitely complex, though its intrinsic nature remains always the same. In uniting with the poet, it does not identify itself with him at all; on the contrary, music offers the poet the expression that he alone could not attain. The expression is so developed that it asserts the constant presence of the inner essence of the phenomenon; the poet, by means of words, thus reconnects the inner essence with its accidental form (only the phenomenon). Thus if they are in harmony the poet and the musician proceed in parallel fashion, and their work becomes the integral expression of humanity. Presenting it thereafter to our eyes, they create dramatic art.

The ideal nature of music makes it the outstanding agent of art; through Time it implicitly participates in poetry, and through Space, in the fine arts, by means of movement as performed by the actor. Its position is so high, its freedom so great that it can oscillate thus in infinite nuances without losing a particle of its character. It is wrong to place music among the fine arts; it is more than one art since it participates in each of them. Plato sensed this when he proposed to base the state on music. For mankind music represents the principle of order. (Obviously, in speaking of music I have in mind something other than a concert piece.)

If we now return to the boy who found the pictures beautiful in themselves, what will he, that intuitive chap, say when we illustrate for him a Mozart sonata with a story or some picturesque explanations? Probably he will wonder why Mozart himself did not explain the sonata and he will ask us where we have read our little tale. If we replied that the notes indicate it, we would give him every right to accuse us of a fib, and we would have every reason to feel humiliated. There is Mozart, defenseless before the child; the child is no longer defenseless before the confidence of the genius; both are profoundly guileless. Do we want to deceive the composer and corrupt the child under the guise of bringing the two closer together? A child will never look for the anecdotic meaning of music unless we put him on that false track. The child can perfectly distinguish the meaning of a thing from its expression. It is we who confuse these ideas. Why then does a child have so much fun in singing a text, and even more, in miming it, as it does with the songs of Dalcroze? Here we touch upon one of the most serious educational problems, which is usually treated with regrettable carelessness and flippancy.

Without preliminaries, let us state at once that music should be introduced to the child only in the form of Dance. If I were rich and socially completely independent I would keep my children, during their first years, away from the influence of any music, whether it be piano or concert, lyric song or dance music. They would have to invent music; while dancing they would get the notion of singing. There is no doubt that the humming of little songs here and there in daily life will have a good influence upon the child's spirit. But I would beware of insisting upon it, and I would choose those songs whose text does not call forth any tales, but merely expresses a mood or an enumeration of things; furthermore, I would not draw attention to that little cantilena the child must hear but not listen to. Whatever story there is must be told the child in words; it cannot yet be time for him to face the enormous problem of music made definite by the poet and that of the poet deified through music. The child must be able for a long time to consider music "beautiful" in itself.

Let us add here as counterpart pictures! For the child, pictures are the first initiation in the fine arts. Experience tells us, I believe, that the child doodling on paper tries to imitate what he sees or knows through touching but has no intention of sketching a series or successive acts. We risk giving him that intention through animating an immobile picture with a story; his imagination then makes him see what the picture no longer contains or does not yet contain, and this dangerously falsifies his first notion of art. We always want to be historical, biographical, anecdotic in the belief that we thus enhance the child's interest, but this happens at the expense of his ingenuousness. When he draws a house and a garden, we urge him to add a little girl leaving the garden, entering the house, lighting a fire (to make the chimney smoke), etc. The child knows very well that this is deceitful, that his sketch does not show anything of the sort, and so he is about to get a lesson in the interpretation of designs that he so naively executed for their own sake and which he finds "beautiful" in themselves.

For a youngster, the notion of a picture must be utterly separated from that of a story. The colored prints decorating his room must be selected without exception for their "beauty in themselves." The pictures should never be spoiled by a printed caption, should never be given a name; the child should simply look at them and let them sink in. Make-believe, innate to the youngster and his greatest enjoyment, will invariably come to him as something alive. His imagination needs no picture or sketch to be stimulated when he is told about the Sleeping Beauty! But when, for instance, the prince enters the room of the Beauty, the child may be placed "just for fun" behind the door, his little sister on a sofa and, at a given signal, the prince will enter the Beauty's room and awaken her. This will not interrupt the reading too much; the reader can read while walking about the room. The whole episode will be animated, and the written tale a guide for the imagination, nothing more. Being immobilized in lines and colors on flat paper, the picture is in itself fiction. To add another fiction to it is to overload it and to wipe out all its artistic and educational value. Consequently books with pictures that illustrate a text should be excluded! I am convinced that no child looking at a beautiful painting will ever ask what it represents if we have not put this paltry and deplorable notion into his young mind. Poor paintings, it is true, always represent something. Hence we should show the youngster only beautiful paintings, that is to say, those which, like the *Creation of Man* by Michelangelo, suppress the anecdote by transfiguring it.

Our Protestant education—which is Jewish and rational—presents the entire universe, including the most sacred ideas, in a historical and chronological form. Therefore the Protestant attains even the most rudimentary notion of art only after laboriously removing those artificial foundations. For the Catholic, the road is shorter, the initiation easier; his impressions are already strongly affected by the Omnipresence, i.e., by the eternal Present, alone, and his dogmas are so obviously symbolic that, for a long time, he is unable to see them as documented reality. The Catholic artist suppresses the anecdote where the faithful Protestant artist still seeks painfully to realize it (Burnand). Are we not often disturbed when looking at a painting which, although very well executed, is still not a work of art? We try to understand this. The only explanation is that the artist subordinated himself to the subject of his choice instead of conquering it. The layman without a feeling for art will always collect reproductions of such paintings; only the artist will collect others. For this reason art cannot and must not be explained.

Jaques-Dalcroze, intuitive in everything, has replaced picture books with mimed songs! What child will even enjoy seeing a series of motionless pictures, if he himself has executed and, consequently, really experienced them? A living instruction is an instruction without images; living art—figuratively speaking— is an art without fiction, unless it implies movement; then it is alive and our own body is at the same time the creator and the performer of the work, but not in a "living tableau!" For nothing, on the contrary, is more dead. To immobilize the living body is nonsense and to try to make a "tableau" is to ignore the essentials of painting (or sculpture).

Two objects must definitely be excluded from the child's education: pictures with captions and the living body frozen in a "tableau." Otherwise he will require many long years to rediscover the very sources of Art and its elements in their simple authentic form. For the child the illustrated book is as much a falsification as is pure music explained by a story.

Just as the child must find for himself words matching the musical sounds (and he does it so well and easily if left alone to improvise his song!) he must be allowed to discover for himself the acting out of the text he sings. It would thus be preferable neither to show him nor to make him execute the Dalcroze songs until we are assured that he himself has tried this thrilling synthesis. The harmony of his moving body with the musical sound is ingrained in him, for dancing is the first expression of his satisfaction and his enjoyment. But dramatization is a decisive step, important and very dangerous unless he is well prepared and well supervised. A young niece of mine, when about to go to bed, insisted that I be the prince who carries her into her castle; after we had performed this action with charming roulades mixed with tender kisses, she fell asleep beaming.

The usefulness of fixing a tale or melody through written signs must be considered objectively: "What do you want? We really have to do this lest we forget the beautiful story and the gay music." The child does not understand the grand air with which we surround reading and writing. Here as anywhere else he must discover what we have imposed on art, and this is, after all, disagreeable.

In the last analysis, the fine arts are the transfigured expression of the

Present; even the arts of Time (music and poetry) express the Present, because they avail themselves of time without submitting themselves to it. Consequently historical and anecdotal ideas have nothing to do with Art, and aesthetic education must take account of that fact. If, later, the idea of dramatizing (plotting) is imposed upon the youngster, it must always be in some stylized (Dalcroze songs, etc.) or symbolic form. Dramatic realism (this would probably not be the youngster's idea, for he would not find it attractive) will be shown him as something ugly and hardly recommendable.—Eurhythmics is, in this respect as in all others, artistic training of the first rank; its importance is inestimable. By definition eurhythmics authorizes the child to express himself in an idealized form that ushers him bodily into the sanctuary of art and thus justifies his urgent need for make-believe. It blunts the spell for him of the illustrated tales by lifting his own self to the level of the work of art. And it does so with no other suggestion than the artistic expression itself, the language of art, music, which in itself is the negation of chronological reality. However, it is effective only under one condition: that the so-called "plastic" element of dramatization be excluded, lest the child look for a spectator and so spoil his imagination. Not until much later can the adolescent, warned by pure eurhythmics, understand that dramatizing does not necessarily involve the spectator; even then the Initiator will need all his eloquence of speech or example to instill this conviction in the student.

For the child the Theme is himself, his integral being, body and soul. If we give him this Theme, which is himself, in its artistic aspect, he will feel unquestionably that he is an artist. From this point to understanding a work of art is only a step, and our books with their historical vulgarization of art can be put aside among the dictionaries once and for all time.

# The Child and Dramatic Art

*Pour l'Ere Nouvelle,* January 1923

We know what is meant by a child or at least we all agree on the significance of the term; and we have modern pedagogy to enlighten us still further and to unite us under the shining emblem of its projects. But what do we know about dramatic art? Can two persons agree on this matter? Of course not. It is therefore necessary for each of us to state what he means by this term and how he interprets it before we bring these two notions, apparently so incongruous, in contact with one another. If I may be permitted, I should like to review briefly my own development of this idea, as presented in my recent book, *The Work of Living Art.*

Our arts are lifeless; only dramatic art avails itself of the living being—the actor—to convey itself to us. If we regard this art as inseparable from an audience as are our other art forms, we place the living yet passive beings (the spectators) opposite the active beings (the actors). This attitude is debatable even from the merely artistic point of view. Ethically it poses a problem: does the human being have the right in art to remain exclusively the passive appreciator sitting opposite other human beings—his brothers—who are sacrificing their personal existence in order to furnish this satisfaction for him?

A strange yet characteristic situation. The terms of this problem suddenly open our eyes to a fact entirely new to us: does dramatic art really need an audience? A picture, a statue hidden away in an attic, do not exist; a spectator is indispensable for them. One can however very well imagine a play being performed without anyone attending it, though it would still certainly exist.

Here we are then in the presence of an art form—dramatic art—whose existence is assured even without a spectator; and, what is more, the addition of an audience is morally disquieting to us. I am speaking here of the idea of dramatic art itself, not as it is seen in our existing theatres. In our period of transition, the idea we form of things does not correspond to their positive realities; these cannot yet fit our means and our intentions. Indeed we are much richer today than we avow publicly and privately, particularly as regards dramatic art.

The ethical problem thus raised by the theatre causes another uncertainty: is it proven that it is harmless to awaken in us fictitious feelings and to give them body and soul by means of our own bodies? Furthermore, are we sure that it is laudable to attend those proceedings and to let ourselves be moved by them? Since I cannot possibly elaborate here on this topic, I may be allowed bluntly to affirm the principle: in dramatic art the artistic question depends on the resolution of the ethical problem; when the latter is resolved, the form of this art will itself be fluid, ever new. How? Why? The answer, it seems to me, is given in advance! That disquieting opposition of audience and actors poses a problem which is probably insolvable; hence, as long as we maintain such a relationship it is our duty gradually to diminish the gulf that separates the spectator from the actor, to thus throw off our egotistic torpor, to take gradually an active part in what we still arrogantly call the performance, and eventually to *live, ourselves and together, the work of art*. Respect for ourselves, for the actor our brother, and the dignity of dramatic art will be our reward.

Let us transfer these ideas into the domain of the child! Every child is a born actor, in the sense that for him imitating is inseparable from learning. If the child appears in public (and how dreadful this is!) he does not want to consider his audience spectators of his imitations. As soon as he becomes conscious of his imitations, he seeks solitude, or, at least, becomes indifferent to his surroundings. When the spectacle of external life has taken hold of him firmly enough to invite him to copy it by mustering his imitations in a fictional form, fiction takes first place in the child's preoccupation; there he finds the supreme realization of his existence; to show his fiction to others seems to him to abandon the best, the truest aspect of life, and he is very shy in revealing its mysteries. At the most he will try to *explain* his fiction to others, but he will by no means exhibit it. The child is rather vexed about this, for at times we make ourselves spectators although we were not asked to; on the contrary, at other times we demonstrate a condescending indifference to what he considers the supreme expression of his person, for which he himself has such a candid respect. He is particularly sensitive in this regard. Besides, why do we always approach the child's serious and tragic life with a smile? The child never smiles while playing, never above all when he is in his grand fictional reality. Our smile is always patronizing, and is therefore an insult that hurts the child, even though he does not dare say so.

I appeal to those who have been children.

Should we then favor the child's predilection for fiction and even stimulate it by having him recite what he did not invent himself? Or should we, on the contrary, lead him as often as possible to reality? These questions, it seems to me, do not touch the heart of the problem. We have nothing to favor, nothing to repress: we have something to respect. Are we showing our respect if we prematurely awaken in the child the superfluous notion of an audience, small as it may be—if we support this notion, dangerous to the point of making us doubt the dignity of the theatre and the rightful existence of dramatic art?

The child already has great difficulty in reconciling in his little brain fiction and reality. The awakening of fictitious feelings is no danger for the child so long as he finds in them, as I have said, the best and truest aspect of his own personality. This awakening is an anticipation which enriches him and allows his often intense sensitiveness to put up with the discouraging dullness of his daily life. Pierre Loti, leaving his twig garden, exclaimed: "Forever getting up, forever lying down, forever eating tasteless soup . . . !" What becomes *immediately* harmful is to suggest to the child the idea that it gives us pleasure to watch him in his moments of fiction. The terrible problem of the opposite groups (actor-audience) is certainly not a problem for the child, but his feelings, so pure when he is left alone, run the risk of being forever corrupted by the idea of *exhibiting himself.* And not merely his feelings, but his imaginative creations too will thereby be fatally affected. Yet, in that respect, do we not, with or without good intentions, spend our time poisoning the child with our looks and our words? A child who wants to exhibit himself, to attract attention, must at once be shown the door. Yet how can we do this if we are the principal offenders?

Practically, these considerations exclude and condemn in childhood any kind of performing, of costuming, of reciting other than in lessons, etc., . . . in short, everything that presumes an audience, including even the parents. The reform is indeed radical, and we have a long way to go!*

---

*In a second article I intend to deal with the difficult question of finding an opportunity particularly of cases when the child himself wishes to have an audience out of a more or less conscious unselfishness or a need for a communion with a group that understands him.

# Costuming

*Pour l'Ere Nouvelle,* April 1923

In the course of my reflections about the child and dramatic art in the preceding issue of this magazine, I mentioned in a footnote the question of finding an opportunity. I admit having done this reluctantly, for my conviction does not allow a compromise, and I am writing the following lines still from the same radical viewpoint.

Time-honored habits have perpetuated in us certain dispositions. Does this mean that it is always desirable to accept these dispositions as natural phenomena and to preserve them? Everyone can discover that a child feels a satisfaction in embodying a fictitious person and then seeks occasionally to let others share in his pleasure, and that this idea gives birth in him the idea of an audience. It does not follow that this is good. Parents, friends and comrades are delighted to watch the—alas—very peculiar expression animating the child's features during his performance and they try as benevolent and appreciative spectators to demonstrate their sympathy and approval. Must this be confused with a *shared* joy?

I mentioned costuming, an essential matter which is ordinarily passed over without too much emphasis. However—with your permission—I shall dare to dwell on that subject.

To see a child dress up makes me sick at heart, to see him costumed makes me sicker still. I defy my reader to find a single child who has maintained the simplicity of his demeanor and the ingenuousness of his person during this sacrilegious act. The majority of women—not all women fortunately—live in a perpetual carnival. Woman is the sex which does not cover itself, does not dress itself, but costumes itself. When does woman ever undress except to dress herself still better? Therefore woman, as everybody will have noticed, is always wholeheartedly in favor of costuming and particularly of costuming children. Forever accustomed to the emotional upheaval which this kind of preoccupation begets, she is blind to the child's trouble, deaf to the corruption of his aims, and insensitive to the distortion of his appearance. To be convinced of this one need only observe the satisfaction with which a woman's eyes follow the child whose disguise she has just accomplished. What I shall call the decisive and irreparable shock escapes the woman; she has been hardened in the pernicious flames of her passion for dressing up and is quite willing to help bring the delicate innocent child into a state similar to her own. Whether one likes it or not, a good three-fourths of costuming is the desire that the child feels, indeed not for fiction, but rather for "having others partake" in his fictional joys, or to be more frank, for showing off.

When I was young, my mother used to entrust us to the care of an elderly lady whose educational genius was indisputable. This remarkable person understood the extraordinary importance fiction has for the child, but she also felt deeply the dilemma of the child who finds himself oscillating between dream and reality, and she tried to make this position as painless as possible. Atavistically, we children yearned passionately for costuming, but she never permitted us to put on the slightest token of a costume. Thanks to this sacrifice our marvelous fictions maintained, during the long hours with her, a nobility, an unforgettable purity. When she left us alone for an hour or two, we turned quickly to costuming as to a forbidden, yet delicious fruit. When on her return she surprised us, her attitude suddenly made the costumes prosaic; and with a word she placed everything under a light of plain and crude reality. We did not need any explanation from her; she made us feel for ourselves that we had defiled the divine fiction and were not worthy of it for the rest of the day.

The question is of such importance that I am inclined to say: Yes, keep all fictions, all festivals, with or without an audience, with or without a stage or curtain—anything one may wish of this kind—but never with the shadow of costuming!*[42]

Then—only then—shall we know what childhood and youth desire and, as a result, what we ourselves desire in the realm of festivals and dramatic art. Let us start from here! My deep, my solemn conviction is that this touchstone will bring us the most remarkable and most humbling surprises.

---

*It stands to reason that everyday clothes have to be in accord with this principle. And that the mamas do not forget that here little girls have the same right to be children as have little boys. Great progress, incidentally, is being made today in this sense due to the influence of sports and general hygiene.

# Picturesqueness

## (1922)

When a drinker signs a pledge of abstinence, he usually is to a certain degree
under the influence of the intoxication of which he wants to purge himself. The
step is surely difficult for him to take, but even so, he does not weigh all its
implications: his organism, warped by the alcohol, and his brain, preoccupied
with too cherished a habit, prevent him from suspecting the emptiness he will
later feel and the intense effort he must maintain to fill this emptiness without
turning again to the dreadful poison. In signing his pledge, he proves that he
has recognized the danger but he cannot vouch that he will accept from the very
outset all implications of his decision. These are revealed to him slowly in a
succession of painful, even agonizing surprises. Oh, had he only known! But
no matter whether or not he realized those implications, he still firmly believed
in the absolute necessity of fleeing from the slow physical and spiritual death
that lay in wait for him. Now he is caught in a struggle between on the one hand
the relapse he secretly desires; on the other, the almost desperate acceptance of
an idea that he somehow sensed when he signed the pledge, but which he has
since lost.

Our life is full of situations in which only faith in a barely grasped truth
can guide us. One may even say that life is the way that it is, and not otherwise,
in order to teach us the value of faith (I am not speaking here of religious
beliefs). As soon as we perceive light on the horizon, life takes pleasure in
placing before our every step a wall to hide it. For this reason the pursuit of truth
often resembles a demolition.

These walls must be knocked down, one after another. Our neighbor thus
sees only the negative work of our life and judges us accordingly. We must
therefore, like the drinker grappling with his abstinence, maintain our confidence not only in the barely glimpsed light, but also in the rightness of our
action in the face of the skeptical and malevolent judgments of our neighbor.

The desperate situation of the fine arts compels us to seek in our tottering contemporary civilization a firm, uncorrupted position that we can safely use as a point of reference. But as on the Venetian lagoon, our pilings waver at the slightest touch. So we must of necessity search elsewhere, and elsewhere find merely ourselves!—A last resort, you say? Of course not! For through myself I understand you as well as myself, since you alone justify my existence! We do not have to love our neighbor *as* ourselves but *within* ourselves. Organized Christianity has separated us; we must join again in an intimate union.

In *The Work of Living Art* I spoke of collective physical feeling, the great Unknown. It was necessary to emphasize this specific point, for we have separated our body not only from our soul, but also from the body of our fellow men to such a degree that physical feeling has become for us a personal mystery of which we reveal nothing. In the present study we can consider this collective feeling—which has created and always will create the beauty of a civilization— as being already virtually achieved. We accordingly enlarge our point of reference by making it the collective being, a perfect whole perceptible to all of us. Is this perhaps to anticipate? I do not think so. It seems, on the contrary, that the advance indications are of a New *Presence.* . . . Its very name must thrill my kind reader, who must have felt it rising within himself. Let us all put our faith in the dimly glimpsed Truth! Let us have confidence in it! Light cannot deceive us. In the conviction of this, I shall proceed.

After the great era of collective creation to which our cathedrals bear witness, the work of art became gradually independent. Ceasing to be a simple community artisan, the artist entered the pernicious path of individualism that led him to decadence. Therefore, one of the first premises for a flourishing art appears clearly to be a sense of solidarity. If the artist has lost this sense, the reason is probably that society gave him ever fewer examples of such a solidarity. But conditions today are no longer the same! All social reforms, without exceptions, are based on the feeling for solidarity and no one would think of disputing the sovereignty of this principle. If the artist refuses to adopt it as a rule of conduct, he will isolate himself from society and lose his rights. We might even say that he has already lost them. His situation is no longer merely an aesthetic problem, but involves also a serious problem in social ethics. We cannot help it; his path is barred. If he does not resolve his dilemma, he must retreat or mark time, for the die is cast. For him it means either to be or not to be, and he knows it. Every day he feels his reputation further damaged; soon what will remain of it? The house is on fire, as the popular saying goes. Oh! If it were only fire, the artist might rise again from its ashes purified and rejuvenated! Unfortunately he is sinking in quicksand too, so that all we see of a good many artists is a lock of wildly fluttering hair.

If artists had held fast to the golden chain of humanity, giving everyone a fine example of loyalty and steadfastness, they would now be our masters. Instead, what are they? Not even entertainers. And we, what have we done to keep them at the top? Nothing, absolutely nothing; and it may be their turn to judge us. Let us consult the New Presence; it will speak volumes about our faults, our negligence, and our sordid egotism toward the artist. We, ourselves, have created the dilettante, and this is saying enough, I think.

Unless we accept the law of solidarity and its duties, we shall fall under the sway of a far more severe law, that of responsibility; for solidarity implies a reciprocal action that we cannot avoid. As far as the artist is concerned, we have hitherto lived as we pleased, demanding everything of him and offering him nothing. The New Presence catches us unaware and, like August the clown, trying to help lay a carpet, we wander hither and thither not exactly knowing which end of the art to seize nor which attitude to adopt towards the artist. The artist watches us with some misgivings, as a storekeeper watches a customer who does not quite know what he wants. Tired of waiting, the artist takes refuge where he is sure not to meet us. He willingly chooses this, but there nothing human can inspire him. Complacently we assume his innate individualism to be responsible for his flight, and we settle back again in the pillows of our old easy chair.

Through what miracle has the New Presence been able to manifest itself in such an atmosphere? The answer is quite simple. We have returned to the source, to the point of departure, to the only solid ground—the ground the artists pushed us away from and then forgot. We have returned to ourselves—our integral selfness, body and soul—and here we have rediscovered our neighbor. The church set us against our own bodies, and when as a result we declined to recognize ourselves, we then lost the power to recognize ourselves in others. The body has taken its revenge; but while this revenge may be sweet, it is also destructive. We begin to be aware of this, which has forced us to return to our starting point. This is the whole miracle which, like everything great, is very simple. But how can we extend this miracle to include the artist who, after all, is waiting for it even though he does not admit it? This will come about through our own action. Since what he offers us is not at all suited for us, we are no longer prepared *to take* from him, we want *to give*. Laymen though we be, if we claim that we are able to give, the artist will obviously have to listen and pay attention to us.

Yet, for all those moments when that barely glimpsed light—the light of an art living in us and we in it—brightens and guides us, life too often interferes and multiplies the obstacles separating us from that light. Therefore, we must demolish before we construct, and this requires sacrifices we are not willing to make. Like the drunkard facing the poison he cannot give up, we lack courage and faith. Habit is a dreadful power that successfully replaces honest judgment. We need a touchstone to warn us wherever our decadent art has imposed upon us ways of feeling contrary to living art, contrary to the New Presence which we want to revive and serve. But there is a problem: we are afraid of this test, for we sense its inexorability.

Let us nevertheless make an attempt in this new direction and, for example, defy what is called, not without apprehension nor some doubt, the *picturesque*. Etymologically this term denotes objects or themes particularly suited to the ends of painting, those which may favorably be presented by forms and colors on a flat surface. Only by extension do we apply the term to literature or to speech. But, and mark this well, this concept does not prevail in architecture or sculpture if a ruin is said to be picturesque; the adjective is not applied to its structure or style, but to its decay and age. Lastly in music the term "picturesque" refers only to certain experiments that are always regrettable and foreign to the aesthetics of music. Even so, we apply the term readily to the purely visual effect produced by various objects without considering the original connotation of the term in painting.

Picturesqueness is thus a quality we judge visually. And we should remember that this quality is exclusive and consequently implies a choice: by choosing this rather than that, we express our tastes and our desire. From this specific point of view, what do we call "picturesque"?—The painter likes to enrich his palette by the number of colors and the variety of their arrangement; this assumes intricate planning in every detail. He does not always seek variety, but it is nevertheless one of his principal objectives, though he may not always be aware of it. He does not hesitate in his choice between an old crumbling wall gnawed away by leprosy and lichen and the properly maintained wall whose cement feeds no parasites. Nor will he hesitate between a chestnut tree with all its branches normally developed, whose injuries have been promptly tended by a conscientious forester, and an old veteran of a tree succumbing to its years and the weather and raising its naked branches as if to accuse heaven.

Or, for that matter, the painter cannot possibly hesitate in his choice between a new school in which everything is conceived, constructed, and arranged for the greatest benefit and the full development of youth, and a seminary that is a victim of the neglect of dirty zealots, but which harmonizes with the very site where it rots. The distinctly functional character, the tidiness and rational proportion of the school, do not furnish a subject for the painter, or at least so we believe.

Does the painter prefer decay, decrepitude, neglect and filth (for here things must be called by their right names) only because neatness, health and strength usually offer fewer themes to be captured in colors and forms? We know that the sentiments of veneration, of nostalgia, etc., are invoked to justify this taste for old and worn-out things. In this way people attempt, more or less consciously, to blend two motives that are quite different. But why does the painter feel the need to defend himself only on this point when otherwise he deems his taste indisputable? Does our ineradicable preference for old furniture, for instance, depend solely on our cult of the past? Is it for the sake of sacrifice to this cult that we go to the second-hand dealer to bargain for rickety tables and poorly-jointed cupboards? The same pretty woman who would never wear her grandmother's dressing gown, though it is an authentic witness of a past rather closely linked to herself, will settle down with satisfaction in an easy chair which is carefully disinfected and renovated, but whose last owners are total strangers to her. Let us not deceive ourselves; the cult of the souvenir is one thing, and our taste for the old is another. The New Presence can put up very well with the one but not with the other. And we must ask ourselves why this is so.

We—some artists and I—have rented an old parsonage in a small medieval town bordering on a very beautiful lake. The whole situation was indeed picturesque, even excessively so! As soon as we arrived, we whitewashed all our rooms and repaired several things in the house which, though they were quite picturesque, seemed incompatible with our own dignity. Yet we never tired of the dilapidated lanes in our neighborhood or of their dirty inhabitants. The least repair on their shacks, even the maintenance of the streets and walls, wrung our tender hearts. It seemed to us an indisputable crime against art, and hence against us. The picturesqueness of the place was for us the foremost consideration. My companions, the painters, sometimes put the blame on nature itself when they returned at noon without having touched their brushes: "Impossible, my good fellow, everything was so monstrously fresh . . . !" For them nature was too beautiful that day. The vineyard is suitable only in winter or late fall; an orchard must be overrun by moss, the poplars by the parasitic mistletoe. If these gentlemen were to construct a shelter for themselves, they would build it with old weathered boards; yet they demand impeccable meals; for the eyes may be defiled, but the palate never! Antiques are manufactured for such persons; the new artificially aged. If it were not for the sexual instinct, they would voluntarily destroy their own youth; but the fish served to them must be absolutely fresh.

I do not exaggerate; on the contrary, out of respect for dear memories, I understate. What sort of depraved sense could push us to such extremes? Our interest in this small town grew from no historical precedent, no personal memory, and especially, alas, no concern for its unfortunate people, ruined by alcohol and debauchery. Our motive must be sought elsewhere. "We love to see," you will say, "the numerous evidences of past generations, a legitimate sentiment deriving from an instinctive sympathy for everything that is or was human. Your new school does not yet bear any trace of life. A blank page, even of the finest parchment, is uninteresting. We want to perceive the grand style, the stamp of past centuries."—"And the present? Has it no style?"—"Perhaps, but we do not yet recognize it; we must wait."—"Wait for what?—sickness, suffering, misery and death?"—"Not necessarily! A particular mansion of the eighteenth century does not evoke such a thought; still it bears the stamp of its era, and this is what makes it dear to us."

Do you think so? Then why do we admire only its style? The recollections of human life are part of the style. Since we must *wait,* as you say, that same mansion, when newly built, would thus have meant nothing to you. Like a naive bourgeois, do you need the sanction of centuries in order to admire it? Do you not recognize heroism in someone unless you are told that he is departing for the Thirty Years War? It is always the present that you find wanting.

The sight of such restorations as the Parthenon in polychrome or the Roman Forum crowded with buildings vexes the artist, not because he has certain reservations regarding the accuracy of the restoration, but solely because he must admit that he prefers by far the ruins to everything new; and that this taste is peculiar to him and would not have been shared at all by the Greeks and Romans. . . .

We are thus faced with two possibilities: either we deplore the present because it seems less desirable to us than the past, and that makes us unworthy of it and thereby unworthy of life; or we divide life into two separate parts, the past (its trees, houses, or whatever) to which we devote all our artistic care, and the present, which occupies merely our material well being. Unquestionably the latter attitude is characteristic of the contemporary painter, and it is what isolates him from his other colleagues in the fine arts. Let me also point out here that what I call the past is not the historic facts *per se,* but everything resulting from the wear and tear of time and, in particular, from the failure to prevent this deterioration, even the complacency to sustain it. The sculptor, the architect and the musician are easily won over by the painter to this perversion, but they never apply it to their own work. Why? The poet often becomes attached to ancient languages, yet he writes his own books "in good French." Only the painter carries into his own art this taste for the worn-out and dilapidated.

Perhaps we are here close to a solution; for if only one of our artists is in the grip of such a perverse tendency, the cause may be sought in the very nature of his work. Let us see what might keep the other artists from this perversity.

The *sculptor's* object is the human body, or more specifically, the movements of this body as expressed in a motionless synthesis that contains both the preceding movement and the following one. No sculptor will choose worn-out, debased, or sick bodies. He may use them on occasion, but it will never occur to him to attribute to them any quality especially beneficial to his art, as the painter does with the term "picturesque." The same can be said of the sculptor of animals.

The *architect,* in arranging space, thinks of the living body. Even when he designs a hospital, he will not give his building a diseased appearance. The architect who constructs faked ruins and "grotesque" walls or who prefers the use of old material is a poor fellow unworthy of any consideration. The painter has corrupted his taste, in bringing him to adopt old material that impairs the youthful beauty of his work and deceives the eye as well as the feeling. Left to himself, the architect would never have thought of such a thing.

The *composer* expresses the impulses of our soul. Without the poet's support he must deal in generalities; with that support he has at once the most extensive and most precise power. But the feelings the composer experiences are eternal; they belong no more to the past than to the future. Music is the perfect art of the present; decay, degradation, and neglect—in short, picturesqueness—is totally foreign to it.

The *poet* indulges in archaism as a sport. He is attracted to it, not by the age of the language, but rather by its youthful directness! Thus the painter is the only artist who takes delight in wear and tear, the filth of objects, the decay of nature, the negligence and superstition of human beings. Unlike his colleagues in the other fine arts, the painter appears therefore to have no clear sense of the dignity of his fellow creatures, and consequently of his own dignity.

Actually, such a view is relatively new. The art historians could easily trace for us the origin and progress of this disease; but a mere chronological account would teach us very little about this deplorable phenomenon. We must delve far deeper into the matter.

The object for the sculptor, the architect, the musician, and the poet is the *living* human being. The sculptor interprets man plastically, and the architect gives him a definite frame in space and detailed arrangements appropriate to his *life;* the musician expresses the impulses of the living soul, and the poet offers in words and ideas what the other three have directly projected into space or time. However, the wide variety of objects that are within the poet's reach bring him close to the painter whose accomplice, alas, he readily becomes in respect to the "picturesque."

The three artists, then, who deal preeminently and exclusively with the living human being, remain untouched by the infection! This fact is extremely significant.

We have taken the taste for the picturesque as an example in order to discover a potential touchstone that may give us a warning whenever art is in danger of sinking into quicksand. The result of this brief inquiry is conclusive: the artist can rely upon the *living* human being and not the historic being; for, in dealing with living man a lie will invariably appear as a lie, insanity will be insanity, neglect will remain contemptible, filth repugnant, superstition disgraceful. The beautiful term "picturesque" will no longer dress them up. What an impoverishment, people will say! Possibly, but the drinker says the same about the alcohol of which he must rid himself. If the "picturesque" must be bought, as in most cases, at the expense of the health, the well-being and the dignity of our fellow men, will we not sign the pledge of abstinence? Undoubtedly the sacrifice is too great for us to weigh its entire impact. Therefore, like the drinker, we must act out of faith in the absolute necessity of avoiding a deadly poison, come what may.

Our signature will be our vow of loyalty to the integrality of body and soul within our fellow beings, and this signature will constitute the touchstone we have sought.—Loyalty is always sensitive; one word can destroy it. Let us rely then on scrupulously observing it; and when, tired of good health, we wish to turn once more to disease, the disease of the painter, let us remember the drinker! In art today all of us are alcoholics. It is high time to "sign" even for those who believe themselves safe and sound, for we are all infected by the "picturesque." But here, as elsewhere, we are in a period of transition; by turning away from monumentality and its outgrowth, the "picturesque," we prepare for centuries of a sanity and a vitality which in our present state of mind we can hardly imagine. *Living* art will be its noble expression. What this art will permit the other art forms and what it will deny them, either by adopting them or by rejecting them, we cannot yet foresee; but in our struggle against the poison of the picturesque, we must begin with respect for the living being, our contemporary.

Alcohol dims our self-knowledge, blunts our sense of responsibility, and thus keeps the imagination occupied without bothering it with scruples about ourselves and others. We easily compare the state of intoxication with a return to the brute; rightly so, but we must add that this return is conscious, willful, and hence comfortable. The absence of scruples about our fellow men would thus characterize the state of the brute, a state from which humanity up to the present time has slowly and painfully emerged. A glance backward, an occasional impulse to return to the primitive condition is definitely a sign of decadence. But does not our nature also sometimes need to return to a kind of "homesickness" for the state of weariness which our ascending as human beings has provoked in us? Do we then not sense that a hidden atavism is awakening to claim its rights and satisfaction?

In the final analysis, this desire for retrogression would explain our taste for ruins, for the careless, the derelict, for the poor condition of buildings and plants, the superstition, the misery, the rags, and for people and landscapes immersed in all this. In Switzerland the paradise of the painters is Le Valais;[43] in Europe it is Italy, Spain, the Balkan countries—in short, wherever such disgraceful indifference creates the "picturesque," the primitive, the uncivilized, the uncultured: the natural state those painters call it, instead of honestly admitting their nostalgia for the state of the brute which other countries have tried to shake off, even if, it is true, they have not always chosen the right means toward this end.

The dauber is no longer in vogue. Our painters insist on a perfectly objective and proper technique, yet they use this technique to depict ancient and grandly weather-stained dwellings with antique furniture, and gardens whose naturalness is false. In this way they remind us of certain exhibition halls "picturesquely" adorned to display objects of an entirely contradictory character. There is a consistent lack of feeling for the human body. Like the ostrich who evades danger by hiding his head, we try to deny dissonance by disengaging ourselves from our environment, taking into consideration only what is outside of us, what our eyes see. Not truly knowing the past, we naturally play at living there. Were it not so, who would dream of living in rooms incompatible with our habits and mode of thinking? What are our fashionable ladies doing in an Empire parlor, in an old Flemish dining room, and so on . . . ? We are not very apt at disguising our true inclinations; why then do we disguise our homes? —Here the two unfortunate tendencies of our restless era come together: our taste for monumentality which I have treated in the preceding essay[44]—and the much less open taste for the "picturesque" and for the past.

So long as the artist enjoyed unlimited confidence, his taste seemed to us beyond question, and we accepted it with closed eyes. Would a painter, when asked to furnish and decorate apartments, ever inquire about the owners' manners and habits? He knew very well that whatever pleased him to do would be blindly accepted as the product of superior taste, more reliable and enlightened than the owners'. This gesture of deference became second nature with us. But today it no longer suits the true state of affairs; we still obey like sheep, but we have lost confidence in our leaders. Hence the great uneasiness which, I think, no one can deny.

We must, must at any price, make a clean sweep and build all over again, but not upon ruins. We must therefore clear away all the plaster across which we stumble. We want our life to be hygienic; let us learn to want an art that harmonizes with such a life. No matter what it may seem, the "picturesque" is basically materialistic, and it will continue to dominate us under new guises, even if, by some chance, we may give up what is too obsolete. Whoever *prefers* to paint the debased and overdressed types of our capitals, the foolish conventions of the stage, the low resorts and the slums, etc, . . . would undoubtedly be quite astonished to hear himself accused of being "picturesque"! And yet he is hopelessly in the grip of this old evil.

Hitherto, I have been obliged to describe the "picturesque" through the ideas best known to us under this label. Now we can define it more precisely and give it a new and far more extensive significance.

At present we are suffering from a neo-picturesqueness which is as puerile as, but far more noxious than, the old kind. It consists of taking the mental, physiological, and social deformities with which our era is infected as the justifiable norm for the work of art. How many artists, for instance, feel themselves disgraced unless they express, always and everywhere with an almost insane persistence, the flabbiness of face and attitude currently typical of a certain category of individuals? With a sense of harmony, which does them credit, they make these degenerates flabbier than they are, and, carrying their effrontery even further, they confer this decadence upon nature which, otherwise, would appear wholesome, straightforward, and vigorous. No longer do they probe into ruins and neglect; no, they complacently fabricate their own, making puppets or caricatures of whatever happens to come before their eyes. They assure us that their desire is to be truthful. They have our blessing! Yet a well-ordered society expels unwelcome truths. Our exhibitions, and lately our museums, have opened their doors to all that beautiful world. The public is apparently willing to recognize itself there and consequently does not require other views. It certainly does not take much for anyone to resemble that world. Shame on the artists who hold up such mirrors![45]

"Picturesqueness" thus results from a preference for something unhealthy and hence gives evidence of a definitely pathological lack of concern for the most fundamental responsibilities we must have toward our fellow men. You will admit that it is impossible to be more despicable.

It is amusing to observe that, in this whole matter, it is the painter who both cheats and is cheated! He imagines himself to be in the *avant-garde* while, on the contrary, he is lost far behind in the past, and it serves him right. He abandoned us, and we pass him by without even turning back to invite him to follow us. What he offers us with his now-familiar lack of fervor no longer touches us. Truly, he is too far behind; our pace is no longer his. His listlessness belongs in a studio; we are outdoors, in the sun; our health is good and robust, and we intend to keep it that way!

# Mechanization

## (1922)

What do we mean by the term "mechanization," and what do we mechanize? Man first tamed animals in order to free himself from certain muscular exertions. The limited development of animals and their more or less passive cooperation then required mechanical assistance, e.g., wheels, adjusted to their strength. This constituted the beginnings of mechanization which, as its name indicates, is by definition inanimate. Forever passive, it waits for the initiative from a living being, and it is we who provide the lever, the wheel, the button to lend mechanization, at our convenience, the initiative it does not in itself possess. Now, Life is this initiative. Consequently it is not life that we mechanize but certain forces of nature, and mechanizing them is synonymous with mastering them.

One must know a thing in order to master it. Although the sciences are the source of our knowledge in this matter, their findings would remain mere statements without the expert's intuition and his discerning imagination. Just as an intermediary, such as a lever or a button, is needed between the machine and us, an intermediary is needed between scientific knowledge and its practical use. Mechanization is this intermediary.

The definition is quite simple, as we shall see; at least, it seems so. In reality it is complicated, because certain practical appliances introduced by mechanization can be considered as a new degree of knowledge calling in turn for a new usage of a new mechanization, as for example the entire field of recording. To record means to capture natural phenomena in their course, that is, in time. No particular use is yet involved, but it already requires the medium of mechanization. Thus it can be seen that mechanization admits of degrees, and that it is permissible on occasion to mechanize mechanization. This, incidentally, corroborates our definition, namely, that mechanization is an intermediary between a scientific discovery and our wish to use it.

Today mechanization has two aims: speed, most frequently identified with economical use of our physical and intellectual forces—and true, simple recording. The development of locomotion, manufacture and notation might be called physical economy. Intellectual economy sometimes benefits from such development, but sometimes the saving is illusory, for, alas, our nervous system has its limitations. Real intellectual economy results instead primarily from methods introduced into our work by mechanization.

Recording, which should not be confused with statistics or systematization, finds its best known and probably strongest expression in the principle of the cinematograph and the phonograph; the latter for time without space, that is, for sound alone, the former for time in space, that is to say, movement. Now, it is characteristic of these two phases of recording that, having entered the mechanized life through time and space, they possess both, and are therefore able to employ them afterwards at will. Recording the sound of a taxi ride concerns exclusively a certain ride, only during the time and for the duration of this ride. The recording does not possess this duration; it merely represents it. And though the record can reproduce it, it cannot modify it without departing from the natural truth.

A film, by contrast, possessing movement in time as well as in space, has therefore captured that movement and has thus the power to modify it. The recording of a taxi is a symbol, but a combination of phonograph and film is reality. Why? The clicking of the taxi meter, I will be told, corresponds to its rhythm in the phonograph. This is not so! The clicking played in reverse, that is, from the arrival of the taxi to its departure, would reproduce precisely the same sequence offered in its normal course. A simple span of time makes us no more possessors of time than would eternity make us! Likewise, in a simple clear projection we do not yet *possess* the image it shows, but as soon as we add the slightest movement to it, the image completely surrenders to us, and we may dispose of it as we please. In order to *possess* time we must have space, and in order to possess space we must have movement, which is the idea of time projected into indefinite space.

For us human beings, any recording, whatever it may be, can concern only time or space or the two together. These are the only conceptions we can record or, at least, the ones that must form the basis of all our recording, for through them we have defined, without reservation, the form of our existence. It would therefore seem that, by forcing these conceptions of time and space into our possession through the medium of mechanization, we will possess life itself or be at the point of possessing it.

The revelations of the subconscious, the double vision into the past and the future, of telepathy and the like, will be recorded by photography, which, no doubt, will eventually disclose for us the graphs of thought. And it is quite probable that we shall eventually come to record the birth of an idea, the process of an invention. In addition, the elements of the external world, barely accessible to our very limited sense organs, have become perceptible with the help of the telescope, the microscope, or even an invisible light revealing to us the inside of solid bodies. It sometimes seems as though our senses were given to us only to guide the recording of objects that they can neither see nor feel!

So we have here an ever higher amount of recording, the greatest part of which in turn is mechanized to serve our wishes. Does this mean capturing Life? If we ever arrived at taming all impulse, would there not always have to be an initial impulse to stimulate this taming? The force of impulse, or let us rather say, of *initiative,* depends on our will. It is, therefore, our will that will consistently refuse to be mechanized, because it takes a will to deliver it up to the operator of the machine.

From a scientific point of view, the problem of mechanization is solved in advance; we shall go as far as our faculties will permit, and catastrophes warn us of the limits that are dangerous to pass. But the ethical problem implied in mechanization, the only one that matters since it alone is a problem, is concerned exclusively with our conception of life, and its solution depends on our free will. To accept as incontestable a recorded scientific statement, and to accept or tolerate thereafter its application in our public and private life, are two entirely different attitudes.

The diplomat and the businessman say, "I have the power; consequently, I have the right." But a man who acknowledges any moral law whatever acknowledges thereby the obligation to choose, and this is not a right, but a duty. Possibilities offered by one or another scientific invention do not have to be applied to practical life. Heretofore, instruction in history has been solely concerned with the past; centuries of culture weigh on our shoulders and so cloud our eyes that the history of humanity hides from us humanity itself, from our own presence and that of our contemporaries.

The development of modern science and its applications begins to weigh upon us in the same manner and, as in the case of the historical tradition, we feel obliged to bear the new burden. Now, it should be noted that in relating everything to ourselves we do not yet sufficiently distinguish between a discovery and its potential use. The discovery in itself does not alarm us; it is our utilitarian preoccupation, which causes us to create new needs for the new discovery, that exercises pressure upon our personal freedom and that causes anxiety. We justly accuse mechanization, the instrument of useful application *par excellence,* of being the modern disease. "Where are we heading?" In truth, things will go for us, as they did for Orgon,[46] only as far as we let them go. That should be the motto for all education on the point. The decline of willpower derives from our belief that we have to adopt at once everything offered to us.

"Time is money," we are told. With this nonsense we accept implicitly an ever more whirling locomotion, an ever more stimulated life and the sanatoriums that these bring with them. "Liberty!" Alas, we see it only in terms of cars and airplanes, or we send it promenading on Hertzian waves.[47]

Our liberty is but a film projected on the empty screen of our existence. We are the spectators who every day buy a seat in the dark to see our liberty parade before us in an artificial light. Passive as we are, we submit to the growing mechanization imposed upon us under the guise of progress and thus assist in the intellectual deformation, the moral decay, caused by this mechanization. We are about to put ourselves at the service of the technology. Our civilization creates an organ before its function is determined, and thus produces monsters whose tentacles agitate blindly in a void.[48]

Art for art's sake, speed for speed's sake, force for the sake of force! Whatever the result, we avail ourselves of them. Like the nouveau riche, we throw our gold out of the window for the sheer fun of throwing. While thinking we are developing our mechanizations to the maximum, we actually depreciate them through our abuse. Certain painful and useless aspects of hard labor to which criminals once were sentenced are now abolished as too degrading for human dignity. Two-thirds of our life, however, is still wasted in that way; like squirrels in a revolving cage, we make money in order to go faster and faster, and we go faster and even faster in order to make money.

Such labor discredits us in our own eyes regardless of the grand aim it lends us, but it stupefies us, and that is all we ask of it. "All the distractions of a spa." Would not this pleasant phrase be applicable on many visiting cards, even the most distinguished?

Yet let us not be ungrateful: our mechanization is not so blind as it would appear, and there is some reason for its present excessive development. If we have rediscovered our body (see *The Work of Living Art*) and its latent forces, we have also become more aware of its limitations. It is therefore natural that we look earnestly at science, to extract from it everything that will augment the expressive powers of our organism.

Whether or not we begin with materialism matters little; it is essential for us to have a *point of departure*. The soul will always be able to regain its rights, since it has tried to serve the body, something the body has never done for the soul, not even during the most debased periods of history. On that account, the growing unconcern with our mores should be regarded as a childhood disease, such as measles or whooping cough, from which our blood will emerge purified, our muscles flexible and our nerves more resistant. Then, and only then, will our body be able to call itself the temple of the soul, the temple which we have turned into a sordid hovel. The soul is here, so we are not building the sanctuary before we have divinity. But neither should we keep the latter waiting too long. *This is the point where mechanization touches upon our moral dignity.*

In becoming accustomed to new instruments for which we still seek a function, we run the risk of seriously changing our sense of values. This will reduce our perception of responsibilities and duties toward others. As a goal in itself, mechanization is inhuman—which does not mean it is useless, for although we may deceive ourselves about the goal, we do not necessarily pursue it with worthless means; it is just that these means should have another purpose. From this viewpoint, sport is a kind of animated mechanization. It must be obvious to everyone that the idea of sport tends to dominate all our activities. The slogan "Time Is Money" is the tyrannous expression of this attitude wherever a personal interest is involved. The degree of speed of a stenographer, the trading by telephone, the automatic recording of stock exchange quotations, a certain type of bookkeeping, and the like resemble sport in their betting on speed. If they were not used, they would lose all value, and consequently, as in any game, their significance lies exclusively in an agreed-upon convention. Yet the sport by its very nature does not serve commercial interests; a truck, however near perfect it may be, is not a vehicle for sport. Sport came to us from England, from a nation with the highest developed sense of personal dignity. This sense induced the Englishman to take his body as point of departure, but his puerile imagination did not go beyond the game, i.e., sport. Physical culture is still unknown in England, and to fill this void, the English people strive to perfect and complicate the combinations of the game.

Our more restless mentality approaches the idea of sport with some apprehension. Though we need it even more, and though we acknowledge physical culture as the only road to reach our goal, we cannot devote ourselves to it with the ease of the English. They are positive; we are tragic. We want to find in sport something for which an Englishman would never look. Let us, for instance, compare portraits of some English sportsmen with those of French or Italians. We note that the features and attitudes of the Englishmen are not those of professional sportsmen. No matter what his profession, the Englishman will always have a somewhat sportsmanlike appearance, whereas pictures of other nationals indicate positively that sport does professionalize them. This is tragic, for sport in itself is as inhuman as the mechanization it represents. We are therefore not privileged to treat sport as Anglo-Saxons do. Our conscience is different. Although we use the same means, our attitude does not allow us to reach the same goal.

Thus, sport, like other mechanizations, gives us a moral problem to solve and should be seriously considered. The dizziness we experience in the face of the myriad aspects of mechanization encourages us to draw a general conclusion by inference; but instead we should proceed from our deepest conviction in order to prove the value and the good reasons for our use of mechanization. We cannot judge, for example, the general importance of the evasive and indefinable motion picture by trying indirectly to define it. We must attack it directly, armed with a weapon that will at the same time serve as a touchstone.

This will be true of every other mechanization. Not one can guide us by itself: our conscience must judge it first. Here, as anywhere else, conscience is the final judge—not conscience in the religious sense of good and evil, but simply our conscious view of life arrived at through meditation, and that is very difficult to maintain in our modern life.—The new attitude we have taken towards our body permits us to re-establish in ourselves the consciousness of our responsibility as a whole being. It is this sense of responsibility that must guide us. We are therefore obliged to guard it solicitously from distractions and the narcotics offered it by modern life, lest mechanization, escaping our control, gain the upper hand; and God knows how far it might drag us if we let it go.

In the preceding chapter I evoked the "New Presence" as a complete personality conscious of its responsibilities. Its integrity could not accept the unhealthy notion of the "picturesque." How will it react to mechanization which, on the contrary, would appear to manifest an excess of health? If our whole self is to be the point of departure, it will have to be the touchstone for all. Then we can, forthwith, establish the New Presence as the arbiter of mechanization as it has been of picturesqueness, and also, though we have not so defined it, of monumentality. It is our own being, at once personal and social, body and soul, the profound conscience of the one conditioning the responsibilities assumed by the other—the being that the church foolishly dismembered, but which modern times have aroused from its lethargy.

The World War demonstrated how feeble our imagination was. We still place imagination in the domain of fantasy, literary invention or artistic fiction, and do not take it seriously; or at least we rarely consider it from the practical standpoint. To imagine, meaning to make oneself an image of something that is not there, is not necessarily a function left to our own will. Everyone now realizes the superhuman creative power of an idea: faith in being the chosen people created the Jew and brought the Germans to war.

It is imagination that determines our actions, which otherwise would be automatic. A man will never lift his hand to his face unless the idea of this gesture is in his mind, that is, in his imagination.

In philosophy, psychology, and the like, we give such phenomena technical terms. This does not alter the fact that all could be reduced to the term "to imagine," for all of them imply an image before their realization. These facts are well known, yet we do not utilize them in those phases of our existence where imagination could be of great service. This indifference distorts and lowers our scale of values; for, in order to evaluate, the object of evaluation must be understood or invoked by imagination. So we submit to deficiencies, and indeed, were it not for our intuition, we would often be rather embarrassed. Unfortunately, intuition has no plastic power; it is able to understand but, lacking in imagination, it cannot create anything new. Therefore we accept established values without consulting our intuition, and this at a time when all those established values have become questionable.

Our intuition, for example, tells us rightly a work of art is so valuable that it must be accepted with little deliberation. But since we do not know how to imagine a work of art prior to its positive existence, we neglect everything that led to this existence, surely also a worthy consideration. This causes continual delays in creating works of art and, for the artist, a waste of his powers. Or we admit theoretically—theory and intuition are often close relatives—the salutary influence of such and such a principle, yet it is still only the result we evaluate, never the principle proper or, above all, the sacrifices involved in its application. Here, if one muses about it, is the obstacle encountered by all our public actions; we judge only by results; imagination fails us. And needless to say, this tends to complicate dangerously the conduct of our private life. One wonders whether it is not urgent to admit imagination as a specific branch of academic instruction or, at least, to encourage it by *pointing it out* and conferring upon it a very high value. In this matter the progressive school is on the right track; for by permitting a child to have a precise understanding of the road traveled to reach this or that goal, the school permits him to learn one road and also to evaluate in his imagination other roads of which he sees only the goal attained.

Every activity that is positive, and not simply mental, is a training in imagination. Any artisan entering the workshop of another realizes immediately in his imagination the road covered, the one still to be traveled, and the goal to be reached. His evaluation is not confined to the result, but includes the entire route. His glances, his attitude testify to it. The intellectual, by contrast, is interested in the road as an activity, but he cannot evaluate it because his imagination fails to show him the goal clearly; he has to wait for it. When the goal is reached, he evaluates the result but loses sight of the road that led to it. The same is true of the work of art; the dilettante sees only the work and applies his taste; an artist conceives the entire route in his imagination, estimates it, and evaluates the finished work, depending on his appraisal of the route. He alone is just and fair.

Our lack of imagination is the cause of almost all delays, procrastination, organizational defects, errors of judgment, and so forth. Socially this is tantamount to a perpetual injustice. In our private life this deficiency is a vice that results probably in the most serious consequences, and it is inhuman to accept it tacitly, for it is the source of our egotism and insensitivity. Nay, even more! Do we not know that we transfer to others the qualities we believe them to have? What is confidence if not a work of the imagination? And confidence is, at the highest level, the creator, creator of energy, creator of happiness.

Imagination can be employed wrongly, no doubt, as for example it sometimes is by diplomats, who should exercise every precaution; but whatever use is made of it, imagination enriches life tremendously and thus amply compensates for its dangers. It there not some cowardice involved in self-control and in the consistency it inspires, both so highly praised by us? Good Lord, where would we be if the history of mankind, if our own history, were the result of eternal self-control! And if, on the other hand, the word "generous" inspires esteem and admiration, do we not sense here a favorable field for imagination, hence, for confidence and its creative power?

To return to our scale of values, it is evident that this scale, if we have one, should inspire our confidence and regulate our actions. Therefore, if the health-giving imagination has no place in our scale, all our activities will be crippled. The New Presence, as we have seen, revived in us a sense of new responsibilities, to which in turn new values must correspond or, at least, some old ones must be adapted. Now, this New Presence is the work of our imagination, sustained by the confidence we have in its prophetic and creative quality. Therefore we shall obtain its proper realization only through a *common belief* in imagination.

The isolated artist believes in his work and completes it, yet our indifference, our coolness towards his work greatly increases his toil. But if the artist is part of a community, if the living forces of many personalities join him, thus giving proof of their faith and substantiating their power, the present indifference, it may be hoped, will yield to him more readily. In this respect, the New Presence should emerge fully. We have stated that it will provide the touchstone for us to evaluate the phenomenon of mechanization that dominates and shapes our entire modern life. In the face of so formidable a resistance, the New Presence must strengthen itself and prove its mettle. It must search for means within reach that will permit it eventually to emerge from the clouds. it is beginning to come to light in every domain: social science, psychology, education, and the like are all filled with the New Presence; only in art does it still generally meet serious resistance. But isolated personalities are not capable of opposing mechanization. Resistance—supposing it is necessary to resist, which is not proven—must come from a community made capable through the harmonious exercise of its faculties. If we exclude art, we deprive this community of the most methodical and regulating element which, better than any other, can bring all the diverse wishes into harmony.

Art has heretofore been communicated to us indirectly through works in which we took no active part. In this manner we shall never arrive at a powerful harmony. Our modern weakness is the result of our consistently passive attitude as spectators and, in particular, as spectators of works of art. This passivity made fatalists of us, especially in art, where we accepted everything offered to us. And artists, habitually not very scrupulous, made fun of us.

Mechanization likewise finds us fatalistic. Its most foolish experiments, its most shameful excesses no longer make us wince. We give in to everything, consent to everything, to such an extent that certain words such as "unacceptable" tend to disappear from our current vocabulary; as for "resignation," we do not dare pronounce it too loudly.

In my book, *The Work of Living Art,* I stated that art should be lived and not merely contemplated. This *life* in art, which makes our whole being at the same time both a creative artist and a work of art, bestows upon us an authority difficult to obtain in any other discipline. The bestowal is, however, *jointly* made, to artist and audience bound in solidarity. This is the very condition. Without it we relapse into a work of art *opposite* an audience, and lose all benefits from our efforts.

We espouse togetherness in almost all phases of our social life. Why do we still hesitate to do this to benefit art, the most powerful source of conciliation? Our difficulties arise from our physical as well as our mental habits. These must be changed—we must resolve to change direction completely and to move on a new path towards a new horizon; and since we are ignorant of both, we must have faith. Every great work, every salutary reform requires this. We so benevolently believe in any scribbler, any harebrained mechanic, the sauciest of poets, that it would be strange not to be as generous to art!

Art has begun to penetrate our life, but it has entered through a back door; the all-powerful fashion of living has bowed down before it; our homes, our belongings, have been ennobled through contact with art. People of a ripe old age remember how different conditions were half a century ago! Art is even found in the details of our machinery. the demand for it echoes a general feeling. And yet a single subject remains untouched by this blissful infection: our own self. We tastefully adorn a sheath, unconcerned about the rust on the blade it encloses. Let the blade also have its turn, today!

Our house is on fire, and our bathrooms will never extinguish the flames. who can deny that music and painting are endangered, that sculpture and architecture are in need of a definite orientation? And why? Because art has strayed into a blind alley from which our body alone can rescue it. I speak intentionally of our body, for in taking such initiative, our organism will naturally carry along in its wake our mentality as a whole. We push further and ever further the culture of the body; it gives us strength and health, but not necessarily balance or beauty, the result of balance. Art will give us this balance. What would the authority of the Presence be without it? Let us not be dominated by our habits: *Let us have inspiration!*

In *The Work of Living Art* I discussed the aesthetic training of our body. I cannot repeat that discussion here and have to consider the matter not only well known but also an accomplished fact, or at least, well on the way to accomplishment. Let us take this point of view. Here we are, working together, in exercises, in actual realizations, collective ceremonies, and so forth, in short, in a current that carries along our body, compelling it, willy-nilly, to continuous activity and wholesome reactions.

This discipline maintains in us a collective corporeal feeling that accompanies us in our professions, obliges us to feel in our body the presence of other bodies under their clothes. This is a kind of silent freemasonry analogous to the mysterious knowledge of the physiognomist but surpassing it by far; for the latter, in studying the face of his fellow man, completely loses sight of his own, assuming that he can preserve it—like an actor who forgets his own physiognomy during two-thirds of his life. The disciple of living art, however, experiences the joy of feeling his body at one with the body of others. This is a tacit exchange. Sexuality, doubtless, has a part in it, but by no means does it determine the phenomenon or its consequences. A pianist observing the hands of another pianist transposes them to his own. Michelangelo had, of necessity, to undress with a glance all those whom he encountered. The crowd in the street would appear to him as though seen through a light mist, their clothing.

For the disciple of living art, this sensation is further intensified by musical expression felt and realized in common. He knows the transfiguration arising from it and handles it automatically in respect to the bodies surrounding him, whereas for us these beings are dressed, and all their gestures are determined and attenuated by their clothes. We have no other conception of them, so that, after all, we do not know them, for even physiognomy depends on the garment, which distorts its expression. The disciple of living art has the power to strip humanity, his brothers, of the contingencies of habits, fashion, professional deformities, and the like, uncovering their purely human qualities, untouched by the centuries. "Modern," that word of which we are so fond, makes him smile gently, for he considers himself as much a contemporary of Sesostris or Alcibiades[49] as of us. His interest in the manifestations of contemporary life is as lively, if not livelier, than in those of any other era, but his judgment prevails. He has a point of comparison, the infallible touchstone: the New Presence! He can accept everything, but within the exact measure authorized by this Presence. Unlike us, he does not throw himself headlong into one or another mechanization, one or another kind of sport or spiritual speculation floating about unattached. Like a captive balloon, he is grateful to the cable that saves him from the caprices of the atmosphere, while permitting him, at the same time, to dominate the crowd.

Let us take an example, although examples limit the general bearing of a demonstration. A musician among my friends knew little about the improvement in phonographs. One of his acquaintances planned a surprise for him and invited him to hear a great singer who was staying incognito at his home. On his arrival my friend was met in the hall with some embarrassment and asked to wait there. Soon his host returned and, with an enigmatic look, placed him close to the wall with the request to remain standing there. He himself stayed nearby, not letting his guest out of sight. Suddenly a magnificent voice arose from the direction of the parlor, filling the apartment despite closed doors. It sang Isolde's Death. As soon as it was finished the two young men, deeply moved, went into the parlor, the musician burning with the desire to accompany this incomparable voice. In the center of the room on a stand, sat a phonograph with its horrible box wide open. The owner pushed his visitor down on a couch and changed the record. The orchestra, still an inferior feature of this dreadful machine, ground on for a moment until two voices rose in "Descend upon us, night of passion" (*Tristan,* act 2). Our musician grew pale and impatient. The record had hardly ended when he took the score of the opera from the piano, opened it at the page of the duet and asked to have the recording repeated. Having assured himself that the piano was in tune with the two voices, he accompanied them, keeping his ear turned towards the sound box. This went on all afternoon; every Wagnerian record was thus played. Our friend played with increasing assurance; no longer did he follow the singers; all three had one identity.

The listener had to acknowledge that he had never heard anything like it, and he invited several friends to come during the evening and hear the miracle. The effect was stupendous; the thought of giving a concert in public even came up, though it was never realized. Our interest in this matter, however, is the impact on the musician and his reaction to it. And I leave it to the reader to extend the meaning of this simple example.

While in the hall, our friend did not for an instant doubt that the voice he heard coming from the drawing room was, as announced by his host, that of an artist, a *living* body. He did not think of the orchestra. The sight of the phonograph so stunned him that he readily obeyed his friend who had pushed him almost violently onto the couch. During the duet two diverse sentiments predominated in him; unable to bear it any longer, he would either throw the whole thing out of the window, or ... or what? Dimly he understood; his body trembled with indignation and the urge to do something; but how to proceed? He was able to wait until the end without incident and then, suddenly, he knew his duty: he must animate this monstrous recording at any price, or else withdraw from it for good. When he felt his fingers, naturally attuned to the voice, move over the keys, he experienced such a calm, such a relaxation that the tears of agony he had hitherto forced back began to burst forth. His intensified anguish was gradually transformed into a state of happiness that submerged him and increased his ability as a pianist tenfold, but at the same time, completely removed him from a sense of reality.

On that first day he was never left alone with the phonograph; then he could not argue about something he did not understand. The following day he had the workings of the instrument explained to him, and his friend left him to himself until evening. As soon as he was alone with "them" our musician put himself at ease, settled down carefully, and played a record with his head in the machine. From time to time he spoke softly to the singers, although he knew that he could not interrupt them and converse with them. Since he had mastered the music completely, he tried to understand the character of the two artists as expressed in their voices, to grasp it accurately from their declamation and accents, as well as from their singing proper and their phrasing. He could have been heard uttering: "Oh, this is how you interpret it, yes, I understand. I shall remember it, rest assured." Or merely: "Yes . . . yes! . . ." When he went to the window for a respite he said nothing, he had only one thought: "They!"

Before evening, when new guests were to be initiated into the miracle, our musician went for a walk, totally unaware of reality, the present, the hour, the day, of himself or others. He experienced a feeling of intoxication at seeing himself an integral part of such a mechanism and, at the same time, a strange satisfaction, almost inconceivable to himself, at having saved "them" from such a disgrace. He tried in vain to bring the two sentiments into accord, and this failure remained the sole cause of his anguish. The fact that he completely forgot where he was or had been left him unworried. He finally found the contradiction quite explicable: in lieu of the food given to a living body, fuel is fed into a machine. This is the tribute we pay to the infamous instrument.

Here we have a human being imbued with the New Presence in the grip of a mechanical phenomenon particularly troublesome to him. He could have indulged in the equivocal pleasure of listening without saying a word or else could have thrown the tool overboard. Instead, he saw himself obliged to act constructively! Was this out of respect for the singers, for Richard Wagner and his work, or for himself? Probably all factors were fused into a single obligation, summed up in these words: "He had to act." And what would he have done if the orchestra had been as well recorded as the voices? No doubt exactly the same; for this was not the issue.

Of all our mechanisms, the phonograph comes closest to attaining personality. The blind are far less isolated than the deaf because, as yet, the tone of the voice is more revealing than the movements of the body or facial expressions. Dramatic art abounds in situations in which someone is implored to speak, if only to emit a sound (a typical example is the apparition of Astarte in Byron's *Manfred*); on the other hand, I do not know of any situation in which an invisible character whose voice is heard is conjured to appear. The phonograph thus violates the most intimate, the most inimitable, and the most particular nature of the personality. And the recording arbitrarily complicates this violation, because the phonograph can raise or lower a voice, accelerate it or slow it down, without modifying any part of the authentic content! If our musician had heard his own voice, he would doubtless have been less impatient. Responsibilities towards oneself apparently are always less urgent; honor is less involved, it seems. But there he was; the New Presence compelled him to act.

In order to draw conclusions from this extreme case, we must return to considerations of a general nature. Mechanical recordings have two distinct goals: one pertains to scientific knowledge, its popularization and purely industrial and commercial applications; the other caters to our pleasure and our distractions or tries to stimulate our amateurish curiosity. Let us discuss the latter, but let us not overlook the fact that any recording, whatever it is, defies both time and space. The infinite does not record either in time or in space, and the finite does not exist in one with the other. Any recorded sound implies a beginning and an end, hence the concept of space. Likewise, any recorded line implies arrested time, at least at its ending. Under these circumstances, all recordings devised for our pleasure will more or less directly concern organic life.

When recordings are widespread, they become technical or industrial and are no longer addressed to individuals. The highest degree of organic life is man and all the manipulations of his personal and social life. For instance, an orchestra piece recorded by a phonograph touches directly, whether one likes it or not, upon the individual character of every member of this orchestra; for the recording is indeed done by systematically violating each of these individuals in the course of his playing. Mechanizations of this sort—film, phonograph, or any combination—seem to pose a very simple problem to the New Presence: do we accept this violation, or do we reject it? Reality, however, is more complex. In fact whether one or another person disclaims it and tries to avoid it wherever he can is of no interest. The violation *is* here. Ignoring Nero's circus will not prevent the cruelties committed therein. The New Presence forbids us to assume the attitude of the ostrich. Fortified by its authority, we assert that we cannot escape a mechanization from the very moment it enters the game. We must discover, therefore, the nature of our responsibility towards mechanization and how we must approach it.

I have said that the conscience of our integral personality—body and soul become one—will be the final judge. This conscience obliges us to preserve its *oneness,* the supreme criterion of our judgment. Everything that tends to lessen, weaken or paralyze its vitality, to insult its collective dignity and thus to injure its authority, must be considered dangerous, and consequently must be attacked. Now, mechanization in itself is not at fault; it becomes so through the attitude it requires of us. In the living theatre the stage is not to be condemned, but the audience! The moving picture itself is a marvel; he whom the film aims to please is the culprit. Once we are conscious of this fact we have to concede that this is true of all our mechanization. Its only danger lies in its use and, since we use mechanization, it is our responsibility.

The same conditions prevail in other fields. When we read something pornographic, it is not the book which is at fault, but we who can be tempted by such a book. The vagaries of modern music and painting are utterly inoffensive in their puerility, but we are ready to welcome them; therefore the disgrace is ours, and, if possible, so is the regret. In this respect we must always refer to ourselves, to our attitude and our intentions, for we are creating life day after day. To do that we have to be strong. Seduction must not take us unawares.

Above all, where we cannot be indifferent, let us oppose to it a humanity whose joys will be more intense and longer lasting than anything that can be offered from outside itself. Here the principle of community and solidarity will render us significant services; for the mechanization of entertainment, requiring our passive attitude, and thus always appealing only to the individual, has nothing to set against this principle. A passive collectivity represents a casual body of individuals as we find it, for instance, in a movie house. Collectivity implies action. We now have in the New Presence a power that can become formidable and capable of resisting questionable and destructive recordings.

Art lives on sacrifices; the force and intensity of it expressly depends on them. The New Presence is the manifestation of Art in our social life and as such cannot evade the obligation of a sacrifice that will make it strong.

From a practical viewpoint, some positive data can clarify the preceding paragraphs without any pretense of exhausting so broad a subject. An institute of rhythmical and body training is at present certainly one of the places where the New Presence affirms the principle of artistic collectivity and aesthetic solidarity with a maximum of abundance and precision. The students who go beneath the surface of their instruction to integrate its echoes into their whole existence arrive at a remarkable degree of intensity. Whether they want it or not, all their thinking and feeling, everything that is offered to them, everything they desire and admire, fear and condemn, passes before the tribunal of the New Presence. And since this tribunal has become an integral part of their personalities, its decrees have at once a sharply individual as well as a courageously, even daringly, collective character.

There is something ingenuous about these students even in their errors of judgment! Everything in them is *alive*. Tradition is maintained only as long as it can participate in this life, sustain and protect it. Never individualistic, this disposition results in a boldness without conceit, a happiness remaining constant through all difficulties. It is with this happiness that all other satisfactions are compared, and the comparison is indeed fearsome; the students can be seen, for example, frequenting assiduously certain places where the public at large seeks and finds only a passing distraction. Observing them attentively, one is surprised to detect two parallel thoughts expressed in their faces, one being the scrupulous desire to know, to understand, not to reject without reason; the other, the resolution made once and for all to consult incessantly with the New Presence and then to yield where authorized, but to resist where required. On the other hand, they find pleasure in a thousand things that escape us. To them, circumstances and objects present themselves in such a light that they stand out as we never suspect and would not even perceive with our less refined taste. In spite of a plethora of impressions, these young people are incapable of being blasé, because their enrichment enjoys eternal youth; the youth of *real* life, not the artificial life of the collector of new impressions.

I refer here to the student of eurhythmics, because in him the New Presence is visible and expressive in a particularly demonstrative manner and thus permits us to touch upon that which constitutes its strength in opposition to modern mechanization. It is then easy to deduce that the New Presence will *never* accept mechanization as an aim in itself—no matter in what form it might appear now or in the future. It will utilize mechanization wherever this may serve to further its own affirmation, and it will do this with the nonchalance of a grand seigneur. The New Presence will tolerate recording as long as it permits occasional animation, as we have experienced with the phonograph, and it will abstain from it whenever any violation is definitely unmotivated and hence unacceptable. It is impossible to deny mechanization; therefore I said "abstain." The attitude of armed expectancy—armed with the New Presence—permits us far more numerous and more powerful reactions than the passive attitude of consenting to everything. And this makes of our modern life, even in its most dangerous and repulsive manifestations, a springboard that reinforces our spirit, and of its provocations a system of tempering that maintains our vigilance and firmness.

I mentioned sport and its analogy to mechanization, both of which the New Presence has to take into account and to which it has to apply its criterion. Although the line of demarcation is doubtless undecided, the results are less, and still less is the road traveled to reach them. Too readily we regard sports as engaging only the body and neglect the influence their training cannot fail to have on our minds. Our illustrated magazines are quite eloquent about this fact, and their sports pictures need no comment.

As in the case of inanimate mechanization and its recordings, we must also oppose sport for sport's sake with an aesthetic, socially strong and well-balanced personality. This is necessary as much for our own benefit as for that of others. He who knows how to convey this collective feeling possesses a treasure which no passion for sport can match. Here is probably our strongest weapon.

There is no need to go into details about sports, as anyone can argue ad libitum about them according to his specific predilection. Besides, the problem is well known; and the difficulty is not caused by ignorance or obstinacy, but exclusively by material interests, rivalries, and purely mechanical impulses of our body that are totally unrelated to health, poise and beauty. Fortunately, the professionals who form their own cliques are an insignificant minority; for their inconceivable prestige can become dangerous. Bravery, especially in war, is at the point of falling forever into disgrace. It is very likely that courage in sport will sooner or later go the same way, and that it may be found very pleasant just to get together for a boxing match, a bicycle race or anything else; even horse races and the questionable sort of people they encourage will be regarded as regrettably childish—and without any value to the equine species, a value still invoked as an excuse for those races.

The World War apparently demonstrated the worthlessness of political principles as means of persuading us to establish pedagogic truth in the victor. Therefore the moment seems to have come for us to quit patronizing all the parasitical and cumbersome manifestations of our public life and to throw them into the old toy basket once and for all. The Anglo-Saxon himself will retract his steps; he has been our leader in physical education, let us teach him poise and beauty. The idea of sport must come down to actual doing; to take sport as an aim is barbarous and very infantile.

The notion will be advanced that sport accepted on its own merit is a school of energy, courage, endurance, self-control, and whatnot! Very well! Who would deny it? But unless these virtues are applied, they are meaningless. The professional in sport develops them to apply them to his sport over and over again. If there ever was a vicious circle, this is it! All the strength acquired, accumulated and then spent again has nothing to do with humanity unless it is employed to help humanity on its happy journey through our poor world. The homestretch, or the outcome of a boxing match are not a sign, I imagine, of a superior mentality of the elite human species. They are, rather, the living symbol of man's return to the brute. This is perfectly clear, and yet no one opposes it. When public opinion will disdainfully turn away from such spectacles, then we shall perhaps see how things stand. And the time may not be so far off as we think, for the extremes touch each other, and the jug goes to the well until. . . .

The genuine opportunist, therefore, does not fear certain excesses. A confectioner lets his apprentices nibble to the full; knowing the capacity of their stomachs, he sleeps peacefully. But we are not tradesmen, and we cannot wait with our protest. However, and this is the main point with which I want to end this chapter of suggestions, if we remove we must replace; if we destroy we must rebuild. The New Presence is here; let us surrender to it, obey it with confidence. How can we not do it? Is not the New Presence in everyone of us the very power we so admire in others?[50]

# The Former Attitude

## (1923)

About a century ago, a cartoonist sketched modern man—to wit, his contemporaries—as an old-fashioned purse in which the entire contents were forced to
one side by a ring, while the rest of the purse, empty and useless, hung loosely.
The cartoon could not have been more apt. The head alone seemed to have
some importance; the body was at its lowly service. Such a concept placed us
consistently apart from beings and objects, and the idea that one could participate in them and participate effectively, never occurred to us. We were satisfied
with words, aided if possible by sight; spectators, listeners or actors, we looked
at or were looked at. We exchanged opinions; works of art *were presented* to
us or we *presented* them to others.

All this took place across a space precisely resembling that of our picture
stage. Eternal spectators, we were always separate from someone or something,
convinced of course that the others were in the same situation. Our entire life
was organized along this line of thinking and upon the assumption that it had
to remain so. Everything had to pass through the filter of our intellect. Our idea
of our own body and that of our fellow men was either purely intellectual or
simply based on sexual instinct. From this point of view, the written "character
sketches," fashionable since the eighteenth century, are entertaining and instructive. The body, dressed formally or casually but never nude, seemed to be
merely a kind of extra. Since social life consisted only of small talk, and solitary
life only of more or less literary writing, these sketches generally satisfied
everybody's idea of himself, but art was the loser and became a mere luxury
like other luxuries. Only architecture and those things related to it (furniture,
interior decoration and gardens) apparently benefited from this attitude; for a
frame was needed for all that gossip and idleness, an environment for this
elegant idling. The body was confined to such a milieu. The architect and the
landscaper used their brains rather than their eyes. To prove this to ourselves

we need only play a vigorous game of tennis near one of those boulevards; then young, out of breath, bursting with joy and health, return to one of these salons of yesteryear.

That is why that life created its own style, for a style has never influenced life. Therefore, a number of modern experiments have failed in the same way, but we are not yet through with this architectural chess game. Since we are unwilling, of all things, to believe that our life itself, our daily existence should determine its surroundings, we embrace the absurdity of living modern lives among the relics of an era forever past and imagine thus to display a refined taste! A retired grocer reading his newspaper in a leather armchair runs little risk for that armchair could instill in its owner ideas and ways to widen his horizon; but the modern and cultured man retrogresses in his easy chair and muddies his imagination. We refuse to take our existence as the point of departure and the norm for everything. Only what interests and flatters our mind seems legitimate to us, and our organism drifts in all directions like the empty purse below the ring. All our art works appeal exclusively to our brains—the small gold-filled space of the purse—and the brain, having no pressing engagement, accepts everything under the express condition that we do not have to leave our orchestra seats.

Thus we make ourselves eternal "spectators" and forget that the performance presented to us, or which we *present,* is still of considerable influence on us. Unless this influence is controlled and coordinated into our way of living, it carries our taste and feelings beyond all reality into a perpetual fiction, whose presence in our midst constitutes a source of infection. The enormous success of sports and mechanization is the direct result of such abnormal relations. Whatever one may say, we feel an urgent need for honesty, and since our arts cannot satisfy it, we must turn somewhere else. Sports and mechanization cannot lie without destroying themselves; and since their existence depends upon our body, they include us in their honesty. The company of a professional in sports or mechanization is sometimes disagreeable or rough, but nobody will dispute that it offers us the pleasure of frankness not found elsewhere. The body taken as point of departure always tells the truth. Why? Because we cannot separate ourselves completely from it, even by using a mirror. This is the whole secret!

It will be asserted that the professional in sports pays for his virtuosity, his success, and the joys of his craft with regrettable gaps in culture and sensitivity. Of course; therefore his life is not an ideal to be sought. He is a victim of our intellectualism; in order to lead us toward a well-balanced attitude, the professional must considerably exceed his aim and suffer for it. We are in a period of transition; violence alone can set us free. Intellectual exertions have failed miserably; now it is time for physical exertions. We must at any price recover our organism, our disciplined and, above all, conscious body. The gulf we ourselves have dug is so wide that it is dangerous to leap across. Some resolutely take the jump, others wait until they can no longer hesitate without disgrace. Our huge intellectual ballast is not suitable to encourage us, it is true. Yet, without it, we would believe ourselves lost, even though we are unquestionably lost with it . . . ! This is why we wait; and so the exciting drama unfolds before us, the spectators. Rather than leave our seats we prefer to detach ourselves from *living* mankind.

Recover our organism? To what ends? Is not the mind the master, the body the servant? Surely; and I may add, as the master, so the servant. Everyone knows that noble birth and a high social position imply respect and regard for those in lower stations. Towards our body, our mind behaves like a parvenu; then the body reacts to it as a flunky. Have we any right to complain of this? Besides, many do not complain; they need a "trained"—that is, fawning—valet. This relationship is debasing. We must seek to change it, for the proper function of our household depends on it. A parvenu, a *nouveau riche,* always lives more or less in a state of anarchy. Our life is hardly better.

Once upon a time, dignity resulted from a carefully ordered existence. We speak of the division of labor; but we should note that this division no longer counts when everyone remained in his place according to the agreement; a life of dignity was easily attained. Such tranquility is no longer possible; today the problem embraces the whole of human life, and nobody can escape it; for our proper place has become a place shared by all mankind.

All great lawgivers have directed their special attention to art, granting it a power of the first rank. Plato based the state on music. Schiller, the prophetic philosopher, could not imagine a superior humanity without an education in aesthetics for everyone. Our recent experiences have made us aware of the civilizing and cultural import of applied science and the intellectual training of our youth. Truly it seems we have no other choice. All that remains is to find the means. Through the present study the author wishes to clarify the question a little and to demonstrate that, here as elsewhere, it is a matter of technique, and that we need to get down to the bare facts.

"The former attitude!" We have abandoned it without knowing what attitude to adopt in its place. Like a stroller who is ill at ease with his hands, we sometimes carry a cane, sometimes an umbrella, for no good reason; we know very well that in so doing we have not made one step towards a relaxed bearing. What may be called the intellectual attitude has prevailed for a long time. It still survives atavistically; a vague respectability, a last gleam of prestige, keeps it among our customs. However, those who retain it have no illusions; their reign is over, their grand airs no longer impress anyone. Even the strictly professional attitude has disappeared. Whether you have the air of an artist or a butcher's helper, the handwriting of a cook, the brow of a thinker, etc., etc., does not mean a thing any longer.

The only professional from the past to hold his own is the peasant. Increasing mechanization, commercialism, and the love of pleasure will not prevent the earth from being the earth. Whatever his clothes, whatever his way of life, he who cultivates the earth always embodies activity at its best and preserves its dignity. Nobody else from the past has survived. The other professions, thrown into confusion, try as best they can to reconstruct themselves; yet, unlike the fortunate peasant, they are not in possession of a firm field of action. Positions have become interchangeable, no longer requiring a specific attitude. Quite the contrary; the more neutral the mode of life, the better its chance to succeed.

And the artists? Is there still a caste that can lay exclusive claim to this beautiful term? Did this group not undergo a profound upheaval like all the others? At the end of his life Goethe lamented that the poet wants to be a painter, the painter a sculptor, the musician an architect, and so on. What would he say today? After all, do not those "interesting experiments" of such and such an artist prove that he is trying to break through the boundaries of his art? Michelangelo made no "experiments" in order to paint the Sistine Chapel. He was placidly satisfied to paint as a sculptor; his masterpiece is undoubtedly a mongrel, but there it is!

That the greatest musical geniuses have dared to conceive imitative music merely shows that music, the divine art, has yet to find its path and purpose. In the theatre we still attempt to create painting, sculpture, animated literature, intellectualization for the eye, etc., as if dramatic art could not simply rely upon itself. Modern architecture is often no more than modeling through a magnifying glass. The sculptor seeks atmosphere, the painter wants to give his lines and colors movement by lumping various attitudes and images together on the same canvas. Finally the musician, alas, thinks he will liberate the art of sounds by bringing to it the sound waves and the jarring rumble of our mechanized life. Having tried to free himself of the signification of words, the poet has found an intermediary that is only an arbitrary composition reflecting his caprice and the insolence of his character. Without wincing, we mix different means of expression, juxtapose, separate, or bring them together, amass or eliminate at random. Art has become merely a series of experiments performed in a vivisecting room, more cynical than anything imaginable. And the public accepts this; provided it smells of blood, anything is considered good. In all this, where does the artist stand?

Whence comes this growing anarchy, this contempt for technical integrity, this mad urge to kick over the traces, to rush blindly into the void? It is quite plain: we want *Life* and we do not know where to find it. In spite of everything, we have maintained "the former attitude," that of remaining *spectators*. We seek outside what is exclusively within ourselves; like a sybarite who exhausts himself and falls into despair by looking everywhere for the treasure he possesses within himself.

# Man Is the Measure of All Things

## A Preface to a New Work

(1923)

*La Revue théâtrale* 8, no. 25 (1954);
included in the English edition of *The Work of Living Art*[51]

This title is the motto of my latest book, *The Work of Living Art*. It expresses all my thought and distills the principles which have guided my labor.

An astronomer knows very well that his calculations concern his eyes and not the stars. When he announces the discovery of a new star, he can only state the day and the hour when his eyes were able to observe it; the star itself is unaffected by his mathematical discovery.

The philosopher is aware that his systems only brush the surface of something that remains forever unknown to him.

The applied scientist makes use of electricity, for example, forever ignorant of what it is that serves him.

The engineer can construct the most colossal machine, the most complicated mechanism; all his knowledge, whatever it may be, is gauged by his ambition and by our needs.

So it appears that in every human endeavor, Protagoras' axiom is the expression applicable to human effort.[52]

However, one main area of our culture, and of by far its most elevated activity, would like to escape that axiom. That is the area of Art.

The artist deals above all with an Unknown, whose presence he finds in nature, or at least in a "nature" that he thinks outside himself.

The painter studies nature in order to reproduce it. Where is that nature?

The architect builds up volumes and arranges them according to his taste. Where does he find his taste?

The poet describes or expresses life and his way of understanding it. Where does he find that life and his vision of it?

All artists imagine that they reproduce and express something presented to their eyes, to their sensibility. They think they are spectators, spectators of themselves, or else of their brothers, or yet of what they call "nature." Their detachment is an illusion. Obviously superior to all other men, because they do not make use of forms established by their intellect for utilitarian ends, or to satisfy their curiosity, they accept the Unknown that forces them to create, without even trying to approach it or to analyze it. For are they not artists!

Now, more than anyone else, the artist works under the categorical imperative of Protagoras. For him, more than for anyone else, man is uniquely and exclusively the measure.

But what is man? Is it man at rest who provides the artist with his measure? Or is it man, feeling and thinking, presenting himself to the searching eyes of him who wishes to reproduce that spectacle?

Is the artist a spectator, an active spectator to be sure, but nevertheless a spectator?

In art, is life a spectacle? Is art the mirror of life as has been said, and how overwhelmingly?

Is art a work necessarily circumscribed by a process which encloses it and limits it?

We have betrayed ourselves, and at the same time, we have betrayed art—we speak of "works of art," which implies the identity of the art and the work.

We have works of art, but do we possess art?

When that question first presented itself to me, like a sphinx barring my path, I was too young to try to answer it, and much too inexperienced to try to solve the problem that is so impassively presented to me.

If art is to be the supreme expression of life, of our life—(we know no other)—it will not be the life of man at rest, not the life of man thinking and feeling. It will be the life of man living, and consequently moving and acting.

Now all our forms of art, that is, all those which produce works of art, are immobile; architecture, sculpture, painting are immobile by definition.

Life is mobile and active. Our art forms derive from a convention which does violence to life by depriving it of its essential principle.

This would not matter if we had with these immobile arts an art form which expressed life in flux, in action; for then our immobile art forms would become concessions to a kind of perfection which is denied to active life: they would become ornaments to that life.

Do we have this supreme art form? This form that can embrace the whole of life in its passionate rhythm and exalt it into a work of art? And supposing

Figure 26. Design of 1926 for *Lohengrin*, Act 2

that we have this art form, what characteristic will distinguish it unmistakably from our works of art frozen in their too gorgeous immobility?

I have omitted the musician from my list of artists. It seems obvious that if a painting, for example, belongs to the category of fine art, music has no place there! No need to dwell on it.

Music speaks neither to our intellect nor to our eyes. It speaks to our ears; and our hearing functions in time, not in space. In music we have an art for which time, time-duration and its variances, are the condition of existence.

The fine arts exist in Space. Music exists in Time.

"Man is the measure of all things." What is the measure of man in time?

Here we are at the heart of the question.

Movement is our only possible measure of time. Does movement occur only in time? No; movement measures space too.

Thus movement is, through time, the measure of man in space; that is, in Space and Time.

Music measures time only; but our sense of hearing, which perceives music, is an integral part of our total organism. In order to measure space, music must therefore pass through that organism.

The human body, living and moving, will be the medium by means of which we shall rescue the art work from its age-old immobility. And since it is living, the work of the human body—of the incomparable Self—will be no longer an art work but a work of art: the Work of Living Art!

We must still distinguish between any movement and movement become a work of art.

Taine tells us—in a formula, somewhat bare, perhaps, but certainly definitive, that "the aim of a work of art is to reveal some essential, salient character, consequently, some important idea, more clearly and more completely than can real objects. It achieves this through a group of parts, whose relationships it systematically modifies."[53]

The spontaneous or voluntary movement must therefore undergo a "modification" in order to enter the portico of art and penetrate its sanctuary. There can be nothing arbitrary in that modification, for art is in essence an obligation.

In passing through our body, music, which springs from an obligation, achieves the transposition of its will into a movement regulated by that will. This movement, become peremptory and imperative, will measure space.

Our whole physical organism, if it submits to the laws of music, will thus become a work of art—and thus only.

But there is still another essential difference between the living body and the media of the other arts, the "fine arts."[54]

The living body is no more a brush or a chisel than it is a canvas or a block of marble. It is endowed with consciousness; and that involves responsibility.

If the work of living art carries our total organism into the domain of art—that living organism carries art itself into the domain of the spirit.

That is the obligation we cannot shirk without failing grossly—how many examples have we had—and falling to the level of the passive, inert instrument.

Music (the musician) is the hand of the sculptor, controlling and directing the chisel. We, *we* are both the chisel and the block of marble.—If we do not see in this situation, surely exceptional, a spiritual responsibility, we surrender the rights of a living being; our work of art will doubtless be mobile, but it will not be living.

The movement of a body that has no responsibility—that is the condition of the marionette. It is for us to choose responsibility.

Today all of us feel the inadequacy of the fine arts; all of us wish to give them movement, and all of us seek the means.

The idea of "modification," of which Taine speaks, is central to our aspirations toward a living art.

One may propose boldly that the question is summed up in the means chosen to effect that modification, without which there is no work of art.

Rhythm is the sole means of "modification." Rhythm is the hyphen that joins time to space, the temporary life of sound to the fleeting life of movement.

The question grows narrower, becomes still more technical. Thus: what kind of music will address itself most directly, more imperatively to the living body; and what kind of living body will be most apt to understand the language of music and to interpret it submissively in space?

Here we are concerned with education, since we are living and hence responsible.

The fundamental principle of modern education is not to inculcate alleged knowledge arbitrarily and by force, but, on the contrary, to light in man the fire of understanding so that it may shine forth and permit him to receive in exchange the light from the fires of others. All education worthy of the name must inspire the need for this exchange.

For us, and from the purely technical point of view, the exchange is effected from music to our body—from our body to music, each influencing the other all the way to its primal source.

Music is the miraculous creation of our most intimate and apparently most inexpressible being. The work of living art, which issues from music, can result only from a radiation from inside to outside, which confirms our educational principles.

Therefore we can reject all other methods.

In our time, the eurhythmics of Jaques-Dalcroze is the only discipline that takes this mysterious and sacred road. Its beauty is a result, never an end. In it we possess the technical means—the exchange, the reciprocal gift. That is its supreme guarantee.

What are its applications?

Our living body can be concerned only with an applied art, that is to say, an art that takes part in life. All art that is expository, ostentatious or scholarly is unworthy of the living body's high function.

Here we touch on the most sensitive point, and perhaps I may be allowed to conclude this brief explanation of principles by raising some probably unforeseen considerations that will enlarge our view.

I have said that we will be the chisel and the block of marble in the hands of the musician-sculptor. But . . . are we not also the statue? Therefore, the work of living art unites in a single organism the means and the end, the instruments and the accomplished work.

Without the presence of a conscious spectator, a statue, a picture, simply does not exist. Since the work of living art is conscious and responsible, it is self-sufficient.

A human body moving under the authority of music needs no spectator; it is both the work of art and its audience.

Living art abolishes the dualism that has killed in us the great Reality of art, that pitiable opposition in which one man is constantly a producer and the other unalterably a consumer. Living art exists solely by virtue of its own power, and without any contribution from a sensibility outside itself.

Living art is not a spectacle.

Nevertheless, living art does not fear to be looked upon, for it lives in broad daylight, thank God! So one may ask what will be the attitude of the spectator faced with a work that is not a spectacle, and consequently is perfectly secure without the help of his presence.

For a long time we have separated art from our life and from our homes, in order to shut it up in museums, concert halls or theatres. Living art knows not these sad compromises: it lives, we live in it, and it lives in us. Living art has restored to us the measure we had lost, the measure of all things: *ourselves!* And if, occasionally, it presents itself to our view, this is only in order to convince us once more. . . . And he who looks upon it, looks not upon a spectacle but upon a triumphant demonstration of Life.

No matter in what frame we wish to place living art, it dominates that frame or overshadows it.

If in the theatre, on the stage—our settings, painted and two-dimensional only, suddenly cease to exist. Their measure is not that of a living being: living art blots them out.

Once more "the triumphant demonstration of life" is affirmed! The body, at the behest of music, commands and orders space. Little it cares for age-old conventions, for deep-rooted customs—all must be cut to its measure, all must adopt its pattern. Is not man the measure of all things?

A new technique arises, not arbitrary, but gravely imperious. The body speaks, and the body demands; one must defer to it, and one must obey.

And the spectator is present at this transformation; he accepts by degrees this high and stern discipline; he consents to the sacrifices it demands of him; within his own organism the aesthetic life awakes. He is no longer a spectator; he becomes a collaborator and understands that he must renounce everything that contradicts the axiom of Protagoras. He wishes he were in the space created by the living body, he too wishes to create that space. Thus he takes part in what he has always regarded solely as a spectacle. He is very close to rising from his seat, leaping upon the stage, participating in this marvelous demonstration of the body's life transfigured by music. Finding himself on the threshold, he ends by wishing to penetrate to the sanctuary: he wishes to *live* art.

I cease for the time. In forthcoming articles I shall describe the various applications of living art, particularly in the theatre and dramatic art, as well as the aesthetic and social reforms that it will draw along in its luminous wake.

# Part Six

# Selected Scenarios

# Introduction to Part Six

The process by which Appia conceived and fashioned his scenarios, as well as their profound significance, has been discussed fully in earlier sections of this book, and described extensively by Appia himself in the essay "Theatrical Experiences and Personal Investigations" in part 1.

The concept of using such an elaborate and effective device for detailing, coordinating, and wrestling into a unified work of artistic expression all the disparate elements of production, constituted, together with his unprecedented prescription for technical reform, his major contribution to the art of the theatre. Its supreme value was not, however, immediately recognized. As he recounted in 1925 in an unpublished letter to a friend,

> In 1892 I completed my scenario for the *Ring,* together with the designs. I was thirty years old. I sent them to Cosima Wagner, along with a letter. Chamberlain, who was well regarded at Wahnfried,[1] presented them to Madame Wagner, and warmly endorsed them. She did not even open them—and Chamberlain returned them to me with his deep regrets. Since then, I have not offered them to anyone.[2]

Gordon Craig recorded in his diary that Appia told him how, a little later, he was granted a personal interview with Cosima. She listened coldly while he explained that his designs were concerned with the pictorial aspect of staging, and in no way went against the music itself:

> She turned to those present and said, "Gentlemen, we are met together for the direct purpose of forwarding the works of Richard Wagner." Appia attempted to remind her that Wagner himself had written, "This art of music is not the completed art of the theatre—this art is only in its infancy." Frau Wagner then turned her quiet head and looked at him while one might count one, two, three, four, and even five. She then dismissed him scornfully, with "All this has no meaning at all!"[3]

Not until 1983 were these scenarios published. The section of the *Ring*—the scenario for act 3 of *The Walkyrie* presented here—is the first portion of it ever to be published in English.

The surviving pages of Appia's scenario for *Carmen* are little more than a fragment of the *mise en scène* he is believed to have prepared in the 1920s. Only a portion of act 3 is extant. However, this can be supplemented by a description of the staging of the beginning of act 2, which Appia presented in Paris in 1903. Appia had been introduced to the Countess Renée de Béarn, a woman of great charm and wealth, who sponsored performances in a private theatre fitted out in her mansion in Paris. She was persuaded to support Appia's plan to stage an experimental production conceived according to his still untried theories. He worked on the project for a year and a half, creating a production from nothing—and one conceived and executed according to totally new ideas; presenting scenes from Byron's *Manfred,* with music by Schumann, and the selection from *Carmen.*

The production opened on 25 March 1903. It attracted substantial interest in Parisian cultural and artistic circles (a host of theatre people, authors, composers and painters attended) and was performed for three nights to great acclaim. Sarah Bernhardt termed it "an exquisite artistic sensation," and it was extravagantly praised by others present, including the highly important actor-director Aurélien-Marie Lugné-Poë.[4]

A review records that Appia presented the nocturnal gypsy scene from act 2, and that his theory that the entire *mise en scène* should be placed in the service of the performer was fully realized. The audience was able to look in upon a scene in which the dancers seemed totally unaware of its presence as they performed with ever greater abandon under the night sky. There were no superfluous details, merely a suggestion of a dilapidated inn, whose windows served to filter what appeared to be candlelight from within, as it mixed with the blue shadows and silvery moonlight outside. The stage presented a marvelously varied pattern as the whirling dancers moved gracefully between areas of darkness and light, increasing their tempo all the while until the curtain fell on a climax of motion, light and music, to an ovation from the audience.[5]

The fragmentary notes for *Prometheus* were prepared by Appia in advance of the production that took place in Basel in February 1925. The idea for it had come from Max Eduard von Leihburg, a friend of Wälterlin and former student of Dalcroze, by whom he had been introduced to Appia's theories and designs. Von Leihburg recognized their potential as a basis for staging Greek tragedy and hoped to persuade Appia to assist in producing it in a translation by von Leihburg himself. It was scheduled to take place in the Basel Municipal Theatre, a mere ten days after the premiere there of the ill-fated production of *The Walkyrie.*

In a previously unpublished letter written almost four decades later, von Leihburg recounts his experience. "I was in Basel studying biology. My *Prometheus* had been published and it was necessary to stage it. So we took the risk, but wanted Appia to undertake the design and direction. I wrote to him.

For five hundred francs he was willing to take it on. . . ." Von Leihburg then tells how, unfortunately, *The Walkyrie* scandal broke just as the production was getting under way:

> In the middle of this Germanic hubbub, *Prometheus* was supposed to be launched like a Greek literary firework. Appia refused ever to return to Basel, the city where an artist couldn't breathe. He sent us a small notebook with the outline for the production [the notes published here] and wouldn't budge from Geneva. There was no alternative except for Wälterlin and me to take over the direction, together with [Dr. Gustave] Güldenstein, a student of Dalcroze and teacher of eurhythmics at the Basel Conservatory, who trained the chorus of women in eurhythmics. . . . So it went well, and would have been some compensation to Appia for all the injustice and betrayal. . . .[6]

Fifteen years earlier Appia had collaborated with Dalcroze on plans and designs for a eurhythmic version of the play, but the project had not gone forward. When he returned to the project at von Leihburg's invitation, he set aside his previous designs to produce a new monumental setting, which abandoned every trace of naturalism in favor of extreme but greatly expressive simplicity. The downstage portion of the set was composed of a vast ramp filling the entire width of the proscenium arch. In fact, Appia wanted to extend it out over and beyond the orchestra pit into the very midst of the audience, but this proved impossible. The ramp, formed of successive platforms, rose first gently, then steeply upwards, to form in the center of the stage a huge, overweening monolith to which Prometheus was chained. Its dark and threatening mass was intended to underscore visually the play's central theme of tyranny and oppression.

Despite the inauspicious circumstances, the *Prometheus* was a substantial success, both as an application of Appia's ideas to the new material of Greek drama, and in the favor it found with the public, including even those critics who had withheld full approval of the *Ring* productions. It did indeed give solace to Appia, who, while lamenting the *Walkyrie* fiasco, pointed out to a friend that, "on the other hand, everyone agrees that the spectacle, the visual element of my *Prometheus* was the most magnificent thing to be seen in Basel."[7]

His remark is fully substantiated by the critical reviews, which, while objecting occasionally to elements of the performance, have unreserved praise for the production concept and setting. One critic noted how "architecturally everything fits into the space, creating a beautiful plastic effect,"[8] while another summed up by suggesting that "in Wagner's operas the theoreticians may find the simple, stylized settings out of place, but here Appia's austerity is in keeping with the simplicity of the ancient scene."[9]

Appia's work on *Prometheus* represents in one sense a sort of aesthetic "homecoming." As he, Dalcroze and a host of disciples frequently point out, their work was greatly indebted to the Greeks, whose suggestive example inspired and informed nearly every aspect of it. Through eurhythmics they aspired to recreate Greek *orchesis;* by changing the occasion of performance, they hoped to achieve something of the Greek sense of a communal festival; the hieratic acting style discarded naturalism from a desire to reconstitute the Greek presentational mode; realistic scenery was abandoned in favor of the more emblematic and abstract style of antiquity. The quintessence of Appia's reforms, and many of his contemporaries' ideas as well, were massively influenced and challenged by Greek example.

While benefiting in its turn from the new type of dramaturgy that its example had in part inspired, Greek drama as produced at Basel provided still further guidance on how stagecraft might be reformed. The rhythm and tempo of its language, which von Leihburg sought to retain in his translation, provided the basis for interpretative and expressive movement through eurhythmics that normally could only be based upon a musical score.[10] It suggested, at least tentatively, a way in which eurhythmics and all that it implied for theatrical art might be applied to the spoken drama—a challenge that had always eluded its supporters, including Appia. "The movement that was born out of impulses in the text itself created a rhythmic use of bodies and voices totally in the spirit of Appia and Dalcroze."[11]

Around 1926 Appia worked on a series of designs, both for operas (*Alceste, Iphigénie en Aulide, Iphigénie en Tauride,* and *Orfeo* by Gluck, and *Die Meistersinger* and *Lohengrin* by Wagner) as well as some spoken drama (*Macbeth, King Lear,* and, a little later, *Faust*). All of them are characterized by their minimalist approach: utter simplicity and economy in their depiction, and a total absence of decorative detail.

A portion of the scenario that Appia wrote to accompany *Iphigénie en Tauride* survives and indicates a similarly austere approach to staging. Indeed, Appia was undoubtedly attracted to the work because it invited such treatment. Gluck himself, working a century and a half before, had consciously composed it with corresponding musical restraint foremost in his mind, and it is not difficult to perceive why his concept, as he described it, would have found such favor with Appia:

> I have striven to restrict music to its true office of serving poetry by means of expression . . . without interrupting the action or stifling it with a useless superfluity of ornaments; and I believed that it should do this in the same way as telling colors affect a correct and well-ordered drawing, by a well-assorted contrast of light and shade, which serves to animate the figures without altering their contours.[12]

Appia strives to realize exactly the same idea in the scenario in effect taking Gluck's pictorial metaphor and giving it literal expression, "to achieve a maximum of *human* value in a framework which is of interest only in its relation to

Figure 27. Design of 1926 for Gluck's *Iphigénie en Aulide*, the Closing Scene of Act 3

the presence of the human being." The setting, while suggestive of a classical scene, provides a supportive but unobtrusive space in which the actions occur, which, in turn, reveal the underlying human emotion embodied in them.

The scenario for Goethe's *Faust,* part 1, is an important and unusual work, and the last that Appia completed. It was accompanied by seventeen very simple designs illustrating all the settings required by the scenario. Conceiving of the play as a "dramatic poem," Appia creates the part of a "Reader" who, in the course of the work, assumes various parts. In accord with the austere settings, Appia dispenses with all the supernatural effects, as well as most of the properties and romantic ornamentation with which productions of the play were usually encumbered. In their place he sought to create powerful visual effects by using stark silhouettes, drapes, and isolating the characters either on an empty stage, or by placing them "à la Shakespeare" in front of the curtain.

In his description, Appia puts forward the idea (not original with him, but never before represented in production) that Faust and Mephistopheles should be thought of as a single character: two aspects of a dual personality, which, although presented by two actors, should be closely coordinated in their gestures and characterization.

The scenario is valuable, not only for such innately interesting qualities, but also because (together with a very fragmentary *Hamlet*) it is one of the rare examples of Appia's work with spoken drama. His basic approach was similar to that used with musical works. It was necessary to formulate the settings according to the principle that only those elements should be present that clarify and articulate the essential conflicts and issues that he perceived in the drama itself. Starting with an empty space, he identified the necessary movements of the characters as these are motivated, not now by music, but by the demands of language and dramatic circumstance. This pattern of movement, generated directly from within the written play, would in turn project the initial outlines of the physical settings.

As with music-drama, Appia was above all concerned that the staging should in no way *displace* the thing the artist had created, but rather that it provide and support the appropriate space for it to *take place.* This in turn means that the designer-director must carefully consider the role of external locale within the drama itself, emphasizing it visually whenever it manifests itself in the drama's action, allowing it to recede at those points where the balance of the piece shifts to questions of internal circumstance and conflict. The immediate practical effect of such an approach is to remove from the play's staging the accumulated and largely irrelevant clutter of many decades of scenic illusion, to restore it as the "dramatic poem" that Goethe had in mind. Thus, at the end of his life, Appia was still concerned with one of the major goals that had inspired and determined his call for reform in the 1890s: to organize the elements of production in such a way that the vision of the creative artist could find authentic and worthy expression.

Figure 28.   Design of 1922 for the Conclusion of *Hamlet*, Act 5, Scene 2
Appia stipulated that Hamlet's body be placed in stark profile against the open sky on the upper platform, with torches placed on each of the four corners.

# The Walkyrie:
# Commentary and Scenario for Act 3

1892[13]

## Setting

The setting presents great difficulty due to its contradictory composition, and its use in *Siegfried* and *Götterdämmerung*. The description which is given in the libretto, together with the scenes whose actions take place in this setting, sufficiently indicate these difficulties, and require a further justification here for the two essential ways in which the conception that follows differs from the description.

(1) The scene ought to provide for the spectator a lifelike impression of a mountain *summit*, a real summit without which the Walkyrie could not be properly arranged. This impression must not be diminished; it must be created by the setting, without making it an isolated object which in *Siegfried* and *Götterdämmerung* one relegates to a corner like a useless piece of furniture.

(2) The trunk of the fir tree, under the branches of which Brunnhilde sleeps, becomes the *subject*, interrupts the harmony of the design, divides one's attention, takes up a great deal of space, and disadvantageously pushes back the rest of the setting. Its importance is minimal, and it ought to be given lesser weight than the overall picture.

Description: The rocks should not rise up but should be sliced through on a horizontal plane with deep hollows, the perspective of which, together with the lateral stones at the peak and the overhang that they bring into view, provides a jutting profile against the sky. This formation greatly enlivens the effect of the actual stage objects and the well-defined nature of its lines does not allow one to imagine a continuation that would lessen the sensation of emptiness a mountain summit ought to suggest. The somberness of the material and the scenic arrangement will be of the greatest importance.

With the exception of the practicable[14] of the summit itself, the setting is shallow. The distance from the curtain to the rear of the stage will be determined by the lighting.

On the right,[15] four or five feet above the stage, a ridge rises sharply to form towards the middle of the setting an unequal platform, half of which drops sharply towards the audience, while the other half descends in tiers onto a second level a little lower than the beginning of the ridge on the right, which in turn descends to the quite narrow foreground.

From the upper platform the rocks rise in unequal steps, extending to the upper left where they end in an overhanging ledge. This is to the rear of an isolated step that extends to the extreme left in the foreground above the cave, and continues the line of the summit by turning sharply downstage before entering the wings. It forms a gradient sloping upwards back to the right, forming in turn the actual summit located a third of the distance from the left of the visible stage picture, and two-thirds of its height. The line from left to right is continuous, and the detail of the overhanging ledge hardly interrupts it. The mountain is cut through in a segment, perpendicular at the overhang, so that any detail that one sees of the slope does not interfere with the clean line of the ridge, except for the vertical elements visible within the slopes, the largest of which is seen in the bend forming the ridge.

At the beginning of the ridge on the right, the ground falls away slowly towards the center to join the lower platform. In the middle of this platform a gently sloping path on the left descends to the foreground past the foot of the rocks. This extends almost as far as the right wing, where it is enclosed by a low mossy rock wall, which then continues to the extreme right foreground. At the foot of this wall the ground rises gently (Brunnhilde's "moss hill") and this formation is underscored by the rocks that extend from the wall on the right, reaching the path along which they stand, and rising back to the level of the lower platform. In the center of the foreground the path turns slowly to the left keeping to the base of the rocks supporting the lower platform, and then drops sharply to disappear into the cave at ground level.

The entrance to the cave is half hidden by a wall at the downstage wing, which rises to rejoin the upper platform. The second wall, which is essential, determines the bend in the crest, leaving a practicable ledge which becomes larger in turn as it reaches the summit.

In the extreme right foreground corner, masked by a downstage rock, is an exit that is between this rock and the one forming Brunnhilde's hill.

Above the wall that defines the boundary between the lower platform at the right and the hill, one must imagine a plateau inclined towards the background

Figure 29.    Design of 1892 for *The Walkyrie*, Act 3

up to the ridge along which trees stand. The wings at the right are narrow and set back, possibly representing the borders of the forest from which one or two trees extend branches over the scene, leaving the sky completely open; their trunks are not seen. To the rear an isolated fir tree may perhaps stand to define the perspective and the supposed formation of the ground, but it remains close to the wing without coming forward; the background must remain completely free.

The wall of rocks to the left of the actor emerging from the cave is vertical at its base but then meets the slope of the ridge in a jumbled pile. Directly above the cave the realistic overhanging entablature forms a kind of vaulting that casts an actual shadow over that entire portion of the set.

On entering the set from the cave, the actor climbs several steps towards the middle of the downstage section to the base of the rocks supporting the lower platform. By following the gently sloping path that passes between these rocks and those of Brunnhilde's hill, he can reach the foot of the steps that lead on to the upper platform. From there, by continuing slowly, he can reach the crest and disappear into the wings directly behind the ridge near the first step at the base of the upper platform. This is assumed to extend onto a ledge on the farther side and is not visible. A platform slopes away to the left behind the set to reach stage level. (Siegfried's exit in *Götterdämmerung.*)

The lower platform begins at one-third of the width of the visible stage from the left, extending up to the wall of rock on the right, which is covered in its second half by Brunnhilde's hill. The upper platform begins at one-quarter of the width of the stage from the right and ends by merging with the levels descending from the ledge.

The steps which straddle the two platforms are of irregular shape, some quite large, leading in an imposing manner to the lower platform. For the audience the impression is of the same terrain in two formations; only the rocks descending to the floor at the left mark the difference in levels.

There are some loose rocks on the path at the left before its descent into the cave; one of them is used to sit upon to the right of the cave as one makes an entrance.

The backcloth shows nothing *but the sky.*

The rocks are of grayish color, here and there some light turf. The approach to the fir trees is green, and the rocks become mossy. The hill has turf. The trees are old and irregular with thin branches covered with lichen. . . . [16]

For this setting, the most important in the *Ring,* one must use the best materials in constructing the practicables to allow easy positioning and movement of a landscape represented three-dimensionally. In particular the function of the rocks requires sturdy practicables that can be adapted to each break in the ridge and *form a sharp profile against the sky.* In the front sections facing the audience the construction can be free, and the edge of the practicable may occasionally disappear behind painted scenery. The rock wall in the foreground can easily be attached to the practicable.

Brunnhilde's hill on the right must be entirely "plastique" and connected to the rest of the setting, and must have nothing in common with a piece of furniture.

The downstage area is slightly elevated, covered at the front with a narrow strip of earth, and dark almost to the base of the incline. Only the direct entrance to the cave at the left and the exit at the right foreground are at stage level. The path is gently sloping but *uneven*, remaining practicable for Siegfried's horse in *Götterdämmerung*. All the other practicables will be very uneven and undulating, and none should resemble a staircase.[17]

The branches of the fir trees throw a light shadow over all of the setting to the right; this painted shadow must be capable of becoming *real* for act 3 of *Siegfried*.

The colors will be blended harmoniously, soft, with *nothing of a reddish hue* in them, and the lichens form a bridge between the very *sober* green of the trees and the gray of the rocks. In front of the cave, an area as far as the lower platform and one-third the depth of the stage, must be painted in a shadowy blue, fresh and transparent, much deeper than that cast on the right by the trees. The actual shadow of the entablature above will blend with the painted shadow.

The gauze at the back must be painted in accordance with the lighting requirements.

Shadows and patches of light on the rocks must be very lightly indicated and the choice of details must be *more than sober*.[18]

The scenic picture should produce a feeling of calm satisfaction and etch itself onto the mind as simple lines, recalled with pleasure.

The accompanying drawings, more finished than the previous ones, have no purpose but to indicate the setting and the formation of the rocks, and have no pretensions to being a definitive artistic product. The portion which is in shadow only gives a very sketchy suggestion of the effect that should be produced.[19]

## Lighting

Two essential elements: movement and repose. In the first the role of light is active, in the second it is of a passive calmness with slight and imperceptible variations, only interrupted by the episode of the Magic Fire, which, because of its magic, has nothing in common with the ambient light.

The sky provides the visual interest until the arrival of Brunnhilde. Then the focus of the drama sets the place of action in the sky that previously served only as a kind of commentary, but now remains, to the end, a living thing. One must therefore treat it as such and consider the projections and the other elements as *actors* whose tasks when taken together have all the importance of an acting *role*.

The act begins during the *day;* it is the storm which darkens the atmosphere; the sky to the rear must remain clear, the bulk of the setting always stands out in silhouette. The foreground is dark with shadows diminishing imperceptibly up to the crest.

After the departure of the Walkyrie, all becomes calm, and everything should serve to create the most limpid sky possible. The projectors have nothing further to do except prepare for the Magic Fire.

The setting of the sun, *very subdued,* diffuses itself slowly and disappears in the same way. The thin crescent of the moon must merge into the surrounding landscape.

Depending upon the arrangement of the projectors, of which there should be a great many, it may be necessary to divide them into two categories: those supplying the backdrop with the vague movement of clouds with slow modulations and streaks of blue sky and those responsible for the *march* of individual clouds in the sky and against the rocks, for lightning flashes, for apparitions (the Walkyrie) and for the Magic Fire. It is absolutely critical to leave as little to chance as possible.

The difficult question will be the arrangement of the lighting itself, to preserve the scenic harmony while rendering the outline of the setting and the actors placed within it, indistinct (with the exception of pp. 210–14).[20] The light must never be so strong as to make the facial expressions really distinct.

An area of diffused light with all the intensity coming from above; therefore striking the slope in the foreground. Natural shadows created by the construction of the set itself cannot be controlled in the alternate light-dark; they therefore contribute to the haphazard effect in the first half of the act. Perhaps towards the end, in order to emphasize the calm and serenity of the atmosphere, one ought to spread a little diffuse light over the scene. The corner of the cave remains completely dark and the shadow of the fir trees on the right, which is a painted shadow, may be taken as *real* because of the diffuse light.

*The Ride of the Walkyrie*

Until electric photography is introduced into the theatre, which in a series of quasi-simultaneous projections can produce an arrangement of movements, the scene of the Walkyrie must always remain incomplete. . . . [21] A realistic apparition will always be ridiculous because of the spectators' literal-mindedness; and no matter what projection is shown, it is always imperfect in a drama of this type. The alternative taken in the scenario remains the only inoffensive solution. It goes without saying that an artist of the first rank should be commissioned to create these apparitions.

*The Magic Fire*

It is not a decorative but a *mimetic* effect. It is a magic act, completely independent of the natural environment, totally in the service of Wotan's will, and therefore created through his gestures. The scenario gives the process of its development.

Projection will be essential. Very little steam and *absolutely no noise or violent movement* (it is not a volcano!). Perhaps a number of small fireworks thrown by hand and well integrated with the core of the flame might be a convenient method. In any case, part of the floor of the lower platform will be specifically constructed for the effect, and in the composition of the rocks of the upper platform one must remember that channels will be necessary for the passage of the fire.

The light that ushers in Wotan is *blood-red* without variation; the Magic Fire is the color of *fire*.

## Scenario

171/2 Curtain: The set in silhouette.[22] The eye only gradually takes in those patterns of the terrain not set against the sky. The foreground is dark. The sky is bright, a rainy gray, veiled with indistinct and variable clouds. A few isolated clouds move from left to right near the summit, chasing and doubling back upon themselves. Everything is in crescendo until 210 when the projections vanish into the setting itself.

Gerhilde is at the highest point of the rock, Ortlinde is below the ledge, Waltraute and Schwertleite near them at curtain rise; climbing during 171/3–4[23] onto the overhang. All four, *erect* facing the sky. 172/1: Gerhilde makes her first cry to the three Walkyrie, then turns towards the sky and her voice is lost upstage. At her call, Ortlinde rejoins Waltraute and Schwertleite on the overhang, all three leaning over the precipice stock still.

The manner of their singing should give the impression of unrestrained savagery and the inflections of their voices should not be coordinated with their movements. They hurl their shouts first to the audience and then upstage. Their movements during the rising flow of the "hojotoho!" are not formulaic. Repetition would become tiresome and silly. The whole body ought to physically reinforce the shout. Adapting a formal pose is undesirable; on the contrary the impression should be of *excessive* life. The expansiveness of the music should not be ritualistically paralleled by physical movement.

Helmwige's voice is heard as if from far away, lest the audience confuse it with that of Gerhilde. 172/4: The Walkyrie brandish their lances. Menacing clouds gather at the left, grow and are shot through by lightning. The clouds stir, at first slowly, and then ever more quickly moving from left to right. 172/5:

A violent lightning flash *emerges from the cloud*. One glimpses a vague color-less form, perceiving only a mane of hair, a cloak, a headband flowing in the wind, a lance, gleams of armor, all shrouded in clouds. A second into 173 a similar apparition is seen coming closer. The two are still only vaguely visible from the lightning, which silhouettes them so fleetingly that one can only sense their immobility, emphasized, moreover, by the rapid movement of the clouds.

173/5–6: Waltraute and Schwertleite descend onto the upper platform; Ort-linde does the same but stops somewhat higher. 174/1: All three are in right profile facing the audience. The cloud reaches the fir tree. Several brilliant white flashes outline the branches, and then the sky regains its initial appearance while, imperceptibly, the number of clouds increases. Gerhilde descends from the summit and stops on the overhang. 174/2: Ortlinde descends, crosses in front of Waltraute and Schwertleite and stops at the right on the edge of the upper platform. Waltraute follows closely and presses against her. 174/4: Helmwige sings from the wings and Schwertleite darts past Ortlinde and Waltraute at the same moment that Helmwige enters through the fir trees.

*Entrance of Helmwige*

At Helmwige's casual gesture, Gerhilde descends to the upper platform, Waltraute goes to meet her. 175/2: Gerhilde signals Waltraute to stand guard for her; Ortlinde goes off *singing* and disappears. The others very agitated. 175/3: Gerhilde darts *laughing* in the direction of Helmwige and Schwertleite, during which Waltraute quickly reaches the summit. 175/4: Helmwige moves into the fir trees *singing*. At Waltraute's first call, Gerhilde and Schwertleite climb as far as the overhang and all three are in right profile. 177/1: A few lightning flashes on the right. 177/2: A violent white lightning behind the trees. Gerhilde descends a few steps and turns suddenly to the left. 178/2: Schwertleite rejoins her; an enormous shape silhouetted in lightning climbs behind the sum-mit of the mountain, breaking through the clouds.

*Entrance of Siegrune*

178/4: "gegrüsst"; in a lightning flash more violent that the others, similar to Helmwige's arrival. Siegrune emerges from the trees and ascends the upper platform while *singing*. 179/1: All face left. 179/2: There is a cloud near the fir trees, the Walkyrie turn, following it with their eyes. 179/2: Two violent flashes in the trees. 179/2: Waltraute descends. 179/3: Gerhilde and Schwertleite re-maining above the overhang, descend while *singing;* soon rejoined by Waltraute who has sung, 179/3, on arrival at the overhang. Helmwige quickly turns from the trees and sings while rejoining Schwertleite, Gerhilde and Waltraute on the left above the upper platform. Gerhilde, 180/1, descends still lower nearer to

Siegrune and Ortlinde who direct their first cry from the edge of the trees. 180/2: Waltraute descends towards Gerhilde; Helmwige reaches the rock over the cave and sings, facing right; Ortlinde climbs onto the overhang and almost disappears upstage where she hurls her cries in all directions. Gerhilde, together with Waltraute, ascends, and Schwertleite comes down to meet them.

181/1: While singing, Ortlinde re-approaches Schwertleite and Gerhilde, who have now rejoined Siegrune above the overhang. Helmwige joins them, moving towards the audience. 181/1: They stand for a moment in a tight group facing right on the steps above the overhang; Helmwige remains alone on her step. 181/2: The group, very agitated, brandish their lances. Helmwige descends, followed by Ortlinde. 181/2: The others, with the exception of Gerhilde, descend. 181/3: Gerhilde follows and quickly overtakes the group who are stationary on the platform, and continues all the way to the right edge, where she shouts into the fir trees. 181/5: The group stirs restlessly while remaining in one place; Ortlinde leaves them to rejoin Gerhilde. 182/1: Waltraute does the same, as well as, 182/2, Schwertleite, who laughs together with Siegrune on meeting Gerhilde as the latter ascends towards Helmwige, who has remained behind. 182/3: Waltraute and Schwertleite laugh as they approach Helmwige and Gerhilde who, descending, reply to their laughter. All four, laughing, rejoin Ortlinde and Siegrune who laugh in turn. Thus they arrive as a group on the extreme right of the upper platform. 183/2: Grimgerde and Rossweisse are heard singing offstage. 184/1: All the Walkyrie rush to meet them in a single movement, while remaining onstage; then return one by one.

[A sense of how detailed Appia's directions are may be had by noting that at this point the act has been running just under six minutes; approximately four and one-half minutes have elapsed from the first cries of the Walkyrie.]

### Entrance of Grimgerde and Rossweisse

Grimgerde is first, turning to reply to Schwertleite; Rossweisse in the middle of the group. Helmwige, from behind, comes forward to reply to Rossweisse, whereupon Siegrune moves onto the summit to keep guard. 185/2: Gerhilde, in front, turns back to speak to the others. 185/4: Thus they all arrive together, all on the upper platform to the left and above. At Siegrune's call they stop suddenly, motionless and attentive. Gerhilde, at the head with Waltraute almost on the overhang; Ortlinde last with Helmwige and Schwertleite; Rossweisse and Grimgerde in the middle. In this order (in vocal sequence) they start to move, 186/2; Ortlinde moves quickly in front of the others, and at 186/3 rejoins Gerhilde and Waltraute. Helmwige does not reach the summit until the last bar of 186/3; the others, variously, before her.

Siegrune stays at her post, and everyone sings at full volume, oblivious of the audience and without modifying their voice on account of their movement. 187/4: "bewegt"; Siegrune descends quickly and stops on the overhang, leaning over one edge as if to see better, and then returns to the summit to talk with her sisters. 188/2: Gerhilde descends, talking with Waltraute; Schwertleite remains on the summit. 188/3: Waltraute arrives on the very edge of the overhang, shouting with all her strength towards the right. 188/3–4: Rossweisse and Helmwige descend, and Ortlinde follows several steps behind. 189/1: While the four dash, *running* into the fir trees, Waltraute, at the second bar, hurls her cry at Ortlinde. Grimgerde and Schwertleite descend quickly; Ortlinde and Waltraute utter their second cry, while moving. Waltraute, in front, pauses, 189/2, on her arrival at the upper platform, to move forward once more, 189/3, while the other three advance quickly towards her. Grimgerde sings while running. 190/1: They disappear into the fir trees.

*Entrance of Brunnhilde and Sieglinde*

190/2: "schnell"; The Walkyrie re-enter, half of them encircling Brunnhilde who *sings during this movement and arrives,* 191/1, on the lower platform, at the extreme left of which she places Sieglinde during the agitated ensemble around them. On entering, one of the Walkyrie places Brunnhilde's lance, shield and buckler behind the small mound, in full view of the audience. 192/1: Broad movement of the Walkyrie in a staggered group *around* Brunnhilde, who remains close to Sieglinde. 192/1: Brunnhilde moves forward onto the steps leading to the upper platform, where she looks anxiously towards the right upstage. 192/2: She ascends a further step. Ortlinde and Waltraute follow from afar; she turns back to speak to them, then descends again onto the *upper* platform, while Ortlinde and Waltraute run up, 193/2, to the summit. 193/3: Brunnhilde on the upper platform, the other Walkyrie ranked between her and Sieglinde. 194/1: Brunnhilde ascends a little, attempting despite her extreme agitation to scan the horizon. 194/1: The Walkyrie ascend, leaving Sieglinde alone. Brunnhilde, returning, 194/2, rushes into the group and arrives, 194/3, near Sieglinde whom she cradles in her arms, as the Walkyrie, having turned back, surround them again. 195: Brunnhilde remains close to Sieglinde. 195/4: The Walkyrie recoil in a *violent* movement. 196/1: Brunnhilde moves away bit by bit from Sieglinde, following the movement of the Walkyrie in such a way that at 196/3 they are all together on the middle of the lower platform and on the steps above; Sieglinde isolated on the left, Brunnhilde alone between her and the Walkyrie. 197/2: They recoil again, breaking up the group. 198/1: Rossweisse, Grimgerde and Schwertleite spring onto the ridge. 198/2: Helmwige, Gerhilde and Siegrune do the same, passing in front of the others, while singing, onto the overhang. Then all six descend again, running. 198/4: The Walkyrie gather around

Brunnhilde who, in anguish, has ascended to the upper platform again, 199/1, to meet them; then mixes with them in great *animation*.

199/2: The Walkyrie detach themselves one by one from Brunnhilde, who speaks to them as they pass in front of her, so that, 200/1, she is left alone in the background at the right of the upper platform; the Walkyrie grouped to one side at the left and above. 200/3: "rettet"; Brunnhilde darts once again onto the lower platform and covers Sieglinde with her body, her head still turned towards her sisters, who remain above in an agitated state. 201/5: Sieglinde, facing forward, presses against the rock behind her.

202: The Walkyrie reassemble one by one above Sieglinde, one or two remaining on the ridge, facing right. 202/1–2: Brunnhilde in her shining beauty, sings "ein Wälsung wächste dir im Schoss," with a large, wild movement of her open hand in front of Sieglinde's body, and then draws back breathless as Sieglinde follows her. 203/1: Sieglinde at the center of the lower platform violently grasps Brunnhilde, who, upright, turns upstage. The Walkyrie *in an unrestrained movement* ascend and descend, looking at the sky, and return at last, some coming down, the others remaining on the upper platform. Brunnhilde, still on the right, yields her arm to Sieglinde, but turns her head, motionless. 204/1: Sieglinde falls to her knees, clasping Brunnhilde's legs. All the Walkyrie approach. 204/2: Brunnhilde *suddenly* steps forward onto the path, raising and dragging Sieglinde. 205: The Walkyrie press around the two women. 205/4: They all set off, climbing hurriedly. Brunnhilde drags Sieglinde hastily into the foreground, and at 206/2, "drängend," lets her go, remaining on Sieglinde's left, facing forward with Sieglinde in right profile.

*"Fort denn, eile nach Osten gewandt!"*

During 207/8–9, the Walkyrie circle around the ridge, sometimes together, sometimes separately, while the storm gathers force. The clouds have changed direction imperceptibly since Brunnhilde's entrance and are now being pushed from left to right in a whirlwind, ever darker but not yet completely hiding the rocks. The eye has grown accustomed to the lack of light so that the scene on the lower platform can be clearly followed, because of the white costumes. The foreground remains dark and Brunnhilde and Sieglinde indistinct; but the sky must be as bright as possible compared to the set, to ensure the silhouette effect above all. 208/3: Sieglinde recoils and at 208/4 sings in profile to *Brunnhilde,* who stands erect and gazes at her, hand raised as if to swear to the truth of her promise. Sieglinde departs by the right foreground.

Figure 30. Design of 1892 for *The Walkyrie*, Act 3
The Walkyrie await Wotan's arrival, with the shadowy figure of Sieglinde kneeling next to Brunnhilde.

*The Approach of Wotan*

210: Clouds cover the summit and the ridge (perhaps a gauze in front of the summit). Soft but *continuous* noise of wind to the right. Ceaseless lightning backstage suddenly making the Walkyrie visible and then plunging them into darkness. Prolonged rolls of thunder. A blood-red light grows in intensity to the right, completely distinct from the general lightning. All that can be done with projections must be used to make the sky look terrifying, emphasizing the right side as much as possible. 210: "Stürmisch"; The Walkyrie are dispersed, some on the upper platform waiting anxiously for Brunnhilde, the others circling around the ridge amidst the clouds. 210/3: Brunnhilde climbs among the others, and *stops dead at Wotan's call.* All the Walkyrie do the same. They fall stock still at once, *caught in mid-movement.* Ortlinde and Waltraute sing while descending. Brunnhilde, 211–1, arrives on the upper platform, welcomed by the "Weh!" of the others. She climbs; Ortlinde and Waltraute come to meet her with "Weh!" They all group around her.

The darkness obscures everything except the broad mass of their movement; these images run beneath it. The light increases without illuminating the Walkyrie. The wind and thunder *uninterrupted and without modulation,* grow as at the approach of a cataclysm. Lightning flashes blend ceaselessly with the light. The sky is a whirlwind from let to right; the summit is lost beneath clouds. 212: Helmwige alone attends Brunnhilde on the overhang; all the others follow them and stretch out into a compact mass above them. 213: The whole scene is like a dark whirlwind in which one can distinguish the Walkyrie only by their singing. 214/1: The wind and thunder are in full crescendo, having reached full volume. They *stop dead* on a great lightning flash without thunder. The blood-red light pierces the fir trees in a puff of smoke, lighting up the ridge and the clouds. The light increases until 214/2, when in a great burst of smoke, Wotan appears. The light dies out at once. The sky lightens bit by bit, just enough to make the figures distinct. The clouds desert the ridge but still obscure the summit. The foreground remains dark.

*Entrance of Wotan*

Wotan, in long strides, reaches the upper platform and crosses it in order to be at 214/3 in silhouette some distance in front of the Walkyrie for "Wo ist Brünnhilde?" Several flickers of light in the sky. 215/1: The Walkyrie *assemble* during the music and at 215/2, "Was thaten," become agitated without changing their place. Those singing "Was thaten Vater" make their movement on "Vater"; the others, on "reizte." 216: Wotan draws back a little, 217/1, "Weichet von ihr," in a movement and manner which make them give way, letting him go, and thereby giving the ensemble that follows the quality of a picture in relief.

217/2: Complete stillness, Rossweisse in the middle of the group. 217/3, second bar: Grimgerde moves a step forward; fourth bar, Rossweisse does the same; 218/1, first bar: Waltraute, the same; third bar, Gerhilde the same; fourth bar, Helmwige the same; the others move very little.[24] 281/2, second bar: Helmwige ascends a step; Gerhilde crosses her; on the last three bars, the entire group in a single movement brandish their lances with arms outstretched. 219/1: A sudden drawing back of the group. All the movement of this ensemble is barely perceptible and enters into the unconscious harmony of the scene for the spectator. Wotan remains on the upper platform until 226/1. 220/5: Wotan has drawn back a moment earlier in order to underscore the orchestral crescendo, returning now with an emphatic movement. 221/2: "Hörst du mich Klage erheben"; he draws back again. 221/3: Wotan in three-quarter profile to the audience almost at the edge of the ridge to the right of the upper platform.

Brunnhilde has moved well away from the Walkyrie, who remain above the platform. 223/2: He turns back towards her, and she finds herself standing a little above him in complete silhouette. 224/1: "Du noch bist"; He moves forward again up to the steps leading to the lower platform; she moves a step toward him. The Walkyrie agitated, but still huddled together, reach the left of the upper platform without advancing further: a moment of suspense. All remain like this until 226/1, when Wotan descends to the lower platform, during which the Walkyrie take over the upper platform and Brunnhilde stays on the steps above Wotan without, 227/1, looking at him. 227/2: He turns back towards her with an imposing stance. 227/4: He makes several steps to the left, still on the lower platform. 228/1: Brunnhilde follows, falling to her knees on the large step above her, against the rock (there are still two steps remaining down to the lower platform). The Walkyrie hurl themselves onto the steps in the greatest agitation.

*"Halt ein, Vater" (Walkyrie)*

Grimgerde and Schwertleite are the first, 228/1, to arrive on the lower platform. Rossweisse and Siegrune follow them; Gerhilde and Waltraute delay, looking towards Brunnhilde, and remain on the steps, followed by Helmwige and Ortlinde. 229/2: Helmwige descends, followed at once by Gerhilde and then Ortlinde. The first to have arrived return to Brunnhilde. 230/1: During the trumpet crescendo, the Walkyrie group themselves one by one around Brunnhilde. 230/2: Gerhilde, Grimgerde and Siegrune go back towards Wotan. Helmwige remains above. 231/2: They all arrange themselves in front of Wotan as a compact group, in a savage and almost menacing way (not on their knees!). The music demands this position, or its expression is false and merely formulaic. 231/2: Wotan takes an angry step towards them; they draw back to Brunnhilde, whereupon she rises up again and waits in suspense. 233/2:

Brunnhilde falls down from the height of two steps. The Walkyrie recoil, terri-
fied, towards the right in a *tight* group, fearful and still. 234/2: "Fort jetzt";
Wotan comes *very close* to Brunnhilde, where he remains until 246/3. 234/4:
The second "Weh" of the Walkyrie is from the wings.

*The Flight of the Walkyrie*

The sky darkens again; up to now the clouds have noticeably diminished.
The clear gaps in the clouds have become more numerous; little by little the sky
has regained the appearance it had at the start of the act, except for the summit
still lost in the clouds. 235/1–2: There are many faint lightning flashes behind
the trees. 235/3: Lightning flashes reach the sky on the right, silhouetting a
group of clouds that the wind is chasing towards the left background. 235/4: A
projection like the earlier one shows the Walkyrie fleeing in the background,
*their backs to the audience.* 235/5: A second projection showing them very
indistinct and distant. The lightning dies down; the clouds diminish. The summit
reappears; the sky brightens. At the start of the following scene there are still
some wispy clouds, but the sky has become limpid and clear everywhere.
256–57 is the point at which the climax of a *restrained* sunset will occur,
confined almost entirely to the background. From 260 night falls; a light bluish-
green. At 266 a thin crescent moon rises behind the trees, dimly lighting the
scene. 237: The foreground remains dark, but the twilight brightens it enough
to make all that happens on the lower platform distinct.

Brunnhilde is on the left of Wotan (from the audience's viewpoint), in the
middle of the set. Wotan is turned in three-quarter profile to the right.
Brunnhilde has fallen to the ground, face down, her hair spread out. 239: She
stands up. 240/3: "zu gering"; Wotan turns a little towards her without making
any other movement. She remains behind him *without coming forward* until 244
when she leaves her first position. 246/3: First movement of Wotan, who draws
himself up and looks at her. 249/1: He moves forward a little on the path,
without looking at her. 249/2: She steps towards him remaining some distance
away. 249/3: He half turns towards her. 249/5: She approaches him; he moves
forward again one or two steps towards the foreground.

In response to his movement she stops, close to him, but still behind.
250/4: "dass sonst"; She takes a step on "sonst." 250/5: A step on "Gott" that
places her on the same level as Wotan. 251/2: "dich selbst"; She finds herself
in front of him, turning in profile to speak to him; "zum Spiel," his movement
is swift. 251/2–3: Wotan turns towards her sharply, and facing her, changes his
position. 252/3: He steps left into the foreground, passing in front of
Brunnhilde, who follows him without moving forward, speaking to him from
behind. 253/1: He turns back to her, sharply, and then faces front. 253/2: At
"vernichten," she does not recoil, and continues. 253/4: "in Schmerz und Leid";

She steps back again at the ferocity of what he says. 254/2: After an impatient gesture during which he does not look at her, 254/3, she climbs imperceptibly one step on to the path. Wotan closes the distance between them, and stops, 254/4, close enough to touch her.

*"Und das ich ihm in Stückenschlug"*

She recoils without moving from her position. On the "rest" they remain *thus*. Wotan regains his composure but does not change position. 255/1: He takes a step along the path. 255/3: He goes a bit higher. 255/4: "Was hast du erdacht, dass ich erdulde?"; Her back is to the audience, remaining behind Wotan who has reached the level of the lower platform. 255/4: He turns towards her. 256/2: She rushes forward, falling onto her knees before, *without touching him*. 257/1: She raises herself somewhat without standing up. 257/3–4: She falls down against him in an *unrestrained* movement clasping his knees. Wotan stands with three-quarters profile away from the audience; she, in three-quarters profile towards it. 258: She will not rise until he lifts her during his farewell, and therefore it is not until 259/1 on "Zagen" that she draws back, so that on 259/2, "freisslichen Felsen," she finds herself on the first steps leading to the upper platform. 259/3: The beauty of his stance should lead naturally to the swelling orchestral sound.

*"Leb wohl, du kühnes, herrliches Kind!"*

Wotan advances holding out his arms so as to let his spear rest unnoticed against the rock. She falls to her knees against him. He lifts her up. Until 265/2 she remains there, supported only by him. The following section—completely lyrical—must be mimed as such but with great simplicity. They remain at the middle of the lower platform. 261/4: Crescendo while in this attitude. 262/1: He relaxes it somewhat. 262/5: They are one in *front* of the other; very solemn. 263/2: He is passive; it is she who gently, with respect and supreme love, fixes her eyes on his and sinks gently onto his chest. Only then, he clasps her, resting his head on hers—the great splendor of the music is *not pantomimic* and it is in the contrasting stillness of the scene that the effect is realized and its significance revealed in all its beauty.

The limpid night is bright enough to make the figures visible, as a vague, silvery light is spread in the sky. 264/1: As noted, she remains thus, well to the right, her raised head clasped by Wotan's hands; *completely still.* 264/2: *Is not to be emphasized by any movement.* 264/3–4: Wotan, still, *without moving*, in a low voice, slowly gathering momentum; returns on "dieser Augen," to his initial tone. Brunnhilde remains still. 265/2: "nach Weltenwonne"; She makes

a vague gesture of tenderness, still gazing upon him. 265/3: "zum letzten Mal";
He leans close to her eyes. 265/4: He leans over her again, as before, with the
caress of his song, and then at 265/5, "dem Unseligen," he slowly stands up.
266/1: She lets go of him—he holds her *facing him,* to kiss her eyes.

## *"So küsst er die Gottheit von dir"*

She sinks back with no other movement. He remains still, holding her,
until 266/3, when, clasping her in both arms before him, he walks slowly to the
mound. Brunnhilde places her feet against the cleft in the earth, so that Wotan
can lay her down. The cleft is *behind* the mound, invisible, and once she is
reclining, he places her feet *on* the mound. He acts *very simply,* in the shadow,
with a simple gesture. He finds the buckler, lance and shield placed against the
rock on the right.

The thin crescent of the moon casts a silvery light. The branches stand out
in fine relief; this is not a lighting *effect*—all is perfectly *calm* and clear.
Brunnhilde sleeps, facing left, turned slightly upstage; in profile to the audience.
267/2: He turns away a little, then faces her once again as before. 267/3: He
recovers his spear from the lower platform, gravely. 267/4: He grasps it powerfully, turns the point against the lower platform (in the direction of the foreground), and *leaves it thus.* 268/4: Whatever device is used for the blows on the
rock, they must sound musically like stone on bronze. His gesture is violent,
and at 269/1 he holds the lance against the rock until 270/3.

## *Magic Fire*

269/1: One flame then two, three, four, etc., emerging from the same point
(the head of the spear), to form a beam of light *without steam.* 269/3: The beam
of light, without diminishing, seems to divide itself into a dancing, shimmering
multitude, remaining compact. 270/2: The central mass of flames spreads into
a large semicircle, sparkling and dancing; a little steam. Everything is based
on the projections that spread out, licking the rocks, intermingling, climbing
rapidly. 270/3: Wotan traces at his feet with the point of his lance as if to mark
a path which turns to his (the actor's) right. He climbs onto the rocks, and with
a sweeping gesture encompasses the ridge, the lance held upright. The fire
follows *precisely* his movement; the core of the light emanating from the point
of his lance, followed by the sparkling and the wild dance of the flames. The
steam, very light, and noiseless, in the wake of the light. The projections
spreading over everything. 270/5: The flames reach the edge of the overhang
and spread out mainly behind the ridge; descending and disappearing *quickly.*
There remains nothing but a *glimmer,* which becomes still. The ridge and

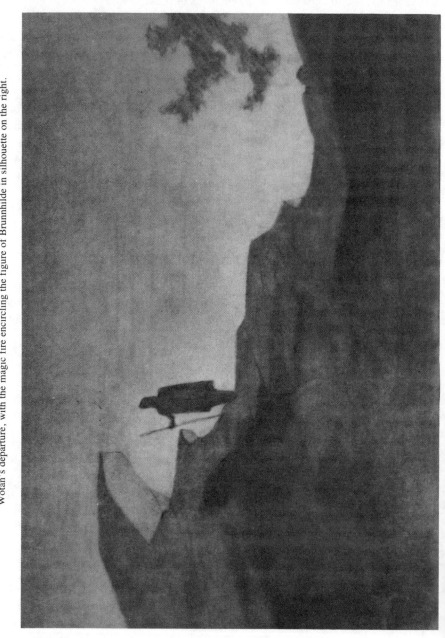

Figure 31. Design of 1892 for *The Walkyrie*, Act 3

Wotan's departure, with the magic fire encircling the figure of Brunnhilde in silhouette on the right.

summit are encircled in steam, which rises slowly, lit from *below* with a red light. In the clear and limpid sky is a high crescent moon and several pale and scant stars.

Wotan has watched the trajectory of his spear and the fire. 271/1: He reaches the steps leading to the upper platform, his head held very high, facing Brunnhilde. 271/5: He ascends as far as the upper platform. 272/1: On the platform above the steps, a hard silhouette against the light, his spear raised high at an angle in Brunnhilde's direction, his arm fully extended. 273/1: He lowers his spear, leaning against it, remaining still, his chest extended towards Brunnhilde. 273/5: He turns slowly to the left, crosses the upper platform, climbing. 274/3: He arrives on the overhang and turns back. 274/5: He disappears behind the rock into the light.

*The Final Impression of Great Stillness*

That Wotan should exit from the same place he entered would be an unfortunate effect, as if it matters to an all-powerful god.

The magic fire, being pantomimic, requires mathematical precision in relation to the music.

# *Carmen*: Act 3

The right half of the stage must be arranged to serve the opening chorus and at the same time to allow for the area of Micaela as well as her last scene with Don José. The other scenes can occasionally make use of this arrangement.

The left half of the stage is assigned to the two card scenes and to Don José on guard duty. It, too, may occasionally be used for other scenes.

The center of the stage in its entire depth serves as a passage, and the slope toward the lowland must be quite noticeable. Escamillo arrives from the center, slightly to the left (that means from the lowlands and the city), for, as he himself says, he is looking for Carmen. Also from the center, but slightly to the right, Micaela enters as though coming from a village near the city.

The sky is cloudless, and the mountains (in the rear, in front of the flatlands) stand out strongly against the bright backdrop.

The right side of the stage remains throughout in a bluish chiaroscuro. The sun strikes only the center and the left side.

For a good effect as well as for plausibility, it is necessary to assume that the act begins in late afternoon, for one does not carry contraband through a city by day. Consequently, beginning with the farewell of Escamillo, daylight is fading—the hues of sunset appear in Micaela's last scene—and a luminous night settles down in time for Escamillo's song from backstage and for the falling of the curtain.

## *Carmen*, Act 3. Scenario
### First Scene up to the Card Scene

227 (239):[25]      Two motionless guards near center stage stand out strongly against the sky.

228 (239):      One of them, as if sent by the other, turns to the right and takes a few steps; then, on the third measure of the third line, he gives a sign in the direction of the wing above, repeats the sign, climbs a bit, and gives another sign; and

| | on the sixth line he descends towards the other guard, who has remained at his place. |
|---|---|
| 229 (240): | The two guards give up their position and go to meet the six soloists, who cautiously cross the ramp down right and group themselves on and against the rocks on the right—the women at the bottom, the men above. |
| 229–30 (240–41): | Tenors and basses backstage, without the counterpoint of sopranos and altos, increase the volume a little. |
| 230 (242): | At the bottom with *"Ecoute,"* a new group backstage (increase in volume). |
| 231 (243): | The soloists take their positions. |
| 232–34 (243–45): | Soloists are seated or lying down. |
| 233 (244): | With the *f* in the first line, Mercedes rises and sings towards right, while leaning against the rock. |
| 234 (245): | Frasquita and Don José join her. |
| 235 (247): | *ff,* all rise and sing towards the right, as if waiting for someone. |
| 235 (248): | *pp,* sopranos and first basses backstage, tenors onstage, seated—as are the second basses. |
| 236 (250): | Two or three of the soloists climb slightly to the right and disappear to the rear in the same direction. |
| 237 (252): | *f,* those in the wings come closer. |
| 238 (253): | *pp,* entering from the wings, they are seen as they descend. The sopranos are on the front ramp. The second basses are on the one farther upstage; but they arrive ahead of the women in order to assist them, etc. Friendly gestures during the ensemble of the soloists and sopranos. |
| 241 (256): | *pp,* very soft and mysterious; all take positions primarily in depth, leaving the side free. |

## Second Scene

Frasquita and Mercedes are in center left, in front of the rock but somewhat in profile. Carmen, behind them higher on the rock, looks down at them.

| 255 (271): | At the bottom, Carmen, remaining on an overhanging piece, begins to sing. The other two talk softly during their musical rest, while leaning against the rock on which Carmen is sitting; but they do not play with the cards and make few gestures. Nonchalantly they take up their cards on page 259 (275). |
|---|---|
| 260 (276): | On the last line, the two get up and sing, swinging their |

bodies around and sideways, and walking to the right to stand apart, thus isolating Carmen on her rock.

## Third Scene (and Exit)

Precisely with the orchestra cue, page 264 (281), Carmen decides to step down and join the others. Her answers preceding this are given from her raised position. To listen to her, the three women—who have their arms on each other's shoulders—walk around rhythmically.

| | |
|---|---|
| 265 (282): | They take the sopranos along on their walk. |
| 266 (284): | On the *f*, all women stop in front of El Dancairo, who has watched them with a smile. |
| 267 (285): | *f*, the circle retreats; then Mercedes moves forward, singing in El Dancairo's face. With some variations, the other two play the same game [during the following passage up to][26] *"Sera même entreprenant."* This causes El Dancairo to make an impatient gesture, which is gracefully cut off by the women at the repeat of the *pp*. Thus, here is frank and lively stage action. At this *pp*, El Dancairo takes two of the women by their arms, etc. They remain on the right. |
| 271 (289): | The three women are grouped against the rock on the left. |
| 272 (291): | The sopranos, moving towards them from the right, answer them. |
| 272 (292): | Second line with the *ff*, the three women advance towards the other women, each in her turn. And the sopranos show their *élan* with the last measure of this page, until on page 273 (294) the entire ensemble forms a kind of a very large procession—partly lyric, partly comic. The women, arms on shoulders, are in front and the men behind them, all moving from right to left. |
| 275 (296): | The music to be strictly observed: the three women with their words, separate from the other women, and turn laughingly toward the men; the sopranos indicate their part by passing the three women and addressing El Dancairo, while the three women leave him and start to lead the procession. |
| 276 (297): | *ff*, the procession is formed from right to left, the three women at the head, then El Dancairo, El Remendado, and a few men. The other men remain and address the processing singing *"En avant!"* The sopranos stay and turn laughing to the three women. |

276 (298):     Second line, the three women, El Dancairo and Remendado and the few men march down towards the flatlands with their backs to the audience.

277 (298):     Third line, they have disappeared. During their exit, the rest of the gang disperses, carrying bundles to safety towards the two wings, but not upstage or center. To the left, José is fully visible against the clear sky. Micaela comes from upstage right; supporting herself on the rocks, she enters the stage and sings her aria at center right a little raised towards the rock. At first. . . .

# The Staging of Aeschylus' *Prometheus*

## (1924)

The large high platform as well as all the characters must stand out in silhouette against the clear, uniform backdrop. Yet this must not prevent the bodies, the faces, and every detail of their expression and gestures from being seen perfectly and sharply. This is the task of well-balanced lighting.

Stairs filling the entire width of the stage lead into the orchestra pit. Doors left and right are needed in the pit for exits.

These stairs are indispensable as much for the characters and their movements as for giving the impression of a mountain summit, without the rock (to which Prometheus is chained) having to be raised too high.

Neutral drapes hanging down to the stairs mask the wings on the right and left. Similar pieces mask the flies, hanging straight without folds. The backdrop is to be in the form of an even cyclorama (if feasible, of the Fortuny type). Experience will show whether a cut-out to indicate the sea is indispensable. Lighting devices are to be installed behind the platform, probably on the floor.

For the final catastrophic scene, four heavy drapes, also of neutral but dark color, are kept invisible in the flies behind the teaser and, in particular, on the left and right. After the last words of Prometheus, darkness grows, and the four drapes fall quickly on the platform and stage, intermingling with and crossing one another in an abrupt fashion that is at once surprising, shocking, and imposing. After they have fallen, the darkness is complete and the main curtain closes.

### Incidental Music

The Oceanides are announced by a very light tremolo of strings backstage on a *single chord*. Upon their entrance, this tremolo fades out imperceptibly.

The final fall of the four drapes during the catastrophe is underscored by a

Figure 32. Design of 1910 for *Prometheus*
The Basel version was more monumental and austere, a gigantic monolith entirely dominating the scene.

strong fortissimo chord (again a single chord) of brass instruments—which, rapidly decreasing, stops abruptly when the main curtain is closed. *This is a major chord.*

No other music. As these chords will then be all the music there is, they are not to be "composed," but simply selected and tastefully arranged.

**Entrances and Exits**

The three men (and Prometheus) enter from the second wing left, move diagonally to the right, and leave through the door in the orchestra pit.

The Oceanides enter from the rear center, stage left, then they form a group and scatter as the scenario suggests.

Oceanos appears suddenly with his first words at the left wing in the rear. It will be seen whether he must be raised instantaneously and how. At any rate, the impression of a trap door is to be avoided.

Io enters from the second wing right, moves diagonally, and exits through the left door in the orchestra—hence crossing the stage in the direction opposite that of the three men at the beginning.

Hermes appears behind Prometheus' rock. He does not seem to be raised by a trap, but climbs quickly, almost straight up invisible stairs. He disappears in the same manner and, if possible, a little further to the right in the rear.

All areas of the setting are thus used and made part of the action.

# *Iphigénie en Tauride*: A Scenario

(ca. 1926)

## General Considerations

The action of this drama is as simple as that of *Alcestis;* the various groupings and movements are only of external and decorative importance and will always gain through very sober planning. The true action—the core of the drama—is in the contest of generosity between the two friends; this struggle is of primary dramatic importance. Even Iphigenia's predicament can be considered of secondary importance, compared to the relation of the two friends.

It is, therefore, the task of the stage director, the designer and the characters to achieve a maximum of *human* value in a framework that is of interest only in its relation to the presence of the human being. This is true particularly in the last three acts. The location for the first act must emphasize the special place of the action: the seashore, the somewhat glaring light and the sanctuary surrounded by trees. Supported by the costumes of the Scythians, the staging will clearly express the contrast between the cult of the Greek Diana and a bloodthirsty and somewhat oriental people. The costumes and movements will fully indicate this contrast; everything around Iphigenia must preserve the simple, uniform, religious atmosphere of Greece. The Scythians, on the other hand, will give the impression of colorful abandon. The two friends are so simply dressed that they will approach the Greek style as shown by Iphigenia and her group and will almost imperceptibly function as a connecting link between the Scythians and the priestesses.

In spite of the costumes and the powerful movements of the Scythians, the spectator must take away from this drama an exclusively and purely human recollection: the framework has been there, but except for the setting of act one, it is completely eliminated by the *living* performance.

## Act 1. Setting

Backdrop sketchily indicating the horizon across the sea and a bit of naked earth. The downstage is bound right and left by two successive wings of very dark green drapes suggesting cypresses. If a stronger suggestion is desired, the folds can easily be held together at the base to indicate the trunk; however, this will weaken the general effect.

Farther upstage a few steps lead to a low terrace, leaving free a small retaining wall on both sides. In the middle of this platform is an altar, made of simple block, like the altar in act 1 of *Orfeo*. Behind it a space for movement, then again some steps in the center leading to the door of the sanctuary. The facade of the sanctuary is of rigid material to the height of a man, so that one can freely lean on it. No particular style of architecture; the pediment cannot be seen; the lines in the stone are inconspicuous and *insignificant*. The door is without ornament and of a darker tone than the wall, which appears to be white marble in the light. This facade is flanked by two slim cypresses, which might be duplicated in the rear if this is necessary to mask the side walls completely. When the door opens, the interior of the sanctuary shows a vague chiaroscuro in strong contrast to the light atmosphere outside.

The proportions of this composition are not strict. The importance of the cypresses near the sanctuary could be increased; that of the cypresses nearer downstage, minimized; more open sky could be shown in the rear; the horizon line of the sea could be raised, depending on whether one wished to locate the sanctuary on the shore or on high ground.

Page 15:[27] Iphigenia falls against the altar, but she may just as well fall on the stairs or against the sanctuary if the altar is omitted, because it inevitably hides her. Yet the altar suggests quite well in advance the drama that is going to follow, and hence it is perhaps not superfluous. Experience will decide this. Without the altar it would seem that the appearance and the movement of the priestesses before the sanctuary ought to be nobler and more stately. An altar in the *center*, on the other hand, focuses the movements.

The character of this setting is perpendicular, which is favorable to the presence of the living human being. The following two settings are likewise basically perpendicular. This arrangement accentuates the presence of the performers so strongly that the setting, barely noticed, vanishes from the consciousness and memory; the dramatic action alone triumphs.

## Lighting for Act 1

The curtain opens on the first notes of the orchestra. The stage is silent and empty, bathed in a warm light (no footlights). Vivid brightness comes from the two openings in the rear, but the sanctuary and its cypresses, as well as the

Figure 33.    Design of 1926 for Gluck's *Iphigénie en Tauride*, Act 1

cypresses downstage, are only softly outlined by the surrounding light. Slowly these silhouettes become increasingly more pronounced; the general lighting rapidly pales. Suddenly at the height of the storm the two openings in the rear become dark.

These light changes at the beginning are essential to bring out the full significance of the scenery.

Page 3: At the moment when Iphigenia and her priestesses silently enter, the openings in the rear become bright again; but although the characters are blended in the silhouette of the sanctuary, they must be clearly visible.

The light is to follow *discreetly* the course of the scene until the storm has passed completely. The lighting then comes to rest as at the beginning, without any variation. The drapes (cypresses) should certainly be of a beautiful deep color, and hang in *large* heavy folds. The floor is neutral, but the stairs and walls are like the facade of the sanctuary. The number of colors is as much reduced as possible; only the play of light and shadow will enliven the picture, in the wake of lively movement. Obviously, the sea should be a uniform blue; uniform too are the floor, the stones and the tree-drapes, each one in its particular color.

It will be necessary to indicate strongly the *outdoors,* since the other three acts are interiors. This, incidentally, is one of the most felicitous arrangements for the action and for expressing its specific inner character.

**Directing the Characters**

*General remarks:* The opening of the sanctuary door will be all the more surprising since the facade is uniform and since the setting remains empty and silent for an appreciable period of time. The priestesses are grouped on the steps and the terrace; Iphigenia, in the center. If an altar is used, Iphigenia approaches it openly and places her hand on the stone with the words: "Que nos mains saintement barbares " (p. 9).

Page 11: Movements leading Iphigenia to the altar below the upstage stairs. Her narration makes it evident that the rigid support of the altar will be very useful to the singer.

At the bottom of page 15: Iphigenia collapses against the altar as she would against a wall. The altar thus loses its significance momentarily.

From the door to the top of the downstage stairs, the entire area of the terrace around the altar is exclusively designated for Iphigenia and the priestesses. No one else will move there; Thoas, the two friends, and the guards do use the stairs downstage, but they do not reach the terrace. The friends exit from where they have entered.

Page 21: Iphigenia falls on her knees against the altar, both her arms pressed against the stone, and, if this is feasible, sings her last words with her head bowed. Then she sinks even lower. The priestesses surround her in silence. No *symmetry* here; this action will be interrupted by Thoas.

Page 22: The chorus of the priestesses becomes rather close and compact to provide, together with the rising Iphigenia, a movement behind Thoas. At this point (p. 33), the contrast between the latter and the Greek element of simple Appolinian beauty must be expressed *suddenly* by means of gestures and movements. Iphigenia and her immediate attendants always preserve their Greek bearing.

Thoas and his guards come from the same wing downstage right. The downstage stairs sharply separate the interlocutors, although Thoas uses them to vary his movements.

Page 28: The Scythians enter from four wings in the foreground.

Page 33: Iphigenia and her priestesses leave, their backs toward the audience, obviously calm, in sharp contrast to the attitude of Thoas. Upon his "Et vous, à nos dieux tutélaires," he stands diagonally on the steps of the downstage stairs, one foot lower than the other and without any sacerdotal mannerism.

Page 34: The chorus approaches Thoas and sings, partly turned towards the sanctuary. If the ballet is executed, Thoas could remain on the steps with his arms crossed and his head bent forward on his arms as though at once pensive and uneasy. Upon the arrival of the two friends through the first wing on the left, he abruptly straightens up, which explains and underlines his words: "De ton arrogance" (p. 38). Thoas steps down to the foot of the stairs.

The end of the act is optional; yet it would perhaps be a good effect to have the light gradually fade in the foreground during the exit of the two friends in order to achieve for the final chorus the following effect: horizon, floor, sanctuary, terrace, and altar in a soft brightness (especially at the top) as against the threatening chiaroscuro from the first upper step of the downstage stairs to the downstage area. Since the lighted part remains unoccupied, the effect of the Scythian chorus downstage will be right, and the curtain will close on a picture expressing beforehand the content of the drama. This kind of anticipation is desirable wherever it is justified, for the audience is unconsciously very sensitive to it and thus is put into the right frame of mind.

## Act 2. Setting

With this act we enter the extreme style expressive of the hieratic simplicity of the inner drama. The design is a spatial composition. It will be easy to add a few steps to the altar if one wishes, but the center and the right side must remain completely empty and bare. If the actress so desires, a seat may be placed at the right for this act, as it will be for act 4, a massive chair without curves (the chair

Figure 34. Design of 1926 for Gluck's *Iphigénie en Tauride*, Acts 2 and 4

in Iphigenia's room will be of wood, less heavy and with cushions). However, this seat does not seem to be necessary for the second act; it would certainly be far better to draw attention exclusively to the altar and the steps leading to it.

In act 4, the spectator will have seen this space arrangement without the seat and will remember it, so the seat then will not have the same disadvantages.

Probably the drapes of this space dedicated to crime will have to be of a somber red—but without any design—and with heavy, tight and deep folds to emphasize the scene of the Eumenides.

**Lighting of Act 2**

Diffuse, soft, and with a chiaroscuro effect. The characters are to be perfectly visible with their slightest gestures. A mystic brightness falls from above left on the altar and the steps supporting it.

Page 53: The brightness from above fades slowly, but the light is diffused softly.

Page 56: Precisely on the *f* (*grave e marcato*) of the orchestra the light is dimmed suddenly, becoming very pale. The light effects in this scene must be very restrained so that, with Iphigenia's entrance (p. 64), the normal lighting of the beginning can be restored without shock, and the whole remains a *living* scene rather than a pictorial spectacle.

The light stays normal and calm until the end.

**Directing the Characters**

*General remarks:* The two friends are seated, half lying on the lower steps of the altar.

Page 49: They are standing together on the stairs in the foreground to emphasize their tension over the arrival of the Official and the guards, who enter through the *center* of the drapes in the rear and also leave through it. Iphigenia and her priestesses enter in a long line from upstage right, walking beside the drapes and across the platform toward the altar.

Page 53: Orestes does not fall on the altar steps but entirely downstage before the downstage steps. Here he sings his aria (p. 54) and falls asleep on the steps in the foreground while the stage darkens.

As stated above, the scene of the Eumenides, if performed as spectacle, completely distorts the character of the whole staging of this drama as here conceived and, consequently, regrettably confuses the audience. This scene must, therefore, be staged according to the Dalcroze eurhythmics. The numerous openings of the setting facilitate the action, whether downstage, on either side, or upstage. Orestes is obviously unconscious during pages 56–57.

Figure 35.    Design of 1926 for Gluck's *Iphigénie en Tauride*, Act 3

His cries (p. 58) are the reaction to an approaching and encircling movement of the Eumenides.

Page 59: "Ah, quels tourments," Orestes slightly emerges from his lethargy and, with each cry, raises and drops his head, though he is visibly not in contact with his surroundings.

The ghost of Clytemnestra comes *very close* to Orestes; this immediate and terrible proximity terrifies him. Entering from the wing downstage left, she disappears into the right wing; little lighting effect.

As regards this matter, it appears to me that apparitions are always made to seem hackneyed and their effects weakened by placing them too far from the person who is supposed to see them. For instance, the ghost of Hamlet's father and the dialogue in his scenes would gain much by bringing them closer to Hamlet.

Iphigenia. Act 2.

The friends in chains.

The Official of the Sanctuary enters with the temple guard; they tear Pylades away and leave.

Orestes alone.

Scene of the Eumenides, with Orestes (apparition of Clytemnestra).

Iphigenia enters (from rear) with priestesses. Orestes is unchained. He exits with two priestesses.

Iphigenia and priestesses, bowl, libation. All leave slowly while singing. Solemn and mournful ending.

# Goethe's *Faust*, Part 1

## As a Dramatic Poem

(ca. 1927)

Carl Niessen, trans. and ed. (Bonn, Fritz Klopp Verlag), 1929. *Theatre Arts Monthly*, 16 (Aug. 1932) (abbr.)

### Introductory Remarks

Goethe called his work "a tragedy." Accordingly, *Faust* is being performed as a drama like any other tragedy.

No matter how it is staged, *Faust* cannot possibly have its full realization as a drama; yet no one in the German speaking world would forego its production.

Thus the problem remains still unsolved. Whether performed on the "Mystery Stage" as Devrient once tried it, on the Relief Stage, the Shakespeare Stage, in the Reinhardt Circus,[28] or in stylized scenery, all productions have hitherto been attempts to present a masterpiece simply as a play.

My point of view is to regard part 1 of *Faust* as a *poem,* a dramatic poem if you will, but a poem nevertheless, in the precise meaning of this word. Its dramatic character permits the transfer of this poem to the stage. In Germany and all countries close to the Germans in spirit and language one can rely on an audience which, if it does not agree with me, at least will be cultured and attentive enough to appreciate my attempt and sufficiently informed to judge it. This audience may not accept everything, but it will be able to understand my motives and to weigh their significance not only for the first part of *Faust,* but, indeed, for any dramatic poem in the future.

In this drama more than in any other the actor himself, his performance on stage, and his *literary* role dominate the production. It may be stated that the scenario of Goethe's poem is more important than the sketches accompanying it, because the sketches in themselves cannot be complete or definitive.

## Synopsis of Scenes

The action begins in Faust's study. This is where Goethe had the unfortunate idea of inserting "Part 1 of the Tragedy."

The Dedication will be read by an actress of middle age who is gifted with a particularly agreeable, dignified, quiet and warm voice. A man would tend to suggest the character of Goethe, which really is not desirable.

This female Reader will stand in the middle of the stage framed by a half-open curtain and slightly in front of another curtain falling in vertical folds. She will not hold a book in her hands but a loosely rolled parchment scroll at which she never glances.

After the Dedication, the main curtain will close slowly, and the three characters of the Prelude on the Stage will arrange themselves informally in front of the closed curtain; they are illuminated by the houselights which had been dimmed for the reading of the Dedication.

The *Poet* will be the Reader. He is chosen to read certain passages of the poem, as will be indicated later. He is basically distinguished from the others by his costume and by the restraint of his speech and gestures.

At the end of this scene, the last verses will be entrusted to the *Director*. They contradict the spectacle that awaits the audience. Goethe was a man of his time, and in addition, he possibly intended to be a little mischievous. At any rate, the Poet will discreetly express his disapproval by gesturing dejectedly and withdrawing. Thus he makes it clear that he not only disagrees with the Director, but that he is determined to oppose him. The *Jester* emphasizes this situation by paying close attention.

The Poet has entered from the right, the Director from the left, and the Jester through the center opening of the main curtain. They exit in the same manner while the houselights are slowly dimmed.

## Prologue in Heaven

This is the real beginning of the *reading*. The Reader never appears in the setting proper, let alone backstage. He is always visible against a vertical panel which is as high as the stage opening and is installed at the spot where the Reader is to stand; this panel, of neutral color, is not part of the setting but is, rather, related to the proscenium, which it resembles in color and texture. It can be pushed forward as desired and also quickly moved into the wings. It must be so built that it does not shake. We shall call it *The Reader's Wing*.

Words given from offstage by an invisible speaker throw a chill on the audience and destroy the harmony of a production.

In the Prologue in Heaven the Lord could not appear anyhow, and the Archangels would always remain paltry figures. So here the reading of the poem is imperative.

The *Reader,* standing, must never become theatrical, that is, affected by the scenic action, but must always be strictly literary though very animated. The contrast between Reader and actor must remain complete.

The costumes and the panel are not enough for the Reader to register visually; he will have to hold his head in a particular manner, addressing neither the audience nor the stage. He will simply read the poem without specific emphasis and without the assumption that anyone is listening to him. He should not in any way seem to be a part or even refer to the action on stage, nor should he show any concern with the spectators' reaction.

And this is not all! He is a *Reader,* not a narrator! How can he show this fine distinction?

The Reader should hold a book in his hands, in both hands. This book should be beautiful and noble, like an old manuscript bound in soft leather. It should have the form that sculpture and painting have made classic. Its center fold should be deep and narrow; its open leaves should form a curve which first rises and then falls.

The Reader must never give the impression of reading! He will never turn a page. The book lies in his hands like an emblem in the hands of a deity. It prevents him from making gestures that might bring him close to the dramatic action, and permits him to make only those restrained, affirmative, negative or neutral movements of the arms that are possible while the hands are firmly holding an important object. The rest of his body shares in this characteristic restraint, thus giving him a harmony and a monumental rhythm in the true sense of these terms. His rhythm then stands out in contrast to the nervous, restless, and, more or less, arbitrary movements of the action on stage.

So as to indicate clearly that this is a reading, the Lord is to be read by the Reader standing *opposite* the place from which Mephistopheles seems to hear His voice coming. A second Reader, used for this scene, will stand at the other side. Since Mephistopheles does not address the Archangels, no dramatic mistake is possible with them.

Mephistopheles will stand in the center, a bit upstage, his head turned upward to the right towards the Archangels, whereas the Reader of the Lord is on the left.

The drapes in the rear are closed, and dimly and uniformly lighted. The traveler in the first wing, three-fourths open, leaves enough space right and left for the rigid panels of the Readers.

A broad beam of light of as even a width as is feasible crosses the inner stage from high up right to the floor left. It touches Mephistopheles's head so that the actor will stand out in a silhouette before the rear curtain.

The setting is not deep. Faust's study could be ready on wagons, for the scene shift must be *very brief*.

*From the beginning,* during the stanzas of the Archangels, Mephistopheles turns his head in the direction of the Lord since, unconcerned about the Archangels, he looks elsewhere.

With the "closing" of heaven, the diagonal beam fades slowly while the two Readers withdraw, each to his respective wing.

For a while Mephistopheles will watch; then he will advance swiftly and, leaving center stage, make a few steps to the left where the Reader of the Lord was and, finally, disappear imperceptibly in the darkness. He will *not* address the audience. His brief monologue is addressed jocularly to himself. His unconcern with the Archangels is in keeping with protocol. The actor emphasizes thereby that he knows the ritual that precedes and accompanies the appearance of the Lord. Patiently he will wait until it is finished.

### General Views on the Characters

The poem of *Faust,* part 1, has only one character: Faust. Mephistopheles represents an integral part of Faust.

On stage, there are two characters, two separate bodies. Thus it is the actors' task to unite them like the front and back of a medal.

The two performers of the single character of Faust—that is, Faust and Mephistopheles—must attempt to resemble each other in figure, attitude, inflection, and gestures. What is required is not identity in these respects, but an interchangeable similarity that rarely appears in both at the same time. Gestures and inflections of Mephistopheles must remind the audience of Faust and vice versa.

The Mephistophelian part of Faust will, in spite of everything, give him a stature that will prevent Faust's degradation, but at the same time, it will emphasize the fated dualism in Faust. The Faustian tone in Mephistopheles will dignify his sarcasm.

Mephistopheles has to change his character hardly at all when he comes in contact with the episodic characters of Martha, Margaret, Valentine, or the ruffians in Auerbach's Cellar. Faust however is *warped* by these mean contacts and is visibly conscious thereof; his conversation with Mephistopheles in the atmosphere of loose morals surrounding the two women is almost pitiable. He tries to hide his shame under a swaggering and vulgar bearing, as is very well indicated in the dialogue. These are probably the passages where it is most obvious that the two characters are one. Mephistopheles rises a notch to join Faust in his fall.

Faust does not talk to Martha, nor will Martha talk to Faust. Faust's remorse about Margaret's fleeting appearance in his life remains superficial; it does *not* reach the depth of his very being. Faust rightly feels that he is immortal, and Mephistopheles is always present to remind him of it.

Wagner comes in contact with Faust only twice, both times before the arrival of Mephistopheles. He plays the part of a confidant during the monologues spoken by Faust in his presence.

It would be wrong to make Wagner a figure of fun, since he has access to Faust's study day and night, and the honor of accompanying him on his walks. Faust expresses respect for him and treats him with gentleness and courtesy.

That Wagner's part borders on the ridiculous is due to the intellectual content of the text, not to his appearance and accent. It may even be desirable to have Wagner look distinguished, in order to stress the amiable folly of his words.

Faust's meeting with the Peasant merely gives him an opportunity to show the dignified manner in which he receives those who address him.

Auerbach's Cellar is a strange example of Faust's split personality. Mephistopheles too must guard against playing the clown; on the contrary, he should strictly preserve the same assumed dignity that Faust thinks it advisable to show during revels, from which he is not as aloof as he pretends to be.

In the admirable scene between Mephistopheles and the Student, the actor will do well to take on Faust's inflections and gestures. Here the effect of identity has an incomparable flavor if Mephistopheles can keep his grand manner as well.

There is no need for the *Student* to behave like a young simpleton, as is usually done; this makes his part too easy. He believes he is in Faust's study facing Faust. This alone gives his timidity an appearance of modesty mixed with an awareness of the privilege he enjoys. The audience watches this important scene with extreme attention, not missing a single nuance. This puts great responsibility upon the actors.

Both the charm and the dignified classic pace of this scene are shattered *suddenly* with the banal entrance of Faust, who is about to undergo his well-known sentimental degradation. The dialogue indicates this with a precision painful to endure.

At the Witch's Kitchen, Faust must show that what he sees there is not strange to him, and that he is embarrassed about it. He again assumes his grand air. Mephistopheles's familiarity is by contrast frank and sympathetic. It will express what Faust in his degradation is trying so hard to conceal.

Faust indeed *begins* to deteriorate when faced with the Woman's image. Of course, this concerns the female body in general, and not yet a sentimental petit-bourgeois girl. Faust may still keep something of his lofty air, although it is considerably weakened in the Witch's sordid environment.

The meeting with Margaret in the street indicates conclusively Faust's degradation. The dialogue becomes commonplace. From this point on, Mephistopheles will gain in stature.

Margaret's role is difficult. Her insignificant personality is so far below the level of Faust, her sentimentality so incapable of elevating her to her beloved, that the audience ought to feel this, but they rarely do. The audience become immediately interested in this episode as if it were a major event. They do not perceive the scene as representing Faust's downfall and the first step toward his subsequent blunders, but resolutely regard the two characters as equally significant, indeed showing even more sympathy for Margaret's fate than for Faust's. Thus the poem, as performed, is in danger of going awry. Fortunately there is the "Forest and Cavern" scene to restore balance.

Stage director and actors will find the effect of this scene impossible to reduce, so they will have to try their best to minimize the importance of the Margaret episode by emphasizing its depressing influence on the hero, Faust, in contrast to the new stature thereby given to Mephistopheles. On this balance between the two characters, which constitutes psychologically the personality of Faust, depends the dignity of the poem, and that of those who witness it.

Martha's part is so effective that the actress should rather underplay it than try to make it a personal success.

In the Garden Scene, during the Walk, Mephistopheles plays a parody of a role that Faust would consider more entertaining than the one given to him. Mephistopheles knows this very well indeed; and Faust, being aware of it, envies him.

This scene is dangerous since it seems to concern only poor Margaret. Faust will stress his *physical* desire, and the uneasiness he feels in employing such means to gain his goal. Mephistopheles is pleased with himself.

Forest and Cavern is one of the principal scenes of the poem. The parallel identity of the two characters is presented to us in a dualism that is plainly visible and superbly expressed. The two actors can never study the dialogue *together* enough, since it is actually a monologue.

The spectator must sense something close to ecstasy.

The second Garden Scene definitely establishes Faust's degradation. The crude intrusion of Mephistopheles therefore offers the spectator justified relief.

Valentine's Street will show us Faust debased enough to allow the serenade and the action following it. With a single gesture Faust could stop this scandal, but he watches it without raising an eyebrow. His duel is a farce, since Faust has reached a degree of flabby baseness that make his flight quite natural.

The Cathedral Scene is merely an episode, but the audience expects much of it. It should therefore be given its emotional value without being turned into a theatrical spectacle.

The dialogue between Faust and Mephistopheles after the Walpurgis Night is like the Forest and Cavern scene, only more brutal. In this scene Mephistopheles must try to resemble Faust. For instance, "She's not the first one (*Sie ist die erste nicht*)"[29] is spoken as if Faust himself is seeking consolation in cynicism.

*The Prison.*—For the first time, Faust faces inescapable reality. It matters little whether this reality concerns Margaret or anything else. This is Hamlet unable to shun action any longer; Faust feels that he has no choice left. Margaret's moving appeal should convince him of this.

Mephistopheles must deliver the words, "Here to me! (*Her zu mir!*)" with the utmost contempt, as if he would say to Faust "Now you see how incapable you are! You are nothing but a shameless intellectual. Let us go on with our adventures!" Faust of course says this to himself too. He does not play a fine role. The only active and noble being at the end is the Reader.

Yet the audience's sympathy must remain with Faust as he is, not with Margaret. The Reader's indignation forces the audience to this position. Only in this way does the first part call for the second, while at the same time it preserves its unity.

### Faust's Study

For the first scene in this room until the setting changes, the lighting should have a romantic atmosphere that varies frequently with the several episodes. This is in contrast to the two later scenes where the lighting is normal and ordinary. The curtain at the window remains closed.

Faust's sleep is his own, not ours. Hence, the light remains unchanged, leaving all commentary to the Reader.

During the entire Poem, the décor should emphasize Faust. Whatever does not concern him *directly* operates through contrast. He always stands out from his environment. For this purpose steps are employed to support his armchair and to separate him from the window. These levels give variety to the movements of Wagner, Mephistopheles and the Student, while contributing to Faust's isolation.

The lack of Romanticism excludes the showing of books and other visible properties. Only the magic book during the first scene in the Study and the Bible during the second are placed open on the reading desk. In order to get the cup and the vial of poison, Faust goes off behind the drapes.

At the beginning, the window is partly visible, and moonlight falls dimly on Faust. With his "O that full moon, thou didst but glow (*O sachst du, voller Mondenschein*)," Faust moves up to the window and gently opens the curtain further. The light increases, accenting Faust in an expressive silhouette. With "Ah me! am I still stuck and forced to dwell, Imprisoned in this musty cursed

Figure 36. Design of 1927 for *Faust*; Faust's Study

cell? (*Weh! Steck ich in dem Kerker noch?*)" Faust violently draws the curtain again and the room is left in uniform shadow. The window is no longer visible.

Lest he risk personification, the Reader as the Earth Spirit enters slowly from the left wing *before* the incantation, about at "How heavenly powers ascend, descend (*Wie Himmelskräfte auf und niedersteigen*)."

The Earth Spirit is assumed to be in the right wing, that is, behind the desk and *opposite* the Reader. He is indicated only by a beam of light. His true presence is in Faust.

The Reader leaves as he entered, unnoticed, upon "And not even like to thee! (*Und nicht einmal dir!*)," not before. Then Wagner enters from left.

With "A festal lofty greeting (*Als festlich hoher Gruss*)" Faust does *not* turn toward the window, but, descending, moves toward the audience to stage center radiant with joy. There he remains until the end without ever turning toward the setting. This is essential.

### Easter Choir

The two Readers, one from right, the other from left, have entered at "So now come down (*Nun komm heraus!*)" at the very moment when the audience's attention is on Faust. The panel for the Reader on the left has already been placed; the Reader on the right (the Angels) lightly closes the curtain from the right side while his panel is being pushed between him and the curtain so as to isolate him from the scenery.

At "What a deep humming (*Welch tiefes Summen*)" Faust remains in the indicated position without turning or suggesting in any way that the chorus originates on earth. This is an inner experience. Goethe himself did not mention that the chorus should come from a nearby church.

The bells begin to ring very softly and, if feasible, simultaneously from right, left, and upstage; this will prevent their assignment to any specific location. They decrease during "rare spices we carried (*mit Spezereien*)" and increase during "Christ is ascended (*Christ ist erstanden*)." Then they decrease again during Faust's monologue and become louder once more, to end in sonorous beauty during the last passage.

Faust does *not* fall to his knees. At the end he stands *erect,* his shining eyes look directly into the audience, not toward heaven.

The choruses are a mixture of recitation and song, sometimes simultaneously, sometimes alternately. Here is the idea: Upon "A festal lofty greeting (*Als festlich hoher Gruss*)" the bells begin ringing almost imperceptibly. The angel choir is widely spread backstage and sings, barely enunciating the words, while the Reader on the right speaks them with great firmness. Then the choir stops, but the bells continue to ring softly, and the Reader on the left speaks "Rare spices we carried (*mit Spezereien*)." At the second "Christ is ascended (*Christ*

*ist erstanden),"* the chorus clearly sings the words but does not yet use full volume. The Reader is silent.

It is difficult to decide the most effective ending without experimenting on the stage. Of course, the third angel choir "Christ is ascended" must burst into magnificent sound as soon as Faust exclaims "The earth has me again! (*Die Erde hat mich wieder!*)." For this last passage, a good number of male singers could perhaps be placed in the orchestra pit in front of Faust in addition to the invisible singers backstage. This would provide a striking effect.

Yet, how to *read* the chorus of the disciples at the same time? Perhaps by interrupting the chorus after "Joy e'er the tomb! (*Freudig Euch los!*)." The Reader would step slowly forward and speak these lines with a very lively and sonorous voice lest he present too great a contrast to the singing. This will lead to "Actively pleading him (*Tätig ihn preisenden*)," a musical passage with a strong crescendo ending with "To you the Master's near (*Euch ist der Meister nah*)," to be executed with extraordinary fullness, especially by the group in the orchestra pit.

At the climax the lights will fade imperceptibly. Faust should *not* return into the setting but exit slowly through the left wing, following the Reader.

**Outside the City Gate**

The intermission should be brief.—This scene, up to Wagner's and Faust's ascent of the rock, is difficult to stage. It takes the dedicated participation by all to assure perfect playing, which alone can make the audience forget its resistance, carrying it away in spite of itself.

Faust's first lines up to "from ice they are freed (*vom Eis befreit*)" are read by the Reader to the audience's left. He *reads* and does not attempt to enliven the pantomimic scene through realistic intonations.—There is no music.

The characters have to fit into this particular atmosphere. They only *indicate* their various parts discreetly without necessarily following the text as it is read. The pantomime has an independence similar to that of the Reader. These two attitudes emphasize the passive and contemplative mood of Faust and Wagner. It will, perhaps, be necessary to separate the pantomime from the area assigned to Faust and Wagner by means of a gauze scrim that will alter the appearance and color of that area.

Faust and Wagner, definite but not dark silhouettes, remain motionless until Faust begins to speak. From then on, the two characters start moving slightly. *Immediately* after the soldiers cross the steps the pantomimic action grows blurred and gloomy, fading out entirely before Faust's "Here I am Man (*Hier bin ich Mensch*)." This is also where the two characters slowly leave their places.

Faust's realistic comment on the walk from the city comes afterwards and

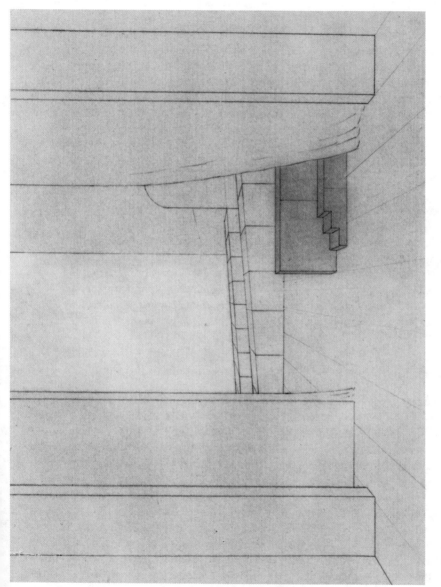

Figure 37.    Design of 1927 for *Faust*; Outside the City Gate

is addressed only to his companion. Wagner obeys the words "Now turn around (*Kehre Dich um*)" for which Faust seems to assume the Reader's inflection. . . .

An undefined peasant music accompanies the shepherd stanzas, which the Reader recites with much charm and humor, but without giving great importance to them.

While the attention of the audience is attracted by the entrance of the old peasant and some extras, the Reader quietly disappears; this brief scene is to be treated "à la Shakespeare," serving as a link between the boldness of the preceding and the truly ideal simplicity of the succeeding scene (On the Rock). A traveler closes slowly in front of the city. The Reader's panel on the left is pulled back into the wings, as the platform of Faust and Wagner disappears on the right. The two parts of the traveler join from left and right.

The steps of the Rock itself are pushed in from the left very slowly and *visibly* with deliberate obvious solemnity while Faust dismisses the peasant and extras with a simple benevolent gesture.

**Scene on the Rock**

Faust climbs step by step the rock he knows so well; he does so in silence and stops occasionally on the stairs. Wagner, sensing the solemnity of the hour, follows him. During this scene he remains generally below Faust on the steps. Upon "The Circle narrows; he is already near! (*Der Kreis wird eng; schon ist er nah!*)," Faust rises. Upon "You're likely right (*Du hast wohl recht*)," Faust begins to descend and to turn to the right.

The intermission should be as brief as possible.

**Faust's Study (Second Time)**

The curtains in the rear are closed. Faust enters from the left. It is an easy matter for him to indicate the poodle's presence through his behavior and gestures. He sits down upon "I have experienced this in ample measure (*Davon hab ich so viel Erfahrung*)." The large Bible lies on his desk.—At "In the beginning was the deed (*Im Anfang war die Tat*)," the Reader enters *from the right*.

The poodle remains invisible on the left where Mephistopheles appears.

It is unnecessary to act out Faust's speeches; hence no steam and no changes in the lighting when Mephistopheles steps forward.

Faust and Mephistopheles should use the steps with dexterity, precision, and much care. The light downstage *right* and the complete immobility of the Reader make his presence scarcely noticeable. He will disappear imperceptibly to the right, speaking his last lines almost with closed lips. Upon "He sleeps! (*Er schläft!*)," the Reader is no longer on stage.

Between the exit of Mephistopheles and the awakening of Faust, there is a long *silence* while the setting remains absolutely unaltered. With Faust's last lines the curtain closes.

### Faust's Study (Third and Last Time)

Faust is seated. Long silence! On "A knock? (*Es klopft?*)," Mephistopheles enters from left.

During Faust's maledictions, the Reader enters unnoticed from the right and later disappears slowly upon "Cease with your brooding grief to play (*Hör auf mit deinem Gram zu spielen*)." Faust exits right, passing in front of his desk.—The Student enters from the left.

In order to give this exquisite scene its greatest effectiveness, Mephistopheles must copy Faust to the point of absurdity, and the Student must move intelligently. Following his entrance speech, he remains stage right. Mephistopheles should not rise suddenly upon "Yet he who grasps the moment's gift (*Doch der den Augenblick ergreift*)" as is usually done; rather, he should bend over the desk after a silent, obscene smile. He does not rise until his "Dear friend, all theory is gray (*Grau, teurer Freund, ist alle Theorie*)," and does not sit down again to write, but remains standing until the end of the scene.

Faust returns from the right.

The magic of the last exit is indicated when the two characters mount the steps in the rear and Mephistopheles holds the curtain apart, revealing that the wall and the window, which the spectator expects to see, have been removed. All that remains is a void into which the actors vanish as the curtain rapidly closes. The entire business is quite unexpected, simple and yet moving.

### Auerbach's Cellar

This scene is very easy and utterly unimportant besides. Faust must separate himself from everyone else with a dignity and a disgust somewhat simulated and hypocritical.

The exit must be handled as naturally as the entrance. No special lighting effects. The sorcery exists in the lines alone.

### Witch's Kitchen

This scene is of interest only as a stimulus for Faust's hypocritical disgust. Faust stands firm and straight on both feet, nobly erect, whereas everything else surrounding him is distorted, abnormal, anarchic, and vile. The monkeys are never erect, and Mephistopheles is too much in his element to behave like a human being.

Faust therefore represents humanity in this odious scene. His bearing will be accented also by the place he quickly takes upon his entrance, against a pillar on the right. He leaves it only for a brief moment when he submits to the hocus-pocus of the Witch.

A ramp in front of the right pillar affords him an impressive position. Behind the pillar he later presumably sees the woman of whom he speaks.

Precisely at Faust's "What do I see (*Was seh ich?*)," a very soft arpeggio of a harp is heard from the wings. As previously, this could hardly be called music but merely serves as an indication of whatever it is that Faust sees.

During the *entire* scene steam emanates continuously from the second wing on the left where the invisible cauldron is assumed to be and whence the Witch leaps out. The slanting lines of the setting are broken and blurred by this moving mist, which also obscures the actors.

The lighting is gloomy and depressing, not red! During the apparition there should be a vague, very discreet, dim light behind the drapes right.

Faust and Mephistopheles enter upstage right through the last wing.

As few properties as possible. Since Faust's rejuvenation is, dramatically speaking, a very ambiguous matter, muffled and evenly spaced gong beats accompany the Witch's absurd declamation of "This you must ken (*Du musst verstehen*)." These sounds fade during the intervention of Mephistopheles "Enough, o Sibyl excellent, enough (*Genug, genug*)."

The musical chord is *not* repeated at the end when Faust demands to be shown the wonderful image again. Fast curtain.

A very brief intermission.

### Meeting in the Street

In front of the main curtain "à la Shakespeare." Margaret comes through the middle of the curtain, opening it a little, and walks toward the left.

Faust enters left and Mephistopheles right, and both move right.

Simplicity.

### Margaret's and Martha's Rooms

Small size and poverty distinguish these rooms from the other settings. The stage floor proper is too good for them; a platform must be built on rollers so that it can easily be moved forward and backward. Furthermore, Margaret's room should change its dimensions depending on the presence or absence of Faust. Here a scenic hierarchy of values is needed; therefore, the frame of the setting should be narrowed immediately after Faust's exit and even further for "All my peace is gone (*Meine Ruh ist hin*)." With "I would give something, could I say (*Ich gäb was drum, wenn ich nur wüsst*)," Margaret's room may take on larger dimensions on account of Faust.

Faust and Mephistopheles come from the corridor through the upstage door left, through which Margaret entered. Margaret exits upstage right at the foot of her bed; she returns the same way.—The mirror, invisible, is assumed to be on the right wall at the head of the bed. The bed is merely indicated by means of drapes, which Faust opens a little and closes on "And thou (*Und du*)."

After the exit of Faust and Mephistopheles, there is a rather long pause. The stage remains empty, and the frame is slowly narrowed before Margaret returns.

The lighting is simple, suitable for an interior, making the characters clearly visible. A little light may perhaps fall from the wing downstage left, suggesting a window, which Margaret "opens" on her return.—No lamp.

## Street

Like the Meeting in the Street, this scene is to be staged "à la Shakespeare" in front of the curtain. But Goethe's precise directions must be observed: Faust is alone for a considerable time. He humbly comes and goes, unable to make up his mind about Margaret. There is nothing of the noble bearing he showed in the "Forest and Cavern" scene.

## Martha's Room

The principle applied to Margaret's room prevails here too, except that Martha's room is larger and appears only once. Merely a few pieces of furniture. Realism is barely indicated. Martha's strong personality makes up for everything.

Through the rather large window Margaret can be seen approaching from right. From her hasty steps we can guess what will happen.

During the entire scene Margaret remains *behind* the table; she does not lead the action.

A small curtain over the peephole in the door helps the first business with Martha and Mephistopheles. He approaches from left without being seen. He stays primarily on the left side of the room and moves to the right only quite cautiously. For his story he takes a stool and sits down in profile to the audience rather than facing it; sometimes he turns three-quarters away while looking casually through the window.

## The Garden

This setting, as something to look at, is not important; but its arrangement is important, because in it is played a long scene entirely made of parallel comings and goings, which must be carefully blocked.

A trellis represents Martha's well-kept garden. On rare occasions, the lawn may perhaps be modestly indicated by painted canvas strips or, better still, by pieces of soft fabric slung around the base of the trellis.

On the other hand, the backdrop, fairly well downstage, should be colored only generally; it should represent nothing definite. This will further emphasize the coming and going of the characters. Shadows on this backdrop must be avoided.

The front part of the trellis folds in the center at a right angle to the footlights to indicate the *garden house,* which marks the end of the setting. To prevent it from shaking, this will certainly need to be supported at the top by ropes, pulley and counterweight. Margaret herself folds up the trellis.

There is no bench until the second garden scene. It should be placed against the downstage ending of the trellis, a little to the left.

*Coming and Going in the Garden:* Faust and Margaret enter talking from the first wing left. Approximately in the center they stop for a moment, then disappear into the right wing.

Mephistopheles and Martha enter from the third wing to the right, in the area between the backdrop and the trellis. They exit left on the same plane without touching each other.

Faust and Margaret return from right using the free area where the trellis pieces meet downstage. Afterwards they exit first wing left.

Mephistopheles and Martha, returning from the second wing left, cross this time, further downstage, between the two trellises. Remaining as briefly as possible in the free area on the right, they leave through the right wing without coming far downstage.

Faust and Margaret, returning through the first wing left, come to center stage, where Margaret picks a flower just behind the trellis. Of course she merely goes through the motion of picking a flower that is not there!

Margaret flees towards the right, pursued by Faust. She hurries back from the upper right wing and, making a semicircle toward downstage, arrives at the end of the first trellis, which she draws to herself; behind it, facing the audience, she waits for Faust, a finger on her lips.

Faust returns downstage right. The rest is easy to stage; Martha and Mephistopheles return from right but avoid the downstage area. Margaret leaves by herself after the others have left, again on the right.

The idealized nature of the garden house is indicated by omitting of the door. Consequently Margaret and Faust pass in front of the downstage end of the trellis which she had pulled away.

For the second garden scene, the first trellis will be restored as it was before. The bench adjoins the place downstage where the trellis had been folded.

## Forest and Cavern

This is probably the most important scene of the entire Poem, not because of its décor, but because it restores majesty to Faust, and within a minor action at that.

Representing a dramatic parallel to the Rock Scene that follows the Walk from the City, it has so magnificent an effect that the entrance and presence of Mephistopheles are almost unbearable.

The effect depends primarily on lines and silhouettes; however, the lighting must not create a romantic impression nor that of a landscape.

Mephistopheles enters downstage right or left; he stays a bit *outside* the atmosphere of the scenery, somewhat "à la Shakespeare." If Faust can in his movements bring out the fine shades of expression, a most pathetic contrast will be the result.

## Fountain and *Mater Dolorosa*

These episodes are brief and unimportant ones, and are decoratively treated as such. The fountain has also been in the setting for the house of Margaret and Valentine. The lighting is somewhat romantic. Martha's window is on the right; Margaret's front door, on the left. She enters with a pail in her hand. Lieschen, with a full pail, returns supposedly from the fountain in the first right wing, and then disappears up the street in the center. Margaret walks to the right where Lieschen came from and where the fountain is assumed to be.

Almost no pause.

The street setting remains for the *Mater dolorosa,* but it is narrowed by a traveler. Only a cut-down flat is visible, representing the wall with the Holy Virgin. In the center an indistinct opening fades into a dark lane.

Not a trace of realism. Margaret is slumped on the floor. Only the area of the flat with the Virgin is lighted, thus indicating suitably the ephemeral nature of the setting.

## Street, for Valentine

Exactly the same setting as for the fountain. The blocking can easily be determined. The corner of Margaret's house is the best area for Mephistopheles. Both he and Faust enter from upstage or the right wing.

It would be good for Valentine to collapse and die against his sister's house, not simply on the floor, and by no means center or downstage.

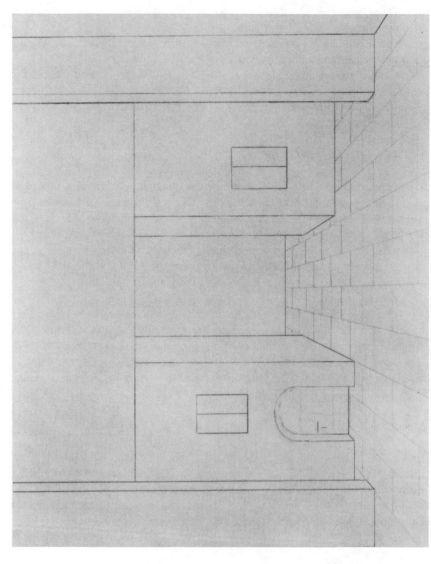

Figure 38.  Design of 1927 for *Faust*; Street

## Cathedral

Like the Prison scene later on, the scene in the Cathedral is especially difficult to place, because it is an episode concerning only Margaret and is of no importance whatsoever. Nevertheless, the audience expects it to be extremely impressive.

Here, then, is the setting that seems to me most likely to solve this problem:

Not the stage, but the auditorium should be considered the space of the Cathedral. For this purpose the house must be lighted.

Two rigid flats close up the stage at the second wing; at the end of each flat is a pillar, equally rigid. Between these pillars, the center stage is closed by a curtain such as may be seen, for instance, in Italy when one enters a church. This curtain can be opened at one side only by lifting and dropping it. It constitutes a kind of modest entrance.

The light one sees when the curtain is lifted is that of an average street in the evening. In other words, outdoor lighting. The light downstage, however, is the same as in the auditorium, the Cathedral, where the audience is.

A brief silence follows the opening of the main curtain.—The stage is empty; then three or four poor people enter timidly and kneel down at both sides facing the audience. Pause!—Margaret enters and holds up the curtain uneasily and hesitantly, politely, allowing a little breathless woman (Neighbor) to pass; the latter kneels before Margaret does.

Margaret kneels almost in the center, close to the woman, perhaps a little more downstage for her gesture at the end of the scene, which would be impressive if she were to bend backward with her arm stretched out and her hand clenched.

The choir, a double male quartet, is placed in the orchestra pit. No female or children's voices. We, the spectators, represent the congregation.

It is evident that, except for the choir, Margaret *herself* should speak the entire dialogue, alternating with two different voices.

The main curtain closes slowly to emphasize the solemnity of the place.

Thus this difficult scene will have no scenic interest but, due to its arrangement, dramatic significance. The audience will surely be conscious of this fact.

## The Prison

A delicate episode that apparently concerns only Margaret, yet it is the last scene of the Poem. The solemn mood must not be dispelled, and the audience must understand that things are *not* yet concluded, that a second part of the Poem must follow.

The plan for the setting is very simple and need not be fully described, except for the use to be made of it and of the traveler. Margaret is not seen at

Figure 39.    Design of 1927 for *Faust*; Prison Cell

the beginning; this emphasizes Faust and the dramatic idea, which must be preserved at all times. And again at the end, Margaret can no longer be seen, whereas Faust remains still within sight.

It is the Reader, however, who becomes most important in this final scene and who drives home its full impact with the last words of the Poem.

The voices at the end must be blended with scrupulous precision. "She is judged! (*Sie ist gerichtet!*)" is to be spoken by Mephistopheles very casually, but his "Here to me? (*Her zu mir?*)" should be accompanied by an intimate and impudent gesture.

Faust and Mephistopheles return to *Life*.

There is a slight pause after Margaret's "I shrink from you (*Mir graut's vor Dir*)" while the traveler is closing. This is necessary to make the dialogue clear.

On "She is saved! (*Ist gerettet!*)" the Reader intrudes almost violently, from downstage left. *Hastily* making a few steps toward the audience, he takes center stage and closes his book with a noble gesture as the main curtain closes.

All this must be executed with precision in order to emphasize the Ending. The final note of indignation should lead the audience back to Faust's character.

"Henry, Henry! (*Heinrich, Heinrich!*)" is heard clearly from the prison, not from above. The emphasis must be simple and natural without any idealization.

At first, the traveler in front of the cell is closed as far as the partition that separates it from the corridor.

Faust needs no lamp but should unobtrusively carry a key.

At the moment when Faust opens the prison door, the traveler parts *very* fast. This business corresponds precisely with Margaret's appearance.

Margaret may, if she so wishes, move freely in the downstage area, but she must never pass beyond the cell partition on the right.

Mephistopheles does *not* use the door at "Off or you are lost and lorn! (*Auf oder Ihr seid verloren!*)." He enters into the dramatic action by passing in front of the cell partition right, yet without going much further. The cell is repugnant to him.

Upon her "Judgment of God! (*Gericht Gottes!*)," Margaret *recoils* to the upstage center area of the cell, where she remains.

Between "She is judged! (*Sie ist gerichtet!*)" and "Is saved! (*Sie ist gerettet!*)" the traveler closes in front of the cell. At "Henry (*Heinrich*)" this traveler reaches the right wing, thus covering the entire setting, while the main curtain closes slowly.

# Notes

## Introduction

1.  Georg Fuchs, "Die Schaubünne der Zukunft," *Das Theater,* vol. 15 (Berlin, 1905), 33.

2.  Lee Simonson, *The Stage Is Set* (New York, 1932), 355.

3.  Lee Simonson, "Appia's Contribution to the Modern Stage," *Theatre Arts Monthly,* 16, no. 8 (Aug. 1932): 642.

4.  Simonson, *The Stage Is Set,* 352, 359.

5.  Adolphe Appia, "Theatrical Experiences and Personal Investigations," an essay of about 1921, included in part 1 of this volume.

6.  Adolphe Appia, *Die Musik und die Inscenierung* (Munich, 1899), 48. Published in English (trans. Robert W. Corrigan and Mary Douglas Dirks, ed. Barnard Hewitt) as *Music and the Art of the Theatre* (Coral Gables, Fla., 1962).

7.  Cosima Wagner, quoted in Dietrich Mack, *Der Bayreuther Inszenierungsstil* (Munich, 1976), 52.

8.  Gernot Giertz, *Kultus ohne Götter* (Munich, 1975), 119.

9.  As Salzmann himself described it, "Instead of a lighted space, we have light-producing space. Light is conveyed through the space itself, and the linking of visible light sources is done away with." "Licht, Belichtung und Beleuchtung," *Claudel-Programmbuch* (Hellerau, 1913), 70.

10. Karl Storck, *Emile Jaques-Dalcroze* (Stuttgart, 1912), 98.

11. H. C. Bonifas, "A Propos des Fêtes d'Hellerau," *Jeunesse littéraire,* 29 June 1913.

12. Serge Wolkonski, "Meine Erinnerungen," ed. E. Feudel, *In Memoriam Hellerau* (Freiburg im Breisgau, 1960), 24.

13. Upton Sinclair, *World's End* (New York, 1940), 5. Sinclair opens his book by using Hellerau as a suggestive example of an attitude towards the humanizing force of art upon life which was soon to be brutally overwhelmed by the First World War.

14. For a fuller account of the work at Hellerau, see Richard C. Beacham, "Adolphe Appia, Emile Jaques-Dalcroze, and Hellerau: Part One," *New Theatre Quarterly* 1, no. 2 (May 1985): 154–64; and "Adolphe Appia, Emile Jaques-Dalcroze, and Hellerau: Part Two," *New Theatre Quarterly* 1, no. 3 (Aug. 1985): 245–61.

15. Bonifas, "A Propos des Fêtes d'Hellerau."

16. Appia used this as a motto at the beginning of *Music and the Art of the Theatre,* together with Friedrich Schiller's "When music reaches its noblest power, it becomes form."

17. Adolphe Appia, *L'Oeuvre d'art vivant* (Geneva, 1921), published in English (trans. H. D. Albright, ed. Barnard Hewitt), as *The Work of Living Art* (Coral Gables, Fla., 1960), 64–65.

18. Edward Gordon Craig (1872–1966), the English actor, director, designer, and writer who, together with Appia, is credited with laying down much of the theoretical basis for the modern theatre.

19. The letter is in Richard C. Beacham, "'Brothers in Suffering and Joy': The Appia–Craig Correspondence," *New Theatre Quarterly* 4, no. 15 (Aug. 1988): 278. Cf. similar remarks at the end of the essay "Art Is an Attitude" in part 4 of this volume.

20. Appia, "Theatrical Experiences."

21. The phrase is used by Appia in "Eurhythmics and the Theatre," an essay included in part 3 of this volume.

22. Appia, "Theatrical Experiences."

23. Appia, in a letter of 25 June 1923 to Gordon Craig included in Beacham, "The Appia–Craig Correspondence," 286.

24. Appia, unpublished letter to Oskar Wälterlin, 12 Jan. 1924, a copy of which is in the Appia Collection, Beinecke Library, Yale.

25. Gordon Craig, *Fourteen Notes,* ed. Glenn Hughes (Seattle, Wash., 1931), 11.

26. Gordon Craig, letter to Barnard Hewitt, 15 Feb. 1960, a copy of which is in the Appia Collection, Beinecke Library, Yale.

27. Appia, letter to Oskar Wälterlin, 12 Jan. 1924.

28. Quoted in Richard C. Beacham, *Adolphe Appia, Theatre Artist* (Cambridge, 1987), 93.

29. Ibid., 93.

30. Ibid., 96. The quote is by Raymond Hall, writing in the *New York Times,* 1 Mar. 1931.

31. "You speak of the use of my designs (at Bayreuth and elsewhere). I know it; I know about this and the exploiting of my ideas in reviews and journals; I'm fully aware of it. . . . But anonymity is part of my entire being. . . . Appia and anonymity belong together. The essential thing is that the Idea is called to life, and lives." Appia in an unpublished letter to Karl Reyle, 10 Sept. 1926, from a transcript belonging to Walther Volbach.

32. Quoted by Jean Mercier, "Adolphe Appia. The Re-Birth of Dramatic Art," *Theatre Arts Monthly* 16, no. 8 (Aug. 1932): 629.

33. Sheldon Cheney, "International Exhibition in Amsterdam," *Theatre Arts Monthly* 6, no. 2 (Apr. 1922): 141. For an account of the involvement of Appia and Craig in the exhibition, see Beacham, "The Appia–Craig Correspondence," 280–82.

34. Oskar Wälterlin, *Entzaubertes Theater* (Zurich, 1945), 18.

35. Ibid., 16.

36. A fuller account of the Basel productions, including a review of the critical reception is in Beacham, *Adolphe Appia*, pp. 118–40. There is also an excellent account in Michael Peter Loeffler, *Oskar Wälterlin* (Basel, 1981), 57–83.

37. Appia's ideas were not officially espoused at Bayreuth until the 1950s, although long before then certain elements of them were incorporated without acknowledgement. For a brief account of the slow evolution of the Bayreuth production style, see the introductory notes to part 2 of this volume.

38. Appia in a letter to Craig, 26 Feb. 1922, quoted in Beacham, "The Appia–Craig Correspondence," 283.

39. Appia, *The Work of Living Art*, trans. Albright, 81.

**Part One**

1. Quoted by Jean Mercier, "Adolphe Appia. The Re-Birth of Dramatic Art," *Theatre Arts Monthly* 16, no. 8 (Aug. 1932): 615.

2. Houston Stewart Chamberlain, *Richard Wagner* (London, 1900), 113. Chamberlain (1855–1927), who married Wagner's daughter, Eva, was Appia's friend and early mentor. It is probably he to whom Appia refers as a particular friend later in this essay. Appia also discusses their relationship at some length in the subsequent essay, "Theatrical Experiences and Personal Investigations," and he is also referred to, anonymously, in the essay "The Intermediary" included in part 5 of this volume.

3. Johann Wolfgang von Goethe, "West-östlicher Diwan" (1819), ed. Ernst Beutler in *Goethe: Eben, West-östlicher Divan, Theatergedichte* (Zurich, 1948), 285.

4. The opera was staged at the new Grand Théâtre in Geneva in 1881, which, perhaps appropriately, burned to the ground in 1951 during a production of *The Walkyrie* precisely seventy-five years after Appia, age fourteen, put his toy theatre to the torch.

5. Anton Hiltl (1831–85), actor, and later Shakespearean director, noted for his use of carefully integrated ensemble with his actors at the Brunswick Court Theatre, which he headed.

6. Otto Devrient (1838–94) staged the production in May 1883, having presented a similar version at Weimar seven years earlier. His father, Eduard, was one of the major nineteenth-century German directors, and the author of the first detailed history of the German theatre.

7. Karl Klindworth (1830–1916), friend and pupil of Wagner. A portion of Appia's scenario for *The Walkyrie*, prepared at this time, is included in part 6 of this volume.

8. Fridtjof Nansen (1861–1930), Norwegian explorer of the North Polar region. When Appia's friend Chamberlain tried to interest Cosima Wagner in his work, she replied grandly, "Appia does not seem to know that the *Ring* was produced here in 1876, and therefore there is nothing more to be discovered in the field of scenery and production." The incident is recorded by Geoffrey Skelton in *Wagner at Bayreuth* (London, 1965), 130.

9. A mountain south of Lake Geneva.

10. The descent (act 2, scene 1 of the opera) was staged at the festival of 1912 held at the Jaques-Dalcroze Institute in the "Garden City" of Hellerau, near Dresden. The entire opera was presented at the festival the following summer. For a complete account of the work at Hellerau, see Richard C. Beacham, *Adolphe Appia*, 62–85.

11. The essay ends at this point, with a note from Appia indicating that the speaker should give résumés of the chapters entitled "The Great Unknown" and "Bearers of the Flame" from his book, *The Work of Living Art*.

12. Appia fails to mention the 1913 exhibition at Mannheim, which included his designs for *Parsifal,* and probably others as well.

**Part Two**

1. Quoted by Marc Roth in "Staging the Master's Works," *Theatre Research* 5, no. 2 (1980): 155.

2. See part 1, note 2, and Appia's remarks about Chamberlain and his influence in "Theatrical Experiences and Personal Investigations," an essay included in part 1. Chamberlain's influence is also discussed in the essay "The Intermediary," in part 5.

3. Appia's own initial experiments, including his production of a portion of *Carmen* in 1903, are detailed in Richard C. Beacham, *Adolphe Appia,* 43 ff. An account of this production is also given in the commentary to part 6 of this volume.

4. The tumultuous Basel productions are summarized in the introduction to this book, and discussed at length in Richard C. Beacham, *Adolphe Appia,* 118–40.

5. Siegfried Wagner, quoted by Oswald Georg Bauer, "Utopie als Aufgabe," in *Bayreuth 1876–1976. 100 Jahre Richard-Wagner-Festspiele* (Munich, 1976), 15.

6. A full account of technical developments and the history of production at Bayreuth is given by Carl-Friedrich Baumann, *Bühnentechnik im Festspielhaus Bayreuth* (Munich, 1980).

7. Quoted by Herbert Barth, *Der Festspielhügel* (Munich, 1973), 201.

8. From the Bayreuth Festival souvenir program of 1955.

9. Appia refers to the series of designs and extensive scenarios for the *Ring* which he prepared in the 1890s. As noted, an excerpt from one of them, act 3 of *The Walkyrie,* is included in this volume. It is revealing to compare Appia's comments here with their more concrete expression in the actual scenario.

10. About the time this article was written, probably in 1902, Appia made the acquaintance of Fortuny who was engaged in lighting experiments that promised to achieve many of the technical advances necessary to any ultimate realization of Appia's crucial new lighting principles. Fortuny was particularly concerned to perfect a method of creating what Appia termed "diffused" light; his efforts culminated in the "Fortuny system," which provided reflected light through the use of a semi-spherical sky-dome enclosing most of the space above and behind the acting area. This system, which came to be widely used in European theatres, was first employed experimentally in Paris at this time.

11. André Antoine (1859–1943), French director and theatre manager, had founded the Théâtre Libre in 1887; and, in 1897, the Théâtre Antoine, both of which were famous and highly influential for their naturalistic style of production.

12. A lavishly decorated auditorium in Geneva.

13. Maurice Maeterlinck (1862–1949), Belgian poet and dramatist noted for his poetic dramas and use of symbolism. His *Pelléas et Mélisande* (1892) was an important example of symbolist drama and a challenge to contemporary staging technique.

14. The quotation is freely translated from Wolfgang Goethe's "Dämon" in *Urworte* (1817), ed. Ernst Beutler, *Goethe, Sämtliche Gedichte* (Zurich, 1950), 1: 523 ff.

15. The manager was Appia's friend and collaborator, Oskar Wälterlin; the musical conductor, Gottfried Becker; the managing director, Dr. Otto Henning; the technical director, Hermann Jenny.

16. The theatre made famous by Appia's friend and artistic disciple, Jacques Copeau (1878–1949), where scenery was reduced to a minimum, and extravagance and spectacle were rigorously avoided.

**Part Three**

1. Richard Wagner, "The Art Form of the Future," in *Gesammelte Schriften und Dichtungen* (Leipzig, 1907), 3: 90.

2. Appia to Dalcroze in a letter of May 1906, quoted by Edmond Stadler, "Adolphe Appia et Emile Jaques-Dalcroze," ed. Frank A. Martin, *Emile Jaques-Dalcroze* (Neuchatel, 1965), 417–18.

3. Quoted by Edmond Stadler, "Adolphe Appia und Emile Jaques-Dalcroze," *Maske und Kothurn* 10, nos. 3–4 (1964): 662.

4. Ibid., 664–65.

5. Quoted by Jessica Davis Van Wyck, "Designing *Hamlet* with Appia," *Theatre Arts Monthly* 9, no. 1 (Jan. 1925): 18.

6. Appia gives an account of his encounter and initial work with Dalcroze in "Theatrical Experiences . . ." an essay included in part 1 of this book.

7. Karl Scheffler in a tribute at Dohrn's funeral, ed. E. Feudel, *In Memoriam Hellerau*, 49.

8. Dalcroze to Appia in a letter dated 28 Mar. 1910, quoted by Stadler, "Adolphe Appia et Emile Jaques-Dalcroze," p. 429.

9. Dalcroze in an undated letter to Appia, in the Appia Collection, Beinecke Library, Yale University.

10. The work at Hellerau has been thus characterized by, for example, Nicholas Hern, "Expressionism," ed. Ronald Hayman, *The German Theatre* (London, 1975), 116.

11. Quoted in Giertz, *Kultus ohne Götter*, 142.

12. Appia thus described the descent into Hades from his production of *Orfeo*, in the essay, "Theatrical Experiences . . ." which is included in part 1 of this volume.

13. The phrase is taken from the title of the book by Gernot Giertz, documenting eurhythmics and Hellerau, *Kultus ohne Götter*. It was first used by Robert Breuer in "Hellerau," *Die Schaubühne* 8, no. 28/29 (1912): 52.

14. In February 1914 the co-founder, director, and tireless exponent of Hellerau, Wolf Dohrn, died, aged thirty-six, in a skiing accident in the Alps. Dalcroze became estranged from the directors of Hellerau shortly after the outbreak of war, and formally ended his connection in November of 1914. In addition to that given in Beacham, *Adolphe Appia*, there is an interesting account of the Hellerau project in Mary Elizabeth Tallon, "Appia's Theatre at Hellerau," *Theatre Journal* 36, no. 4 (Dec. 1984): 495–504.

15. For these plans, see Jessica Davis Van Wyck, "Working with Appia," *Theatre Arts Monthly* 8, no. 12 (Dec. 1924): 815–18.

16. Appia dedicated *The Work of Living Art,* published in 1921, to "Emile Jaques-Dalcroze the faithful friend to whom I owe my aesthetic homeland." The estrangement between Appia and Dalcroze, after such a close and passionate association, must have been painful. A former student remembered many years later how Dalcroze recounted that he received a letter which Appia stipulated should be sent only after his death. In it he sought to reconcile the differences between them. Dalcroze, profoundly moved, recalled that "it was like a voice from beyond." The account is from a letter in the Appia Collection, Beinecke Library, Yale, dated 13 Feb. 1969.

17. Isadora Duncan (1878–1927), the American dancer who revived a form of *orchesis,* ancient Greek dance, using flowing robes and bare feet. She was an important precursor of modern dance.

18. Goethe, "Generalbeichte," from *Gesellige Lieder* (1801–2). Ernst Beutler, ed., *Goethe, Sämtliche Gedichte* (Zurich, 1950), 1: 89–90. Translation: "To disaccustom us to Half [Measures], and to live steadfastly in Wholeness, Goodness and Beauty."

19. Quotation from Houston Stewart Chamberlain, *Richard Wagner* (London, 1900), 196.

20. The *Werkstätte* refers to the furniture factory which Wolf Dohrn and Karl Schmidt set up at Hellerau, under the auspices of the German Werkbund, an organization devoted to the development and promotion of the applied arts in German light industry. By 1910, the factory and first twenty-four homes had been built, with a population of over 2,000 projected for the summer of 1911, to rise ultimately to the maximum of 12,000. The construction and arrangement of Hellerau were scrupulously overseen by a commission which approved every building and generally safeguarded conditions, maintaining, for example, a ratio of one to five between developed and open land to ensure that Hellerau's inhabitants would be free from the squalid and cramped conditions prevalent in the industrial quarters of most cities, including neighboring Dresden.

21. Friedrich Schiller, *Hymn to Joy,* trans. Natalie MacFarren (London, 1902). Schiller's poem is, of course, used by Beethoven in his Ninth Symphony.

22. Serge Wolkonski relates an anecdote about a visitor to one of Dalcroze's classes at Hellerau:

> I remember during one practical session, the door up above was opened, and a man who didn't wish to disturb the lesson walked quickly across the gallery, opened the door opposite, exited, and shut the door. We, however, heard it in the music, which amusingly accompanied each step of the visitor up to the slamming of the door. It was delightful: without suspecting it, the man became the presenter of a eurhythmic pantomime. (In E. Feudel, ed., *In Memoriam Hellerau,* 11)

23. An interesting account of a fundamental difference of opinion between Appia and Dalcroze over the use of costumes in *Orfeo* is given by Hélène Brunet-LeCompte, *Jaques-Dalcroze* (Geneva, 1950), 161–62. Dalcroze spent a great deal of money on representational costumes, while Appia insisted that the pedagogic nature of the exercises should be emphasized by using the students' normal leotards and tunic, as described in this article. Upset by their disagreement, Appia left Hellerau in some haste, and had to be reassured later by Dalcroze of the esteem in which he was held. See also Beacham, *Adolphe Appia,* 71.

**Part Four**

1. Beacham, "The Appia–Craig Correspondence," 286.

2. It is found in the English edition of *The Work of Living Art*, 131.

3. Beacham, "The Appia–Craig Correspondence," 278.

4. Gordon Craig, quoted in Denis Bablet, "Edward Gordon Craig and Scenography," *Theatre Research* 11, no. 1 (1971): 21.

5. Walter Fuerst and Samuel Hume, *Twentieth Century Stage Decoration* (London, 1928), 4.

6. The French title "Art vivant? ou nature morte?" is a play on words; the French expression for "still life" is "nature morte."

7. Shortly after he wrote this essay, Appia undertook to apply his ideas to the design and staging of a spoken drama, *Hamlet*. Together with the American Jessica Davis Van Wyck, he prepared a scenario and fourteen settings. Van Wyck published an engaging account of their work and its results; "Designing *Hamlet* with Appia," *Theatre Arts Monthly* 9, no.1 (Jan. 1925): 17–31. See also Beacham, *Adolphe Appia*, 97–104.

8. Appia's friend and collaborator Jean Mercier has recorded how, at their initial meeting, Gordon Craig identified the way in which Appia's theory of reform was dependent upon music: "Craig wrote his name on the tablecloth and next to it that of Appia. He drew a circle around Appia on which he wrote the word 'music.' Admirable symbol of truth! The two pioneers of contemporary dramatic art rested their reform on the same base—the actor. But Craig was free in his reform; the reform of Appia was dominated and directed by a major force, music."

9. Dana Rufolo-Horhager has discussed the many ways in which the ideas put forward in "Monumentality" have found expression in the Schaubühne am Lehniner Platz, in Berlin, the theatre used by the director Peter Stein; "Adolphe Appia's 'Monumentalité' and Peter Stein's Schaubühne," *Theatre Research* 9, no. 1 (1984): 29–38.

10. Richard Schechner, "Towards the Twenty First Century," ed. James Schevill, *Break Out!* (Chicago, 1973), 379.

11. J. L. Styan, *Modern Drama in Theory and Practice* (Cambridge, 1981), 2: 92.

12. Ibid., p. 157.

13. This narrative closely echoes the account that Appia gives of his own early disillusionment with the theatre in the essay "Theatrical Experiences . . ." which is included in part 1 of this volume: "I was conscious of the flimsiness of the settings and the flatness of the stage floor. . . . Afterwards I toured the theatre alone, murmuring to myself: 'Is it for this that these thick walls were built, this massive construction?'"

14. This is almost certainly a reference to the use of "Über-marionettes" called for by Gordon Craig, most recently in an essay of 1907, "The Actor and the Über-marionette": "The actor must go, and in his place comes the inanimate figure—the Über-marionette we may call him, until he has won for himself a better name." J. Michael Walton, ed., *Craig on Theatre* (London, 1983), 85. Craig and Appia did not meet until 1914, but it is likely that long before then Appia was aware of the ever self-publicizing Englishman and his iconoclastic ideas.

15. A Parisian museum that exhibited wax figures.

16. Lucien Jusseaume (1861–1925), Parisian artist who was the chief designer for the Opéra-Comique for twenty-five years. His symbolist settings for *Pelléas et Mélisande* of 1902 caused a sensation and initiated a new style. Appia had met him in Paris and benefited from his help in a private presentation of Byron's *Manfred* with music by Schumann, and the first scene of act 2 of *Carmen.* See Beacham, *Adolphe Appia,* 43–45, and the brief account in the commentary to part 6 of this book.

17. Houston Stewart Chamberlain, *Richard Wagner,* 196.

18. Richard Wagner, "Opera und Drama," in *Gesammelte Schriften* (Leipzig, 1907), 3: 135.

19. Friedrich Schiller, "Über die Ästhetische Erziehung des Menschen in einer Reihe von Briefen. Zweiundzwanzigster Brief," ed. Gerhard Fricke and Herbert Göpfert, *Sämtliche Werke* (repr. Munich, 1967), 5: 638. Appia placed this motto at the beginning of his book *Music and the Art of the Theatre.*

20. Arthur Schopenhauer, *Die Welt als Wille und Vorstellung,* ed. Paul Duessen, *Sämtliche Werke* (Munich, 1911), 1: 308. This is the second motto used by Appia in *Music and the Art of the Theatre.*

21. The Procuratie Vecchie, and the Procuratie Nuove; the arcaded buildings that enclose the Piazza San Marco on three sides.

22. This is an abbreviated version of a text Appia prepared for presentation on 3 April 1919 at the Olympic Institute in Lausanne, accompanied by slides illustrating his designs. It may have been written by Appia at an earlier date. Appia refers to the occasion in a letter to Gordon Craig of 30 Nov. 1918: "Someone has asked me on behalf of the Olympic Institute (President Baron de Coubertin, a charming and serious Frenchman) for lectures with slides; one of my friends will read them. I will be pleased to see my designs (about 15) enlarged on the screen! The slides are wonderful." See Beacham, "The Appia–Craig Correspondence," 278.

23. Cf. a statement by Appia in the above-mentioned letter of 30 Nov. 1918, to Craig, referring to his "vision of *The Hall,* a kind of cathedral of the future, which reunites in a vast, free and *changeable* space, all the expressions of our social life, and in particular dramatic art, *with or without spectators.*"

24. This article was written in the autumn of 1920 and may have been intended to serve as the introduction to the projected further volume of essays that Appia mentioned during this period, following the completion of *The Work of Living Art* in May 1919.

25. This essay was prepared for the International Exhibition of Theatre Design held at Amsterdam in January 1922, where (as noted in the introduction to this volume) Appia's work was prominently displayed. It was published again the following year in Milan at the time of Appia's production of *Tristan* at La Scala.

26. Cf. the observation by Dalcroze to Appia when confronted by the newly completed hall at Hellerau: "I never go into it without shivering from pleasure, but also from apprehension, because I ask myself if we know how to profit as we must from this suggestive place. . . . Do we know how to give life to these virgin spaces, animate these lines, and awaken these echoes?" Quoted by Stadler, "Adolphe Appia et Emile Jaques-Dalcroze," 440.

27. Cf. "About the Costume for Eurhythmics," an essay included in part 3 above.

28. Appia probably has in mind the abstract settings of such contemporary designers as Oskar Strnad, Gerard Bucholz and Heinrich Heckroth, who adopted the architectonic elements of his settings without always heeding the essential requirement that they be closely coordinated with the emotional qualities, as well as the stage action of the piece to be performed within them.

29. This lecture by Appia (who was intensely shy, and afflicted by a stutter) would have been given to the students of Dalcroze at the Geneva institute by someone (possibly his friend Henry C. Bonifas) acting on his behalf.

30. Felix Arvers (1806–50), poet and author, and a collaborator of Eugène Scribe, the author of "well-made" plays.

31. Jeanne Julia Bartet (1854–1941), an actress who, since 1879, had enjoyed renown at the Comédie Française.

32. Giacomo Meyerbeer (Jakob Liebmann Beer, 1791–1864), a German composer who worked in Italy and later Paris; composer of extravagantly romantic and grandiose operas, including *Les Huguenots*.

33. Cf. Bernard Shaw on Wagnerian production at Bayreuth which he considered to be in the "quaintly old-fashioned tradition of half rhetorical, half historical-pictorial attitude and gesture," with the acting "conceived as *tableaux vivants*, with posed models, instead of as passages of action, motion and life." George Bernard Shaw, *The Perfect Wagnerite* (repr. New York, 1967), 129.

34. *L'Arlésienne* (*The Maid of Arles*), a play by Alphonse Daudet (1840–97), with choral and orchestral music by Bizet, first presented in Paris in 1872; *Manfred*, a "dramatic poem" by Schumann (Lord Byron's poem adapted for concert or stage), first presented in 1849; Appia himself staged a scene from it in Paris in 1903. Cf. n. 16 above.

35. Appia refers to the "Asphaleia System," first employed in continental theatres early in the century, which allowed sections of the stage floor to be raised, forming platforms of various heights, which could even be tilted or rotated.

36. The Austrian director, Max Reinhardt (1873–1943), was renowned for his creative use of the revolving stage, having first employed it to great effect at the Deutsches Theater in Berlin to stage *A Midsummer Night's Dream* in 1905.

37. Appia was on friendly terms with Georges Pitoëff (Russian and later prominent French director), Craig and Copeau, and had probably met Stanislavsky as well.

38. At the time of composing this essay, Appia had in fact just completed a visit to Florence, remaining from the middle of May to late in June 1922.

39. The name of a very popular series of guidebooks.

40. The Piazza della Signoria, the main square of Florence, dominated by a massive palace.

41. John Ruskin (1819–1900), British author and art critic, who wrote extensively about the art and architecture of Italy.

42. A novel by Julius Stindl (Wilhelmine Buchholz, 1841–1905), published in 1883 as *Buchholzens in Italien*.

43. Gustave Doret (1866–1943), Swiss composer and conductor, who collaborated with René Morax in an important festival, the Fête de Vignerons of 1905. Appia attended and wrote of such festivals that they "have taught us that art must spring forth from the heart of all of us and

must be represented by all of us," in the essay "Style and Solidarity," which is included in part 3 of this volume. His own work on the Fête de Juin of 1914 in Geneva was influenced by the Vevey festivals. Together with Jaques-Dalcroze, Doret did much for the preservation of Swiss Romande folk songs.

44. Cf. Dana Rufolo-Hörhager on Peter Stein's Berlin Schaubühne:

> Certainly this stage space is strikingly reminiscent of Appia's words in "Monumentality": a space which can be adapted to the needs of the presentation at hand; an auditorium which is contiguous with the stage; a floor which can be modulated by means of hydraulic levers; a diffused lighting source: all this is realized in the Schaubühne. Also in the use of decorative and construction materials, the Schaubühne recalls Appia's words to mind . . . the interior of the building features basically the three non-decomposable materials of concrete, glass, and brass. The Theatre itself has walls of greyish concrete. There are no decorations or materials, as Appia recommended. . . . The neutral interior of the vast performance hall has been designed to accept whatever range of colors, motifs, and materials a scene-designer might choose to use. ("Adolphe Appia's 'Monumentalité' and Peter Stein's Schaubühne," 37)

45. The lecture was for a conference held in Zurich early in 1925, shortly after the Basel debacle which was to result in the cancellation of Appia's planned presentation of the complete *Ring*.

46. H. Taine, *Philosophie de l'art* (Paris, 1881), 1: 41–42. Appia, who was particularly fond of the quote, discusses its implications at length in the earlier essay, "Comments on the Theatre."

47. A page of the manuscript is missing at this point.

48. The incident occurs in Homer's *Odyssey,* book 8. The minstrel sang of the quarrel between Ulysses and Achilles.

## Part Five

1. Quoted in Giertz, *Kultus ohne Götter,* 131.

2. Hellerau, in an almost uncanny way, serves as an allegory for the moral catastrophe that overtook Europe in the course of this century. Born of such hope and idealism, the "Garden City" was transected by Hitler's autobahn; the Dalcroze Institute was used as an SS training site; at the end of the war its luminous cloth was pulled down to make bandages for those wounded in the destruction of Dresden; and today it serves as a recreation hall for the East German military, to which all access by the public is strictly forbidden.

3. Friedrich Nietzsche, "Richard Wagner in Bayreuth," in *Werke,* vol. 2 (Leipzig, 1922), p. 376.

4. See amongst numerous examples, Plato's *Republic* 3.398 ff., or Aristotle, *Politics* 8.5–7.

5. John Sturrock, "Introduction," Marcel Proust, *Against Sainte-Beuve and Other Essays,* trans. and ed. John Sturrock (London, 1988).

6. Appia, letter to Gordon Craig, 7 Jan. 1922. Beacham, "The Appia–Craig Correspondence," 282.

7. About this time Appia became interested in and visited the Goetheanum, the spiritual retreat established at Dornach in Switzerland by Rudolf Steiner and his followers. Volbach, *Adolphe Appia,* 173.

8. Ibid., 129–30. As well as the testimony, much of it unpublished, in accounts by *inter alia*, Oskar Wälterlin, Jean Mercier, Paul Bonifas, and Karl Reyle.

9. Susan Sontag, *Against Interpretation and Other Essays* (London, 1967), 8.

10. Jacques Copeau, "L'Art et l'oeuvre d'Adolphe Appia," *Comoedia* (12 Mar. 1928). Reprinted in Volbach, *Adolphe Appia*, 207–8.

11. Craig, letter to Appia of 22 Feb. 1917; Beacham, "The Appia–Craig Correspondence," 276.

12. Gottfried Keller (1819–90), Swiss author. Appia refers to a character in Keller's story, "The Misused Love Letters," in *The People of Seldwyla and Seven Legends*, trans. M. D. Hottinger (New York, 1929).

13. Homer, *Odyssey*, book 8.

14. The reference is to Wagner's opera, *Die Meistersinger von Nürnberg*, for which Appia prepared a scenario about the time this essay was written.

15. The phrase is attributed to Napoleon after meeting Goethe.

16. Appia is playing here with the suggestion of a comparison between Mr. A. and theatrical art: to the uninitiated such art is thought of as painted on canvas; others think of it as three-dimensional (like a staircase).

17. *Dr. Festus* is the title of an album of satirical sketches by the Swiss artist Rodolphe Toepfer (1799–1846).

18. Alphonse Daudet (1840–97), French novelist and playwright.

19. H. Taine, *Philosophie d l'art*, (Paris, 1881), 1: 41–42.

20. René Martin (1891–1977), Swiss painter, decorator and sculptor, born in Paris, and died in Greenwich, Connecticut. He was a friend of Appia, and in 1922 did the portrait of him (standing in front of his design for the sacred forest of *Parsifal*) which is illustrated in this book.

21. Dr. Louis Paul Amédée Appia (1818–98), Adolphe's father, a physician who practiced in Geneva and was one of the founders of the Red Cross. He was a modest and hard-working man, a strict disciplinarian and moralist.

22. Alexandre Rodolphe Vinet (1797–1847), Swiss (French-speaking) Protestant theologian, critic historian and essayist.

23. Charles Augustin de Sainte-Beuve (1804–69), French writer and critic, member of the Academie Française. He was famous for his magisterial (if somewhat patronizing and philistine) judgments and a critical "method" that consisted in interpreting works of literature largely by reference to the external features of a writer's biography and character. *Histoire de Port-Royal*, a chronicle of Jansenism in five volumes, was written 1840–59.

24. A celebrated family of seventeenth-century Jansenists, including Antoine I (1560–1619) of Paris, barrister, an opponent of the Jesuits; Angélique (1591–1661), his daughter; Mère Agnès (1593–1671), another daughter, abbess of Port-Royal; Robert Arnauld d'Andilly (1588–1674), his son; another son, Antoine II (1612–94), the most illustrious of the family, a theologian and polemical opponent of the Jesuits, writer, and Cartesian philosopher.

25. Sainte-Beuve, *Histoire de Port-Royal*, 5 vols. (Paris, 1840–59).

26. Port-Royal was a convent of the order of Cîteaux founded in 1204 near Chevreuse; dissolved in the sixteenth century, it was re-established by Angélique Arnauld in 1609, and it later

became a Jansenist center whose adherents followed an ascetic and solitary life. At the end of the seventeenth century, after the Jansenist purges, its members were dispersed and the convent was closed in 1709.

27.  François Charles-Marie Fourier (1772–1838), French socialist, writer and reformer, coined this term in referring to his idea of utopian social communities.

28.  Ralph Waldo Emerson (1803–82), American poet and essayist.

29.  Literally, "an artist of life."

30.  Orthopedic equipment to strengthen the muscles. Sandow was a British health expert.

31.  A mountain south of Geneva.

32.  Jean Jacques Rousseau (1712–78), French philosopher, author and social reformer. Johann H. Pestalozzi (1746–1827), Swiss educational reformer.

33.  Pierre Jeaneret (1896–1967), Swiss designer and architect, who, for a time, collaborated with his famous cousin Le Corbusier.

34.  A village in the alpine region southwest of Munich, famous for the Passion Play performed there by its inhabitants every ten years.

35.  This is probably a reference to the French composer Gabriel Urbain Fauré (1845–1924), with whom Appia was on close terms from about 1880, and who is believed to have taught him theory and counterpoint for a time.

36.  Appia's metaphor appears to anticipate Bertolt Brecht's description of conventional theatre as "culinary."

37.  A character from the comic play of 1860 by Eugene Labiche (1815–88), *Le Voyage de M. Perrichon.*

38.  The reference is almost certainly to Appia's friend the Englishman Houston Stewart Chamberlain (1855–1927), whom he met about 1884. For a description of this important relationship, see Volbach, *Adolphe Appia,* 31–40.

39.  Josephin Péladan (1859–1918), French author, opponent of naturalism, and follower of Wagner.

40.  Henri Bonifas (1887–1952), pupil and collaborator of Jaques-Dalcroze, later professor of psychology at Geneva. He was a friend of Appia, about whom he published several articles.

41.  Appia attributes this idea to Robert Burnand (1882–1953), French writer and historian, who wrote books on Napoleon III and on everyday life in nineteenth-century France.

42.  It was over the issue of costuming that Appia found himself in his only significant disagreement with Dalcroze in the preparations for the Hellerau Festival of 1912. See part 3, n. 23.

43.  The area of the upper Rhone valley.

44.  The essay is found in the preceding part of *this* volume.

45.  Appia evidently has in mind what he considered to be the grotesqueness of certain contemporary portrait art, e.g., works by Kokoschka, Munch, Schiele, etc.

46.  A character in Molière's *Tartuffe.*

47. An electromagnetic wave, artificially produced as a means of transmission in radio telegraphy. First fully investigated by Heinrich R. Hertz (1857–94), German physicist.

48. Appia deals with a concept widely explored through contemporary dramatic and cinematic art, e.g., Georg Kaiser's *Gas Triology* (1917–20), Karel Čapek's *Rossum's Universal Robots* (1921), Fritz Lang's *Metropolis* (1926), or (a few years later), Chaplin's *Modern Times* (1936).

49. Sesostris, the name of three Egyptian pharaohs of the 12th dynasty (1970–1850 B.C.); Alcibiades (ca. 450–404 B.C.), Athenian statesman, adventurer and general, intimate of Socrates.

50. Appia added a somewhat curious postscript to this essay:

> I have included graphology in animated mechanization. Here is my reason: a novice who wants to paint a tree against the light on a beautiful summer morning will paint the trunk brown, the foliage green, *because he knows* this trunk is brown and the foliage is green. Thus the picture does not really show what the painter actually sees. Similarly, the graphologist proceeds by taking his client out of his environment, disregarding the ever-changing light that determines the aspect every hour of the day; he *knows* from the handwriting the fixed shades of the person's character and cannot truly relate to any moment of his subject's life. Thus, the graphologist does not discover the *living truth*—the only one, after all, that matters—but a dead truth. His portrait is that of a mummy—it has authenticity and immobility; movement and light are wanting; that is to say, *Life*.
>
> The *living* truth is not found in what we *know* of a human being, but in what we see and feel of him in ourselves. Ignoring this, the graphologist makes of his knowledge a mechanical recording—no matter how remarkable it may otherwise be; hence he deserves our profound sympathy.

51. This translation by Barnard Hewitt was published as an afterpiece in the English edition of Appia's *The Work of Living Art* (Coral Gables, Fla., 1960), copyright Walther R. Volbach. Appia subtitled it "A Preface to a New Work," but, as noted earlier, the precise nature of that work (or the relationship of this preface to several other pieces with a claim to that function) is unclear.

52. The phrase is a fragment attributed to the Greek Sophist philosopher of the fifth century B.C. Appia evidently referred to himself as Protagoras to some of his friends; Beacham "The Appia–Craig Correspondence," 284.

53. H. Taine, *Philosophie de l'art*, 1: 41–42.

54. Cf. Appia's letter to Gordon Craig of 30 Jan. 1919 in which he speaks of "the legitimate existence of the *Work of Living Art* separate from the dramatic idea, and as something sufficient unto itself . . . !—even without witnesses, without spectators . . . ! The result will be that dramatic art is a living art like industrial art is to fine art: in other words, an applied art. I'm sure I'm right!!" Beacham, "The Appia–Craig Correspondence," 279–80.

## Part Six

1. Haus Wahnfried, home of the Wagner family. Chamberlain later married Wagner's daughter, Eva.

2. Appia, in a letter to Karl Reyle, 4 Mar. 1925, in an unpublished manuscript belonging to Walther Volbach.

3. Taken from the unpublished account in Gordon Craig's *Daybook III*, as recounted by Appia.

Entry for 13 Feb. 1914. The copy of the *Daybook* is at the University of Texas at Austin, Humanities Research Center.

4.  Volbach, *Adolphe Appia*, 79.

5.  The account is taken from Hermann von Keyserling's article, "Die erste Verwirklichung von Appias Ideen zur Reform der Bühne," *Allgemeine Zeitung* (Munich), 6 April 1903.

6.  Max Eduard von Leihburg, unpublished letter to Walther Volbach, 18 Sept. 1960.

7.  Appia, in a letter to Paul Boepple, autumn 1923, the Swiss Theatre Collection, Bern, Switzerland.

8.  *Basler Anzeiger*, 13 Feb. 1925.

9.  *Basler Nachrichten*, 12 Feb. 1925.

10. A challenge that was of increased interest to Appia at this time. See the subsequent remarks concerning the scenario for *Faust*.

11. Loeffler, *Oskar Wälterlin*, 82.

12. Christoph Willibald Gluck, preface to *Alceste*, trans. Eric Blom, in *Kobbe's Complete Opera Book*, ed. the Earl of Harewood (London, 1922), 43.

13. This is only a portion of *one* of the scenarios Appia prepared in the early 1890s, most of which were never published until their recent appearance in the initial volumes of the French language *Collected Works*. A brief description, along with six designs illustrating the act, was included in *Die Musik und die Inscenierung* (1899). This translation was prepared by Mr. Neil Monro-Davies.

14. The term is that used by Appia himself to identify the solid scenic elements that he called for in place of the conventional painted flats and cutouts normally used in the theatre of his day. They are, of course, essential for realizing Appia's innovative conception of stage setting as a three-dimensional *space* rather than a *picture* contrived from painted flats.

15. Appia always describes the setting as seen from the audience, and his practice has been followed here to avoid any possible confusion that might result from converting it to the modern convention of giving stage directions (i.e., stage right, stage left), as seen by the actor.

16. A short section of the scenario has been omitted, in which Appia refers to practical adaptations necessary for employing this setting elsewhere in the *Ring*.

17. Wagner's Bayreuth setting of 1876, which, with very minor alterations, remained unchanged through the first decades of this century, consisted of the standard painted cutouts, executed with a good deal of superfluous pictorial embellishment. Painted rocks and tree trunks rose incongruously from the flat stage floor, and the summit itself was essentially a staircase masked by an arrangement of painted flats.

18. Once again, Appia probably intends an oblique reference to practice at Bayreuth, where the painted sets were characterized by overblown romanticism, and occasionally outlandish decoration and lurid *trompe l'oeil* effects.

19. Appia insisted that his designs were meaningful only when examined together with his complete descriptive scenarios. The essence of his scenic reform was that stage settings should *not* be thought of (or evaluated) as essentially *pictures*, but rather as *spaces* in which a particular series of dramatic actions was to take place, and whose elements, arrangement and dimensions must emanate from within the drama itself.

20. The pagination refers to a standard edition of the libretto used by Appia that was published by Karl Klindworth. Pages 210–14 contain the climax of the storm, just prior to Wotan's entrance, during which Appia stipulated that "the summit is lost beneath clouds. . . . [T]he whole scene is like a dark whirlwind in which one can distinguish the Walkyrie only by their song."

21. In production the "Ride of the Walkyrie" had always been a major problem and embarrassment. In 1876 at Bayreuth, a rather crudely executed static image of a Walkyrie on horseback was projected and moved across the backdrop. The effect was unsatisfactory and much criticized; it was replaced in the 1896 staging by children dressed as Walkyrie and flown in on wooden horses across the upstage area. Appia, writing several years before Edison's first motion picture, foresaw that technology could provide a solution.

22. The transcript of Appia's scenario is at places in a somewhat unfinished state, not in terms of its detail which is very great indeed, but in its punctuation and syntax. Here its punctuation has been regularized, the text divided up into additional paragraphs, and the broken phrases or sentences that occur from time to time have been completed. Even so, there are ambiguous passages where Appia's intended meaning is not altogether clear, and the text offered here has occasionally entailed a small amount of guesswork. The reader is reminded that unless specifically noted otherwise, Appia always gives his stage directions and descriptions from the spectators' viewpoint. Occasionally the translator has had to resort to more modern terms in order to convey adequately the actual meaning.

23. Except for occasional direct quotation from the actual dialogue (which has been left in German), Appia bases his description on page and bar references drawn from the libretto as published by Klindworth. These have been retained (although occasionally simplified) for the general sense of the staging they convey (as well as a suggestion of the moment-by-moment progression), even without ready access to that edition. If read together with any text of the libretto, a tolerably clear picture of the details of Appia's intended staging emerges.

24. Appia drew attention to this moment in his short published account, *Staging Wagnerian Drama* (1895).

    The Walkyrie have hidden Brunnhilde among themselves and are busy softening the temper of their father. The musical passage is very short, but the incomparable polyphony should here correspond to a spectacle that visualizes this polyphony; all the while the Walkyrie remain a unified group. We here have a light counterpoint, in which the successive entries reflect their timid supplication in a wholly individual way; thus each of the Walkyrie should underline her vocal entry by a step forward. The last bars have an irresistible glow of their own; the intertwining of the voices will have to make itself physically felt, always, of course, relying strictly on the musical notation. Thus the whole group, bent towards Wotan, will rise and step back right on cue with the hard chords of the god's crushing word. (*Staging Wagnerian Drama*, trans. Peter Loeffler, (Basel, 1982), 45)

25. The page numbers given first are those provided by Appia, and refer to the French edition published by Choudens in Paris in 1882. The numbers in parentheses refer to the standard score of Schirmer (New York), trans. T. Baker.

26. Words in brackets are not in Appia's manuscript.

27. The page numbers refer to the edition of Novello, published in New York by H.W. Gray Co.

28. Otto Devrient (1838–94) presented *Faust* in Weimar in 1876, and seven years later in Leipzig on a stage considered to be an adaptation of a medieval format divided into three sections.

Appia gives an extensive account of this production in the essay, "Theatrical Experiences and Personal Investigations," which is found in part 1 of this volume. The Relief Stage refers to the Munich Künstlertheater, which opened in 1907. In 1889 the Shakespeare Stage was founded in the Bavarian Court Theatre. Karl von Perfall (1824–1907) was its general manager, Jocza Savits (1847–1915) served as stage director, and Karl Lautenschläger (1843–1906) was technical director. Max Reinhardt (1873–1943), the renowned Austrian director, presented a number of plays commencing with the *Oresteia* in 1919 in a converted circus, the Grosse Schauspielhaus. He did not, however, stage *Faust* there.

29. In Appia's manuscript all quotations are inserted in German. The English translations are from the version by George Madison Priest (New York, 1932).

# Select Bibliography

Appia, Adolphe. *Music and the Art of the Theatre,* Trans. Robert W. Corrigan and Mary Douglas Dirks. Ed. Barnard Hewitt. Coral Gables, Fla., 1962.

———. *Staging Wagnerian Drama.* Trans. Peter Loeffler. Basel, 1982.

———. *The Work of Living Art.* Trans. H.D. Albright. Ed. Barnard Hewitt. Coral Gables, Fla., 1960.

Bablet, Denis. "Edward Gordon Craig and Scenography," *Theatre Research* 11, no. 1 (1971): 7–22.

Barth, Herbert. *Der Festspielhügel.* Munich, 1973.

Bauer, Oswald Georg. "Utopie als Aufgabe," in *Bayreuth 1876–1976.* Munich, 1976.

Baumann, Carl-Friedrich. *Bühnentechnik im Festspielhaus Bayreuth.* Munich, 1980.

Beacham, Richard C. *Adolphe Appia, Theatre Artist.* Cambridge, 1987.

———. "Adolphe Appia and Eurhythmics," *Maske und Kothurn* 29, no. 1–4 (1983): 141–52.

———. "Adolphe Appia and the Staging of Wagnerian Opera," *Opera Quarterly* (Autumn 1983): 114–39.

———. "Adolphe Appia, Emile Jaques-Dalcroze, and Hellerau. Part One: 'Music Made Visible,'" *New Theatre Quarterly* 1, no. 2 (1985): 154–64.

———. "Adolphe Appia, Emile Jaques-Dalcroze, and Hellerau. Part Two: 'Poetry in Motion,'" *New Theatre Quarterly* 1, no. 3 (1985): 245–61.

———. "'Brothers in Suffering and Joy': The Appia–Craig Correspondence," *New Theatre Quarterly* 4, no. 15 (1988): 268–88.

Bonifas, Henry C. *Adolphe Appia.* Zurich, 1929.

———. "A Propos des Fêtes d'Hellerau," *Jeunesse littéraire* (29 June 1913).

Brunet-Lecomte, Hélène. *Jaques-Dalcroze.* Geneva, 1950.

Carter, Huntly. *The New Spirit in the European Theatre.* New York, 1926.

Chamberlain, Houston Stewart. *Richard Wagner.* London, 1900.

Cheney, Sheldon. *The New Movement in the Theatre.* New York, 1914.

———. "International Exhibition in Amsterdam," *Theatre Arts Monthly* 6, no. 2 (Apr. 1922): 140–42.

Copeau, Jacques. "L'Art de l'oeuvre d'Adolphe Appia," *Comoedia* (12 Mar. 1928).

Craig, Gordon. *Fourteen Notes.* Ed. Glenn Hughes. Seattle, Wash., 1931.

Feudel, E., ed. *In Memoriam Hellerau.* Freiburg im Breisgau, 1960.

Fuchs, George. *Revolution in the Theatre.* Ithaca, N.Y., 1959.

Fuerst, Walter, and Hume, Samuel. *Twentieth Century Stage Decoration.* London, 1928.

Giertz, Gernot. *Kultus ohne Götter.* Munich, 1975.

Goethe, Johann Wolfgang von. *Eben, West-östlicher Divan, Theatergedichte.* Ed. Ernst Beutler. Zurich, 1948.

_____ . *Sämtliche Gedichte*. Ed. Ernst Beutler. Zurich, 1950.

Hartmann, Kristiana. *Deutsche Gartenstadtbewegung*. Munich, 1976.

Hayman, Ronald, ed. *The German Theatre*. London, 1975.

Jaques-Dalcroze, Emile. *The Eurhythmics of Jaques-Dalcroze*. London, 1912.

_____ . *Rhythm, Music and Education*. London, 1921.

Keyserling, Herbert von. "Die erste Verwirklichung von Appias Ideen zur Reform der Bühne," *Allgemeine Zeitung* (6 Apr. 1903): 6.

Kindermann, Heinz. *Theatergeschichte Europas*. Salzburg, 1968.

Loeffler, Michael P. *Oskar Wälterlin*. Basel, 1979.

Macgowan, Kenneth. *The Theatre of Tomorrow*. New York, 1921.

Mack, Dietrich. *Der Bayreuther Inszenierungsstil*. Munich, 1976.

Martin, Frank A., ed. *Emile Jaques-Dalcroze*. Neuchatel, 1965.

Mercier, Jean. "Adolphe Appia. The Re-Birth of Dramatic Art," *Theatre Arts Monthly* 16, no. 8 (Aug. 1932): 616–30.

Moussinac, Léon. *The New Movement in the Theatre*. London, 1931.

Nietzsche, Friedrich. *Werke*. Vol. 2. Leipzig, 1922.

Oenslager, Donald. *Scenery Then and Now*. New York, 1936.

Pretsch, Paul. *Cosima Wagner und Chamberlain im Briefwechsel*. Leipzig, 1934.

Proust, Marcel. *Against Sainte-Beuve and Other Essays*. Ed. and trans. John Sturrock. London, 1988.

Reyle, Karl. "Adolphe Appia's Basler 'Ring,'" *Basler Nachrichten* (2 Sept. 1962): 19.

Roth, Mark. "Staging the Master's Works," *Theatre Research* 5, no. 2 (1980): 139–57.

Rufolo-Horhager, Dana. "Adolphe Appia's 'Monumentalité' and Peter Stein's Schaubühne," *Theatre Research* 9, no. 1 (1984): 29–38.

Sainte-Beuve, Charles Augustin de. *Histoire de Port-Royal*. 5 vols. Paris, 1840–59.

Salzmann, Alexander von. "Licht, Belichtung und Beleuchtung," in *Claudel-Programmbuch*. Hellerau, 1913.

Schevill, James, ed. *Break-Out!* Chicago, 1973.

Schiller, Johann Christoph Friedrich von. *Sämtliche Werke*. Ed. Gerhard Fricke and Herbert Göpfert. Repr. Munich, 1967.

_____ . *Hymn to Joy*. Trans. Natalie MacFarren. London, 1902.

Seidl, Arthur. *Die Hellerauer Schulfeste*. Regensburg, 1912.

Shaw, Bernard. *The Perfect Wagnerite*. Repr. New York, 1967.

Simonson, Lee. *The Stage Is Set*. New York, 1932.

_____ . "Appia's Contribution to the Modern Stage," *Theatre Arts Monthly* 16, no. 8 (Aug. 1932): 638–45.

_____ . *The Art of Scenic Design*. New York, 1950.

Sinclair, Upton. *World's End*. New York, 1940.

Skelton, Geoffrey. *Wagner at Bayreuth*. London, 1965.

Sontag, Susan. *Against Interpretation and Other Essays*. London, 1967.

Stadler, Edmond. "Adolphe Appia und Oskar Wälterlin," *Neue Zürcher Zeitung* (26 May 1963): 5.

_____ . "Adolphe Appia und Emile Jaques-Dalcroze," *Maske und Kothurn* 10, no. 3–4 (1964): 660–72.

Storck, Karl. *Emile Jaques-Dalcroze*. Stuttgart, 1912.

Styan, J. L. *Modern Drama in Theory and Practice*. Vols. 1 and 2. Cambridge, 1981.

Taine, H. *Philosophie de l'art*. Vol. 1. Paris, 1881.

Van Wyck, Jessica D. "Designing *Hamlet* with Appia." *Theatre Arts Monthly* 9, no. 1 (Jan. 1925): 17–31.

_____ . "Working with Appia," *Theatre Arts Monthly* 8, no. 12 (Dec. 1924): 815–18.

Volbach, Walther. *Adolphe Appia, Prophet of the Modern Theatre*. Middletown, Conn., 1968.

Wagner, Richard. *Gesammelte Schriften und Dichtungen.* Vol. 3. Leipzig, 1907.

Wälterlin, Oskar. *Bekenntnis zum Theater.* Zurich, 1955.

———. *Entzaubertes Theater.* Zurich, 1945.

Walton, J. Michael, ed. *Craig on Theatre.* London, 1983.

Zinsstag, Adolf. "Die Prostitution eines Kunstwerkes am Basler Stadttheater," *Rundschau/Bürger-Zeitung* (Basel) (6 Feb. 1925).

# Index

Actors: first step in play, 200; movement, 102–3, 296; music transfigures, 211; supreme, 193
Allan, Maud, 120
Appia, Adolphe: aesthetics, 38, 73; concept of mission, 40; creativity, 2, 13; devastated by attacks, 31; father, 45; inward-looking, 37; mother, 44; neglect, 2; obstacles, 44–45; reform proposals, 247; scenic vision, 55; shyness, 2; visionary, 23
Appia, Adolphe (Writings): "About the Costume for Eurhythmics," 124; "Actor, Space, Light, Painting," 162; "An American Lecture," 39; "Art Is an Attitude," 163; "The Art of Living Theatre," 166; "The Child and Dramatic Art," 250–51; "Comments on the Staging of *The Ring of the Nibelungs*" ("Notes de mise en scène pour *L'Anneau de Nibelungen*"), 82–84; "Comments on the Theatre," 162; "Curriculum Vita," 40; "A Dangerous Problem," 248; essay on Sainte Beuve's *Port-Royal*, 249–50; "Eurhythmics and Light," 123–24; "Eurhythmics and the Theatre," 121; "The Former Attitude," 252; "The Gesture of Art," 165, 248–49; Goethe's *Faust* scenario, 394–97; "Ideas on a Reform of Our *Mise en Scène*" ("Comment reformer notre mise en scène"), 84–85; "The Intermediary," 250; "Introduction to My Personal Notes," 37–38; *Iphigénia en Tauride* scenario, 392–94; "Living Art or Dead Nature?," 163; "Man Is the Measure of All Things," 252; "Mechanization," 251; "Monumentality," 165, 246; *Music and the Art of the Theatre (Die Musik und die Inscenierung) (La Musique et la mise en scène)*, 9, 38, 55–63, 84; "New Forms," 248; "The Origin and Beginnings of Eurhythmics," 68, 120, 123; "Picturesqueness," 251; Prometheus scenario, 390–91; "Reflections on Space and Time," 248; "The Reform and the Theatre at Basel," 85; "Return to Music," 119–20; "Rhythmic Spaces," 120; "Richard Wagner and Theatrical Production," 85; *Staging Wagnerian Drama (La Mise en scène du drame wagnerian)*, 38, 59, 84; "Style and Solidarity," 120; "Theatrical Experiences and Personal Investigations," 38; "Theatrical Production and Its Prospects in the Future," 164; "The Theme," 250; *The Work of Living Art*, 20, 21, 69, 195, 196, 297, 343
Appia, Geneviève, 161
Architecture, 222–23; aesthetics, 231; for drama, 191; Florence, 225; Greek, 224; influences on activities, 227; modern technique, 231–32; Munich, 225; Paris, 224–26; space for the living body, 254–55
Art: active engagement, 14; artificial life, 73; choice, 311, 314, 316; decision, 284, 290, 299, 312; dilemma in modern culture, 245; duality, 297; essence, 282, 283, 290; ethical and social function, 245; evaluation, 365; example, 299; expresses ideas, 262; expression of life, 73–74; expression of present, 340–41; human solidarity, 246; independent, 350; laws of aesthetics, 75; liberating force, 285; living human, 355; man the measure, 239–40; outside of time, 334; phenomenon not central, 280; sacrifice, 258, 259, 314; source of balance, 367; symbols, 299, 303; technique, 75; to be lived, 367
Artaud, Antonin, 166, 249
Artisan, and artist, 280
Artistic, definition, 284
Art works, acts of violence, 335
Attitudes, elements beyond phenomena, 282

Basel Theatre: dissidents, 31; inauspicious circumstances, 29; lighting, 27–29; *Rhinegold* well received, 30; *Ring* abandoned, 31; Wagner's *Ring* (1924–25), 27, 114; the *Walkyrie* problems, 30

Bayreuth: Appia's acceptance, 86–88; Appia's designs rejected, 10; dead tradition, 108; impressions, 49; reforms, 86

Bernhardt, Sarah, 390

Bière, Switzerland, 3

Boepple, Paul, eurhythmics in Basel, 146

Brunswick Theatre: artistic director, 65; use of platforms, 49

Chaikin, Joseph, "Open Theatre," 166

Chamberlain, Houston Stewart, 41; helped Appia observe and analyze Bayreuth, 82; Richard Wagner, 66; scholar and philologist, 66; *The Wagnerian Drama*, 66

Characters, 98–99

Charity, giving ourselves, 328–30

Cheney, Sheldon, American critic, 25

Child, born actor, 344

Choreography: method needed to score, 90; musical body training, 6

Claparède, Edouard, professor, University of Geneva, 144–45

Collective creation, cathedral era, 350

Color, painting, 212

Conductor-composer, conventional signs, 202–3

Copeau, Jacques, 216, 252; French Director, 25; Vieux Colombier Theatre, 166

Costumes, 99; black tights, 154; eurhythmics, 154; footwear, 99; gray tights, 155; white or gray tunics, 156

Craig, Gordon, 163, 216; on La Scala, 24

Creative periods: eurhythmics, 9–18; "Living Art," 20–33; "Wagnerian," 2–9

Dalcroze, Emile Jaques-, 120–26; choreography for *Orfeo*, 123; collaboration with Appia, 13; conservative, 123; Dresden, 146; eurhythmics, 10–11, 63, 300; genius for synthesis, 142, 143; importance to Appia, 119; indifference to, 145–46; living art, 340; production, 63; pupils individuals, 141

Dalcroze (Jaques-) Institute: exhibition arrangement, 195; musico-luminous sense, 151; principles, 149

Dance, eurhythmics, 156

Designer-director, role, 6

Desmond, Olga, 120

Devrient, Otto: actor, 49; setting for *Faust,* 65

Dohrn, Harold, 146

Dohrn, Wolf: eurhythmics, 246; Hellerau; 146; Hellerau founder, 120; social experiment, 11–13

Doret, Gustave, score, 227

Drama: time patterns, 206; without music, 209

Dramatic art: architecture for, 191; based on duality, 297; imaginary, 292; living beings, 294, 297; movement, 192; origin, 288; performance normal, 291; tells a story, 337

Duncan, Isadora, 120, 128; living art, 170

Dresden, *The Ring of the Nibelungs,* 54

Eurhythmics: act of devotion, 302; aesthetic education, 136; Appia's experience, 68; Appia's impressions, 67; beauty its principle, 217; costume, 124, 154; demonstration (Dresden), 11; demonstration effects, 62; elements of music, 196; essential quality, 141; experimentation, 63; harmony, 300; importance to Appia, 119; influence on spectators, 137; influence on theatre, 135; key to staging, 39; living art, 171; "musical-gymnastic" exercises, 10; New Presence, 372–73; personal experience, 145; revelation, 69; self the work of art, 341; sense of active participation, 137–38; sensory equilibrium, 150; in spoken drama, 392; theatrical reform, 121

First World War, artistic change, 25

Flaubert, Gustave, 324

Fortuny, M. Mariano, reflected light, 103

Fuchs, Georg, theatre reform, 1

Geneva: Fête de Juin, 124; pageant (1914), 20; pageant hall, 20

Gluck, Christoph Willibald, *Iphigénia en Tauride,* 392

Goethe, Johann Wolfgang von, 222; biographic, 322

Gorter, Nina, Dalcroze collaborator, 146

Grotowski, Polish Laboratory Theatre, 166

Güldenstein, Gustave, 391

Hair styles, 99

Held, director of Geneva Conservatory, 143

Hellerau: living art, 138; to be universalized, 247; utopian community, 13

Hellerau festivals: critics' reactions, 15–18; destroyed by war, 18; Gluck's *Orfeo* (1912), 15, (1913), 18; lighting system, 14–15; new performance art, 14

Hellerau Institute: costume development, 154, 156; public link, 157

Human body: effect on the stage, 102; lighting, 103; means of expression, 185; scenic order, 178; spoken drama, 181; three-dimensional settings, 103

Imagination: confidence, 365–66; determines actions, 364; training, 365

Internationalism, and artistic creation, 237

*Iphigénia en Tauride:* lighting act 1, 426–28; act 2, 431; setting act 2, 429–31

Jaques-Dalcroze, Emile, *See* Dalcroze, Emile Jaques-
Jeaneret, Pierre, 323

Klindworth, *Rhinegold* score, 56
Kurvenal, 146

La Scala (Milan), conservative, 23–24
Leihburg, Max Edouard von, 390–91
Leipzig, Goethe's *Faust,* 49–52
Life: goal an attitude, 278; initiative, 359
Lighting, 91–93, 177, 184; actor first element, 188, 216; anticipated development, 9; console, 15; costumes, 155, 156; diffused, 7; effects limitless, 103; exterior settings, 94; flexible, 176; formative, 7–9; Gluck's *Orfeo,* 15; Hellerau, 123–24; innovative concepts, 1; interior settings, 94; luminous atmosphere, 150; luminous sound, 150; movable spots, 9, 15; painted scenery, 92–93, 188; reform, 215, 216; role, 13; sensory education, 150; settings, 106; shadows, 94, 212; soul of *mise en scène,* 7; space, 138; suggestive, 93; supremacy, 181; technicians (electricians), 94; with music, 150, 177, 178
Living art, 170; all join in creating, 246; artist, 303; audience an obstacle, 72; audience unnecessary, 71, 296, 300–301; demonstrations, 197; eurhythmics, 383; the human body, 138; purely human qualities, 368; self-sufficient, 384; in space and time, 382; theatre, 170–71; to be experienced, 70–71
Lugné-Poë, Aurélien-Marie, 390

Mechanization: aims, 360; ethical problems, 361; intermediary, 359; moral decay, 362; recording, 360; responsibility, 371
Mercier, Jean, 247
*The Misanthrope,* production, 235
*Mise en scène:* austere limitations, 182; basic elements, 101; created by spectator, 237; hierarchic principle, 69; locations, 56; painted scenery, 103, 192–93; performer, 41–43, 55; three-dimensional space, 138; unity, 57; Wagnerian contradictions, 59
Molière, Jean Baptiste, 241
Monumental work, duration, 227
Music, 261; art of the present, 355; art of time, 334, 340–41; basic element, 216; bodily art, 217, 298; controls production space, 6; controls time, 176, 206, 207; determines time elements, 295; dictates expression, 296, 298; emotional expression, 297; and eurhythmics,

129; expresses ideas, 261, 262, 338; lyric drama, 181; means and technique, 128; movement and meaning, 297; phenomenon, 210; rhythm, 295; sensory education, 150; social, 301; teaching external, 127; time values, 204

Nature, study of phenomena, 279
New Presence, 171, 351; arbiter, 364; collective feeling, 350, 372; complete personality, 364; compulsion to act, 370; imagination, 366; living art, 352; mechanization, 373; point of comparison, 368; reciprocity between life and art, 246; responsibilities, 366; sacrifice, 372
Nietzsche, Friedrich, artistic reform, 247

Onlookers, 277–88, 328; attitude, 280–82

Painters, picturesque decay, 352, 354, 355
Painting, 223; art of space, 334
*Parsifal* (Wagner), symbols, 299
Péladan, Josephin, 331
People's theatre: architect, 230–31; definition, 229; sociable atmosphere, 232–33
Period of transition, living art, 356
Picturesque, definition, 357–58
Pitoëff, Georges, 216
Plato, and music, 263, 338
Playwrights, separated from presentation, 5
Poetry, 259–61; art of time, 334, 340–41; words, 261
Production: art of, 183; designer-director, 6; principles, 6
Projection, 94–95
Proust, Marcel, 249
Psychology, human phenomenon, 279

Recording: film in time and space, 360; goals, 370–71; phonograph for time, 360
Reflected image, 288–95
Retreat, 315; attitude, 314; plan, 316
*Rhinegold* (Wagner), designs, 27
*The Ring* (Wagner): scenarios, 59–62, 84, 413–15; scenic analysis, 3
Romanticism, scale of values, 56
Ronconi, Ludovico, Théâtre du Soleil, 166
Ruskin, John, 221

St. Denis, Ruth, 120
Salzmann, Alexander von: Appia concepts interpreter, 14–15; Russian painter, 13
Scenario, indicates performer's actions, 41
Scenic design, 31 (see also Settings); actors' space, 183 (see also Space); illusion, 5
Schechner, Richard, 166; "Performance Group," 166

Schiller, Johann Christoph Friedrich von, 178
Schmidt, Karl: Hellerau city founder, 146; social experiment, 11–13
Schopenhauer, Arthur, 179, 210; on music, 20, 337; philosopher-artist, 240–41, 278, 288
Sculpture, 233; art of space, 334; object the human body, 354
Senses, development, 149
Settings, 95–98; atmosphere, 106; design, 56–58, 106–7; dictated by music, 3; dictated by performers, 84, 105–6; lighting (see Lighting); painted scenery, 101–2, 105, 182, 184, 208, 211, 212, 239; the *Ring,* 65; simple, 7; three-dimensional, 7, 194–95; visualized, 4
Shakespeare, William, 241
Simonson, Lee, 3; on Appia's original premises, 1
Sinclair, Upton, on *Orfeo,* 18
Soleure, Switzerland, Swiss annual music festival (1905), 144
Sontag, Susan, 250
Space: actors', 193, 194; designs for bodily rhythm, 13, 65, 155; eurhythmics, 136; living, 63; movement, 194, 200, 255; organic vision, 65; quality of, 255; use of, 1
Spectators: seek outside themselves, 378–79; separate, 375–77
Sport: doing, 374; influence on minds, 373; physical culture, 373
Staging: actors first factor, 48, 183; adaptation, 236; dependent on spectator, 236; drawing-room comedies, 213–14; emotional meaning, 4; idealistic, 238; inspired by text, 238; with music, 209; practical, 3; to present dramatic action, 235; realistic, 238; theoretical, 3; variety of levels, 7, 45
Stanislavsky, Konstantin, 216
"Study sites," 69–70; flexible space, 39; to involve all present, 39; lighting, 39; moving bodies, 39; music, 39
Style: qualities: 131–32: responsibility in arts, 133
Symbols, 285, 311; eternal meaning, 290; form, 287; lasting truths, 301–2; universality, 299

Tableaux vivants, Geneva pageant (1914), 20
Taine, H., 239, 382; aim of art, 297–98; unified dramatic work, 176

Teaching, transmission, 320, 327
Tessenow, Heinrich, architect, 13
Theatre: actor essential factor, 104; art form, 5, 22–23; bare and empty hall, 197; contradictory conventions, 5; emotions, 288–89; exhibitions, 197; experimental productions, 85; motifs, 179; open performance area, 14; Parisian monotonous, 48; phenomenon, 179, 180; productions, 58, 204; rational hierarchy, 77–78; real event, 14, 182; to reform public taste, 105; role of actor, 22; scenes extension of actors, 6; significance of episodes, 56
Théâtre Antoine (Paris), 104
Theatre reform: Georg Fuchs, 1; practical, 1; theoretical, 1; two premises, 4
Time: dramatist, 203; musician controls, 203; projection into space, 201; quality of, 255; uncertain, 200–201
Toscanini, Arturo, 23, 25
Transition period, 196
*Tristan and Isolde* (Wagner): La Scala (Milan 1923), 23; little understanding, 24; negative criticism, 24

Values, scale, 366
Vilar, Jean, Théâtre Populaire, 166
Vinet, Alexander, criticism, 305–6
Volbach, Walther, 161

Wagner, Cosima: dismissed Appia's staging, 38; hostile to reform, 30
Wagner, Richard: dramatic music, 265–66; genius suffers duality, 109; modern staging, 112; musical drama, 208; new art form, 81; reform necessary, 105; staging problems, 82–84; symbols dependent on men, 299; traditional scenic illusion, 81–82
*The Walkyrie:* designs, 27; lighting, 401–3; scenario, 403–12; setting, 397–401
Wälterlin, Oskar, Basel Theatre director, 27, 30, 114
Werkbund, applied arts, 13
World War I. *See* First World War

Zinsstag, Adolf, Basel Wagner Society, 30–31